THE ARCHITECTURAL NETWORK OF THE VAN NEURENBERG FAMILY IN THE LOW COUNTRIES
(1480-1640)

ARCHITECTURA MODERNA

Architectural Exchanges in Europe, 16th – 17th Centuries

Vol. 4

Series Editors:

Krista De Jonge (Leuven)
Piet Lombaerde (Antwerp)

Advisory Board:

Howard Burns (Venice)
Thomas DaCosta Kaufmann (Princeton)
Jean Guillaume (Paris)
Konrad Ottenheym (Utrecht)
Ulrich Schütte (Marburg)

THE ARCHITECTURAL NETWORK OF THE VAN NEURENBERG FAMILY IN THE LOW COUNTRIES (1480-1640)

Gabri van Tussenbroek

BREPOLS

Cover illustrations: Dordrecht, group of merchants. Anonymous engraving (GAD, Inv.Nr. DI 452 d) and 's-Her-togenbosch, The screen of the Sint-Jans Church. Photograph by A. Schull, before 1866 (RDMZ, Neg.Nr. 14.087).

This research was carried out with the financial support of the Vlaams Nederlands Comité (VNC), a joint initiative of the Nederlandse Organisatie voor Wetenschappelijk Onderzoek (NWO) and the Fonds voor Wetenschappelijk Onderzoek Vlaanderen (FWO).
The translation of this work was brought about with support from the NWO.

Translated from the Dutch by Titus Verheijen and Whitney A. Byrn.

D/2006/0095/80
ISBN 2-503-51847-8

Printed in the E.U. on acid-free paper

TABLE OF CONTENTS

Editor's Preface

By Krista De Jonge

No joint architectural history of the Southern and Northern Low Countries, which roughly correspond to the present-day states of Belgium and The Netherlands, exists as yet for the Early Modern Period. The political and military frontier, which originated in the Dutch Revolt and which was only consolidated with the Peace of Westphalia in 1648, became firmly established in Belgian and Dutch historiography of art and architecture during the course of the nineteenth century. When, after a short period of unity under William I (1815-1830), the Belgian and Dutch Kingdom went their separate ways, both developed their own architectural histories with a particular nationalistic bent. The architectural past was used to reinforce national identity and to give meaning to the new borders. The research project *Unity and Discontinuity. Architectural Relations between the Southern and the Northern Low Countries 1530-1700* financed by the Vlaams-Nederlands Comité, which is an initiative of the Nederlandse Organisatie voor Wetenschappelijk Onderzoek (NWO) and the Fonds voor Wetenschappelijk Onderzoek Vlaanderen (FWO), sought to correct this view. Carried out jointly at the Catholic University of Leuven and at the University of Utrecht in 1997-2000, it addressed four levels of continuing interaction between the North and the South, of which the building trades was one. This is the subject of the present book, which was developed as a dissertation at the University of Utrecht under the direction of Koen A. Ottenheym.

Gabri van Tussenbroek's work takes the period of (relative) unity under the last Dukes of Burgundy of the House of Valois and the early Hapsburg rulers as a starting point for what could easily be called a family saga, were it not that this highly interesting narrative highlights the continuing unity between the southern and northern parts of the Low Countries even after their separation. On the basis of little-known or unpublished archival material, as well as of a new examination of surviving buildings, the author paints a complex picture of the Netherlandish professional world of the sixteenth and early seventeenth century. The Van Neurenberg family network linked Namur and Maastricht in the Mosan region with Cologne, Nijmegen, and Amsterdam; its history is that of the enduring success of a particular material, the Mosan carboniferous limestone. But this is not only a phenomenon of the *longue durée*. The professional careers of the family's principal representatives illustrate how urban building practice in the North rapidly emancipated itself from medieval traditions after the Revolt, and how social emancipation soon followed. Here the first seeds of discord can be found, which will ultimately divorce professional developments in the North from those in the South. This highly original study serves as a long-awaited complement to the seminal book published over eighteen years ago on the Keldermans family, the Van Neurenberg's famous counterparts from Brabant, stone traders, stonecutters, sculptors, architects and engineers.[1]

The editors particularly want to thank the Netherlands Organisation for Scientific Research, which gave generous financial support for translating the dissertation into English.

The series *Architectura Moderna*, founded in the year 2000, is dedicated to Netherlandish architecture from the early modern period, set within its European context. It intentionally carries a title which evokes the debate of *antique vs. modern*, the focal point of Netherlandish architectural theory of

---

[1] J.H. van Mosselveld et al. (ed.), *Keldermans, een architectonisch netwerk in de Nederlanden.* 's-Gravenhage 1987.

the late sixteenth and early seventeenth century. The reader may catch the echo of well-known treatises, such as Hans Vredeman de Vries's *ARCHITECTURA Oder Bauung der Antiquen auss dem Vitruvius* (printed in Antwerp, 1577), Charles De Beste's *Architectura. Dat is constlicke Bouwijnghen huijt die Antijcken Ende Modernen* (written in Bruges between 1596 and 1600), and Salomon de Bray's and Cornelis Danckerts's *Architectura Moderna ofte Bouwinge van onsen Tyt* (published in Amsterdam, 1631). However, the series not only focuses on the theoretical tenets underlying contemporary Netherlandish architecture, their origin and their reception (see the first volume on *The Reception of P.P. Rubens's* Palazzi di Genova *during the 17th century in Europe: Questions and Problems*, 2001, edited by Piet Lombaerde), or on aspects of patronage within a European perspective (see the second volume on *Trade in Good Taste. Relations in Architecture and Culture between the Dutch Republic and the Baltic World in the Seventeenth Century*, 2004, by Badeloch Noldus), but also welcomes studies which explore Netherlandish construction history in all its aspects (see the third volume on *Hans Vredeman de Vries and the Artes Mechanicae revisited*, 2005, edited by Piet Lombaerde).

ACKNOWLEDGEMENTS

This publication is the result of a study undertaken in the years 1997-2000. It is part of the research programme *Unity and Discontinuity. Architectural Relations between the Southern and the Northern Low Countries 1530-1700* financed by the Vlaams-Nederlands Comité, which is a joint initiative of the Nederlandse Organisatie voor Wetenschappelijk Onderzoek (NWO) and the Fonds voor Wetenschappelijk Onderzoek Vlaanderen (FWO). The programme was directed by Ms Prof. Dr.-Ir. Krista De Jonge (Catholic University of Leuven, Dept. of Architecture of the Faculty of Engineering) and Prof. Dr. Koen A. Ottenheym (Utrecht University, Faculty of Arts, Dept. of Architectural History). The initial results of this research were presented during the international colloquium 'Unity & Discord' held on 23-25 November 2000 at the Catholic University of Leuven.

The manuscript of this publication was publicly defended at Utrecht University on 8 May 2001 under the title *Bouwen voor stad en land. Overzicht van het handelsnetwerk van de aannemersfamilie Van Neurenberg in de Noordelijke en Zuidelijke Nederlanden (1480-1640)*. First of all I would like to thank my supervisor Koen Ottenheym for his unabated genuine interest, his critical eye and the freedom he gave me, vis-à-vis the execution of the research. The department of Architectural History at Utrecht University was a pleasant place to work; here I could freely exchange views with colleagues on the substantive sides of the research, but also with regard to the practical problems and worries that writing entails. I would therefore like to express my thanks to Dr. Lex Bosman, Dr. Rob Dettingmeijer, Dr. Elske Gerritsen, Dr. Badeloch Noldus, Dr. Freek Schmidt, Dr. Marie-Thérèse van Thoor and Dr. Pieter Vlaardingerbroek for the enjoyable cooperation. Dr. Charles van den Heuvel and Prof. Dr.-Ing. Dirk de Vries, who were indirectly involved in the study, also deserve thanks as do Dr. Jean-Louis Van Belle, Dr. Herman Janse, (†) Drs. Joris Snaet and Dr. Francis Tourneur.

During the long process that preceded this book's creation I relied on the help and support of a large number of people. I would like to express my thanks to Ruud Koopman, Jörg Soentgerath and Annemie De Vos M.A. for selflessly allowing me to use their unpublished data. Other people who were involved in various stages of the creation of this publication, who gave their opinions on the structure, approach or text, also provided an essential contribution to the research. That is why it is my pleasure to be able to thank Dr. Ad van Drunen, Dr. Ronald Stenvert, Drs. Vincent Theunissen, Drs. Rolf de Weijert and Drs. Hans Willems, who helped me compile the index. Ronald Glaudemans, responsible for the creation of a number of drawings in this book, also deserves my thanks.

Other people who I would like to take this opportunity to thank for contributing in one way or another are Dr. Thorsten Albrecht, Ir. Dik Berends, Ir. Harry Boekwijt, Drs. Chris de Bruijn, Dr. Thomas Coomans, Prof. Dr. Guy Delmarcel, Prof. Dr. Wim Denslagen, Drs. Jan Dröge, David Gedge, Dr. Oscar Gelderblom, Prof. Dr. Eric Groessens, Ir. Rob Gruben, Drs. Jan van der Heiden, Ir. Taco Hermans, Hein Hundertmark, Prof. Dr. Henk Kars, Bart Klück, Gerard Overeem, Dr. Juliette Roding, Ulrike Schwarz M.A., Ir. Bram Steketee, Drs. Marnica Stoop, Ir. Herman Strijbos (†), Daan & Truus, Titus Verheijen and Drs. Ester Vink.

I would also like to thank Prof. Dr.-Ing. Johannes Cramer, who enabled me to work on this book's manuscript while I was a postgraduate researcher at the Post Graduate Research Group Art Research – Building Archaeology – Monument Care (Graduiertenkolleg Kunstwissenschaft – Bauforschung – Denkmalpflege) (Technical University Berlin – Otto-Friedrich University Bamberg).

Finally, I would like to express my thanks to the NWO, which supported this publication financially, and to the series editors of *Architectura Moderna*, Prof. Dr.-Ir. Krista De Jonge and Prof. Dr. Piet Lombaerde (Higher Institute of Architectural Sciences Henry van de Velde) and the advisory board of this series, who generously enabled me to publish this book.

Berlin, August 2005

INTRODUCTION

The need for buildings and housing is as old as mankind. Cave dwellers looked for housing among the rocks, the Batavians built their homes of poles and straw, and the Romans fired bricks with which to build. Nevertheless, the similarities between construction in classical antiquity and contemporary construction are relative. The first time we see a situation that is similar to today is during the Middle Ages. In the eleventh century, construction materials were exported to the Northern Low Countries from the Eiffel, in order to build churches and later houses. During the late twelfth century the brick firing process was reintroduced and the more the woodlands of the northern Low Countries became depleted, the more the timber trade's importance increased, necessitating timber acquisition further afield. Materials were obtained from one of the staple markets in Deventer, Dordrecht, Venlo or Amsterdam, from the precursors of what we today call 'builders merchants'. Roof constructions or house facades could be ordered ready-made and these could be adapted to the most specific requirements and wishes.

This book deals with the building industry and the materials trade in the sixteenth and seventeenth century. It attempts to answer the questions how building contractors and stone merchants operated at the time, how their field of operations was delineated and what their influence was on architecture. To this end, we will focus on the Van Neurenberg family of merchants (Fig. 1). The family operated over a period of one hundred and fifty years from the towns of Namur, Maastricht, 's-Hertogenbosch, Dordrecht and Amsterdam. Members of the family were involved in important construction projects, such as the Antwerp town hall, the tower of the Old Church in Amsterdam, the cloth hall in Nijmegen and the rood screen in the Sint-Jans Church in 's-Hertogenbosch. They experienced all the principal changes to the construction industry in their time and were compelled to capitalise on these changes in order to maintain their position in the market. Social and family ties ensured that the descendants of the Van Neurenberg family were part of a much larger network of (stone) merchants who, particularly during the second half of the sixteenth century and the seventeenth century, would manifest themselves as interest groups.[2]

This publication follows the family over time using a number of themes and small case studies. It sets out to ascertain to what extent there were influences on architecture, which can be immediately linked to the materials used and the trade in those materials. In other words: did the Van Neurenberg family and the group of stone merchants from the Meuse Valley, of which they were members, influence the development of architecture through their working methods? Apart from this question, the book also deals with the organisational characteristics and composition of the family.

Families of merchants and building contractors

Family businesses were active throughout Europe in the past, often holding a leading position in the field of industry in which they operated. If we focus on construction in the Low Countries, then it is without doubt the Keldermans family who had a far-reaching influence on the construction industry during the fifteenth and sixteenth century. As a combination of master mason, sculptor and stone merchant, they were responsible for a wide range of projects such as castles, churches, urban homes and fortifications. The travelling master mason thereby implemented his own stylistic vision and expert-

---

[2] See also Meischke et al. 1997 for the development of the Namur stone trade, e.g. pp. 59-61.

1. Coat of arms of the Van Neurenberg stone trading family. Anonymous water colour, eighteenth century (Photograph by A. Molendijk 1996, Collection Museum Mr. Simon van Gijn, Dordrecht).

ise which not only applied to the Keldermans family, but also to other master masons and stone merchants, such as Van Boghem, Darkennes, Hanicq, De Prince, Schairt or De Vleeschouwer.[3]

The advent of the Renaissance in architecture seemed to prolong this tradition for the time being. Nevertheless the construction industry was subject to more changes than just the renewal of stylistic vision. Materials trade and stylistic export would diverge even more and the traditional master mason would be forced to adopt a different position within the construction industry. The richness of this issue, which is not merely art historical, but also touches on socio-economic aspects, complicates dealing with the question of whether the materials trade influenced the construction process. To be able to provide an answer to the question to what extent the materials trade was responsible for changes in the construction industry, we require insight into the materials trade's position within the construction industry and within the sector of industry it operated in, its social and professional networks and the trade politics involved.

Over the centuries, master masons and building contractors were invaluable in erecting buildings. However, their day-to-day practice has hardly warranted extensive study and its influence on the construction industry is therefore much less researched than that of the architects responsible for designing the buildings. The impression Andries Vierlingh provided of the construction industry in the sixteenth century is far from positive. Vierlingh was the steward of Steenbergen and in that capacity was deeply involved in hydraulic-engineering. Towards the end of his career he committed his experience and knowledge to paper.[4] His opinion on the building contractors he had dealt with was extremely negative. To him they were poor people with no particular background who would not hesitate to take on a construction job having submitted a bid for half the real cost in order to get a copy of the builder's offer. The copy then acted as a guarantee for outstanding monies. They used this as 'proof' of credit worthiness and fell to drinking, whoring and gambling, so that sometimes a quarter of the contract price had already been spent before actual construction had even started;[5] often building contractors barely had enough money left to purchase tools and materials. Additionally, their work ethic also left much to be desired. When the members of the polder authority made their daily rounds, work was done in earnest. However, this appearance of industriousness was only a ruse; as soon as the officials had gone the men would drop their tools and start drinking and playing dice. To heighten the illusion a few men were hired to work for half an hour in order to give the dike warden the impression there was a big crew on the job. When he left they were sent again. Those eager to work were chastised or threatened with a beating. The principal's supervision was totally inadequate and agreements were, to a large extent, based on trust.

Naturally, this scenario is only one side of the story. There are also examples of construction projects where building contractors did good work, and construction was finished within the set terms. Nevertheless, Vierlingh's accusations are an undeniable aspect of daily life. Sixteenth-century construction contracts always seem to emphasise the delivery period and quality of work expected. Moreover, the agreements quite often featured a penalty clause, which was indicative of the bad experiences people had had.

At the start of the sixteenth century, the construction industry was still entirely based on medieval patterns with subdivisions of carpentry, bricklaying and stone masonry. Master masons usually came from the materials trade, had direct ties to the quarries, and were often responsible for both the design and execution. Construction companies were often organised along family lines. Materials could be delivered pre-fabricated and assembled on site. The trade in pre-processed materials meant that architectural shapes could be disseminated across a wide area; a method primarily applied by stone traders from Brabant.[6]

[3] Haans 1989 and Janse, De Vries 1991, pp. 33–37.
[4] Vierlingh 1920.
[5] Ibidem, p. XIII.

[6] Van Mosselveld 1987 passim, Meischke 1988, pp. 114–127 and Van Tussenbroek 2001b.

2. The Low Countries, areas of stone origin (drawing by author).

After the political separation of the Northern and Southern Low Countries in the sixteenth century, trading relations between the two regions were only partially maintained.[7] Because Dutch soil held no significant stone deposits, dependence on imports remained. During the preceding period Holland and Zeeland had primarily used Belgian calcareous sandstone from the area around Brussels and dark carboniferous limestone from Hainaut. In the centre and east of the Northern Low Countries

[7] Concerning the political aspects: De Schepper 1987.

4

they used sandstone from the county of Bentheim, calcareous sandstone from the diocese of Münster, Hohenleihe tuffa stone and Drachenfels trachyte from the Eiffel, and carboniferous limestone from the area around Namur (Fig. 2). Diversity decreased in the new situation and it was Namur stone from the Meuse region and in particular Bentheimer and Obernkirchner sandstone, which would predominate.

The supply route for Belgian calcareous sandstone was closed off in 1585 when the Schelde was blockaded. Although this fact is well known and we know that the flow of goods along the Schelde ended in that year, we do not know to what extent this influenced construction. In other words, did the organisation of the construction industry undergo changes due to the disappearance of this influential flow of goods? Or did matters develop the opposite way? Did changes to the way construction was organised ensure that the stone merchants from Brabant managed to survive the politically unstable situation?

The same question can also be applied to stone deliveries from the Meuse Valley. As a result of the ever-increasing tolls on the Rhine and the abolition of Venlo's staple rights in 1545, the influence of the Mosan trade increased. Here too it is unknown as to what extent this shift was an influence on the development of the construction industry or architecture. However, it is known that merchants from the Ardennes were much better at dealing with the conflicts between the regions. They managed to reinforce their market position in spite of the war, thereby cornering a large proportion of the Republic's stone market.

Earlier research in this field

Research into the organisation of the construction industry has occurred for quite some time from a local angle. From the 1880s to the 1920s there were a large number of publications that contained town accounts, construction accounts, bylaws and related matters.[8] The attention to the organisation of construction would continue until the Second World War. Researchers attempted to answer questions such as how the stone trade had been organised, who was entitled to make designs and which stonemasons and master masons were involved in which projects.[9] The advent of modern archiving made this data available to the public for the first time.[10]

This interest continued to a limited extent after the Second World War.[11] It was primarily societies for the preservation of historic buildings that continued to investigate construction practice. In the 1950s R. Meischke first attempted to write a complete overview of the organisational and design practice in the Low Countries before 1650. In articles which have since become classics, he described construction practices in the fourteenth and fifteenth centuries and design practices in the sixteenth and early seventeenth centuries.[12] Simultaneously, the results of architectural historical field studies were collected and compiled with archival data, published in countless articles, primarily in the *Bulletin KNOB*. The works of H. Janse, A.J.L. van de Walle and F. van Tyghem are early surveys of the medieval construction industry.[13]

Nevertheless, it can be stated that attention to the history of the construction industry was marginal after the Second World War. For an exhibition in 1987 in the restored Markiezenhof in Bergen op Zoom,[14] the book *Keldermans, een architectonisch netwerk* was published, in which a num-

---

[8] For example, Van Zuijlen 1863–1866, Muller 1883–1885 and Kleintjes and Sormani 1911–1919. See also Van Tussenbroek 2000b. Attention to stone from a historical or geological angle has existed for much longer. Van der Woud 1998, in particular Chapter 3.

[9] Muller 1881–1882 and Nanninga Uiterdijk 1907, among others.

[10] Bos-Rops, Bruggeman 1987, p. 17.

[11] For example, Parmentier 1948.

[12] Reprinted in Meischke 1988, pp. 46–113 and 127–208.

[13] Bom 1950, Van de Walle 1959, Janse 1964, De Vlieger 1964, Van Tyghem 1966 and 1978.

[14] Van Mosselveld 1987.

ber of articles provide insight into the practices of this family of master masons in the fourteenth, fifteenth and sixteenth centuries. A short time later, *Werk en Merk van de Steenhouwer* was published, in which H. Janse and D.J. de Vries provided an inventory of the existing knowledge of the stone trade, the organisation of the construction industry and stonemasons' activities.[15] From the 1990s the number of publications pertaining to the organisational and architectural historical aspects of the construction industry has increased.[16] Furthermore, research into the history of architects' practice has also intensified.[17]

As far as the material-technical side of the trade in stone is concerned, the standard work is *Natuursteen in Monumenten*,[18] which deals with the geological aspects and other characteristics of various stone types. There are countless publications in this field, which will not be mentioned here.[19] In Belgium interest in the history of the construction industry also is increasing. There J.-L. van Belle's *Les maîtres de pierre d'Arquennes* was published in 1990.[20] In a wider European context the conference publications from the *Centre International des Recherches Glyptographiques* were published, which has been active since the end of the 1970s. A practical geological guidebook to Walloon stone types was published in 1996 and allows one to distinguish between the large varieties in types of stone.[21]

State of the research

The construction industry was strongly tied to regional customs. In spite of the fact that the main lines are often the same, it is important to take these regional and traditional factors into account as they regularly explain differences in processing, shape or application. Mutual differences can also be discerned in the organisation of construction between the towns. For example, the town fabric lodge developed early in Haarlem and Amsterdam, while this development took place much later in, for example, 's-Hertogenbosch. The power of the guilds, which was sometimes of great importance for the construction organisation in a town, differed greatly.

The past hundred years have only seen a limited number of publications on the Van Neurenberg family. The first person to acknowledge the Van Neurenberg family in Dutch literature was J.J. Weve in 1889.[22] In Belgium the family was referred to as the most important historical family of master masons as early as 1867.[23] In 1902, the *Bulletin NOB* featured a short contribution by M.G. Wildeman under the title 'Guilloardius van Norembergen'. The piece opened with the question: "What do we know about the abovementioned sculptor or stonemason?" Wildeman provided some information on a tombstone Van Neurenberg had supplied, but was primarily interested in other information.[24] In 1912, M.F. Courtoy made a more structural attempt to provide an overview of the family's history, while Buschman, 1918, and Juten, 1922, provided correct information on individual construction projects.[25] The doctoral thesis *Het steenhouwersgeslacht van Neurenberg en de donkere Belgische steen* by H. Huis-

---

[15] Janse, de Vries 1991.

[16] For example, see the introductions to the series *Huizen in Nederland* by R. Meischke and the books *Houten kappen in Nederland* and *Van Aaks tot Zwei* by H. Janse.

[17] Ottenheym 1989, Kolman 1993, De Vries 1994, Huisken 1995, Gerritsen 2004, Vlaardingerbroek 2004 and Noldus 2005. Articles with comparable themes in the *Bulletin KNOB* can also be explained by this renewed interest. See also Roding 1993, Kolman, Stenvert 1994, Hermans 1996 and Hoekstra 1997.

[18] Slinger 1980.

[19] Including, Van der Kloes 1893, Schroot 1918 etc. For the time being however there is no survey of the insights into stone gained over the past twenty years. For Walloon literature see Cnudde 1987.

[20] He had already written *L'Industrie de la pierre en Wallonie (XVIe et XVIIIe siècles)*, Van Belle 1976. The year 1994 saw the publication of his encyclopedia of stonemasons' and quarry marks for southern Belgium and northern France. Van Belle 1994. Other publications that should be mentioned which deal with Belgian territories are Lalemann 1989 and 1995 on stonemasons' activities in Ghent, Nys 1993 on Tournai stone and Diversen 1994, in which various authors studied the construction history of the Onze Lieve Vrouwe Cathedral in Antwerp.

[21] De Jonghe et al. 1996.

[22] Weve 1889, pp. 8-9.

[23] Piot 1867, p. 43. This refers to Coenraad IV.

[24] Wildeman 1902, pp. 309-310.

[25] Courtoy 1912.

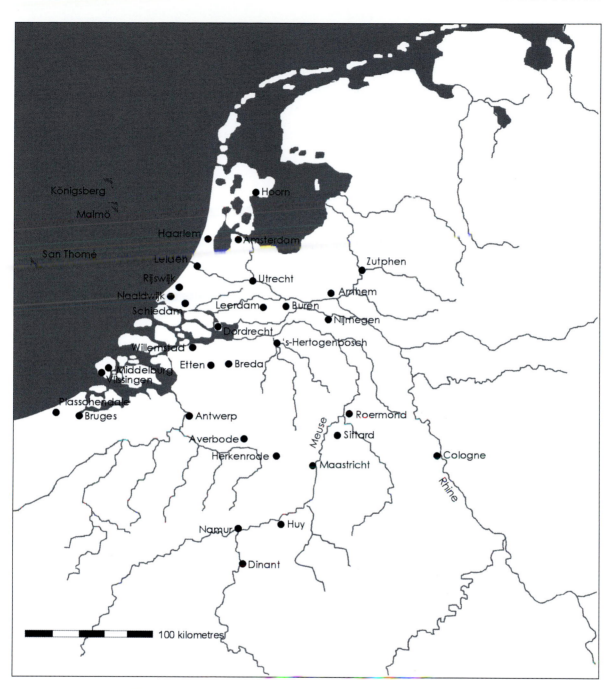

3. The Van Neurenberg family's area of activities between 1500 and 1640 (drawing by author).

man from 1986 provided more extensive information[26], and this was followed in 1992 by the publi-cation 'Het huis Nieuwe Haven 29 en zijn bewoners tot 1864'. by the same author in cooperation with Chr. de Bruyn.[27] There are countless other articles and publications in which the family is mentioned, though often only in passing.

---

[26] Huisman 1986.   [27] De Bruijn, Huisman 1992.

Although the Van Neurenberg family were one of the most important families of building contractors in the sixteenth and seventeenth centuries (Fig. 3), a large number of questions remain unanswered. For example, there is little insight into the underlying trading politics, which partly determined the activities, the range of actual activities, the company's relationship to shifts in the construction industry, the contacts and cooperation with other families and any possible political influences on the company.

The research: sources and method

There are three categories of sources available for research into the stone trade and the use of stone in the past. The first is the buildings themselves. As far as possible these have been examined for original applications of stone. The manner in which the stone was processed was also studied. This analysis made it possible to ascertain to what extent stonemasons' traditions were congruent in the north and south. The second category is comprised of archival sources: invoices, contracts, etc., but also drawings, designs and pictures. During the research into the sources the lack of a family archive was sorely felt. The third category is the existing literature, which in many cases proved to be the starting point for further research.

This research combines a number of disciplines and their methods: history, building archaeology and architectural history. The data culled from the historical sources were, where possible, related to the archaeological evidence. The partial surveys carried out for the benefit of this research were not aimed at tracing the building's entire construction history, but at finding (and documenting) stone elements relevant to this study. The results of the abovementioned research were then inserted into a much wider historical framework and related to the organisation of the construction industry.[28]

Emerging from the research, the Van Neurenberg family's role can be seen as a *pars pro toto*: the developments their activities underwent fit into the broader picture of the construction industry as a whole. The research into the family itself is however definitely not intended to be an independent prosopographical study.[29] The objective was cataloguing the spread of trade on the basis of the family's history in relation to other families of stone merchants. In that sense it is the entrepreneurial behaviour of a group that originates from a more or less defined area, which is central to the research. Detailing the interconnections between families of stone merchants increases the understanding of entrepreneurship and helps us understand more about the success of a product from a particular trading context, in this case Namur stone.

[28] The option of carrying out petrological research was considered, but due to the low expectations for this type of research vis-à-vis this study, it was not carried out. One of the main problems which played a role in this decision was the large area in which the stone applied can be found and the limited knowledge on past operation. Petrological analysis should serve to solve the question from which quarries the Van Neurenberg family acquired their materials. The ideal situation would provide a petrological link between stone in a building and a particular quarry, on which – moreover – written data has been retained. A methodological problem is that Namur stone has the same composition over a larger area, with vertical fluctuations. To solve this difficulty it would require a large number of samples in order to carry out a chemical analysis of trace elements in which a relevant statistical separation would have to be found. It should therefore be ascertained which layer was mined in the sixteenth or seventeenth century for every quarry, to be able to determine an overlap with the reference material, etc. An attendant problem is that not every bank was mined. Many thanks to Prof. Dr. H. Kars, Rijksdienst voor Oudheidkundig Bodemonderzoek, Amersfoort. See Kars 1983, Paepe, Pieters 1994, Ansorge, Schäfer 1994 and Klaua 1998 for more information on this method.

[29] For more information on the prosopographical method see Stone 1971, Roorda 1979 and De Jong 1996.

PART I

1500–1570: THE START OF A NEW TRADING ERA

I. The Construction Industry in the Sixteenth Century

Sixteenth-century society

A fifteenth-century manuscript from Nürnberg features an illustration of a stonemason called Coenraad. He is seated on a two-legged stool and holds a marteline (Fig. 4). He is using it to square a block of stone. Beside him on the ground there are a number of tools such as a set square, which enables him to check whether his work is straight, a scantling, to use later when profiling the stone and a simple spirit level.[30]

Such an illustration provides a great deal of information on the daily work of a simple stonemason in the late Middle Ages. However, it gives no insight into the way in which his work was organised and which rules he had to follow. At the time, most stonemasons worked for church fabric lodges. In the Low Countries, in the fifteenth century, the fabric lodge was still the principal centre for stonemasons' activities.[31] A hundred years later, this situation started changing dramatically when the large church construction projects had been completed or were on hold, and the towns were starting to vigorously and confidently take over the role of patron for the construction sector.

This development in the construction industry was not isolated. Major changes were also taking place elsewhere in society. For example, the Hapsburgs made great efforts to get all the Dutch territory under their dominion. Not until 1543 could Charles V impose his rule on the last province, Gelre. This made the Hapsburg Low Countries an almost continuous territory, with the exception of the Prince-Bishopric Liège, where the Prince Bishop managed to retain his secular and ecclesiastical power until the French Revolution. Charles V reinforced the unity created with centrally led administration and regulation, which was reticently accepted by the towns who, previously, were accustomed to administrative autonomy. Moreover, Charles' expensive political expansion was a heavy burden on the Low Countries, which faced continually increasing taxation.[32]

An important consequence of this centralisation, which started as early as the fifteenth century, was the local aristocracy lost its important position in the country's administration. This loss of position led to a partial disappearance of the aristocracy as patrons for major construction projects. Moreover, during this time a social shift from the aristocracy to a rich citizenry became apparent.

4. Brother Coenraad, 1425/36 (Hausbuch der Mendelschen Zwölf-brüderenstiftung, fol. 31v, 4r. Stadtbibliothek Nürnberg).

[30] Binding 1993, p. 287. Hausbuch der Mendelschen Zwölf-brüderenstiftung in Nürnberg, ca. 1425/36. Fol. 31v, 4r.
[31] Among others, Meischke 1988 and Koldeweij 1989.
[32] Groenveld, Schutte 1992, p. 75.

11

Urban patricians in the north were increasing and new building commissions ensued. For example, new town halls were built in Gouda (1450), Vianen (1500), Woerden (1501) and Alkmaar (1509).[33] New social strata were emerging in the towns, which were slowly preparing for important administrative positions.

Around 1500, the focus of international trade in the Low Countries lay in Antwerp. The town had surpassed Bruges as the centre of trade. Towns in Zeeland, along the access route to the Schelde, benefited from this turnaround and underwent rapid growth. Antwerp was also a significant transhipment port for products from Brabant and Flanders. In the north, Dordrecht was an important trading town that later would be superseded by Rotterdam and Amsterdam. In the northeast there were the Hanse towns along the IJssel river: Zwolle, Kampen, Zutphen and Deventer, which played a vital role in the trade with Northern Germany.[34] In the southeastern quadrant the majority of the required materials was transported on the Meuse River. Venlo, which was ruled by Gelre, was still an important staple town in the early part of the century, however it increasingly became a hindrance due to its function as a staple market for industrial towns such as Namur, Liège and Maastricht. Traders from these towns would soon assert themselves and penetrate the markets in the north.

The Roman Catholic Church was confronted with counter movements. The separation, which became predominant during the revolt against the Spanish, appeared during the first half of the sixteenth century. It was precisely at this time that work was taking place on many large construction projects. From approximately 1450 onwards there was a boom in ecclesiastical construction activity, which saw the completion of important churches. Around 1530, a number of these buildings were completed or work on them was halted, which resulted in fabric lodges closing.[35] Craftsmen and master masons therefore lost their fixed source of income and were forced to start working as building contractors or to find employment in the stone trade. A few were lucky enough to be appointed town master mason, a position that had been combined with the fabric lodge master for some time.[36]

The end of the fabric lodges resulted in the disappearance of a long-time, important supplier of knowledge and materials. Moreover, the schism in the Church threatened the funding of new and still uncompleted church building projects. These factors ensured that a number of projects were not completed.[37] Social priorities had shifted and the position of the stonemasons shifted accordingly. They too managed to free themselves from the traditional structures that ensured they could maintain their position within the changing society.[38]

The end of Gothic architecture and the introduction of the Renaissance

The fabric lodges were responsible for the design and technical realisation of church buildings and their influence radiated to smaller towns in the surrounding area.[39] Another core of construction activity was the stone trade. This trade had been on the rise since the start of the fifteenth century. Flexible stone merchants proved to be much better equipped to cope with changes in demand or fashion. Telling examples are found at the end of the fifteenth and the start of the sixteenth centuries, when the Utrecht and 's-Hertogenbosch fabric lodges had lost so much influence that they acquired part of their products prefabricated from stone merchants.

---

[33] Meischke 1987, p. 88.
[34] Jappe Alberts 1980, p. 14.
[35] Peeters 1987, pp. 163-169.
[36] Van Tussenbroek 2001b.
[37] These included the Sint-Rombouts tower in Mechelen, the Sint-Lievensmonster tower in Zierikzee, the Sint-Jacobs

tower in Antwerp, the Sint-Laurens Church in Alkmaar and the New Church in Delft, all of which construction was suspended around 1530. Van Langendonck 1987, pp. 40-41 and 51 and Van den Berg 1987, p. 71 and 81.
[38] Peeters 1987, Van Tussenbroek 2001b.
[39] Meischke 1988, p. 54.

An important stone trade family was the Keldermans family, seven generations of whom are known from sources between 1380 and 1557.[40] Because the knowledge acquired was handed down from one generation to the next and the members of the family were active over a large area in the Northern and Southern Low Countries, a rather homogenous, prefabricated product was disseminated across a large area. This prefabrication usually concerned stone from the area around Brussels, which dominated the market in the northwest of the Low Countries via the staple town Dordrecht. There are other cases in which other parts of buildings, such as roof constructions, were delivered readymade. This practice existed as early as 1400.[41] To a great extent the spread of styles was determined by the dissemination of stonework and the activities of the stonemasons from the Southern Low Countries and the Rhine Valley.[42]

The first signs of the renewal of architectural stylistic vision in the Low Countries started with a few Italian motifs for the Entrance of Charles V into Bruges, in 1515.[43] In painting, stylistic innovations had existed for much longer and around this time many painters journeyed to Italy to study the art historical treasures there. However, it would take until the end of the twenties before the first Renaissance-like buildings were realised, among others in Breda, Brussels, Buren, 's-Hertogenbosch, IJsselstein, Mechelen and Zaltbommel (Fig. 5).[44] In Zaltbommel and Nijmegen the first innovations came from the Meuse Valley. It was the Liège Prince Bishop's court that acted as a centre of modernisation. A brief spate of construction in Renaissance styles took place here. This style was linked to the trade in Namur stone.

5. Zaltbommel, Maarten van Rossumhuis, 1537 (Anonymous Photograph, approximately 1910, RDMZ, Neg.Nr. 83.651).

The building trade in the sixteenth century

Traditionally the building trade was very loosely knit and there were large regional differences as far as the use of materials, construction, profiling, layout and allotment were concerned. Staple towns played an important role in the construction materials' trade. Town patrons purchased the required materials there; stone and wooden structures could be ordered prefabricated there.

Population growth had consequences for the building activities to be undertaken. At the time towns were still regularly hit by fires — Harderwijk in 1503, Zaltbommel in 1524, Delft in 1536, Breda

[40] Van Wylick-Westermann 1987, passim.
[41] Janse 1986, p. 89.
[42] Janse, De Vries 1991, Chapters 3, 4 and 5.
[43] Kuyper 1994, p. 1.
[44] Vos, Leeman 1986, p. 11.

in 1538 — whereby large areas were destroyed. There was therefore a demand for a well-organised trade in construction materials to enable rapid and effective construction. However, older materials were also often used. As far as the development of structures and construction methods is concerned, it was not the styles from the south that brought on modernisation. This development was entirely separate. In this context it was precisely elements such as function, regulation, social shifts and economic aspects that marked the changes in town construction. The town bylaws, which generally did not undergo alterations for hundreds of years,[45] were adapted when circumstances required. For example, urban fires were an important reason for the 'stonifying' of towns: building in wood was discouraged by town authorities and even outlawed for some parts of buildings. There are also many known examples of towns providing subsidies for building in stone and tiling roofs.[46]

Building archaeological research has revealed that the developments in timber and stone structures occurred independently. This impression is confirmed by historical studies into the construction industry, in which guild rules prescribed the strict separation of, for example, carpenters and bricklayers.[47] For example, innovations in wooden structures in the Northern Low Countries to a large extent originated in the south[48]; however, in the centre and east of the Low Countries there are influences from Münster and the Rhine Valley.[49] Several areas of influence can be identified when it comes to fired materials: the reduction in brick size in the Northern Low Countries spread from the province of Holland. Because brick production was primarily a local matter, there were exceptions to the general development. Places where bricks retained their large size for a longer period included Utrecht or the towns along the IJssel. On the other hand, the spread of pantiles took place from the east.[50]

The use of stone reveals similar regional differences. As the map of the areas of origin shows (Fig. 2), it was primarily the waterways that determined the best place to get the stone. There is, for example, a high concentration of Ledian and Gobertinger in the west of the present-day Netherlands, a lot of Bentheimer sandstone in Overijssel and Münster stone in the east.

It is these factors that make general statements on the construction industry an extremely precarious matter. Construction in the Low Countries at the start of the sixteenth century was largely a direct continuation of medieval tradition. This medieval tradition applied to the stylistic vision, the organisation of the construction industry, the use of materials and construction principles and each of these aspects underwent its own development. A study into the development of architecture in the Northern and Southern Low Countries in the sixteenth and seventeenth centuries should be more than the analysis of only one of these aspects. It is precisely the interplay of a large number of factors that can explain changes in a particular sub-field. If the Meuse Valley stone trade's influences on the construction industry in the north are then also discussed, the focus should be on more than just the stylistic development, construction principles or the craftsmen involved. It is this encompassing vision that this publication will try to illustrate in the coming chapters. To start with we shall examine that part of the construction process on which everything depends: the material or more specifically, stone.

[45] Meischke 1988, p. 208-262.
[46] See, among others, Maaseik. Glaudemans 1999, pp. 85-86, Van der Heijden, Molhuysen 1981, p. 33 and Meyer, V.d. Elzen 1982.
[47] Kolman 1993, Chapter 3 and 4.
[48] Janse 1989, Chapter 1.
[49] This concerns the dissemination of ridge pieces and link-beam posts.
[50] De Vries 1985.

II. THE TRADE IN NAMUR STONE

Around 1750, the town master mason of Veere, Adriaan Bommenee, wrote concerning the quarries near Brussels, "All manner of work that one could wish for can be ordered from and finished at these quarries, from that type of stone [...]; all manner of low and high pilasters [...] columns; entire blue facades for houses, etc. If you manage to explain and express yourself properly by means of paper or wooden moulds, or through good and fine drawings, which have been accurately drawn."[51] When Bommenee committed his memories to paper, the practices he described had existed for hundreds of years. Products delivered ready made existed as early as the eleventh century; they came from the Eiffel and later from the Meuse Valley, and Hainaut and Brabant. Prefabricated stone products were also supplied down the Weser. But although the practice had been known for quite some time, this manner of working was primarily characteristic of the period this book focuses on. The Van Neurenberg family of stone merchants was, as will be revealed later, a prime exponent of the delivery of finished products to order. Under the influence of the changing construction industry in the north, this method of working became increasingly prevalent during the sixteenth century.

Stone from various quarters

In contrast to timber and brick, stone has always been a foreign product in the Northern Low Countries. That people were prepared to go to great lengths to obtain this stone is proven by the many construction traces of foreign stone types, which can still be found in the Low Countries.

Almost without exception, the supply of stone took place over water. There was a busy trade over the Rhine as early as the tenth and eleventh centuries, where tuffa stone, trachyte and basalt from the area around Andernach were ferried over it. In the thirteenth and fourteenth centuries, the area around Brussels and Tournai became the principal place stone where originated. Here the Schelde was the most important artery. In the sixteenth century the Meuse also started to play a role, when Namur stone and marlstone were supplied over this river. Furthermore, calcareous sandstone from Baumberg was supplied over the Berkel and the IJssel, while sandstone from the County of Bentheim was transported to Zwolle over the Vecht, and from there to the west.

Two factors determined which type of stone to choose. First, the stone had to be suitable for the intended purpose. For example, Namur stone, a hard homogenous limestone that is nonporous, was used for quays, dripstone mouldings, thresholds and coverings. Marlstone, a very soft, porous type of limestone was not suitable for these applications, but was good for detailed decorative work. The second factor in determining which stone to use was the supply. To this end, the transport routes between the various quarries and the construction sites have to be examined. The question of which quarry could supply the right stone for the lowest transport costs or the standard range at the nearest staple market, often proved to be the determining factor.

---

[51] *In deese putten kan men alle werk bestellen en laaten claarmaaken dat men van die soort van steen begeert te hebben [...]; alderley soorten van laage en hooge pilasters; alle soort van laage en hooge reghtstaande frontwerken; colommen en entercolommen; geheele blauwe gevels voor huysen etc. Als men sig maar wel ten reghte weet te expliceeren en uyt te drukken door papier of houte malle, of door goede en nette teykeninge, die aecoraat op de voetmaat geteykent sijn.* Bommenee 1988, pp. 139-140.

Origin of stone in the sixteenth century

We can roughly distinguish between four geographical areas that played a role in the supply of stone in the sixteenth century. These are the surroundings of Brussels-Hainaut, those of Namur-Liège-Maastricht, the diocese of Münster and the County of Bentheim. Furthermore, we can distinguish a number of minor areas that played a less significant structural role in the materials trade. The stone referred to here is only encountered incidentally. An example of such stone can be found in Harderwijk. Here it was prescribed that graves had to be covered with "*Lijflantssche* stone or another hard stone."[52] This choice is an obvious one as Harderwijk was part of the Hanse. Ships that sailed north with cargo, took on, among other things, stone in Scandinavia, which served as ballast for the return journey.[53]

German stone types: Münster stone, Bentheimer sandstone, Obernkirchner sandstone and tuffa stone

So-called Baumberger or Münster stone was supplied from the Münsterland over the river Berkel, between Coesfeld (Germany) and Arnhem. Baumberger was transported west over the Overijsselse Vecht, the Lippe, Ruhr and Rhine. This type of stone was used from the end of the fourteenth century onwards, particularly in the east of the Low Countries.[54] Baumberger stone is a calcareous sandstone variant with a high percentage of lime, which makes it relatively soft. There was a risk of the stone becoming damaged in transit; therefore it was usually worked at its destination, which means its area of origin had minimal influence on the finished product.[55]

It is not surprising that Baumberger stone was primarily used in Gelderland and mainly in high-status buildings. Stone was a luxury product that added status, and moreover Münster was geographically favourably sited for Gelre and vice versa. Well known examples of Münster stone in Gelderland can be found in the southern portal of the Eusebius Church and the Devil's House in Arnhem,[56] the decoration of House Twickel in Delden, the Sint-Stevens Church, the Latin school and the town hall in Nijmegen and the Cannenburgh in Vaassen. Münster stone was also applied at Buren castle.[57] In addition to decorative work on the exterior and for stone window frames, Baumberger was also frequently used for interior work. The fireplaces and decorations at Schloss Horst are famous.[58] A well-known Utrecht master, Colijn de Nole, frequently worked in this type of stone and the fireplace in Kampen's council house is an example of his work.

The trade in Bentheimer sandstone underwent great highs and lows.[59] After a revival of trade in the second half of the fifteenth century, relatively little Bentheimer stone was used during the sixteenth century.[60] Only in the first half of the seventeenth century did the trade fully flourish and enor-

---

[52] *Lijflantssche stene off mit anderen herden stene.* Berns 1886, p. 30.
[53] This trade helps explain why a town on the Zuiderzee like Harderwijk mentions Scandinavian stone as the material for gravestones. Scandinavian stone types could be sold in the Low Countries. The relative scarcity of stone will have ensured that this was not a usual occurence and that the stone was used in the harbour town itself.
[54] De Vries 1994, p. 122.
[55] This practice is also known for marlstone. This method is still used. During a recent restoration of Maastricht town hall the new parts were supplied as semi-manufactured products and then detailed on site.
[56] Today only part of the arch is original. During two restorations the remaining original work on the outside was

replaced by German limestone.
[57] See also Beelaerts van Blokland 1931.
[58] For the other stonemasons involved, see Klapheck 1915.
[59] See Voort 1968, 1970 and 2000 for an overview of the working of Bentheimer sandstone.
[60] In addition to Utrecht's Cathedral and the Old Church in Amsterdam, Bentheimer sandstone was also used in Tiel at the start of the sixteenth century. For example, the mayors, aldermen and council of Tiel wrote a letter to the town of Zutphen on 17 March 1501. The letter reveals that stonemason Johan van Zutphen, who was working on the Sint-Maartens Church in Tiel with his son, had been to Bentheim to buy sandstone there for the church in Tiel. See M.M.D.-H. 1961, p. 142.

mous quantities of stone from the quarries near Bentheim and Gildehaus were used in the Republic for more than one hundred years. The trade in Bentheimer sandstone took place almost exclusively over the Overijsselse Vecht, after which the stone was transhipped in Zwolle, because that town had staple rights to this stone. During the sixteenth century, stone quarrying was widely dispersed, which hampered the material's competitive chances. This situation would only change in the seventeenth century when almost all the leases on the quarries were owned by Dutch merchants.[61]

Perhaps of greater importance in the sixteenth century was Bückeberger or Obernkirchner stone, which was shipped to Bremen over the Weser. The first important shipments of this stone to the Low Countries took place relatively early. The listing of a shipment of the "best Buckeberg stone" for the town hall in Antwerp, which Anthonis van Seron supplied in 1561, is conspicuous.[62] Although Antwerp was relatively close to the quarries of Gobertinge and Lede, people preferred the yellow Weser stone. It is therefore interesting to examine an explosive conflict that took place in 1563. On 31 August of that year, the Bremen council wrote a letter to Hennemann Blomingk, the responsible official of the Schauenburg on the Weser, in which they confirmed that Bremen stonemason Hinrick Lifflender had purchased stone in Obernkirchen from Albert Hesselenn. In order to transport the stone to the Weser Lifflender had rented eight carts. Previously, it was the Bremen stonemasons who purchased stone in Obernkirchen and controlled the trade of this material over the Weser. However, before Lifflender managed to ship his stone Nicolaas Mido, a representative of the abovementioned Anthonis van Seron from Antwerp, took the carts from him. Mido, who was from Antwerp and was also active in the stone trade in the Weser area, claimed he had the exclusive rights to break and sell the stone concerned. He therefore threatened to not only take away Lifflender's carts, but also the stone. Tempers flared and resulted in Hinrick Lifflender punching Nicolaas Mido.

The story had a historian-friendly conclusion: Mido reported the fracas to the official and urged him to imprison Lifflender. However, before he could be arrested Lifflender escaped and fled to Bremen, leaving the shipment of stones he had purchased behind. The Bremen council demanded the return of the stone in its letter, threatening the confiscation of all Obernkirchner stone shipped over the Weser when it got to Bremen if Lifflender's stone was not returned.[63]

The above information suggests that a license had indeed been obtained from Antwerp to break and sell Obernkirchen stone in the early sixties. Simultaneously the dominance of the Bremen stonecutters hindered the people from the west from quarrying. All the material passed Bremen and traditionally was stapled here, in which case the Bremen stonecutters were responsible for the trade.[64] Bremen looked after its interests well. In 1576, "bockeborger" stone was again purchased in Bremen from Emmeken Markus for the repair of the town hall in Antwerp; apparently the town had given up trying to quarry their own stone in Germany.[65]

Finally, we can mention another type of stone, namely tuffa stone. Tuffa stone had been shipped to the Low Countries from the Eiffel for hundreds of years, sometimes in combination with trachyte and basalt lava. Tuffa stone originated from various quarries and varied in composition.[66] Although the use of tuffa stone decreased in the Northern Low Countries after the advent of stone types from Brabant, this type of stone was applied well into the sixteenth century. Examples include the Sint-Maartens Church in Zaltbommel and the Sint-Jans Church in 's-Hertogenbosch. In contrast to what older lit-

[61] See Voort 1970 for more on this subject.
[62] [...] besten Buckebergschen steen [...]. Janse, De Vries 1991, p. 18.
[63] See Bremisches Jahrbuch, Bd. 16. Bremen 1892. p. 86.
[64] A well-known example is Lüder van Bentheim, who at the close of the sixteenth century would supply the facades for the town hall in Leiden. See Albrecht 1995 passim.

[65] Janse 1994, p. 95. An example of the Southern Netherlands activity in Northern Germany can also be found at Schloss Reinbek near Hamburg. See Wendt 1996.
[66] Both trachyte tuffa and phonolite tuffa had already been used in combination since the Middle Ages.

erature suggests, the contacts with the Eiffel continued for much longer. Material was obtained from Andernach for the vaulting of the Sint-Walburgs Church in Zutphen as late as 1533, whereby also the help of a master mason from Andernach was requested. It is remarkable that during this period tuffa stone was primarily applied in ecclesiastical buildings and not in government or private structures. A possible explanation could be older trading ties, which the ecclesiastical principals continued to use until the construction projects were completed or halted.[67]

'Belgian' stone

Two principal 'Belgian' stone type trade flows can be distinguished: Mosan trade and Schelde trade. The latter was primarily influential in the provinces of Northern Brabant, Zeeland and Holland. The stone was more often than not exported ready-made; subsequently it is easy to point out the influences that were imported into the north. As far as this influence is concerned, the abovementioned trade of the Keldermans family is the most well known example.[68] Stone from, among other places, Lede, Balegem and Gobertinge, but also from Hainaut and northern France was shipped north over the Schelde. A good example of this route is the well-known Blue Tower of Gorinchem, which was executed in stone from Hainaut. The many tributaries of the Schelde played an important role in this construction. Because there was no connection between the Schelde and the Meuse, and upstream transport from Gorinchem and Dordrecht was impractical, the Schelde trade's influence in Gelderland and the east was much smaller than it was in Zeeland and Holland.

The stone trade from Brabant boomed at the close of the Middle Ages and tailed off shortly afterwards. Around 1750, Adriaan Bommenee wrote, "[...] in the fourteenth, fifteenth and sixteenth century, all public places and buildings were made of white *arduyn* or brick with white *arduyn* layers in between. But now this stone is no longer used in the united Low Countries; and in Flanders and Brabandt the same stone is also little used."[69] The waning popularity of this type of stone seems to have started before the year 1600. Research has revealed that the thickness of the stone applied and the height of the blocks decreased around this time, which indicates that the seams were running dry,[70] and probably necessitated people from Antwerp such as Anthonis van Seron buying stone in Germany during the second half of the sixteenth century. In the Northern Low Countries, the political situation was also an important factor in the stagnation of supplies of stone from Brabant. The closing of the Schelde in 1585 marked the end of exports from the Schelde basin to the Northern Low Countries. With the exception of a brief resurgence during the Twelve Years' Truce, the old situation was never restored.[71]

Trade over the Meuse played a much bigger role. Much more carboniferous limestone from the province of Namur can be found in Gelderland than in the rest of the country. However, Namur stone had already been used in Utrecht and Dordrecht in the fourteenth and fifteenth centuries. Early examples of the use of this type of stone can also be found in Deventer.[72]

---

[67] For more on tuffa stone see Van Kempen 1997.
[68] See Van Mosselveld 1987, passim for more on this subject.
[69] *[...] in de 14, 15 en 16 eeuwen heeft men gaan bouwen alle publicke plaatsen en gebouwen met witten arduyn of met gebacken steen en witte arduyn speklaagen daardoor. Maar nu is die steen in de geünieerde Neederlanden buyten gebruyk; en in Vlaanderen en in Brabandt werdt deselve meede weynig verwerkt.* Bommenee 1988, p. 157.

[70] Examples have been found in the Hanswijk Church in Mechelen, the Sint-Michiels Church in Leuven and the Begijnhof Church in Brussels, where at least in the columns smaller blocks were used after a halt in construction work at the start of the seventeenth century. Further research will be required in order to make definitive statements on this matter.
[71] Janse, De Vries 1991, p. 11.
[72] Bloemink, Roetert Steenbruggen 1991, p. 51.

Marlstone

A brief discussion of marlstone will ensue before we move on to Namur stone. Carvers or carpenters also used this material, a light yellow, very soft limestone, although it is classified as a stone.[73] Marlstone is often named after its place of origin, such as Sibbe or Sichener. Other names for marlstone are Maastricht's chalk or *tuffeau de Maastricht*.[74] The stone is found to the south west of the Geul River into Belgium, to the south west of Maastricht. Marlstone was used in prehistoric as well as Roman times. From the tenth century, the stone was also used as a construction material and from the twelfth century it was demonstrably used in combination with Namur stone. Almost two hundred extraction sites have been used from the Middle Ages to the present. The usable stone is between twenty-five to seventy-five centimetres thick. Early applications can be encountered in the western end of the Onze Lieve Vrouwe Church in Maastricht and the middle aisle of the Sint-Servaas Church in Maastricht. Valkenburg castle (twelfth century and later), Kessel (possibly twelfth century) and Stein (around 1200), and the churches of Voerendaal, Baexem, Bergen, Grathem, Heel and the Munster Church in Roermond (first half of the thirteenth century) all show marlstone.

6. Nijmegen, Stratenmakers tower: marlstone application, 1537-42 (photograph by author).

Only in the 1530s and 40s was marlstone used outside the Duchy of Limburg. The factors involved are primarily the same as those dealt with for the Namur stone trade, and will consequently be discussed below. Marlstone applications were diverse: on the one hand the material was used for decorative purposes, such as the Maarten van Rossum House in Zaltbommel or the refugium Mariënhage in 's-Hertogenbosch. On the other hand, marlstone was used for the construction of fortifications and rounded guntowers (*rondelen*), such as in the Stratenmakers tower in Nijmegen (Fig. 6), and a number of bastions in Ravenstein and in Deventer, around 1560. The rood screen in the Sint-Peters Church in Boxtel (1607-1608) and the church in Heusden (1638-1639) also involved the use of marlstone.

Relatively little research has been carried out into the quarrying and dissemination of marlstone. The material's popularity seems connected to its properties (easy to work, low transport costs) and its favourable geographical location. Marlstone proved eminently suitable, particularly when the need developed in Gelderland to carry out large-scale fortification renewal.[75]

[73] Janse, De Vries 1991, p. 8.
[74] *Tuffeau* is the French name for very soft limestone. Slinger 1980, p. 55.

[75] The favourable price ratio vis-à-vis brick played a role. (Unpublished lecture by J. Soentgerath, Bouwhistorisch Platform Zeist, 9 February 2000.). See also Stevenhagen 1999 and De Vries 1994, p. 62.

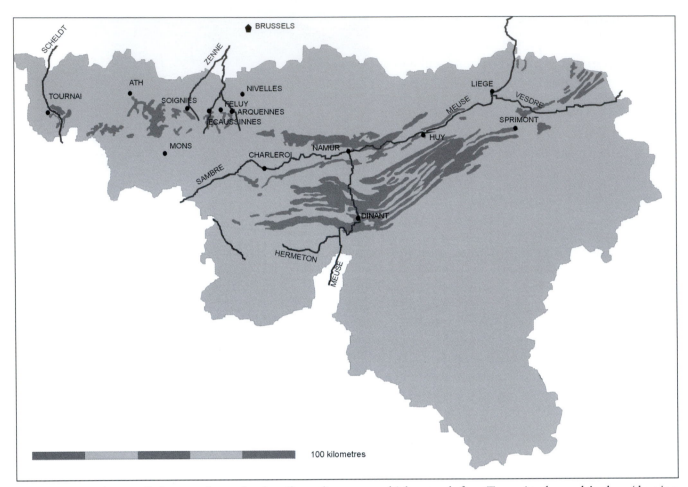

7. Namur stone is part of a large package of carboniferous limestone, which extends from Tournai to beyond Aachen (drawing by author).

Namur stone

The influence of stone from the Schelde basin would decrease dramatically during the second half of the sixteenth century due to a great extent to the wartime circumstances. Nevertheless, the stone trade between north and south did not grind to a complete halt. On the contrary, during this period the trade in Namur stone even increased. At this juncture, the history and characteristics of the trade in Namur stone will be elucidated in order to better understand the shifts in trade and the manner in which traders and building contractors from the Meuse Valley worked. The incomplete bibliography of this type of stone is a great hindrance. In contrast to Obernkirchner or Bentheimer sandstone very little has been written about Namur stone. That situation is in some ways similar to that of Tournai stone, concerning which, L. Nys wrote in 1993, "The medieval stone quarries of Tournai have never been the subject of any kind of study whatsoever […]."[76] J.-L. van Belle expressed a comparable idea regarding stone from the Hainaut basin, "The study of the history of the stone industry in Belgium and that of the Walloon country in particular, is a recent development."[77] However, although the older

[76] *Les carrières médiévales du Tournaisis n'ont fait l'object d'aucune étude, assez curieusement si l'on considère la richesse et la masse de la documentation qui concerne la question.* Nys 1993, p. 54.

[77] *L'étude du passé de l'industrie de la pierre en Belgique et en Wallonie en particulier est une préoccupation récente.* Van Belle 1990, p. 7.

20

8. Namur, Saint-Loup Church. The appearance of Namur stone from various banks differs considerably (photograph by author).

9. Namur, Saint-Loup Church. Deeper within the Namur stone banks the layers become thicker, the texture rougher and sunken fossils are encountered (photograph by author).

literature often has major lacunae, it is still possible to gain an impression of the history of the trade in this stone.

Composition and appearance

Namur stone is also referred to as *arduin* or *Meuse stone*, but these terms have led to a great deal of confusion both in the literature and in daily use. *Hardsteen* is also used as a term for Namur stone, although this term actually applies to *petit granit*, a carboniferous limestone that also contains small crinoid fossils, which originates both in the Meuse Valley and from Hainaut. In Belgium Namur stone is also referred to as *calcaire mosan*. The main component of all types of limestone, and therefore also of Namur stone, is carbonic lime ($CaCO_3$), which is white. However, contamination with carbons and hydrocarbons (bitumen) gives the stone a colour that varies from grey to black. The stone developed from reef lime and has a content of over ninety percent calcium carbonate. It is part of a large package of carboniferous limestone, which stretches from Tournai to Aachen (Fig. 7). It is geologically related to Tournai stone, crinoid and black marble. Further east, the geologically related Aachen bluestone can be found, which has its own quarrying history.[78]

[78] See Kasig 1984, passim for more on this variant.

The deposition or stacking of the abovementioned reefs, sand and organisms has created a thick stone package, which consists of various repeating layers. These layers are made up of various banks, while the banks themselves are, subsequently, characterised by layering, which can sometimes be seen with the naked eye. The layers are structured according to the same pattern, whereby the thickness of the banks decreases the higher up the layers one looks. Simultaneously the stone's structure is finer there. The lowest banks therefore harbour large uninterrupted blocks with a less fine structure. Moreover, the bottom banks are contaminated with fossils (Fig. 8 and 9).

Visual analysis has demonstrated that in the Northern Low Countries only a few variations of varying petrological composition were used in the past. This variation concerned stone that developed during three periods: the Devonian; the fourth Palaeozoic or Primair period, ca. 390 million years ago; and carboniferous, 350-270 million years ago.[79] The stone from the *Viséen* was used most commonly in construction and also for export.[80]

Quarrying

Bommenee described the work in and around a quarry during the first half of the eighteenth century in his memoirs. He was well informed having visited a quarry and because his son had worked at one for a few years. Particular customs and methods sometimes continued to exist for hundreds of years.[81] Due to this lengthy tradition it is reasonable to examine the principles of stone quarrying on the basis of Bommenee's description. Bommenee describes the quarries in Hainaut as follows, "The stone pits are all open [...]. When a quarry is first dug, you have to get approximately eighteen to twenty feet deep before you start finding good stone. Whether the stone found at the top is not suitable for the job, as some would have it, is unknown to me, but I believe the top layers are not as good as the bottom layers, which is the case due to old age and due to rain and the air, which have affected the stone since the creation of the world, alongside the sun's rays."[82] What Bommenee is alluding to is the layered character of the stone. Not every bank is suitable for quarrying, so that sometimes material has to be removed before operating the quarry. This upper material can be used to burn lime, but is not appropriate as a building material. The good banks are broken out of the mountain; holes are sawn or

10. Stone quarrying took place in the same manner for centuries. Example from Carrara (photograph by author).

[79] Goossens 1994, Nijs, de Geyter 1985, pp. 13-14.

[80] In the application of Namur stone, Comanne distinguishes between various types: here this type concerns the *grès houiller*, used during the Roman period in the area around Liège; limestone from the *Viséen*, (also referred to as *pierre de Meuse, Namur stone* or *blauwsteen*); and *tuffeau*, a marlstone-like variant found downstream from Liège. Moreover, some variants were applied as black marble. Comanne 1992, p. 394. See De Jonghe et al. 1996, fiche 21, 24, 25, 26, 28 and in particular 31 for more information.

[81] See, among others, Janse 1964, Van Tyghem 1966, Van Belle 1990 and Nys 1993.

[82] *De steenputten sijn alle open en daar gaat men in met een afloopende april ofte afril soo men die begeert te benaamen. Als een put eerst werdt aangeleght, soo moet men wel ontrent 18 à 20 voeten diep sijn alvoorens men goede steen gaat vinden. Of die steen van booven niet na den eys rijp is, sooals sommige willen seggen, is mijn onbekent, maar ik geloof dat de boovelagen soo goet niet sijn als beneedelaagen, dat sulks is door ouderdom en door den reegen en de lught, die van de schepping der weerelt tot nu toe daarop gewerkt heeft, beneevens de straale van de son. Bommenee 1988, p. 141.*

11. Les Grands Malades near Namur. Drawing by General de Howen, 21 April 1821 (Collection Société archéologique de Namur).

drilled into a thick horizontal piece of stone, after which iron wedges are hammered in and the stone breaks (Fig. 10).

Many quarries lay adjacent to bodies of water,[83] which had both great advantages, but also quarrying drawbacks. The open face quarries were often hilly areas, with the pit's bottom at a relatively low level; consequently at this depth the water hindered quarrying. Bommenee had the following to say on this matter, "To one side of the stone pits there runs a brook, which comes down from the mountains. There it is only around a foot deep and four to five feet wide. And that water flows so fast that the brook did not freeze over during the harsh frost of the year 1740. There is a waterwheel on this brook [...], that is turned by the brook water [...]. The wheel was connected with three pump buckets which worked day and night, to continually get water from the quarry, that continually enters the stone pit due to rain, hail, snow, and otherwise."[84] The problem Bommenee described was much less prominent in the Meuse Valley quarries; the stone there was found in the deeply eroded banks of the Meuse so that work generally took place above the water level (Fig. 11).

[83] Nys 1993, p. 69.

[84] *Ter sijden de steenputten vooren gemelt, loopt een beeke waater, die uyt het gebergte komt vlieden. Die is aldaar maar ontrent een voet diep en 4 à 5 voeten breet. En dat waater heeft soo een sterke gank, dat die beek aldaar in de strenge vorst van 't jaar 1740 niet is toegevroosen. Op deese beek werkt een waaterrat [...], dat door scheepsplanken voor waaterborden daar onderaan hangen van 't beekwaater gestaadigh word ront gedreeve. Aan dit rat hangt ook een gank met kammen in een scheijfloop en dat scheijfloop is vast aan een eijsere krukas en daar hangen 3 pompemmers aan en daar pomp dat werk meede, dag en nagt, om gestaadig waater uyt de careerput te haallen, dat aldaar door reegen, haagel en sneeuw, als anders, gestaadig in de steenput komt.* Bommenee 1988, p. 141. In Hainaut the problem of water in the quarries became an issue around 1600.

12. Schönau, construction of the Cistercian monastery. Anonymous drawing, sixteenth-century (Germanisches Nationalmuseum, Nürnberg, Hz. 196).

In order to be able to keep the labourers working, the quarry operators had to take precautions. Operational continuity was of great importance, which becomes apparent if the (scant) information on the number of labourers working at the quarries is examined. In Bentheim there were a couple of dozen per quarry, depending on the demand for stone.[85] At the end of the seventeenth century, one Namur quarry had twenty-two labourers present spread over a whole year. On average approximately ten men worked at any one quarry simultaneously.[86] Historical illustrations of stone quarries also point to the same number (Fig. 12). Naturally, the total number of labourers was much higher. Among other things, proven by the fact that during the demolition of hospital buildings and the church of the Knights of St. John, for the construction of Castle Vredenburg in Utrecht in 1529, several hundred Namur 'pioneers', probably stonebreakers, worked in Utrecht.[87]

Although work in the quarry created a great deal of waste, not much material was actually wasted. Bommenee, "There is always a great deal of waste at the stone pits, which is worked off the rock. The bosses burn this waste into lime and use this to fertilise their farmland and fields, as they have a large number of dependents";[88] thus allowing the conclusion that operators sometimes had farmland and used the proceeds thereof to partially pay their employees in kind. But also "they need a lot of horses to drag stone up out of the stone pits and to transport stone to the quayside in Brussels. They also need the horses to work their land, as they harvest a lot of rye. When the harvest is ripe everyone who works at the stone pit has to pitch in to harvest it."[89] Any lime left over after fertilising the land was sold.

Not everyone did the same work at the quarry. Roughly the same three-way subdivision is encountered in the various areas: stone breakers for the quarrying and heavy work, stonecutters, who processed the stone into a trading product and the operators, who maintained contact with market.[90] One of Van Belle's most important conclusions in his research into a Namur quarry in the year 1685 was that the operator owned all the parts of the trade, as was also the case at the quarries in Hainaut.[91] Moreover, production at quarries could also be fully geared towards the orders of traders from the north.[92]

Processing: finishing and identifying marks

Surface treatment

Besides the question when the trade in Namur stone increased and which factors played a role, it is also important to examine the actual quarry products. Research into materials provides data on

[85] Voort 1968, p. 96.

[86] Van Belle 1983, pp. 102-103. Naturally, the size of a quarry has to be taken into account when making such determinations. The lease contract, which regulates the activities of the stone breaker(s), is of crucial importance. In the limestone quarry Rüdersdorf, just to the east of Berlin, such a group consisted of eight people.

[87] Hoekstra suspects that these people, the total number of whom varies from source to source from 184 to 400, were experienced in the stone quarries and were therefore used for the demolition. They were of no use for anything else. Hoekstra 1997, pp. 118-119, n. 21.

[88] *Op de steenputten valt seer veel afval, die van de steenen werden afgewerkt. Dien afval brande de baasen tot kalk en mesten daar hun landerijen meede en hunnen weyen, want soo een sleept veel*

gevolg na sig, want voor eerst soo betaallen veel hun volk die in de putten werken met booter en melk op reekening en om de 3 à 4 weeken reekene sij af. Bommenee 1988, pp. 141-142.

[89] *[...] hebben sij veel puurden noodig om de steen uyt de steenput op te sleepen en om de steenen te brengen te Brussel op de kaay. Ook hebben sij de paarden noodigh om hun lant te labureeren, want sij winnen aldaar veel rogge. Als den oogst daar reijp is, soo moet het alles helpen om in te saamelen, dat op de steenput werkt.* Ibidem.

[90] Nys 1993, p. 90.

[91] Van Belle 1983, pp. 112-113.

[92] Germain 1981, p. 218, [...] *lors que les taillieurs de pierres ont vendu et livré de la marchandise à des marchants qui les viennent achapter aux falises, comme font ordinairement les marchands de Hollande.*

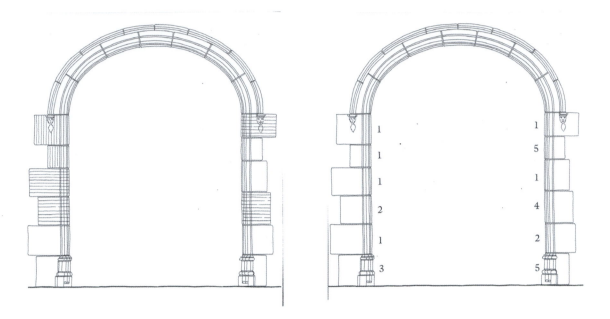

13. 's-Hertogenbosch, The Ruische Gate consists of Namur stone and crinoid stone. On the left the way in which the stone was placed; on the right the historic stone finishing (1. Smooth; 2. Sixteenth-century stroke; 3. 'Dutch' stroke; 4. Bush-hammered; 5. Rough, later stroke (drawing by Ronald Glaudemans).

14. Hasselt (Belgium), refugium of Herkenrode Abbey. Finishing Namur stone using a pointed chisel (photograph by author).

processing. A stone in a building can be read in various ways. Think for example of identifying marks, surface treatment and positioning of the piece of stone (Fig. 13).[93]

After the stone was taken from the quarry and was cut into manageable blocks, further processing took place at the quarry or in the surrounding area. Studying the surface treatment of the stone, in particular, provides an indication of the way work took place, the tools that were used and the development of processing techniques. Stonecutters used various tools and those used for finishing the piece of work left traces on the stone (Fig. 14).[94] The most important of these were the pointed chisel, the charring chisel (a wide, thin chisel) and the bush hammer. Research into stone cutting work on

---

[93] *L'Observation d'un bloc, de n'importe quel bloc de pierre, mis en oeuvre dans une construction se prête à une multitude de lectures.* Bavay 1989, p. 11. Compare to Doperé 1998. This study discusses the surface treatment and the marking of a number of applications of Gobertinger stone. In De Jonge 1998, research was carried out into the geological composition

and surface treatment of the stone used in Boussu Castle, by J.-L. van Belle and F. Tourneur, in particular pp. 109-113 and 145-149. See also Hochkirchen 1990 for the surface treatment of stone.
[94] See Janse 1998, pp. 26-28 and Van Tyghem 1966 for more information on stonecutter's tools.

15. Overview of historic stonemasons' tools (Collection atelier Hofsingel, 's-Gravenhage, Photograph by G.Th. Delemarre 1951, RDMZ, Neg.Nr. 41.240).

Namur stone has revealed that finishing techniques changed around 1500. In the Middle Ages the stone axis, the hatchet and pointed chisel were often used. For harder types of stone or for rough work it was primarily the marteline that was used. Over the course of the fifteenth century, slagging was improved, which led to improved iron quality.[95] The harder the iron became the more the charring chisel was used. Its use can be seen in the surface treatment on the stones, the charring and later the stroke.[96] Over the course of the sixteenth century this stroke became increasingly narrow.[97] In the sixteenth century, it was primarily the charring chisel that was used, although other tools were also used for surface treatment (Fig. 15).[98]

The surface treatment of the Namur stone found in the Northern Low Countries has various forms. A few fifteenth-century examples, such as the Zoudenbalch house in Utrecht and the Ding House in Maastricht show traces of surface treatment with a pointed chisel. Where stroke occurs a slow development can be discerned, as Table 1 reveals. It seems as if the manner of finishing smooth surfaces became more refined during the sixteenth century. In the seventeenth century, the development indi-

[95] Klein 1965, p. 64.
[96] Overeem, Karsemeijer, 1987, RV blad 01-13. Charring entails processing the stone's surface with a single stroke thereby resulting in a grooved or ribbed surface.
[97] See Comanne 1992. See also Doperé 1994. A similar development can also be seen in the stone from Ecaussines. In the sixteenth century they employed a stroke of 32/36

strokes per palm and for mouldings this number was even higher. In the seventeenth century, the number of strokes decreased to 24, only to increase again to 28 strokes in the eighteenth century. Many thanks to J.-L. van Belle, 15 April 1999.
[98] Comanne 1992, pp. 397-398.

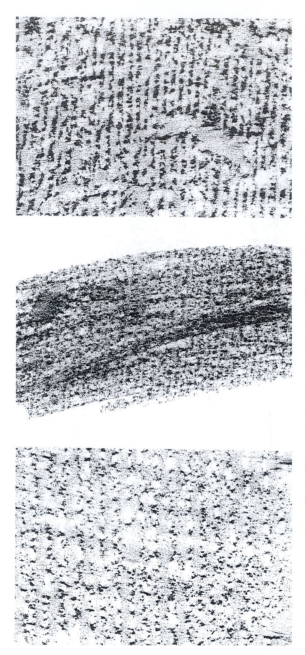

16. Indication of the development of surface treatments for Namur stone in Nijmegen's cloth hall (1540, thirty-three strokes), the Reformed Church in Willemstad (1595, forty-seven to fifty strokes) and Maastricht town hall (1659, twenty strokes) (drawing by author).

cated here was reversed and there was a tendency to make the surface treatment rougher. The bush hammer, a hammer with a surface consisting of a number of points, was used very sparingly from the seventeenth century onwards (Fig. 16).[99] Only in the eighteenth and particularly in the nineteenth century did the use of this tool really become common.[100]

Placing and use of the stone

There are roughly two ways of placing a stone in a structure. The stone can be applied as it was found in the quarry, in exactly the same position as it was formed due to deposition in nature; this placement is known as *en lit*. It can also be placed in deviation to its original quarry position, whereby the stone can be put on its side or at an angle; this is known as *en délit*. Stone placement reveals the choices made in its processing because the processing determines how the stone will be applied.

In general there was no standard method. It is preferable to use the stone in accordance with its quarry position, but due to the nature of the material this position is not always possible. A Namur stone column shaft, for example, will generally be placed *en délit*, because it is impossible to quarry a homogenous piece that can be placed *en lit*. The layers in the bank were simply not high enough. The column is therefore horizontally mined from the quarry instead of vertically.[101]

Stone tong holes

Another element that reveals something about the way the stone was worked, are stone tong holes, made to help position the stone in the structure. Stone tongs are scissor-like tools that help grasp the stone. The tongs have two bent arms, which cross each other at the centre of rotation and meet at the top in a loop with a chain. Putting the tongs onto a stone and then hoisting them up automatically tightens the tongs' grip. To provide grip small holes

[99] Thanks to Francis Tourneur. Comanne 1992 lists medieval applications. However, these are not unequivocal. Later processing needs to be taken into account. See also Janse, De Vries 1991, p. 41.

[100] For more on this problem, see Friederich 1988, passim.
[101] For placement according to the quarry position, see Bavay 1989, passim.

Town/building	Date	Stroke per palm
Heeswijk, gate in the castle's bailey	XV	Pointed chisel 11 (randslag 14)
Maastricht, Ding House, side façade	ca 1480	Pointed chisel
Utrecht, House Zoudenbalch	XVd	Pointed chisel
Duurstede, castle's bailey	ca 1485	19-25
Utrecht, gate of House Loenersloot	ca 1500	27
Herkenrode, abbey gatehouse	1531	31-33
Nijmegen, cloth hall	1536-1543	33
's-Hertogenbosch, Baselaars gate	ca 1540	31-33
Middelrode, Seldensate castle's gate	ca 1540	30-31
Willemstad, Reformed church	1595	47-50
Venray, southern gateway of St. Peters Banden	XVId	None
Maastricht, town hall	1659-1664	20-23

Table I. Overview of stroke development on Namur stone.

were made on either side of the stone at its centre of gravity, and these can sometimes still be discerned in the finished structure. The use of stone tongs seems to have originally been a German phenomenon, although it was also used a great deal in the Meuse Valley.[102] Stone tong holes in Namur stone have been found in Utrecht (House Loenersloot, Nieuwe Gracht), Nijmegen (Church arch) and Herkenrode (gate building).

Stone tongs were not always used. Alternatives such as the grapnel, which involved cutting a hole into the top of the stone, did not leave traces in the visible surfaces of the stone. However, unless destructive research is permitted it is impossible to ascertain whether a grapnel was used.

Identifying marks

The majority of Namur stone that was used as construction material does not bear marks.[103] Marks were used more in one area of origin than in the other. Moreover, they were sometimes applied with chalk or graphite. In sandstone these marks can sometimes still be recognised hundreds of years later due to the porous nature of the material.[104] It is unknown whether such written marks were also applied to Namur stone. So far, no traces of these have been found. Another possibility, although it can seldom be studied, is that marks were applied to the enclosed side of the stone. Such practices were applied to a number of Balegem stone window frames, which were found in Nijmegen.[105] A mark was

[102] See Janse, De Vries 1991, pp. 75-78.
[103] Janse, De Vries 1991, p. 61. See Janse 1981 pp. 141-144 for more on the disappearance of mason's marks.
[104] Examples can be found on the Paleis op de Dam in Amsterdam, the Cellebroederspoort in Kampen and the Hooglandse Church in Leiden.
[105] Many thanks to Jörg Soentgerath. Such marks on the 'inside' could also be for mortar or something similar, as

these have been discovered in Breda on archeological finds. In 's-Hertogenbosch a mark was found on the inside of a gate at the Baselaars convent made of Namur stone. The small gate can currently be found in the depot of the Department of Bouwhistorie, Archeologie en Monumenten of the Municipality of 's-Hertogenbosch, in a disassembled state. See also Van Tussenbroek 2000, p. 89.

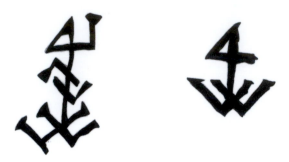

17. Coenraad II and Coenraad III van Neurenberg's marks (after GAA, archief van kerken en kloosters, inv.nr. 116 and SAA, Insolvente Boedelkamer 1562).

also found on the inside of the stone (from Lede) of the Palace of Breda.[106] It is hardly possible to distinguish between areas where marks were or were not applied to stone. A crude demarcation would be to state that the mason's marks stop short of the Meuse and Rhine. Fewer mason's marks are found in the areas where merchants from Brabant, Hainaut and the Meuse Valley were active, than in the areas where influences from Bentheim or the Weser area can be pointed out.[107] However, it should be noted that in the Belgian areas mentioned there may perhaps have been fewer mason's marks, but assembly marks and supplier's marks were common. Exceptions occur when stone has been cut to size at the construction site.

When studying the scarce marks on Namur stone it is possible to distinguish between mason's marks, quarry marks and assembly marks. Although the inventory of marks is not as advanced in the Netherlands as it is in Belgium, it is possible to state that examples from the Meuse Valley are found less often than those from the Schelde basin, Hainaut or the east.[108] An adequate explanation has not yet been found. The trade at various staple towns may perhaps have played a role in the way materials were marked by merchants. Mason and supplier's marks unmistakably had an administrative function, whereby the manner of administrating and checking may have influenced the use of the marks (Fig. 17).

Mason's marks should be viewed as check marks. The hypothesis that these marks were made as conditions of payment seems implausible. Stonecutters were usually paid on a daily basis, which does not necessitate the marking of the production. Marking in order to check the stonecutters' productivity therefore implies payment per unit. The mason's mark as a check mark for the quality supplied seems more plausible. The stonecutter could then be held responsible if his work showed any flaws. Although the system of markings on stone still is not fully understood, an increasing amount of data points in this direction.[109]

Attributing a mark to a particular stonecutter should take place with the utmost caution. As far as the distribution of marks is concerned, at least two systems existed concurrently. As far as research has been able to ascertain, some stonecutters used a personal mark. On the other hand, marks were also allocated by the principal and, during larger construction projects, the fabric lodge. The stonecutter was then allocated a check mark for the duration of the project, which he was supposed to apply to his work.[110] If the stonecutter then left for anoth-

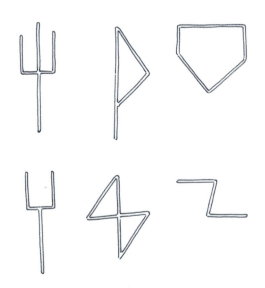

18. Liège, Saint-Jacques Church. Stonemasons' marks, fifteenth century. Not to scale (after Chevalier 1973, p. 64-69, figs. 1-6 and 8).

[106] Van Wezel 1999, p. 187. Marks have also been found in Germany on stone surfaces not immediately visible. Großmann 1993, pp. 159-162.
[107] Janse 1992, p. 277. However, the merchants from Brabant did use mason's marks.
[108] For an overview of 'Belgian' marks see Driessen 1992 and Van Belle 1994.
[109] Janse, De Vries 1991, p. 50, already pointed this out.
[110] Sauer 1962-1963, pp. 467-468 and Bouttier 1991, p. 28.

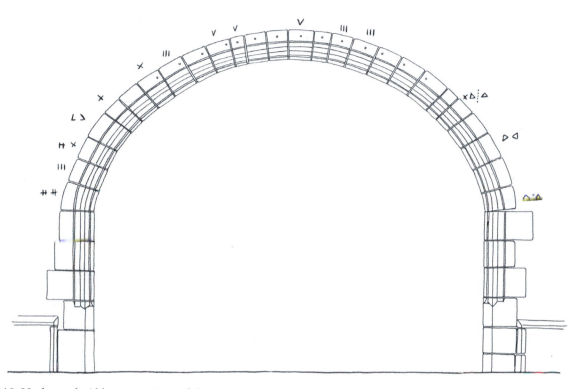

19. Herkenrode Abbey, overview of the pair and assembly marks scratched into Namur stone on the gate build-ing, 1531. Not to scale (drawing by Ronald Glaudemans).

er job, then someone else was allocated his mark. This fact makes dating buildings on the basis of mason's marks problematic. Of course there are examples of marks that can be linked to a single person who used them for an extended period of time, and who worked in the same place for an extended peri-od. Mason's marks on Namur stone dating back to the first half of the fifteenth century have been found in the Saint-Jacques in Liège (Fig.18). But after this time, the use of mason's marks on this type of stone gradually declined.[111]

The quarry mark is a different kind of mark. Quarry or supplier's marks are primarily a fea-ture of the stone trade in Hainaut. The marks of a large number of merchants from this area are well known.[112] This is not the case in the Meuse Valley, although there are a number of marks, which could possibly qualify as supplier's marks.

Finally, assembly marks characterise the trade in ready- made parts. In order to know how the pre-fabricated parts were to be assembled at the construction site, the individual parts were marked. This type of mark occurs regularly on Namur stone. The way in which the parts were marked differed considerably. There are roughly three ways in which this marking took place.

The first determining factor was the thickness of the layer. If the layer to be applied consisted of several pieces, these could be given marks, the so-called pair marks, in order to later reunite them.

[111] A further explanation has to do with the manner of trad-ing: almost all stone was cut to size at the quarry and not at the construction site. Research on the Saint-Jacques Church in Liège has revealed eight different marks in the choir (ca. 1420). The work completed during a subsequent building campaign, between 1514 and 1538 has revealed no mason's marks. However, the work does show more assembly marks. Chevalier 1972, p. 70.
[112] Van Belle 1994, passim, Laleman 1989.

20. Herkenrode Abbey, gate building, detail (photograph by author).

The mutual disposition of the layers made little difference, as long as the total height of the assembled parts was correct. If the piece in question was a large gate, such as that of Herkenrode Abbey or the refugium of Herkenrode in Hasselt (Belgium), a large number of different marks were required (Fig. 19 and 20).[113] An interrelated system of assembly marks in the building was not necessary.

However, there is internal logic among the marks that indicate the difference between left and right, the so-called position marks. An example of these marks are in the gate of the Van Deventer hospital in 's-Hertogenbosch.[114] Here the left-hand posts were given a star and the right-hand ones had a triangle. A logical system with pair and position marks can also be found in the southern portal of the church in Venray (Fig. 21a).

The third system is even more complex as it concerns actual spot marks. In this system there is no room to move blocks as all the elements have been given their own particular place. There are various grades of refinement in this system. A relatively simple example is the gate at Springweg 102 in Utrecht and the gate of Seldensate Castle (Province of North Brabant) (Fig. 21b). In both these examples, Roman numerals have been applied which run across two blocks. This means the positions of the parts was determined in advance. Genuinely spec-

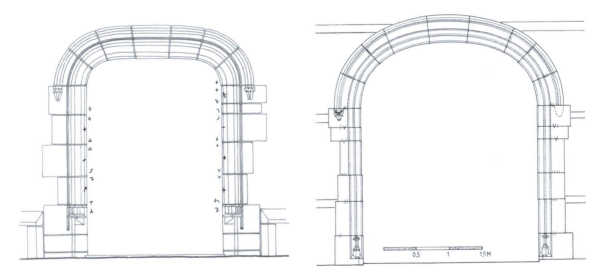

21a and b. Venray, Sint-Petrus-Banden Church, southern portal (approximately 1560) and Seldensate (Middelrode), gate building (approximately 1530). Assembly marks. Not to scale (drawing by Ronald Glaudemans and Mark Bimmel).

[113] For examples of such marks in Alden Biesen and Sint Truiden see Driessen 1992, passim.

[114] Documented in the building by Ad van Drunen, in June 1980.

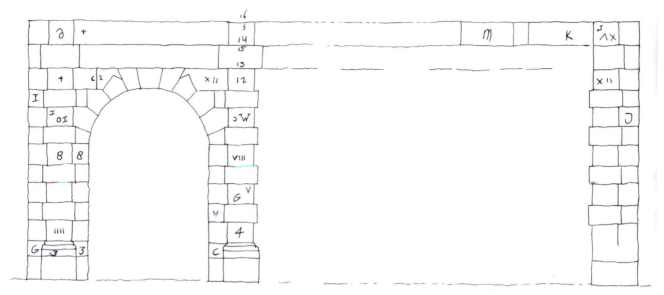

22. Dordrecht, Groothoofdse Poort, system of marks indicating horizontal and vertical order, around 1615. Not to scale (drawing by author).

tacular are the spot marks on the Groothoofdse Gate in Dordrecht (Fig. 22). Here an ingenious system of letters and numbers in various shapes explain the structure of the gate. The complex structure of the gate, which was not made on site, forced the building contractor to clearly mark the individual blocks so they could be correctly placed on site.

Colour

A number of buildings, such as the gate in Middelrode and the church portal in Venlo bear traces of coloured finishing. Other studies have revealed that stone was sometimes given a coloured layer in the past. This practice probably had less to do with protection against the weather than with emphasising the sculpted parts, which seems almost contradictory.[115] Why hide expensive stone behind a finishing layer? However, one should realise that some shapes are easier to execute in stone than in brick, which makes the choice easier.[116]

This does not mean that Namur stone was usually painted. Most of the examples of Namur stone in this study do not bear any visible traces of paint. Many historical stone applications have a regular stroke, which makes the presence of a plaster layer much less plausible. The removal of some paint layers during repairs or restoration should be taken into account. Whether paint on the stones that do bear traces of colour was applied during construction, or at a later date, is hard to ascertain.

The transport of materials over the Meuse

An important factor in the production process was the shipping of the stone. In some cases it was traded by the quarry operators, in other cases, merchants from the north came to collect the ordered

---

[115] Crèvecoeur 1999, p. 135-136.
[116] The literature provides us with a considerable number

of examples of colour on stone. See Denslagen, De Vries 1984, in particular pp. 49-52.

and prepared stone themselves. Transport to the north was a complex process. To a great extent transport depended on the presence of water, whereby the Meuse caused further complications for the captains who travelled downstream. When examining the river conditions, the Meuse upstream of Venlo is characterised by a large fall and is very shallow. North of Venlo the situation is different; here the fall is much less pronounced and the river is deeper, which proved problematic for captains from the north, as they could not travel any further than Venlo. Both the Romans and the Normans had adapted to this hindrance by using small and large ships.[117]

The importance of trade was great enough for these problems to be overcome. Countless products including draper's goods, timber, stone, marlstone, lime, slate, coal, furs, metal goods, grains and wine were traded downstream over the Meuse. The import of fish, wool, salt, dairy products and pottery took place in the opposite direction. Bulk transport vessels were preferred for the transport of these goods.[118] The difference between both parts of the Meuse, as far as ships' tonnage is concerned, was less than sixty *last* herrings (approximately ninety-six tons) south of Venlo and over sixty *last* north of there.[119] The largest vessels could transport approximately 270 tons, though only over the Meuse downstream from Venlo.[120]

Transport regulations

A limitation that affected stone merchants and quarry operators concerned a number of official regulations regarding transport. Transport was subject to its own guild structure and was, in many cases, not carried out by the merchants themselves. Only members of a captains' guild were allowed to work as a captain, and one precondition entailed owning a *Coppelye*.[121] A *coppelye* was a group of several vessels, the principal of which was the *roefschip*, a ship with a deckhouse, i.e. living quarters on deck. A smaller *paetschip* was attached to the deckhouse vessel, and the former had a *pont* or ferry behind it.

More often than not, the *roefschip* was a *hoogmast* or *hoogars*. This type of ship had a carrying capacity of approximately 140 tons, which means that it could transport some 1,600 bags of salt and four to five other shipments of various goods. A *hoogars* had a tonnage of approximately 100 tons. In comparison, a cubic metre of Namur stone weighs 2.7 tons, which means a *hoogars* could transport approximately thirty-seven cubic metres of stone.

The *paetschip* or *pedde* was used for shipments up to sixty tons.[122] A ferry with a tonnage of thirty-five tons was primarily used transhipping the cargo if the draughts of the *roefschip* or *paetschip* were too deep. The ferry was also used to transport the horses the captain brought along to the other side of the river, which was sometimes necessary when the towpath changed banks.[123] These horses were primarily used when travelling upstream. A *coppelye* with a *hoogmast* required five to seven horses. Two to four horses were sufficient for a *hoogars*. Towing horses could be rented from countless places along the river. Downstream, the current, sometimes aided by sails, carried the ships.

The transport of materials was controlled by strict rules. The captain's area of operations was usually limited to the riverbed. As soon as they moored in a harbour, the rest of the transport of their cargo was taken over by town porters. A number of stone contracts have separate clauses for the transport of the material from the quayside to the construction site because of these rules. After all, the town

---

[117] Knoors 1978, p. 18. On the Meuse as a river and trading route see Breuer 1969, in particular p. 74ff.

[118] For the history of the Mosan trade before the thirteenth century, see Rousseau 1930.

[119] Knoors 1978, p. 19.

[120] See Van Beylen 1970, Chapter 6 for more on the types of vessel used.

[121] Breuer 1969, p. 89ff., Knoors 1978, p. 19.

[122] A *paatschip* was approximately thirty-nine metres long and 2.6 to 5.85 metres wide, with a depth of 1.3 metres. Its draught was between sixty and eighty centimetres. In the seventeenth century, a ship of this size cost some 800 guilders. Breuer 1969, pp. 91-92.

[123] Ibidem.

was a separate governing body with distinct regulations that could not be controlled by the merchant who had engaged the captain.

A large number of captains were active under the regulations between Liège and Dordrecht. They transported materials, but also traded in them and had as in the case of Dirk Engelen, rapeseed purchased in Holland, turned into oil in Venlo.[124] A captain whom researchers are more familiar with is Jan Conincx van Elsloo. Conincx was the second husband of the abovementioned Dirk Engelen's widow and expanded the latter's transport company.[125] In the 1590s, he would specialise entirely in the transport of stone. It was the services of such captains that the Van Neurenberg family would use for the transport of merchandise.

Tolls

Once all the requirements had been met and the stone had been loaded aboard ships at the quarry, there were a large number of other hindrances encountered on the way north. Sometimes these were locks or water mills, but much more often and more structurally they were the dozens of tolls. The toll system had existed since the eight century. Landowners levied tolls to generate income and later to finance bridges and maintain roads. The toll the captains had to pay depended on the ship's cargo. Toll could be paid for with money, but it was often paid in kind.[126]

Transport and the system of many tolls dramatically increased the price of stone. Between the southern starting point of the Meuse, Charleville, and Dordrecht, there were thirty-seven tolls.[127] More-over, market tolls could also be expected at certain times, if annual fairs were being held along the route (Fig. 23).[128] How heavily the tolls influenced the price of stone, is illustrated by an example from the close of the fifteenth century. When, in 1488 in Deventer, the tolls on the Vecht to Bentheim became cost prohibitive, it was decided to purchase a large shipment of Namur stone. Long distance transport was still cheaper than incurring the tolls on the Vecht.[129]

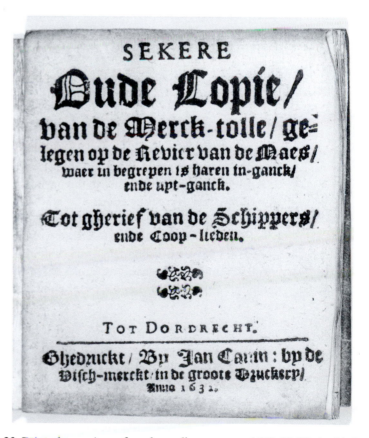

23. Printed overview of market tolls, rates etc., 1632 (GAD, Archief van de gemene Maashandelaars, Inv. Nr. 945).

[124] Other well-known captains include Peter Henricx, Jan Hillen, Celis Artsen, Henrick Maroyen, Jan and Arent van Hingen, Jochum Schoncken and his two brothers, Nicolaes Royen, Vaes Lemmens van Dilsen, etc. See Meulleners 1886, p. 94.

[125] He married Mercken Engelen on 26 December 1580.

[126] […] Alle de blauwe steen die is te bekoome bijna voor niet en den arbeyd is goedkoop, maar 't voeren per as 7, 8 à 9 uuren verre en dan de Henegouse reghten en de Brabandsche regten en de inkoomende regten en dan de scheepsvragt, dat is # 32-:-: Vlaams voor een pleytslaadinge, die maar 32, 33 en 34 last voeren kan, soodat de vragt en 't lossen saamen komt op # 1-:-: per last van 4,000 lb. Amsterdams gewigt. Daarbij soo grosseeren de steenhouwers extra en daarvandaan komt het, dat de steen alhier soo geldig is. Bommenee 1988, p. 142.

[127] Bauduin 1962, pp. 117-121. Meulleners 1886, p. 92 mentions Roermond, Asselt, Kessel, Venlo, Grubbenvorst, Middelaar, Grave, Batenburg, Oyen, Zaltbommel, as just a selection of toll towns. See also Van Houtte 1972, p. 301. There were also many tolls on the Rhine, at least forty between Mannheim and Dordrecht. Frijhoff 1998, p. 158.

[128] GAD, Archief van de gemene Maashandelaars [Archive of the Organised Meuse Merchants], Inv. No. 948.

[129] Janse, De Vries 1991, p. 13.

35

Stone was also affected by the fact that some tolls distinguished between rough stone and finished blocks. During this period, the Lith toll cost sixty percent more for a ship with "worked Namur stone" than for a cargo of "rough or unworked Namur stone".[130] Here the fact that stone had been worked resulted in an additional tax for the toll. On the other hand, sometimes toll exemptions existed, mostly concerning materials for ecclesiastical buildings. For example, in 1536 exemptions were provided at the tolls of Orsoy, Buederich and Lobith for a wooden raft from the Gnadenthal Monastery near Neuss for a house in Nijmegen and from the toll at Huissen for wood and stone for the construction of the Eusebius Church in Arnhem. However, exemptions were sometimes also provided for secular purposes.[131] Exemption or taxations were often the cause of lengthy disputes between towns and landowners. In particular, the fact that tolls were such a heavy burden on the price development of goods ensured that exemptions were highly prized and sometimes intensely fought for.[132]

In addition to certain goods being exempt from tolls, particular citizens or merchants from specific towns were also occasionally exempt from paying tolls. What mattered in these cases was who owned the cargo and not who owned the ship. The captain had to be able to show a toll letter, which proved that the cargo's owner was a citizen in a town exempt from toll.[133] It was of the greatest importance to the competitive position of merchants that they could trade their wares toll free and this is also the reason why some captains and traders involved themselves in the toll business. For example, Meuse captain Jan Jansz Trip (1530?-1580) leased the toll by Tiel from the Count of Meurs in 1578. In 1585, Prince Maurits made his son Jan Trip supervisor of the toll by Zaltbommel.[134]

Transport over water involved a large number of problems. As well as with tolls, the captains had to deal with factors that complicated transport such as low water levels, overly strong currents, water mills and sand banks. Nevertheless, the advantages of transporting stone by ship far outweighed those of transport over land. No matter how little water there was, the loading capacity of the smallest *pleit*, eight to ten tons, was still much more than that of a cart and horses. Moreover, transport over land also involved tolls and poorly maintained roads.

Quarrying and export history of Namur stone

The quarrying and export history of Namur stone reveals that after overcoming all the quarrying and trading difficulties, a definite profit margin still remained. The stone from the left bank of the Meuse, to the north of Namur, was already being used in the High Middle Ages. Eleventh-century tombstones have been found in the immediate surroundings, while written sources have come down to us from the thirteenth century onward.[135] In a charter from Liège dating back to 1229, Henri, Abbott of the Cistercian monastery of Val-Dieu allowed the abbot of the Monastery of Val Saint-Lambert to operate the quarry at Herbatte (Namur). He reserved the right to break as much stone as he wanted for his own monastery, thus showing that the stone was already of regional importance as a construction material at this time. In 1203, a group of rebels took over a ship loaded with Namur stone ready to be shipped to Liège for the rebuilding of the bishop's palace in Huy.[136]

[130] GAD, Archief van de gemene Maashandelaars [Archive of the Organised Meuse Merchants], Inv. No. 265.
[131] Classen 1951, p. 138.
[132] GAR, Town magistrates archive. The list of disputes resulting from tolls was long. See Inv. Nos. 789, 790, 791 and the *regestenlijst*, listed in Van Bree 1989. The GAD, Archief van

gemene Maashandelaars [Archive of the Organised Meuse Merchants], lists countless such conflicts.
[133] Knoors 1978, p. 23.
[134] Klein 1965, pp. 24-25.
[135] Courtoy 1946, passim. For Roman applications of Meuse Valley blue stone, see Anderson, Groessens 1996.
[136] Courtoy 1946, p. 18.

There are a large number of quarries on the left bank near Namur. In 1289, there were already ten quarries being worked. In the fourteenth century this number increased and the stone industry became an important source of income for the town. Blocks for fortifications were cut, but also for fonts, tombstones, architectural elements and chimney parts.[137] Stone was also exported to other regions. For example, father and son Joris and Jean d'Osnon supplied Namur stone pillars for the monastery of the cathedral of Saint Lambert in Liège in 1370.[138] A number of fifteenth-century quarry operators' names have also been preserved. They provide an impression of an important industry that not only supplied ordinary Namur stone, but also black marble, which was basically a variant from the same bank. The operators were active on the Count of Namur's land, but some monasteries also had their own quarries, such as, for example, the monastery of Onze Lieve Vrouwe and the Abbey Salzinnes. The latter supplied the stone for the bridge over the Sambre near Vocaing in 1418.[139] During the sixteenth century the type of stone determined the appearance of a large number of buildings. In 1582 a traveller wrote that Namur was a beautiful town "because it is built using beautiful stones of marble, and the colours are now ash blond, then black again, then white, then reddish again, then dappled in different colours, and all the town's roofs are tiled in slate."[140]

However, it was only in the sixteenth century that stone from the Meuse Valley really became an important export product. The trade in and application of Namur stone long remained limited to part of the Meuse Valley. A few early examples in the Northern Low Countries can be considered incidental. In the Middle Ages the stone never held the position that, for example, the tuffas and trachytes from the Eiffel or in the fourteenth and fifteenth century that stone from the Schelde basin held. In addition to twelfth and thirteenth century examples from Maastricht, such as the Onze Lieve Vrouwe Church, the Old Bridge over the Meuse, the columns of the Dominican Church and the second town wall, Namur stone was used between 1321 and 1382 in the cathedral tower in Utrecht and between 1391-1394 in the Buur Tower in the same town.[141] In the fifteenth century an increase in the use of Namur stone in the north can be seen. Simultaneously, the production of prefabricated products, such as baptismal fonts and tombstones, increased in the South. These were readied at local yards or at the quarry and then exported north.[142] Namur stone was also applied more often as building stone in the north. For example, in 1429 the round bastion Engelenburg in Dordrecht was clad in Namur stone, in 1467-1468 House Zoudenbalch in Utrecht had a Namur stone facade and in 1470 the second part of the Lebuinus tower in Deventer contained a staircase turret with roughly hewn steps of Namur stone. In 1488 a large order of Namur stone was shipped to Deventer,[143] for the crenellations of the Noordenberg tower. Master Johan Oesterhuys, the town tower master journeyed to Namur to provide directions. Marthen van Namur supplied the stone via Gorinchem. The Bourgogne tower of the castle in Wijk bij Duurstede, dating back to approximately 1490 is also comparable and used Namur stone in its construction.

It would go too far to list all the known deliveries and applications of Namur stone here; suffice it to say the stone had an increasingly large range during the abovementioned period. In 1490, the stone was applied in Zwolle[144], and around 1495 it can be seen in the House Het Zeepaard (Wijn-

---

[137] Ghislain 1984, passim.
[138] Courtoy 1946, p. 18. Other operators and merchants from this period are known by name.
[139] Ibidem, p. 27.
[140] [...] pour estre bâtie en belles pierres de marbre de couleur tantôt cendrée, tantôt noiré, tantôt blanché, tantôt rougissant, tantôt diversement tachetée, et pour estre entièrement couverte d'ardoises. Rousseau 1937, p. 18. Incidentally, this does not mean that the town was completely made of stone. A large proportion of the buildings were still half-timbered.

[141] Slinger 1980, p. 51 mentioned medieval examples of Namur stone, the tenth and eleventh century churches of Andelst and Alphen a/d Maas. However, the application in Alphen is almost certainly a later repair.
[142] Courtoy 1925, pp. 59-62. See also Comanne 1992 concerning this increase in scale.
[143] Bloemink, Roetert Steenbruggen 1991, p. 51.
[144] Janse, De Vries 1991, p. 13.

straat 113) in Dordrecht, which has an entirely Namur stone facade[145], while also other facades in Dordrecht were executed in Namur stone. Namur stone was also common in Utrecht around 1500.[146]

This tendency, which emerged around 1500, would continue to develop strongly during the first half of the sixteenth century. Liège and Namur's expansionism was an important factor in opening up new markets, which would eventually lead to direct contact between Liège and Dordrecht. Exports increased as a result of the increase in quarrying, industry and forestry around Liège. The causes of this increase were technological advances and the refinement of existing techniques.[147] Merchants from the Meuse Valley saw Holland, which was becoming more important, as an interesting market. However, they were seriously hampered in their desire to expand their trading territory by Venlo's staple right.[148] Because of this staple right all the products and goods from the south had to be stapled (i.e. traded) in Venlo, which made direct contact with the market in the west impossible.[149] Venlo's staple right came under heavy pressure from merchants who attempted to circumvent the right and appealed against it. Other towns also supported them in this effort. Previously, Venlo had been part of the Duchy of Gelre, which was the last to be added to the Hapsburg Netherlands in 1543. Due to a shift in political interest, the Duke of Gelre's support for stopping or at least not taking over trade from the south waned, allowing the towns in the Meuse Valley to open a direct route north quite quickly. In 1545 Venlo's staple right was officially abolished.[150]

Examining the development of the trade in Namur stone indicates that the abolition of Venlo's staple right in 1545 was no more than a formality. Years earlier, traders from the south had managed to circumvent the staple right, as proven by deliveries in Nijmegen. During the years 1533-1545, Willem I van Neurenberg supplied large shipments of Namur stone for the fortifications, the Hezel gate and other gates. He also supplied building materials for the cloth hall and the town hall. Around 1530 the stone had already been applied in the Sint-Stevens Church in Nijmegen and in 1535, Andries de Fyrole van Namur supplied 807 feet of Namur stone for the town's quay wall.[151] Jan van Naemen supplied Namur stone for a "summer house" in Grave Castle's herb garden.[152] Around 1540, Namur stone was also purchased in 's-Hertogenbosch. The merchants in this case were Lambert, Claes and Jan van Namur.[153] During the years 1545-1548 there were once again purchases of Namur stone in Deventer. Stone was purchased from one Peter Comess from Namur for the Welle and the harbour. A messenger was dispatched to Namur via Venlo and Peter Comess delivered the stone himself. People from Deventer also purchased 100 feet of Namur stone in Amsterdam for the meat hall during these years.

The number of examples mentioned here will also be limited. In 1553, Michel Votron, stonecutter in Namur, supplied a gallery of blue stone for Rijnsburg Abbey near Leiden. However, these were not used there and were sold again in 1560 to Aert Coebel, collector general of Holland.[154] In 1553 Claes van Namur supplied a shipment of seventy-two feet of steps for the gable of a house for

---

[145] The wood of the floor above the second story, in the loft, and the frames that provide access to the staircase turret were dendrochronologically dated 1493-1496. De Vries 1997, p. 220.

[146] See for example, Springweg 102, the gate to the former Elisabethsgasthuis and supplies to the Cathedral between 1487 and 1502. Examples elsewhere include Vianen town hall.

[147] Think, for example, of the invention of the water pump, the improvement of iron producing methods, etc. Knoors 1978, p. 28.

[148] This staple right was an unwritten law that resulted from the necessity for captains to tranship their goods if they were sailing upstream.

[149] Knoors 1978, p. 28.

[150] GAM, Oud Archief, Indivieze Raad, No. 940. Incidentally, in this document Maastricht captains stated that they had had freedom of passage for much longer. However, this testimony seems slanted. Knoors 1978, p. 28 states that Venlo's staple right was abolished as early as 1515. See also Thurlings 1945, p. 12.

[151] Janse, De Vries 1991, pp. 13-14.

[152] Ibidem.

[153] It should be noted that where the 's-Hertogenbosch bills refer to Namur stone, this may now and again have concerned blue stone from Hainaut when taking into consideration the merchants involved.

[154] Janse, De Vries 1991, p. 14.

the churchwardens in Dordrecht. Around 1555, Coenraad II van Neurenberg and Jacob Pierson Lambillon supplied tombstones for the Old Church in Amsterdam. In 1559 Master Henrick, town bricklayer of Zwolle, travelled to Amsterdam to purchase blue floor tiles and returned with 600 of them. The abovementioned Jacob Lambillon supplied Namur stone for the Utrecht town's cellar in 1561.[155]

Price developments and standard products

However tempting it might be to draw up a list of price developments for Namur stone on the basis of what little archival data exists, it nevertheless proves to be a risky undertaking in practice; many factors determined the price the buyer had to pay for a product. The transport of stone was a considerable expense. However, that was not the only expense incurred. In order to properly compare the prices all factors have to be taken into account. Initial considerations include the quarry's lease price, the duration of the lease, and the period the operator was granted to work the pit for this sum.[156] Then this data has to be taken into account in the price of an unworked foot of stone. A secondary factor was the wages and other costs required to quarry the stone and possibly work it. Both these factors determine the price of a foot of stone at the quarry, whether worked or unworked stone. In addition to the lease agreement and wage fluctuations this price can be viewed as a reasonably constant factor; however, the cost of transportation determines the large discrepancies in price between towns in the north.

In order to determine the price level in the north and how this developed, it is important to know exactly how many tolls the stone passed through en route to its destination and whether the merchant had (a) toll exemption(s) and, if so, where. Furthermore, the problem is even more complex; in addition to the distance, the number of tolls and the nature of the toll exemption(s), the nature of the material supplied must be known. Was it ready made or was it unhewn stone? After all, prefabrication influenced the amount of the toll. The price per foot of arch pillars or steps, for example, cannot be compared. Finally, market tolls also influenced price development. Some market tolls can be ignored such as that of Alem, which was only levied one day a year.[157] Others, such as that of Gorinchem, were levied four times a year, for fourteen days at a time, and therefore definitely influenced the price of stone in the north;[158] so it is also important to know exactly when the stone was shipped.

The above considerations primarily pertain to the cost price of the stone, which is difficult to calculate in practice. Generally, merchants had sufficient experience and insight into these factors and accounted for them when determining the sales price of their wares; therefore, the prices of various types of stone in a single market can be compared. Often a fixed price was determined in advance into which the merchant incorporated a substantial profit margin. At the end of this study the cost price of stone will be discussed further, whereby an attempt will be made to gain insight into the national price differences, the prices of various products and the relationship between the price of Bentheimer sandstone and Namur stone.

The products of the Namur stone trade varied widely depending on demand from the north. Contracts, bills and other archival sources list arch elements, steps, cymas, window frames, columns, blocks, tombstones and plinths. But there was also specially ordered work, supplied in accordance with designs from the north, where the northern foot measures were used. Now and again, the measures

---

[155] Janse, De Vries 1991, p. 36. Other merchants that can be mentioned here include Michel Voltron, Henry Henckaert and Jan Misson, who in 1560-63 supplied Namur stone for the construction of Antwerp's town hall. Namur stone was also used in the town hall of The Hague. Finally, there was

a delivery in 1567, once again supplied by Jan Lambillon, for a lock in Spaarndam.
[156] See also Voort 1968 concerning this matter.
[157] Knoors 1978, p. 22.
[158] Ibidem.

used create considerable problems for researchers: every town had its own foot measure that varied from 26.8 to 39.5 cm. The largest foot used in construction measured approximately 32.6 cm. The foot was subdivided into inches, usually twelve of them, but sometimes ten, eleven or thirteen. To maintain local unity of measure, the foot measures were sometimes indicated in places accessible to all, such as the floor of the Onze Lieve Vrouwe Church in Maastricht, the Hezel gate in Nijmegen or the town hall in Leiden.[159] Contracts for stonework usually explicitly stated the measure used. Moreover, sometimes an example of the measure was made and sent along to the quarry.[160]

It is known that in Bentheim and Hainaut standard products were manufactured during the winter when stone breaking had become impossible due to the low temperatures.[161] This case was probably the same at the quarries around Namur. Different prices were charged for the various products, and standard rates may have applied. The more labour a product required, the more the price per foot rose. To what extent stockpiling took place is unknown. The delays that occurred in some deliveries by Van Neurenberg make it seem more likely that the winter was used to get rid of any backlog rather than to build up stock.

It is not always clear from where the designs for the Namur stone that occurs in buildings in the Northern Low Countries came. Deliveries of Namur stone to the cathedral in Utrecht reveal that ready-made arches were delivered around 1500 and in 1514-1515 gutters of Namur stone arrived; the Utrecht fabric lodge designed both of these elements.[162] However, the window frames in the bailey of the castle of Wijk bij Duurstede, which dates to ca. 1490, have Meuse Valley characteristics and were almost certainly supplied ready made after a design from the quarry.[163]

Much fewer unworked products seem to have been delivered. Processing at the quarry had advantages for all the parties: lower transport costs, early discovery of weak spots in the stone, the disposal of waste material, etc.

---

[159] For more on historic measurements, see: Berends 1996, RV blad 01-1 - 01-12.
[160] See Chapter XI and XIII.
[161] See Voort 1968 and 1970, and Bommenee 1988.

[162] See Peeters 1985, pp. 42-45 for information on the purchase of stone for the Sint-Jans Church in 's-Hertogenbosch.
[163] The same applies to the stone cross-windows in the bailey of the castle of Heeswijk, for example.

III. The Van Neurenberg Family and the Building Trade

Family businesses: training and organisation

A relatively large number of families can be identified as being active in the stone trade or stone cutting. This fact is hardly surprising, given that education improved considerably during the fifteenth and sixteenth centuries, and more people were being better educated, especially among town officials. Nevertheless, training to be a craftsman still primarily depended on working in the trade.[164] Only at the close of the sixteenth century would theoretical interest in education become more important. Furthermore, the traditional training within the trade continued to exist for a long time. Parents sent their child to be apprenticed to a master and paid handsomely to achieve this end. In exchange the master provided the youth with room and board, an upbringing and thorough training in the craft. The apprenticeship usually lasted four years.[165]

Training in one's own sector of industry was of course the obvious course of action. This practice often continued from generation to generation causing some family names to appear in the building trade for hundreds of years. Affiliated to the stone trade they expanded their activities and networks of contacts where possible. This focus on a specific sector of industry seems to have been a conscious and obvious political move. When it came to family businesses, they often specialised in a single type of stone linked to the geology of the area in which they lived. For example, the De Prince family was known for its deliveries of dark limestone, while the Keldermans family's trade focused more on the white stone from Lede and Gobertinge.[166] The Van Neurenberg family is consistently associated with Namur stone and sometimes also marlstone and marble, while the Stuerman and Hagen families, on the other hand, traded exclusively in Bentheimer sandstone.[167]

Taking over his father's company was an obvious step for a son. At home he would receive good training and make contacts with patrons and stone merchants in his youth. Taking over a company that had already made a name for itself, had inherently more certainty than entering into a new trade; although eminence within the trade did not always guarantee a flourishing business.[168] The Darkennes family of stonecutters in 's-Hertogenbosch, for example, managed to stay afloat with decreasing levels of success during the sixteenth century, with a concomitant decline in their social status.[169] Differences can also be observed in the careers of various members of the Keldermans family. These differences are the result of a combination of factors including the status within the family, social status, contacts within the building trade and personal talent.[170]

Another important factor to be considered is the creation of a network through marriage. The Van Neurenberg family' case reveals to what extent targeted marriage politics were a tool with which to gain a foothold in the stone trade from within the Meuse Valley. Marriages allowed them to turn competitors into partners, which not only reinforced their own position, but also that of their partner.[171] However, it was not just the family that offered a safety net and a context within which the activities took place. In order to be able to ply a trade one had to be a guild member, although this

---

[164] Schuttelaars 1998, p. 328f.

[165] For more on this subject see Van den Heuvel 1946, p. 620ff. and Van Deursen 1991, p. 137ff.

[166] Janse 1986, p. 173ff. The Keldermans family is also known to have supplied stone from Avesnes, possibly acquired through a middleman.

[167] Olde Meierink 1991, passim.

[168] See Mathias 1995, pp. 6–8 for more on taking over one's father's business and risk reduction.

[169] Kennis 1997. See Van Tussenbroek 2001b for more on the business activities of Darkennes.

[170] Van Wylick-Westermann 1987, passim.

[171] Mathias 1995, pp. 10–13.

played less of a role for merchants. To this end, people took a master test, swore an oath and paid an annual sum. They also had to be registered as a citizen in the town in which they wanted to join the guild or they were not allowed to work at their trade. The image the late-medieval guilds provide is however multifarious and complex, the differences between guilds per town and per period are large. For example, in Brussels stonecutters, bricklayers and sculptors were united in the stonecutters guild,[172] while in Amsterdam the stonemasons were united with the bricklayers, plumbers and slate layers in the Guild of St. Barbara.[173] In 1521 in Utrecht the stonemasons were even part of the same guild as the grain buyers.[174] In Namur, the stonemasons and bricklayers had incorporated themselves as a guild as early as 1421. In 1433, nineteen master stonemasons, thirty-seven mates, fifteen apprentices and twelve foremen had joined the guild.[175] The guild was formed to protect the stonemasons' trade in the town and also provided modest social security. The work at the quarry involved certain risks. Serious accidents happened where labourers died or were so seriously injured that they were no longer able to work. In 1481, the guild decided to set up a few small houses, cells, where the disabled could live if they could no longer provide for their own accommodation.[176] This room complex was dedicated to St. Fiacre and in exchange for the room the inhabitants were only asked to maintain the nearby guild chapel. The stonemason's guild of Namur had its own chapel dedicated to Notre Dame of Neuf-Pont. The guild met here on special occasions, with the priest of St. John the Baptist of Namur's approval. The chapel and the little houses were near the principal quarry.[177]

Organisation of the work: merchants and stonemasons

The Van Neurenberg family's activities cannot be described by a single term because around the year 1500 traditional stonemasons closely resembled medieval master masons and building material merchants both. When examining the Van Neurenberg family it is obvious, particularly in the beginning, that they still operated within this tradition. Coenraad I van Neurenberg was active as a stonemason, a master mason and as a merchant in Namur stone. Other stonemasons, merchants and master masons also conform to this image. Pragmatic factors often determined to what extent people operated in a particular field. For example, the Van Neurenberg family always remained active in the materials trade, particularly as distributors and processors of stone. As far as is known, they never operated a quarry. Their continued use of suppliers is probably attributable to the fact that they were usually located too far from the quarries. After all, other stonemasons, master masons, etc., did shift to operating their own quarries. A good example is the De Nonon (or Nonnon) family.

The De Nonon family, five generations of which are known in the stone trade, specialised in black marble. Their work can be found from Brussels to Mons and Bruges. At the close of the fifteenth

---

[172] Janse 1964, p. 24.
[173] Janse, De Vries 1991, p. 27.
[174] Ibidem. In 's-Hertogenbosch there was a subdivision into cabinet makers and barrel makers guilds, to which cabinet makers belonged, a carpenter's guild, to which the bricklayers and slaters belonged and a painter's guild to which the wood carvers belonged. With regard to the activities that the fabric of the Sint- Jans Church and the town government had carried out, the operation of the guild obligation right for stonecutters was rather lenient. A 1560 bylaw reveals that carpenters, bricklayers, stonecutters and slaters employed by the town and the fabric lodge of the Sint-Jans Church were free and exempt [vry ende exempt] of their guild's legislation. Van den Heuvel undated pp. 31-33, 44-45, 172.

[175] Colart 1941, p. 47.
[176] L.L. 1895, p. 388.
[177] Ibidem, p. 383. Incidentally, the stonemasons were traditionally protected by the Quattuor coronati. These were Roman sculptors or stonemasons who, as Christians, had refused to make an idol of Aesculapius for Emperor Diocletian. The refusal made the emperor so furious that he had them beheaded. The names of the four crowned men (so-called because of their martyr's crowns) were Severinus, Severianus, Carpophorus and Victorinus. Their holy day is 8 November. Dezutter, Goetinck 1975, pp. 102-106.

century Jean de Nonon operated the Corroy quarry, near Herbuchenne. He reached an agreement with the Magistrates of Dinant who allowed him to repair the old road in order to once again make the quarry accessible to carts. In exchange he received an eleven-year lease on the quarry. After this term was over, this privilege was maintained, although he had to pay the town the sum ten Rheinish guilders annually.[178] Jean de Nonon was married to Catherine Bodry. Their children, Jean, Hubert, Marye and Magritte continued to pay this annual sum. Hubert probably continued the actual business. On 16 September 1510 he concluded an agreement with Don Diego Floris, treasurer and general collector of Margaretha of Austria, for the delivery of four marble sheets, ten feet in length and of varying widths. On 13 May 1512, Hubert de Nonon declared that he had been paid "for certain pieces of marble"[179] On 9 July 1519, Hubert and his wife drew up their last will and testament. Hubert owned a few houses in Dinant and he operated two quarries of which his eldest son Jean inherited one. Two brothers, Hubert and André, inherited the other quarry near Corroy and had to pay an interest to their sister Catherine.[180]

It was this type of merchant who would eventually succeed in setting up large trading companies with impressive workshops, a large sales market and a wide range of clients. The clients primarily consisted of the church, the court and the aristocracy. And it was precisely the latter group that owned most of the estates on which the quarries were located. The position of merchants from the north reveals that they often were not active at the quarries themselves. They acted as coordinators, provided the acquisition and maintained contacts between patrons, workshops and quarries. It may seem that when referring to trade, we are primarily referring to distribution; however, there were also stonemasons and merchants who operated quarries, as the example of the De Nonon family shows.

Composition of the Van Neurenberg family from 1465-1570

It seems obvious to suppose that the Van Neurenberg family originated in Nürnberg. However, there is absolutely no proof that this was the case. During the fourteenth and fifteenth centuries people migrated to the Low Countries from Germany, whereby stonemasons and master masons were made the supervisors of major construction projects in the north.[181] Unfortunately, very little is known about the Van Neurenberg family before 1500. In Germany, the name Conrad in connection with stonemasons occurs frequently. At the start of the fifteenth century, one Master Conrad worked on the Carthusian Church in Cologne. The name Van Neurenberg also occurs several times. For example, sources mention a sculptor Albert von Nürnberg, who worked in Berne around 1400.[182] During the fifteenth century one *Coynraid Noerenberch* was imprisoned in Aachen for quite some time.[183]

Although the names are the same as the Van Neurenberg family there is no certainty regarding any possible family ties.[184] Names can also be misleading. For example, between 1494 and approximately 1518 a Willem Coenraadsz worked in Kampen.[185] Although the name is exactly the same as that of Willem I van Neurenberg, son of Coenraad I, he is not a member of the Van Neurenberg family. This Willem is possibly the son of bricklayer Coenraad Wesselsz or that of Coenraad Petersz van Straesberch.[186]

[178] Courtoy 1952, p. 25.
[179] Ibidem, p. 26: *pour et à cause de certaines pièces de marbre.*
[180] Ibidem.
[181] Meischke 1988, pp. 11-18.
[182] Huisman 1986, p. 6.
[183] AS, X 49 (Urkunde-Fehdebrief). Many thanks to Jörg Soentgenrath.

[184] Naturally, the spelling of the surname fluctuates wildly from source to source. The 'Van Neurenberg'spelling has been adhered to throughout this text.
[185] Kolman 1993, p. 195ff.
[186] Ibidem, pp. 190-192.

24. Maastricht, 1575. Engraving by Simon de Bellemonte (GAM).

Nevertheless, the family did not suddenly emerge from total obscurity; when Coenraad I first appeared in Maastricht, he was already a renowned master, in charge of major commissions. It is possible that he and his father, who was most probably called Willem, worked in the fabric lodge of the Dom in Utrecht. In the year 1474-1475, one Wilhelmus Conrardi received payment for work on the church.[187] There is no doubt that during these years, when the northern transept was built, stonemasons and masters were recruited from the south.[188] In December 1503, a messenger was dispatched to Cologne to find one Master Willem, "who makes tracery".[189] In the following year, Willem van Noerenberch was mentioned and worked for the church for a total of 225.5 days,[190] which placed him alongside the likes of Andries Keldermans on the list.

This does not prove that Willem Coenraadsz is the same person as Willem van Noerenberch, or that the latter was the Maastricht Coenraad van Neurenberg's father. However, a strong possibility exists: as observed in the previous chapter Namur stone was regularly used in Utrecht around 1500. Furthermore, there is a similarity of names at the start of the sixteenth century and it is plausible for Willem to have originated in the south. Around 1500 the first reference to a Van Neurenberg who can be connected to the merchant family occurs. At that point in time, the Van Neurenberg family was located and active in Maastricht and not in Namur. The Van Neurenberg family started out in the stonemasons' trade and not in the stone trade or quarrying.

Coenraad I van Neurenberg (approximately 1465 – approximately 1542)

The oldest known member of the family central to this study was called Coenraad.[191] Maastricht was part of his immediate field of operations, although the traces he left behind are scant (Fig. 24). He worked as municipal fabric and work master of the Sint-Servaas in Maastricht.[192] Like the town mason

---

[187] Jappe Alberts 1976, I, p. 622.
[188] The list of masters includes names such as 'De Wael' and 'Van Namen'(Namur). Janse, De Vries 1991, p. 143.
[189] Jappe Alberts 1976, II, p. 633.
[190] Ibidem, p. 834.
[191] Furthermore referred to as Coenraad I.

or architect the fabric was a position within the town's administrative body and whose job dealt specifically with the construction and maintenance of churches. The name Van Neurenberg does not occur again in the town's citizenship lists.[193] The registers of birth, marriages and deaths of the various parishes do not feature the name either.[194] A major impediment to studying the data concerning Coenraad I van Neurenberg in Maastricht is the lack of the town accounts for the period 1400-1590.[195]

A little more is known about his activities in the town's surrounding area. The first time Coenraad was mentioned in a contract was on 26 August 1502. He was not directly contracted for the work, but acted as a mediator between Averbode Abbey and master Johannes van Geel, for the construction of the abbey's chapel. Coenraad was referred to as "our friend master Conrard van Nurenborch, stonemason from Maastricht".[196] A few months later, on 2 November, Coenraad himself was awarded the commission to make a rood screen for the abbey.[197] This contract refers to him as "Master Coenraet van Noerenborch, town master of Maastricht".

The contract for the rood screen of Averbode Abbey proves that Coenraad had his own workshop where he worked stone from the quarry. Having his own workshop meant that he had contacts with building patrons and with the quarry, which reveals something of his social standing. Whether he actually worked the stone is unknown. Coenraad was active in Maastricht for a long time. In 1521 he became embroiled in a conflict with the town of Maastricht and his citizenship seems to have been revoked. A notice dated 4 March 1521 says that if Coenraad repairs his mistakes, he will be allowed to return to the town and he will be forgiven.[198] The conflict pertained to inferior work, as will be explained below.

The fact that Coenraad lost his citizenship does not mean that the mistakes referred to were the only reason for his temporary absence from the town. It was also possible for a citizen to 'outlive' his citizenship. If a citizen stayed somewhere else for a longer period of time, the original town of residence could decide to no longer recognise him as a citizen. This type of occurrence would not be unusual for a stonemason and stone merchant with a large working area. Naturally, the Maastricht local authorities would have tried to conclude the still current conflicts to their advantage upon Van Neurenberg's return. Buying back citizenship was probably no more than a formality so that the reading of the protocols seems much worse than it actually was. Possible secondary explanations for Coenraad's absence are easy to find. As early as in 1502 he took on potentially lucrative commissions from outside the town as his name crops up in both Averbode and Herkenrode.[199]

In spite of the scant information, it can be assumed that after 1521 Coenraad moved back to Maastricht. This argument is proven by the fact that in 1525 he was the sheriff of the *vrijheid Sint Pieter* near Maastricht and appears in the magistracy of Maastricht in 1531 and 1534 as a member of the town authority.[200] In this position, he took a seat with the town administration for a year as the neighbourhood representative. The year 1534 is also the last known reference to Coenraad I in Maastricht. Hereafter, his name occurs once in 's-Hertogenbosch, in 1542, where he was involved in the construction of a bulwark in Namur stone. Due to his relatively advanced age (approximately seventy-five years old) it is reasonable to assume that he died not long after this time.

[192] Dickhaut 1987, without page number.
[193] GAM, Burgerboeken Maastricht 1482-1666.
[194] GAM, Registers of birth, marriages and deaths for the town of Maastricht.
[195] GAM, Index of archives of the Indivieze Raad.
[196] ...magistri Conrardi de Nurenborch, lapicide de Trajecto amici nostri. Lefèvre 1935, p. 343.

[197] Lefèvre 1927, pp. 427-428. This contract reveals that Coenraad had a workshop in Maastricht.
[198] GAM, Indivieze Raad, Inv. No. 50, Fol. 1.
[199] Van Tussenbroek 1999a, pp. 86-87.
[200] Eversen, *Alphabetische lijst der magistraatsleden van Maastricht*. Reading room gemeentearchief Maastricht. Doppler 1910, p. 113.

Willem I van Neurenberg (approximately 1490 - after 1548)

Coenraad had at least one son Willem who was also active in the stone trade. The first reference to Willem as an independent building contractor dates back to 2 June 1515. Assuming that he was around twenty-five years old at the time, he must have been born around 1490. Undoubtedly Willem obtained his education in his father's company. In the aforementioned contract of 2 June 1515, he committed to the construction of the Carmelite Church in Huy. Research has also revealed a contract dated 10 October the same year for the creation of an altar for the abbey in Averbode. In this contract his freedom and independence were limited more than they had been in Huy, which raises the question to what extent Willem actually functioned independently around 1515. Taking over the company was a slow, gradual process that was only really completed when his father died. It seems obvious that due to the size of the operation and the simultaneous completion of several construction jobs, Willem was more a master mason and supervisor, concurrently running the business and acquiring new commissions, than a craftsman working with hammer and chisel on a daily basis.[201]

On 28 November 1525, Willem, who at the time was burgher of Maastricht, handed over interest to the Brotherhood of the Curates of the Sint Servaas Church.[202] Willem's commissions reveal that he was slowly, but surely spreading his wings. Not only was he working independently more often, he also expanded the business' field of operations. In 1527, for example, he was responsible for the construction of a rood screen for the Notre Dame in Dinant and later during the thirties and forties he could often be found in Nijmegen engaged in all manner of commissions. The latter commissions were clearly the result of the increasingly strong Meuse trade in the north and the disappearance of Venlo's staple rights. Nevertheless, Willem's hometown continued to be Maastricht, illustrated by the fact that in 1535, the year after his father's last mention in Maastricht sources, he was a member of the town authority. Incidentally, 1535 is the only year he is listed as a member.

The last commission Willem is known to have carried out was for the crossbowmen's guild in Maastricht. On 13 December 1548, Willem started legal proceedings against the crossbowmen concerning a building he was to erect. The crossbowmen requested that he abstain from this course of action and instead they would properly re-examine the agreements and contracts and see how to rectify the situation.[203] The above illustrates how work was passed from generation to generation and that the family managed to maintain their position in the town for over fifty years. Whether Willem, like his father before him, acted as town fabric is unknown due to the lack of town accounts.[204]

Coenraad II van Neurenberg (approximately 1520 - 1595)

Willem was married to the daughter of Jan Schaers and Loelen Bollen[205] and had a son who also joined the family business. The latter was called Coenraad II and was probably born in Maastricht around 1520. This Coenraad II had an illegitimate child with Anne van Vuecht of Maastricht in 1548,

---

[201] Comparable building contractors also ran their businesses in the same way, such as, for example, Keldermans. Van Mosselveld 1987, passim.
[202] Doppler 1910, pp. 112-113.
[203] Nuyts 1892, p. 94.
[204] The so-called *resolutieprotocollen* have not been examined. In 1539 one Willem van Neurenberg worked as a jurist and was involved in a revolt in September 1539. As a result he

was banished in 1540 for ten years. At that point in time, this Willem was the governor of the bricklayer's trade. The possibility that he and Willem I van Neurenberg were one and the same, cannot be excluded. Geurts 1993, pp. 120 and 267. The stonemasons belonged to the bricklayers' guild that had two deacons or governors. Wishaupt 1976, pp. 7-9.
[205] Ibidem. Loess Bollen is mentioned as sheriff in the same document.

who was officially recognised in 1569.[206] The child was also called Coenraad (III). A year later, in 1549, Coenraad II married Jeanne Dembourg (or Demry, as the genealogical table of the family states), and that same year they had a son, Charles. The marriage was probably entered into for economic reasons: Willem I gave his son a house in Maastricht and an allowance and Jeanne brought a house in Namur and the sum of three hundred florins into the marriage. She probably died in 1574.[207]

The earliest known reference to Coenraad II in his father's business dates back to the first half of the forties, when he was involved in the construction of the cloth hall in Nijmegen. Coenraad provided support to his father, accompanied stone transports and transported money to Namur. Although Coenraad was assigned with responsible tasks now and again, he did not operate independently and his activities can be viewed as part of his apprenticeship. The first delivery Coenraad carried out independently dates back to 1545. On 2 May of that year, he promised to supply stone

25. Zutphen, Sint-Walburgs Church, contract signed by Coenraad II van Neurenberg for the delivery of worked stone in 1545 (GAZ, Archief van de kerkvoogdij van Sint-Walburg, Eigendommen algemeen: OUD a 2 (1660).

during the autumn or Lent for the Sint-Walburgs Church in Zutphen (Fig. 25).[208] A year later, he supplied a shipment of blue Namur stone for a staircase turret in the same church. This shipment consisted of thirty-six blocks of stone for steps, four cymas for the outside of the tower, 150 feet of mullions and twenty-five feet of tiles.[209] The shipment was intended for the extension of a spiral staircase.[210]

The next known delivery was in the fifties, when Coenraad and Pierçon Lambillon supplied tombstones for the Old Church in Amsterdam.[211] The name Lambillon is also connected to the trade in Namur stone and the cooperation between the two families was to continue after this first job. They were jointly responsible for supplying Namur stone for the crowning of the Old Church in 1565.

Other important commissions Coenraad II supplied stone for can be found in Bruges and Cologne, where he supplied the entrance hall for the town hall from a design by Cornelis Floris. In the early sixties, Coenraad returns as the supplier of stonework for the town hall in Sittard, based on a design by Maximilian Pasqualini. The shipment to Cologne is, as far as is known, his last delivery as an independent building contractor. In 1571 Coenraad entered the service of the Count of Namur, with whom he already had extensive contacts due to the stone trade.

[206] Courtoy 1912, pp. 509-511.
[207] Ibidem, pp. 509-510. In 1589 Coenraad remarried at a relatively advanced age with Isabeau le Maréchal. This marriage does not seem to have resulted in children.
[208] GAZ, Archief van de kerkvoogdij van Sint-Walburg, Eigendommen algemeen: OUD a 2 (1660).
[209] Ibidem, Eigendommen algemeen: Doos 36 no. 4e. See also Meinsma 1901, p. 29 and Ter Kuile 1958, p. 216.

[210] Work started on the tower on 12 May 1547 and Coenraad was not involved with it. No trace is left of his shipment. Half of the northwestern corner of the tower was blown off in 1945. The lower third of the tower turret had a square cross section, which was lost. Three octagonal parts surmounted this square cross section. Ter Kuile 1958, pp. 220-221.
[211] Bijtelaar 1962, p. 56.

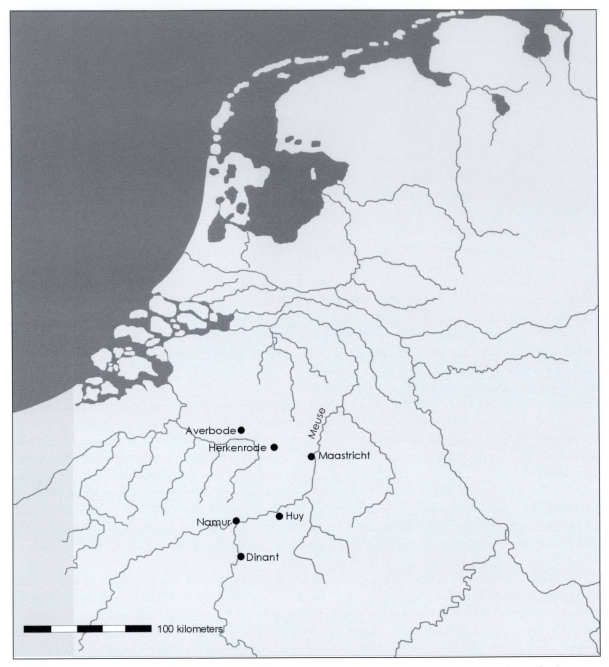

26. The Van Neurenberg family's construction activities in the period up until 1530 (drawing by author).

Business operations and acquisition (Fig. 26)

Coenraad I is known to have worked on the refugium of Averbode in Maastricht. This house was in the Bouillonstraat, near the Sint-Jan and the Sint-Servaas Church.[212] Little can be said concerning the actual activities other than that they probably concerned a conversion or expansion. The house

---

[212] Gerits 1965, p. 33.

27. Maastricht, Artillery tower *Haet en Nyt*, ca. 1515 (Photograph by G. de Hoog, 26 October 1912, RDMZ, Neg.Nr. 2001).

had been purchased by Gérard van der Scaeft as an existing house and probably required some adaptation in order to be able to function as accommodation for the clergymen from the abbey.[213] Few details exist on the other activities for the town during this period. Probably the majority of Coenraad's work

[213] Of the building activities nothing more is known other than that Coenraad worked "on the house in Maastricht". See Lefèvre 1927, p. 429.

as town fabric did not consist of design work, but of maintenance to bridges, pavements and of course fortifications. The wall around the new town was completed during the first quarter of the sixteenth century and included the famous, Namur stone clad round guntowers Hate and Spite (*Haet en Nijt*) and The Five Heads (*De Vijf Koppen*) (Fig. 27).[214] Coenraad I van Neurenberg also executed work on the gates and cladding. In the year 1521 sources reveal something about the conflict between Coenraad and the town of Maastricht; the town demanded that Coenraad repair the work he had done, which was deemed inadequate. Coenraad had executed the work in question in 1501/1502 between the Linderkruis gate and the Hochter (Bosch) gate.[215] To this end, Coenraad must get a number of people to stand as surety for him and would also get some extra work as a result. If he agreed, he would be allowed back into town and the old conflict would be resolved.[216] The proposal was submitted to Van Neurenberg,[217] who then indicated how he expected to complete this work, after which the council decided to set up an eight-man arbitration committee on Monday 15 September 1521.[218] The town and Coenraad each appointed four people to the committee.[219] Both parties came to an agreement in October 1522, after which Coenraad was given the responsibility for completing the work.[220]

On Monday, 23 March 1523, the town commissioned Coenraad, emulating earlier agreements, to repair the wall adjacent to the Linderkruis gate with marlstone blocks.[221] He would also make other repairs where necessary.[222] The dispute arose because a section of wall had fallen. His son, Willem van Neurenberg, who had been appointed as one of the arbitrators by his father, declared that he could repair the downed wall for 150 guilders. The town commissioned him for that job.[223] Coenraad himself had been contracted to rebuild the stretch of town wall between the Linderkruis gate and the Hochter gate.[224] Twenty guilders would be deducted from his remuneration for this work.[225] As far as the existing conflict was concerned, it would require further discussion, primarily relating to its financial conclusion. In June 1526, Coenraad requested a final judgement from the town that would put a definitive end to the matter.[226]

Another activity that little is known about is Coenraad's work on the Sint-Servaas Church. Although he is mentioned as the "work master of the honourable church of Sint Servaes", it can no longer be ascertained what his activities were. No major work was carried out on the church in the first half of the sixteenth century. Coenraad may possibly have been involved in the church's maintenance.[227] Parts that may have been touched by the master include the new cloister, the refectory and the royal chapel.[228]

Coenraad I and Willem I van Neurenberg, and Averbode

A very important patron for Van Neurenberg in the early years of the sixteenth century was the abbey of Averbode. Between 1501 and 1530 Abbot Gérard van der Scaeft led this abbey.[229] It is

[214] Van Nispen 1926, pp. 82-83.
[215] See Morreau 1979, p. 46.
[216] GAM, Archief van de Indivieze Raad 1521-1527, Inv. No. 50, Fol. 1.
[217] Ibidem, Fol. 5.
[218] Ibidem, Fols. 8 and 65.
[219] Ibidem, Fol. 65.
[220] Ibidem, Fol. 72. On 15 October 1522, Coenraad declared before the bailiffs and sheriffs that he would stand surety for the contents of the agreement. Fol. 78.
[221] Referred to as *Sicheneren bluecken*.
[222] GAM, Archief van de Indivieze Raad, Inv. No. 50, Fol. 85.
[223] Ibidem, Fol. 101.
[224] Ibidem, Fol. 102.
[225] Ibidem, Fol. 104.
[226] Ibidem, Fol. 244.
[227] Dickhaut 1987.
[228] The sources for the church's building history are very limited as far as data on later conversions and repairs are concerned. See Berends [without year] with many thanks for the provision of the unpublished manuscript.
[229] Lefèvre 1934, p. 247. He was preceded by the Abbots Arnold de Valgaet (1458-1473) and Barthélemy de Valgaet (1473-1501).

conspicuous that the name Van Neurenberg only appears in the abbey accounts after Van der Scaeft became abbot.

Van der Scaeft, who was born in Hoogeloon around 1460, was well known in Maastricht. After studying law, he became imperial notary public and notary public at the Prince-Bishop's court in Liège.[230] In 1490 he was ordained as a priest at the abbey of Averbode. In his position as notary public, Van der Scaeft had purchased the house in the Bouillionstraat in Maastricht for the abbey of Averbode around 1488-1489, to function as a refugium.[231] The house's caretaker was Antoon van Lymborch, who acted as the abbot's trusted representative and intermediary in 1502-1503. His name also occurs in the referees' contract between the abbey and Coenraad van Neurenberg of 9 September 1504, which pertains to the delivery and finishing of a rood screen Coenraad had supplied.

This contract provides good reason to assume that Coenraad I and the abbey of Averbode in Maastricht had made contact with Abbot Van der Scaeft playing a central role.[232] A few years before Van der Scaeft's appointment as abbot, the abbey had largely been destroyed by fire, which led to major construction work that, in addition to Jan van Gheel and Coenraad van Neurenberg, also involved Matthijs and Laurys Keldermans.[233] Van der Scaeft was high on the social ladder: his position as notary public and later as abbot provided prestige, which allowed him to function as an intermediary. For example, he was the representative for the abbey of Tongerloo, in negotiating with Adriaan Florisz of Utrecht, the future Pope and then professor in Leuven, concerning the position of the abbey with the Archduke and future Emperor Charles V.[234]

Activities for the abbey

Coenraad himself acted as intermediary for the abbey and was also involved in the purchase of building materials. He also acted as supplier.[235] In a contract dated 2 November 1502 he agreed to take care of the construction of a choir screen in the abbey church with Abbot Van der Scaeft. The screen was to consist of eight pillars, two whole ones and six half pillars, cut after the same scantling which was 8.5 feet high in total. The two whole pillars were intended for the front of the screen. At the rear there was a passageway with Namur stone, with two additional small columns on either side. A pulpit was mounted on the screen. The screen consisted of three vaulted bays and was made of marlstone and Namur stone. The contract stipulated that Coenraad would make the screen in Maastricht. Once the work was finished, which was to be accomplished within a year of the contract's conclusion, it would be transported to Averbode at the abbey's expense. Master Coenraad would help install this work himself or with a labourer in Averbode. The marlstone used required that the work be installed unfinished and then cut in situ.

Scantlings or patterns, on the basis of which Coenraad was to work the stone, have been briefly mentioned. That Coenraad was responsible in this case for the design of the screen is proven by the following phrase, which relates to details that will be carried out "after the contents of the design which my Lord of Averbode has kept with him". It seems that Coenraad was not only responsible for the construction aspect of the screen, but also for its finishing. The screen was not in Averbode for long. In 1517, it was sold to the church of Balen-Neet, where it no longer exists. Coenraad I acted as Averbode Abbey's witness in this sale.[236]

---

[230] NNBW V 1921, pp. 668-669.

[231] Gerits 1965, p. 34.

[232] Van der Scaeft was appointed abbot in 1501 and would retain this position until 1532. However, he had already been Abbot Van den Valgaet's coadjutor for some years, when the latter was no longer able to fulfil his duties properly. Valvekens 1936, passim.

[233] Ibidem, p. 119.

[234] Ibidem, p. 124.

[235] Anno 1517 (*anno XVII ii februarii obtulit Magister Conrardus nobis et deliberavit, suis vehiculis et expensis in Averbodio xvm leyen*) Coenraad purchased 15,000 slates for Averbode Abbey. Gerits 1965, n. 25.

[236] Gerits 1967, pp. 154-155. The reason for the sale is unknown. Master Coenraet van Tricht and Jan van Geel valued the *lycoep* at 4 Brabantse guilders, when the screen was sold on 3 November 1517, "which my Lord and the buyers must pay immediately".

As well as the screen, Coenraad made stonework for mullions and the tracery for a Gothic window. Moreover, he would supply three altar stones and a fireplace, as per agreement. The latter deliveries, which more or less accidentally ended up in the principal contract for the screen, provide insight into the daily practice of his work. A screen was an exception, a major commission that was not an everyday order. The fact that anonymous work was also made, such as fireplaces and window frames, puts the major commissions into perspective to some extent, and shows that Van Neurenberg acted as a supplier of parts for buildings as early as the start of the sixteenth century.

Coenraad's son Willem also worked for the abbey and subsequently acted as an early independent contractor. In 1515 Willem made a marlstone altar, "after a design and better than he showed in Averbode".[237] The altar was supposed to reach up to the top of the vault, probably to the same height as a side chapel and was to feature a large number of sculptures. It is uncertain whether the altar was made in Maastricht, even though it seems likely due to what we know of Coenraad I's methods. Willem was only to receive room and board for the time he spent in Averbode putting the altar together. He had asked for fifty guilders for his work, which was reduced to forty after some negotiation. Here we see the father's business contacts being passed on to the son. The latter made good use of the existing contacts and continued his father's work. Once the altar had been finished it would be valued by Coenraad, "and by another craftsman [...] without guile",[238] thus leading to the conclusion that the commission for the altar for Averbode Abbey was executed under Coenraad I's supervision. After all, the latter could hardly be seen as an impartial master who could objectively value the work after completion.

Herkenrode Abbey and Abbess Mechtildis van Léchy

The activities at the abbey of Herkenrode near Hasselt (B) are comparable to those in Averbode. Here too, the contacts were made in Maastricht. As the work master of the Sint Servaas Church, Coenraad I was the ideal person to approach for building commissions. Mathias Boers, a canon from Hasselt, probably acted as the intermediary for Herkenrode Abbey. Boers landed Van Neurenberg the commission for the construction of a side chapel dedicated to saint Servatius in the Sint-Querinus Church in Hasselt.[239] The abbey of Herkenrode may have come into contact with Van Neurenberg through its contacts with the other church.

Abbess Mechtildis van Léchy of Herkenrode (1519-1548) can be considered the female equivalent of Gérard van der Scaeft. Under Mechtildis' regime, the abbey underwent major construction activities. During the period that she was an abbess the church was converted (from 1521 onwards), and the eastern and western abbey buildings, a covered gallery, a Gothic gatehouse (1531), the abbess' accommodation and outbuildings (watermill, a bakery and brewery) were built. Of the abovementioned construction activities, Coenraad van Neurenberg was definitely responsible for the conversion of the church and the abbey buildings. Earlier, in 1512, he had built the so-called "withuis" for Mechtildis' predecessor, Gertrudis van Léchy.[240]

Activities in Herkenrode

Just as Abbot Gérard van der Scaeft had been the driving force behind the construction in Averbode, the Abbesses Gertrudis (1491-1519) and Mechtildis (1519-48) van Léchy were the driving force in Herkenrode (Fig. 28). After the sacking and destruction of the abbey in 1509, the abbey entered into a new period of growth and prosperity under the influence and patronage of Prince Bishop Erard de

---

[237] Lefèvre 1935, p. 50

[238] [...] ende van enen andere werckman [...] sonder argelist, Lefèvre 1935, p. 50.

[239] Dickhaut 1987, no page number.

[240] Various, 'Voormalige Abdij Herkenrode', p. 12.

la Marck of Liège.[241] A number of new buildings were erected for which Coenraad I was one of the principal master masons. The best craftsmen and artists were employed for the rebuilding of the abbey. In 1532, for example, the high choir of the rebuilt church was paved with majolica tiles by Peter-Frans van Venedigen, a ceramicist from Antwerp of Italian extraction.[242]

On 22 October 1512 the first contract between Gertrudis and Coenraad was signed. This contract concerned the construction of a house, which was to provide accommodation for the nuns. The house was demolished in 1812. The next commission was awarded on 29 March 1520. Mechteldis van Léchy concluded a contract with Coenraad to "build a square chapter house of brick" in Herkenrode.[243] A chapter room must have been located there previously because Coenraad promised to "move" the tombstones that were in the chapter room.

The next contract is from 7 March 1521. On this date, it was stipulated that Coenraad "would make and continue the old church, which stands between the new church and the new chapter house, following the new chapter house in all its ways and fashions, connected to the old church by means of a cross vault".[244] The building seems to have been executed entirely in the traditional stylistic vision. Nothing is known concerning the detailing. Furthermore, he was to build a dormitory, a staircase to the dormitory, a bathroom, a second staircase, toilets and a cloister gallery.

On 16 January 1522, Coenraad was commissioned to build a small gate and to continue work on the gallery, which formed the connection to the infirmary.[245] Although this job did not signal the end of construction activities on the abbey's grounds, Coenraad did not return after 1522. In 1531, Mechtildis had a gatehouse built which was roofed on 9 December of that year (Fig. 29). The

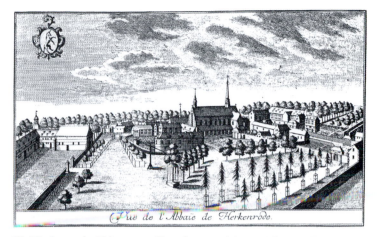

28. Herkenrode Abbey near Hasselt around 1740. After De Dijn 1982, p. 105, Nr. 67-68).

29. Herkenrode Abbey's gate, 1531 (photograph by Ronald Glaudemans).

[241] De Dijn 1982, p. 20.
[242] Ibidem. During this period, Antwerp was an important centre for luxury ceramics production. The tiles were influenced by Italian styles. Van Dam 1991, pp. 10-11.
[243] Grauwels 1982, p. 25.
[244] Dickhaut 1987.
[245] Based on De Dijn 1982 and Bollen 1977.

front of the gate has a Gothic column, which bears the coat of arms of Cardinal Erard de la Marck, while the rear of the column bears the coat of arms of Mechtildis van Léchy. Attribution on the basis of archival documents is not possible at this point in time. Taking into account the marks system and the similarities with the refugium in Hasselt, the work could also have been made by Lauwereys Ballen. The latter indeed built the brewery (1547-1550) on the abbey grounds and the refugium of Hasselt Abbey (1542-1544).[246] Ballen was probably a close relation of Coenraad, as their grandmothers shared the same surname.[247] On 2 November 1534, the abbess commissioned Michel Vocken to build two gates, and on 8 May 1538 the altar of the oratory or private chapel of the abbess was consecrated. The bay-like expansion was demolished in 1886.

The abbey was sold in 1797, after which some of the buildings were turned into a spinning mill. After the sale of the church's fixtures and fittings, and two disastrous fires on 17 March 1824 and 12 June 1826, the abbey fell into decay. Thanks to a number of eighteenth-century inventories, and the remaining buildings, it is however possible to gain an impression of what the abbey once looked like.[248]

The Carmelite nuns' church in Huy

On the second day of June in the year 1515, Willem entered into a contract with Brother Arnulph Doprebay, rector of the Carmelite nuns in Huy.[249] The Carmelite nuns had a half-finished church, as was also the case in Herkenrode and Willem agreed to finish the church. To this end twelve pillars of Namur stone had to be delivered, on which he would then build pointed arches in brick. The twelve pillars for the church had to be made like those located in the Sint-Querinus Church in Hasselt.[250] Furthermore, he was to supply a number of window frames, a spiral staircase and a door. Moreover, he agreed to raise the collars, the campanile and the roof of the nave to the same height as the church's choir, and to make a brick gable with a round window in it. This involvement in the church's roof is interesting; normally the medieval master mason did not execute this type of work because it was not his speciality, however he did supervise the work. Willem would undoubtedly have subcontracted the construction of the roof to a carpenter, while still retaining final responsibility.

Willem was to bear the work's risk and would also be responsible for supplying the materials, the labourers and staff. He would receive a sum of 575 guilders for this job, a considerable sum when compared to the forty guilders he received for the altar in Averbode. Moreover, Willem received two hectolitres of grain and six barrels of beer as a contribution towards the costs, which also had a considerable value. The abovementioned Arnulf was to provide a room with two beds and sheets and blankets as lodgings for the labourers. These labourers were probably foremen employed by Willem. He sent them to supervise the work, possibly using local craftsmen.

An additional condition in the contract was that the nuns were to teach and support a little girl for two years. This girl was probably one of Willem's daughters, and in including this clause it was a way for him to ensure she received a good education. Furthermore with a better education she was a more suitable candidate for marriage, which would allow Willem to build ties with a family of higher social status.

A second contract specified that Willem was to demolish the temporary part of the church building at his own risk. He would remove the rubble and waste, and build a new wall in Namur stone

---

[246] Dickhaut 1987. See also Meischke 2000, p. 76.

[247] See Doppler 1910, p. 113.

[248] The nineteenth century saw the demolition of the "withuis" in 1812, the abbey church and part of the convent in 1843 and the majority of the abbess' accommodation in 1884.

[249] Van der Made 1955-1957, pp. 177-180.

[250] This reference probably relates to Sint-Querinus Church in Hasselt, in which Willem's father was involved.

the same height as the new choir wall. Furthermore, Willem was to build a gateway of Namur stone that was 5.5 feet wide and eight feet high, and above this gate he would place a window with iron-work. Brother Arnulph would pay him another hundred guilders for this work and for the other two contracts; Willem's wife would receive twelve cubits of cloth from the prioress once the construction had been completed. Willem was also given the material the demolished wall provided, with the exception of the gate.

These contracts prove that Willem's activities went a good deal further than just supplying stonework to order or for finishing. Willem was responsible for the entire project and therefore also for the construction. It is also said that Willem made drawings on the basis of which the job was to be executed. All this once again confirms the suspicion that the Van Neurenberg family still worked in a very traditional manner at the start of the sixteenth century.

Willem executed the work together with a number of labourers, which he had brought from Maastricht. Due to the scope of the job and his simultaneous commission to make an altar for Averbode Abbey, it is unlikely that Willem spent all his time working on the church. Although it was not explicitly stated in the contract, it seems clear, as evidenced through the Keldermans, that he came to check on the construction site work, to give orders and to supervise.

The rood screen of the Notre Dame in Dinant

Thanks to an eighteenth-century description another project has been identified. This project concerns eight window frames and a rood screen for the Notre Dame in Dinant. No contract has been found for this screen and it has not been preserved.[251] Twenty years after its erection in 1527, it was destroyed when French troops took Dinant. Pillaging soldiers confiscated the richly decorated columns under the tribune. These items accidentally returned to Dinant, after which the screen was restored in 1580.[252] The restored version has not been preserved either. An eighteenth-century description lists four 'black marble' columns.[253] Although Coenraad I Van Neurenberg supplied a screen for the abbey of Averbode, his participation regarding the screen in Dinant is only speculation. The four columns indicate that the screen had the same floor plan as that of Averbode, which was also flanked by four columns on either side. The window frames mentioned, which have largely disappeared, featured flamboyantly shaped tracery.[254]

Conclusion

There are two major components to the main theme that runs through the early period of the Van Neurenberg family's history, the first being the family's activities. Because they were part of the late medieval building tradition the family's descendants were relatively high on the social ladder of the construction industry at the time. The early commissions can be seen as an oeuvre. Even though very little is known about them, the designs for the screens, altars and build-ings were made in-house. The family provided the design, the materials and the execution them-selves, which defines Coenraad I and Willem I as 'master masons', rather than stonemasons or materials traders.

---

[251] Steppe 1952, pp. 168-169, Timmers 1980, p. 27.
[252] Steppe 1952, p. 168.

[253] Ibidem, p. 169.
[254] Timmers 1980, p. 27.

Their personal contacts constitute the second component.[255] These contacts were the basis for the network that provided Coenraad I and Willem I van Neurenberg with commissions in the area. For Coenraad in particular, construction in Maastricht had a central place in his work. A number of important institutions came to him with commissions that, in turn, led to his name becoming known in the surrounding area. Here too, there is a medieval tradition at work. Familiarity and personal contacts helped expand the business.

Willem I van Neurenberg's career was given a head start thanks to his father's contacts. He was in an ideal position to become acquainted with the trade and perhaps more importantly, the network of potential clients, from the inside.

---

[255] Assembling a network through marriage relationships will undoubtedly have taken place during this period. The scant source material and the lack of information on families related by marriage means this information will be dealt with in the next section.

IV. Expansion of Activities (1530-1570)

Expansion of business operations: new contacts and activities

The Van Neurenberg family's activities were not limited to the south of Limburg or the Meuse Valley. As early as the end of the 1520s, the family had contacts with the north (Fig. 30). It was the family's position in the building trade that determined the expansion of its area of operations. The trade in building materials and the access to these materials were central to this expansion: it was precisely the materials marlstone and Namur stone that were in demand in the north. Construction activities required an enormous quantity of stone and buyers benefited from a guaranteed, continuous supply. The latter could only be realised after direct contacts between the north and south had been established and after the obstacle of Venlo's staple rights had disappeared.

This case was particularly true in Nijmegen: the building campaigns for the fortifications required a great deal of stone that was more easily processed. Marlstone was ideal in this respect. Namur stone was eminently suitable for cladding the fortification's walls, particularly those parts that were in water. Nijmegen's town accounts reveal that during the 1520s, direct contacts developed between the town and Maastricht pertaining to the building materials the town wished to purchase. Various marlstone and lime merchants came to the forefront and the Van Neurenberg family's position ensured that they too were involved in the export to the north.[256] Moreover, undertaking commissions in the wider surrounding area led to increasing renown and to the opportunity to expand and enlarge the company.

How large the company exactly was, can no longer be ascertained. This type of data is all too scarce. The total size probably concerned several dozen stonemasons, foremen, etc. who worked for the Van Neurenberg family in various capacities. In comparison, Cornelis Floris is known to have had countless employees who incidentally were a burden to him occasionally. "One will come down ill, the other will walk out," he complained and moreover, as workshop master, he also ran the risk of an employee damaging a piece.[257] In connection with the construction of the town hall in Antwerp, Floris employed twelve sculptors as mates between 1562 and 1565. In 1595, Floris' son Cornelis declared that his father had had twenty-six or twenty-seven apprentice sculptors since 1550, of which three had lived with him from time to time.[258] When this situation is compared to that of the descendants of the Van Neurenberg family, it becomes apparent that they were no ordinary guild masters. Ordinary guild masters were often unable to employ a single labourer, let alone trade and pre-finance construction projects.[259] However, insight into the size of the Van Neurenberg family business remains a problem.

An element that influenced the activities and that had very far-reaching consequences was the marked change undergone by the building trade's macro-organisation. The result was the development of strong specialisations among craftsmen, master masons, merchants and designers. It is surprising to see how well these changes can be tracked in the daily practice of the Van Neurenberg family. Over a period of just a few years, the range of services the family business provided changed dramatically as they flexibly capitalised on the demands of their time and the market. Particularly when it came to cooperating with other master masons, or deliveries after other people's designs, they revealed themselves as true market opportunists. The last vestiges of the medieval methods and traditions disappeared rather quickly, although traces can be found in the north. For example, Willem van Neurenberg was,

---

[256] Janse, De Vries 1991, p. 33.
[257] Huysmans 1996, p. 78.

[258] Ibidem.
[259] Van Deursen 1992, p. 14ff.

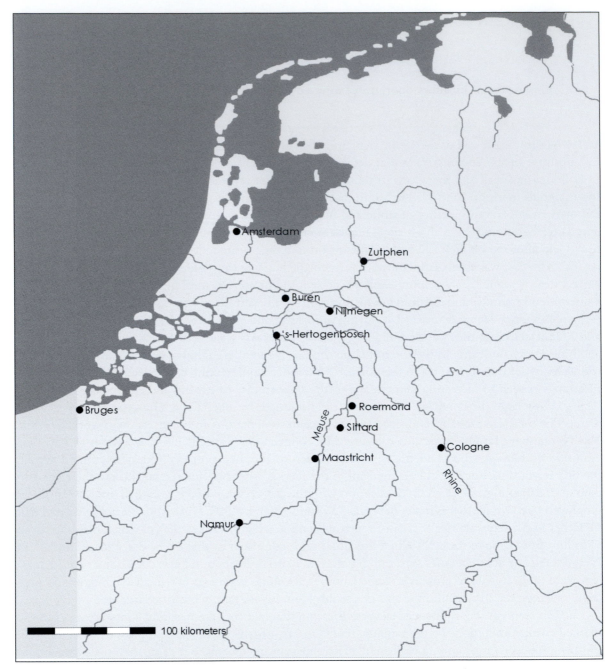

30. The Van Neurenberg family's area of activity between 1530–1570 (drawing by author).

like a genuine medieval master mason, responsible for supervising the construction of the cloth hall in Nijmegen. He was also known in that town as the lockmaster.[260] Nevertheless, the medieval construction process was starting to dissolve.

[260]Willem probably first came to Nijmegen as a result of a commission for locks.

Nijmegen

It did not take long for Willem van Neurenberg to become established in Nijmegen. He had been acting as a supplier of Namur stone in the town from his base in Maastricht since 1533. He appears regularly in the town's accounts, both under his own name and referred to as Willem Lock Master (*Wilhelm Sluysmeister*).[261] This name probably refers to the construction of a stone lock, possibly the *Sochweijdense sluis* (now referred to as the *Blauwe Sluis*), which was built in 1532. In that year foreman Uwen Petersz was paid for taking master Quirijn Petersz, the town bricklayer and Master Derick stonemason to the lock.[262]

In 1533 a messenger was sent from Nijmegen to *Wilhelm Sluysmeister* "for the sake of the building stones". Such entries occurred another four times that year. In 1533 Willem supplied a total of 2,881 feet of blue stone.[263] Moreover, Willem stayed in the town that year in order to inspect the cellars under the cloth hall. After this inspection he was commissioned to supply new stone for the building.[264]

In 1534, a messenger was sent to Maastricht on four different occasions. On one of these occasions it was stated that they went to request Master Willem's presence.[265] In this year, Willem supplied a total of 3,280 feet of stone, the majority of which was intended for the harbour.[266] This same year the mayor and aldermen decided to give "the lock master, Master Willem, for his loyalty in supplying blue stone at the harbour" town clothing, a sort of town uniform.[267] In 1535 a messenger was once again dispatched to Master Willem.[268] This year Willem also supplied a shipment of stones, although the shipment had already been ordered in 1533 or 1534. The shipment totalled 400 feet. He was also paid for working on the new round guntower in the harbour.[269]

In 1536, no new stone was purchased from Willem, but he continued to supply stone for previous orders he had not yet filled.[270] The first reference to Master Willem van Neurenberg in Nijmegen's town accounts under his own name occurs in 1539. He supplied 150 feet of stone for the Crane Gate.[271] In 1540 this entry was followed up by his further involvement in the cloth hall, which will be discussed in a separate chapter. Willem also supplied Namur stone for the town hall. On 30 April 1542, Nijmegen sent a letter to the town of Liège that stated it had grey stone purchased in Namur by Willem van Neurenberg. Symon Boesse and Krijn van Eijsden transported this stone to Nijmegen. At Liège they had been forced to pay toll rights in direct violation of the privileges. The town now requested to have these monies reimbursed and to allow similar shipments to pass toll free in the future.[272] Willem also worked on the *Bussenhuis*, the armoury hall, in 1542.[273]

---

[261] Examination of a few years of the town's accounts has revealed that Willem van Neurenberg and Willem Sluismeester were one and the same. Both merchants were responsible for the supply of Namur stone and marlstone. Willem Sluysmeester had supplied stone to the town between 1533 and 1539, Willem van Neurenberg supplied stone after that. The name Willem Sluysmeester then reoccurs in 1542, "When Willem Lock master came with the first stone" (*Doe meister Wylhem sluyssmeister, mytten yrsten steen quam*) (SR 1542, p. 106). The accounts for these years also mention one Master Willem, whose surname remains unknown. It is conspicuous that Van Neurenberg and Sluysmeester worked on the same projects, including the town hall. "Sent Bernt van Asselborn to Maastricht and because he had to stay four days, paid him 3 Brabant Guilders, which amounts to 6 Guilders" (*Bernt van Asselborn to Trycht gesandt aen meister Wilhem an die steyn vant gewanthuys nae to vernemen ende aldoer vertuven moest 4 dage, hem gegeven 3 Brab. gl., vz. 6 gl.*) (SR 1541, p. 11). Conclusive proof of whether Willem Sluismeester is the same person as Willem I van Neurenberg is provided by the 1542 bill, when *Meister Wylhem sluyssmeister* was paid for the blue and Sichener stone he supplied for the town hall. Master Willem's son, Coenraad, took the money, a total of 661.5 guilders, to Namur (SR 1542, p. 118).

[262] SAN, Oud Archief Nijmegen, Inv. No. 701.

[263] SR 1533, p. 99.

[264] SR 1533, p. 111.

[265] SR 1534, pp. 145-146.

[266] SR 1534, pp. 168-169.

[267] SR 1534, pp. 194-195.

[268] SR 1535, p. 15.

[269] SR 1535, p. 35.

[270] SR 1536, p. 101.

[271] SR 1539, p. 55.

[272] SAN, OAN. Minuut in Inv. No. 2647, Fol. 5. The source actually refers to "having Master Willem van Neurenberg purchase Namur stone".

[273] SR 1542, pp. 113-114.

Activities for Duke Karel of Gelre

Willem van Neurenberg's work on the town walls of Nijmegen should be viewed in the light of the construction activities of Duke Karel of Gelre (1467-1538). His building campaigns provided a major impetus to the building trade in Gelre. The renewal of the fortifications in Nijmegen was an undeniable part of this impulse. During this period, Gelre was still an independent province, but it was nevertheless under a great deal of outside pressure. Karel tried to withstand this pressure and was greatly aided by competent commanders in chief such as Maarten van Rossum.

A request from Willem van Neurenberg to the Duke proves that he not only worked for the Duke indirectly through commissions from Nijmegen, but also directly.[274] Willem asked him to pay the 310 golden guilders that had been promised to him in the presence of Gelis van Riemsdijk, the responsible official in the Land of Maas en Waal and Jacob Kanis, Mayor of Nijmegen. It is unclear what kind of commission this money concerned. However, it is plausible that Willem's activities pertained to the construction of the Blauwe or Sochweijdense Sluis in the Land of Maas en Waal. The lock is located on the most important watercourse in the area and an undated request from Willem not only mentions the official of the Land of Maas en Waal, but also the recipients of the funds. The touring of the lock in 1532 by master Quirijn Petersz, the town bricklayer, and Master Derick, the stonemason, reveals that work was taking place on the lock.

On 13 July 1536, Willem declared that he had received sixty golden guilders from Jan van Vuerssen on behalf of Karel of Gelre for a blue stone tomb, which Willem had shipped from Mook to the Duke (Fig. 31). The tomb was to be set up in Nijmegen, in the Sint-Stevens Church and consisted of eleven pieces of Namur stone. Rense van Holthuysen was responsible for transporting the stone from Mook to the Sint-Stevens churchyard in Nijmegen. The tomb, which was that of Anna van Bourbon, Karel of Gelre's mother, can still be found in the choir of the Sint-Stevens Church. Anna

31. Declaration by Willem I van Neurenberg dated 13 July 1536 (RAG, HA, inv. Nr. 147, nr. 1596, neg.nr. zw1-4).

32. Nijmegen, Sint-Stevens Church. Funerary monument of Anna van Bourbon (photograph by Jörg Soentgerath).

[274] RAG, toegang 0001, Inv. No. 1481 (Red No. 1815), Karel van Egmond pack.

van Bourbon was laid to rest in Sint Stevens Church in 1469, though the tomb only gained its current shape in the sixteenth century (Fig. 32). The tomb featured Gothic-style copper side plates made by Willem Loemans in Cologne before 1512. The stonework was renewed later and the copper plates were then shortened somewhat.[275] The new tomb had Renaissance profiling which makes it one of the earliest examples of a Renaissance tomb in the Low Countries and moreover the supplier is known.

Another occasion, on which Willem worked for the Duke of Gelre, was the construction of the Moerken's gate in Roermond, which the Duke financed. Willem had received the commission for the job, but refused to start before he was certain of payment. After two high-ranking officials ultimately guaranteed that someone stood surety, Willem was obliged to find someone to stand surety for himself and who would assure that he would finish the job, which he duly did. When the matter had been arranged accordingly, Willem started building the Moerken's gate.[276]

's Hertogenbosch

While Willem earned well working on commissions for Nijmegen and the Duke of Gelre, simultaneous activities in 's-Hertogenbosch, which capitalised on the political conflict between Habsburg and Gelre, seem to have been quite profitable for his father Coenraad, too. Although there is as yet no proof, there are many clues which suggest that Coenraad I was also active in Buren and 's-Hertogenbosch, where his name appears in conjunction with that of Alessandro Pasqualini.

It is believed that Pasqualini came with the Count of Buren from Bologna, where Charles V had been crowned emperor in 1530. Subsequently, the master mason would play a role in the introduction of innovations in fortification architecture in the Low Countries. Cooperation between Pasqualini and Van Neurenberg can primarily be deduced from the preparations for the construction of a bastion outside the Orthen Gate in 's-Hertogenbosch.[277] In 1541, plans were made for the renewal and improvement of 's-Hertogenbosch's fortifications and the old gate. Sand, lime, brick and Namur stone were purchased. The Namur stone was supplied by the lodge master of the Sint-Jans Church, Jan Darkennes.[278] However, the plans also included the construction of a bulwark outside the gates, which was to assume the defensive function.

Initially, the town administration paid one Keyser the bricklayer, "so that he upon the orders of the committee members had a plan for the bastion designed by a painter which was to be built outside the Orthen gate and which plan has been changed some three times." It is unknown who this Keyser was. Keyser was not the only one to supply a design. The town accounts also feature an entry paying an apprentice from Namur for the design of a bastion for the Orthen Gate. Perhaps both parties were approached simultaneously.[279]

The fact that a third design was also commissioned shows that the town administration gave thorough consideration to their choice of design. Master Alexander [Pasqualini] was called out from Buren, "having good knowledge of bastions and other fortifications". Pasqualini made a design on paper. After quite some consultation, the town's administration decided to acquire 'more certainty' concerning the bastion to be built by ordering a scale model.[280]

---

[275] Lemmens 1969, p. 95.

[276] RAG, Oud Rechterlijk Archief der stad Arnhem, Inv. No. 388. Many thanks to Jörg Soentgerath.

[277] For more extensive information on this see Van Tussenbroek 1999a and Glaudemans and Van Tussenbroek 1999.

[278] SAH, stadsrekening 1540-1541, Fol. 193. 300 feet of Namur stone for pillars was purchased from Master Jannen,

the lodge master. The lodge master referred to is probably Jan Darkennes, See Van Zuijlen 1863, p. 585 and Kennis 1997, p. 138.

[279] Van Zuijlen 1863, p. 575.

[280] Ibidem, pp. 584-585. "A draft or plan on paper, very artfully and subtly drawn and designed with pens".

Once the mayor and aldermen had approved the design work could actually start. Annuities were sold to finance the project and raised a total of 1,294 Carolus guilders and three stivers.[281] In August and September of 1542, messengers were sent out to nearby towns to fetch diggers for the work on the Orthen Gate.[282] Pasqualini himself was not charged with the execution of the work. A "Master Coenraad, an artist and master of his trade" was fetched from Buren to help build this work and supervise it.[283] Master Coenraad and his man Peter from Nijmegen (not unlikely master Quirijn Petersz, the town's bricklayer) came to 's-Hertogenbosch. His daily wage amounted to ten stivers. Van Neurenberg's presence in Buren and Nijmegen means that the Master Coenraad referred to here, can most probably be identified with master Coenraad I van Neurenberg.[284] Executing the Orthen Gate is in line with Coenraad's previously documented activities.

How far the work progressed is impossible to ascertain and even the materials purchases are hard to subdivide into purchases for the gate and for the bastion (fig. 33). In any case, Master Coenraad and his help received their weekly wage on a number of occasions. However, they were primarily occupied with other matters. When Coenraad and his mate could no longer be used, they were sent away.[285]

The entrance hall to the town hall in Cologne

The entrance hall to the Cologne town hall is one of the principal examples of Rhine Valley, Flemish-influenced Renaissance architecture.[286] The design drawings, which have been preserved, are unique. These drawings by several designers provide insight into the design history of the entrance hall.[287] There was a "hall in front of the burgher's house" in Cologne as early as 1404.[288] After expansions in the fifteenth and sixteenth centuries, the last old parts were demolished in 1570. The first designs for a new entrance hall date back to 1557 however. There are two drawings by Cornelis Floris de Vriendt II from Antwerp from that year. Five years later, sculptor Lambertus Suterman (Suavius) from Liège made a design, but there are also two anonymous drawings and an undated drawing by Hendrik van Hasselt who was also a sculptor. None of these designs were executed as drawn. Nevertheless, Cornelis Floris' design can largely be recognised in the entrance hall. The master stonemason, Willem Vernukken handled the actual execution of the work.[289] On 16 February 1571, he submitted the plans for the staircase in the entrance hall to the town administration.[290] On 26 March of that year, Vernukken was ordered to provide a detailed drawing of the upper story of the entrance hall. Vernukken regularly received commissions in Cologne for design drawings or cutting stone.

The motive for calling in Coenraad van Neurenberg from Namur was the fact that he was the supplier of an expensive type of stone that was to enhance the prestige of the entrance hall.[291] A contemporary description of the entrance hall, illustrates this case, whereby the "sixteen columns made of

[281] Ibidem, p. 576.

[282] Ibidem, p. 581. SAH, stadsrekening 1541-1542, Fol. 139. Frans the bricklayer (Darkennes), Roeloff stonemason and Lambert, Claes and Jan van Namur were paid for unloading blue stone. Frans Darkennes was a cousin of lodge master Jan Darkennes. See also Kennis 1997, p. 142.

[283] Van Zuijlen 1863, p. 585.

[284] Although Coenraad does not occur in the book of burghers, it is noteworthy that one *Jan soon Heronymus Stroewel van Norenborch* was a burgher in 's-Hertogenbosch precisely during the years 1541-1542. SAH, microfilm poorters [burghers] books in the reading room.

[285] Van Zuijlen 1863, p. 585. See also Van Tussenbroek 1999a for more on this matter.

[286] Kiene 1991, p. 127.

[287] See Paczkowski 1997, in particular pp. 257-261 and Huysmans 1996.

[288] Ibidem, p. 130.

[289] Merlos 1895, p. 896.

[290] Kiene 1991, p. 139.

[291] In the beginning, there had been plans to have the work made in Namur. Later, those involved opted to have a stone merchant come to the town. Ennen 1876, p. 284.

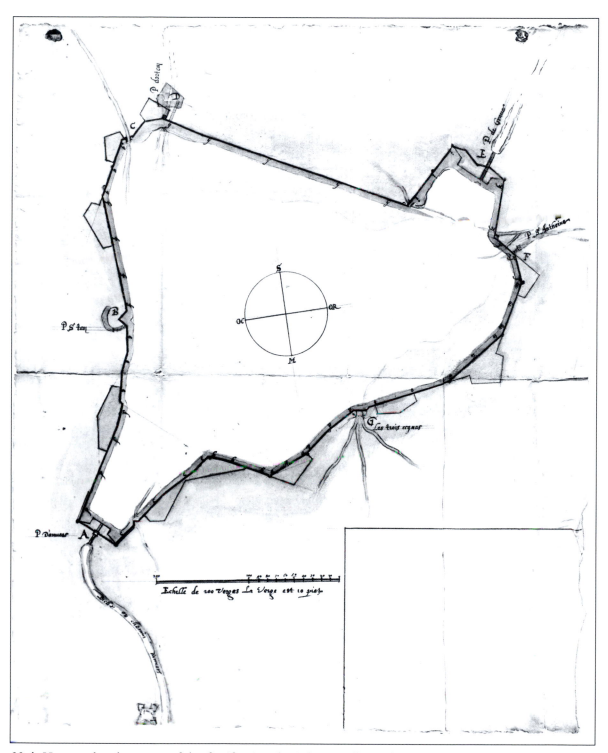

33. 's-Hertogenbosch, survey of the fortifications by Sylvain Bollin and Sebastiaan van Thienen, 1614 (SAH, Stb.nr. 39.842, Neg.nr. 20.920).

single pieces of hard black marble", were referred to separately.[292] The council protocols of 23 July 1567 reveal that the town's stewards had several designs made for the planned entrance hall of the council house.[293] The passage in which they actually decided to build on 30 March 1569 is interesting, because they were of the opinion that it was right to have the bottom pillars made of Namur stone.[294] This passage suggests that the choice of material was important for the building's status, since it is referred to explicitly and separately. Namur stone was clearly seen as exclusive and prestigious. However, what is more important in this context, is that the choice of patron (or supplier) for the material was the motive for contacting Van Neurenberg.

After the Cologne council decided to use Namur stone for the columns, the town building inspector (*Ratsumlauf*) Johann van Bingen and master mason Willem Vernukken[295] left for Andernach to purchase materials at the end of April 1569. Another planned trip to Namur was cancelled due to war.[296] Instead, Coenraad II van Neurenberg was asked to come to Cologne to discuss the delivery of stone. Coenraad was also to ensure the delivery of a chimneypiece.

On 25 September 1570, Willem Vernukken complained that he was short of stone and that Coenraad van Neurenberg was not abiding by the agreement.[297] Coenraad was punished by the postponement of the payment for the chimneypiece, which he had supplied for the council house.[298] Vernukken was provided with funds with which he could fetch the stone required. Unfortunately in this instance it is not clear whether these funds actually concerned Namur stone or not. On 4 October, he complained again about lacking 500 feet of stone, but in this circumstance it concerned Münster stone. It is therefore possible that Vernukken had a two-fold problem, which is not unlikely if the rest of the story is taken into account. On 13 December Coenraad accused Willem Vernukken of working on the entrance hall incorrectly and moreover, he was accused of embezzling money.[299] The accusations were discussed, but the conflict was not resolved: the situation worsened and it seemed as if Vernukken was so annoyed by the job that he threatened to give the commission back and leave the work to another master. The other master was Coenraad II van Neurenberg. While he was slandering Willem Vernukken, Coenraad was simultaneously conducting negotiations with the town administrators. They intended to award the job to Coenraad in the event that Vernukken stopped.[300] In the end, Vernukken was not found guilty of anything and finished the job. Thus it seems highly likely that Coenraad's accusations were purely slander. Coenraad van Neurenberg failed, but not by much. By conspiring with the town's administration and maligning Vernukken he almost managed to procure a job that was already underway. Besides illustrating his personality and moral stance, this example also says something about his business politics. He obviously did not wish to limit himself to supplying stone; he wanted to act as an independent master mason just as his father and grandfather had done. Keeping the medieval tradition was no longer possible and Van Neurenberg would increasingly be employed as a specialist within the construction process.

The entrance hall was the only part of the council house to emerge from the Second World War relatively unscathed, as bombing destroyed the rest. In the 1870s the entrance hall was radically restored by the town's master mason, Hermann Weyer (Fig. 34). The latter used the designs that, at the time, were wrongly attributed to Willem Vernukken as the basis for his restoration.[301] This restoration

---

[292] Paczkowski 1975, p. 94. Georg Braun, Deacon of St. Maria ad gradus in Keulen, gave this description in his *Stadsboek*.
[293] Paczkowski 1975, p. 95.
[294] [...] *so wurde für gut angesehen, die unttersten Pfeiler von Namurer Steinen anfertigen zu lassen*. Kiene 1991, p. 133.
[295] See Glißmann 1998, passim for more on Vernukken.
[296] Kiene 1991, p. 145.

[297] Merlos 1895, p. 897.
[298] Ibidem, p. 626.
[299] Ibidem, p. 897.
[300] *Meine Herren haben für gut angesehen, mit dem Meister von Namur zu reden, auf den Fall Meister Wilhelm meinen Herren länger zu dienen nicht unterstehe, ihm alsdann fürderhin das Werk zu vergönnen.* Quoted by Kiene 1991, p. 145.
[301] Kiene 1991, p. 127.

34. Cologne, town hall, entrance hall (after Vogts 1930).

resulted in a partly renewed entrance hall, which no longer resembled the original. Nowadays, the columns' stone is sanded, which gives the material a matt grey colour. Originally the situation was different. Old photographs show that the columns were polished, which makes the stone gleam revealing its deeper colour.

The town hall in Sittard

In Sittard Coenraad II Van Neurenberg also supplied stone for the new town hall, formerly cloth hall, designed by Maximilian Pasqualini (1534-1572), the eldest son of Italian master mason Alessandro Pasqualini.[302] The town hall was demolished in the eighteenth century.

The building's precursor had been heavily damaged on 22 October 1542 by Charles V's troops led by René of Orange.[303] The new construction did not start until 1561.[304] The new town hall was to have a different function than the old one. The cloth trade had declined considerably. After negotiations between Duke Willem V of Jülich and the town administration, which lasted from 1555 until 1564, it was decided that the ground floor and first story of the new building would be made available to the town administration.[305] The two areas would house the court for the bench of aldermen, the council chamber, the so-called burgher house and the archive. The second floor and the loft were intended for the duke and would also be used to store the unsold grain, for a price, that belonged to traders from outside town.[306]

In 1561, master Maximilian Pasqualini went to Sittard to discuss the construction of the town hall. During this period, Maximilian was the master mason for Jülich the duchy to which Sittard belonged.[307] Alessandro's second son, Johan Pasqualini (1535- circa 1580) was also involved in the construction. Master Johan Brandt van Weissweiler carried out the actual construction and Master Gobbels from Puitzloon carried out the carpentry work on the town hall.[308] Master Johan van Roermond was not only responsible for covering the roof and both towers in slate, but also for supplying the slates.[309] "White Rijmberg stone" was also used in the town hall and Thomas Maeneschen van Rijmburgh supplied it.[310] Coenraad II van Neurenberg supplied the Namur stone, which was used for doors, window frames, steps, benches and pavement, totalling over 4,500 feet and valued at approximately 1,700 guilders. After master Alexander Libisch had executed the preparatory measuring work, the work was given to master Johan Brandt.

The first stone was laid for the new town hall in 1563. It was completed around 1567, with the exeption of the stonework. Coenraad II's delivery was delayed, which meant Master Johan had to incorporate stonework into the building later than planned incurring additional costs.[311] Maximilian Pasqualini also ordered Master Johan to demolish the new house's stone staircase because it was too high and narrow.[312]

The Namur stone for the town hall was delivered made to order. In order to make small alterations to the stone (holes), a stonemason or bricklayer from Maaseik named Jacob Vinck was employed, because Master Johan did not dare do this work himself. In September 1561, a messenger was sent to Namur on several occasions "because of the Namur stone". However, the stonemason was not home

---

302 See Simonis 1971, Chapter 5 for more on the town hall.
303 Oremus 1993, p. 3.
304 Ibidem, p. 7.
305 Roebroek 1981, p. 141.
306 Ibidem, p. 143.
307 See Van Mierlo 1991, pp. 163-165 for more on Maximiliaan.

308 Oremus 1993, pp. 19-20.
309 Ibidem, p. 21.
310 Ibidem, p. 14.
311 Ibidem, p. 18.
312 Ibidem.

which led to additional costs because the messenger had to wait for an answer. In October a messenger was sent to Jülich to Master Maximilian with regard to patterns.[313] In July 1562 discussions were still ongoing with Coenraad regarding the stone. What the problems were exactly is unclear. But it is clear that things were serious, "Sent messenger to Jülich on 7 July to request that the master mason [Maximilian Pasqualini]'s brother Johan come here and discuss the Namur stone with Master Coenraad".[314] In 1564, another messenger was sent to Namur, and once again he had to wait a few days before he received an answer. The stone was finally delivered on 23 March 1566, after which master Alexander Libisch could measure it to check whether it corresponded to the order.[315]

Excavations in 1980 revealed six marlstone block foundations, which suggest that the western side probably featured a colonnade and half the building had an underlying cellar.[316] The town hall burnt out on 2 September 1677 when French troops razed the town for the second time. The ruin would only be demolished ninety-eight years later. In spite of repeated requests from the town administration, the Duke did not cooperate in the reconstruction. The town restored the tower's clock and bells in 1712. The building remained a ruin until part of the brickwork was demolished in 1743. Between 1775 and 1776 the last remnants were removed.[317]

Cooperation with other stone merchants

Some of the Van Neurenberg deliveries were not made as independent entrepreneurs. In a few instances they cooperated with other stone merchants. The Van Neurenberg family's aid was probably required for these deliveries because of time constraints, or because the size of the shipment was impossible for a single merchant to handle.

Cooperation with Lambillon

The first collaboration that will be discussed is between Coenraad II van Neurenberg and Jacob Pierçon Lambillon from Namur and concerns stone deliveries for the Old Church in Amsterdam in the 1550s and 1560s. Lambillon, like Coenraad, was also from a family of stone merchants, stonemasons and sculptors; there were also family ties between the two families.[318] Four Lambillons occur in sources: Hubert, active in the fourteenth century,[319] and Jacob Pierçon, Lambrecht and Pieter, who were active in the sixteenth century between ca. 1555 and 1575. Lambrecht de Lambillon made the sepulchral monument for Jean de Ligne, Count of Arenberg in 1569. This monument was installed in the church in Zevenbergen.[320] Pieter is known to have been a stone merchant and he provided material for the Emden town hall in Germany in 1574.[321] Within the context of this research, the most important descendant of the family is Jacob Pierçon. In addition to his involvement in the Old Church in Amsterdam, he also delivered stone for the New Church (also in Amsterdam) and for the town hall cellar in Utrecht, in 1561. On 24 July 1567, Jan (Jacob?) Lambillon, "merchant from Namur", received a commission to build a lock near Spaarndam.[322] The dates of birth and death of the various members of the Lambillon family are unknown.

---

[313] Ibidem, p. 31.
[314] Ibidem, p. 32.
[315] Ibidem, p. 15.
[316] Roebroek 1981, p. 146.
[317] Ibidem.
[318] GAD, index of the Walloon Church (Waalse kerk).

[319] Hubert de Lambillon is the odd one out. He also came from Namur and worked on the erection of the monument to Philip the Bold under Claus Sluter in 1397 and 1398.
[320] Janse, De Vries 1991, p. 36.
[321] Ibidem.
[322] Vierlingh 1920, pp. 240-248.

Jacob Pierçon and Coenraad II van Neurenberg first collaborated on the delivery of tombstones for the Old Church in Amsterdam. The construction of the new Maria chapel for the Old Church, to the north of the choir, had been started in 1552, but was not yet finished by 1559. This dating is based on the furnishing of the chapel, though it does not mean that the stonework had been placed yet. Henrik van den Berg probably oversaw the construction project.[323] Henrik had previously worked as the chief stonemason in Gouda for the rebuilding of the church, which had burnt down in 1552, but after six months he had been "fetched by the Amsterdammers". It is believed that the chapel was roofed a year later, in 1553.[324] Building materials were sold which seem to have come from the outside wall, which was demolished. The chapel's windows bear the date 1555.

Coenraad II van Neurenberg and Pierçon Lambillon's involvement in the new chapel was limited to the supply of tombstones. In 1555 they sent two ships of Namur stone to Amsterdam for the Old Church. A year later, Pierçon Lambillon sent seven double tombstones and two singles.[325] Neither supplier was involved in the construction. Their names do not occur in the accounts, and more importantly, none of the vertical work features Namur stone.[326] It is hard to reconstruct how the contacts between Namur and Amsterdam came to be. It is possible that the purchase of expensive types of stone for the new altar may have played a role in the contacts. A more likely option is that tombstones made of Namur stone had been delivered earlier. The number of suppliers was so low that when the demand for this stone increased, Coenraad or Pierçon were some of the first people considered.

Cooperation with Misson

Van Neurenberg also cooperated with Remi and Jan Misson, and other Namur stone merchants, for the delivery of stone from 1565-1566 for the construction of a town gate in Bruges.[327] The accounts reveal that the magistrates of the town offered the three men wine; thus leading to the conclusion that they travelled to Bruges themselves, most likely for negotiations concerning the stone. The bill shows that the government of Bruges paid stonemason Ambrosius van Cattenbrouck for the delivery of all manner of material and the setting up of the gateway, which concerned "all the stone".[328]

Various types of stone are mentioned in the Bruges sources for the period up to 1564. From the year 1528 onwards these sources concerned "Escosijns" (Ecaussines), "Parijsch stone", "hard stone"[329], stone from Avesnes, white stone, blue stone, alabaster, blue stone from Tournai, white hard stone from Ghent, Reinsche stone, Rance marble, black marble and black touchstone. Only in the year 1563-1564 is "stone from the land of Namur" mentioned for the first time. Shortly afterwards, on 24 March 1565, there is a contract for a tabernacle for the church in Gestel, which used a great deal of Namur stone. Coenraad's delivery for the gateway follows a few months later. The deliveries of marble from Rance, black marble and black touchstone, a Misson speciality, cannot be ignored; the stone from the Meuse basin points to direct trading contacts, which can also be found in connection with the construction of the Antwerp town hall during these years.[330]

---

[323] Bijtelaar 1962, p. 55. More recently see Janse 2004, pp. 136-146.
[324] Ibidem.
[325] Meischke, etc., 1995, p. 116, n. 91. The archive of the Old Church in Amsterdam retains a letter from Hans of Maeseick, innkeeper at the Gorcom inn in Nijmegen, dating back to 1555 in which he informs the churchwardens in Amsterdam that Coen van Neurenberg had sent them two ships of Namur stone. On 16 January 1556, Pierçon Lambillon writes that he has sent seven double and two single tombstones. Ibidem.

[326] Bijtelaar writes that the chapel first had a temporary floor of "Keulse steen". After tombs had been sold in the new chapel, the temporary floor was removed and was replaced by tombstones.
[327] Parmentier 1948, p. 89, n. 71.
[328] Ibidem, p. 65.
[329] Probably also stone from Ecaussines.
[330] See Van Tussenbroek 2001a for more on the Misson's marble trade.

On 13 July 1570, Johan Michon (Jan Misson) concluded a contract for the delivery of stonework for a lock in Steenbergen near Willemstad.[331] The specifications of the work to be delivered were drawn up in Dutch and French. The assumption can therefore be made that the job was tendered to various possible contractors, which can also be supported by the fact that Misson is mentioned "as being the least and lowest bidder for the delivery of blue stone".

It was from this circle of merchants, suppliers of stone for hydraulic-engineering work, facade cladding, town gates, etc. that the marble trade was to develop. The patron determined the demand for a particular type of stone. It is therefore not surprising to encounter Charles Misson almost annually between 1599 and 1613 in the accounts of the court in Brussels in connection with marble deliveries.[332] These deliveries were special elements made of stone from the area around Namur intended for doorframes, black marble fireplaces or a basin for a fountain in the garden.[333] Misson, for example, supplied two sculpted window frames for an alcove in the palace and a mantelpiece made of black marble from Dinant in 1609.[334]

Misson's activities should be placed in the circle of which Van Neurenberg was also active and overlaps with that of court suppliers such as Robert de Nole, who was the court sculptor during the time Misson supplied stone there. To what extent both families were active in the same market is proven by the fact that Coenraad II van Neurenberg, stone merchant and since 1571 master mason to the Count of Namur was succeeded on 20 October 1595 by Charles Misson, as "stone mason to the count of Namur".[335]

In summary, the flourishing of the Van Neurenberg family as an important family of stonemasons and merchants can be linked to a number of factors. Firstly, their success was due to continuity in vertical personal relations (family relations). Secondly, it was due to continuity as a result of horizontal personal relations (social contacts). Thirdly, there was a favourable economic change: the abolition of staple rights in Venlo. Fourthly, the family had an aggressive acquisition policy. Fifth, cooperation with other stone merchants created contacts with new patrons. And finally, the Van Neurenberg family provided a product for which there was a specific demand.

---

[331] Vierlingh 1920, pp. 226–230. This order concerned the delivery of 5,900 feet.
[332] Brussels, Algemeen Rijksarchief, *Rekenkamer* 27502–27509. Many thanks to Krista De Jonge, 13 April 1999.
[333] De Jonge et al. 1998. pp. 191–219.
[334] Ibidem, p. 195.

[335] He may possibly be one of Jan or Remy Misson's sons. Algemeen Koninklijk Archief te Brussel, Audientie 1235 'sculptures'. In this document it is explicitly said that Coenraad van Neurenberg has passed away. His position is *vacant par le trespas de Coenraet van Nurenberge*. Many thanks to Krista de Jonge.

V. THE STONE TRADE AND THE TOWN BUILDING COMPANY. VAN NEURENBERG AND THE BUILDING OF NIJMEGEN'S CLOTH HALL

This chapter will examine the deliveries and construction projects of the Van Neurenberg family from the perspective of the building patron and the town, in order to gain insight into the place the activities described in the previous chapter occupy in the construction process as a whole. This does not so much concern the supply as the demand for Namur stone and the services of building contractors such as the Van Neurenbergs. Nijmegen will be used as case study because Willem I van Neurenberg supervised the building of a new cloth hall there between 1533 and 1545.

Guilds and principals

The discussion of urban construction in this period is to a great extent a discussion of the guilds. The power of the guilds differed from town to town.[336] During the sixteenth century, the stonemasons of Bruges were part of the bricklayer's guild that had three subsections: the bricklayers, the stonemasons and the paviours. In principle, the stonemasons who were guild members were the only people who had the right to process or trade in stone in the town. However, there are recorded instances of stonemasons from outside town asking the Bruges guild for permission to import their work.[337] Conversely, Bruges stonemasons were active in the surrounding area to the extent that no other regulations applied there. Attracting 'foreign' mates to the town caused major friction within the guild as proven by a document dating back to 6 July 1547. In this document the aldermen of Bruges made a judgment in a dispute between the bricklayers' guild and stonemason Michiel Scherier. Scherier had employed two mates from outside town, but he had only used them very briefly. At the guild's behest they had been imprisoned because Scherier had not asked the guild for permission to allow both mates to work in his workshop. He had recruited them because there were no suitable stonemasons available in Bruges who could work for him. From the guild's perspective, the idea was to protect the interests of the Bruges stonemasons. In the end, the guild decided that the mates would be allowed to continue to work for Scherier as long as he paid a certain sum of money annually for each foreign mate, which Scherier considered an amenable solution.[338]

Nevertheless, not every stonemason from outside town was allowed to work in Bruges. In December 1560, stonemasons Joost Aerts and Jan de Smet asked for permission to employ as many mates as they needed.[339] This request mentioned the precedent set by Michiel Scherier's case. In addition to the abovementioned reason for hiring "foreigners", it was also indicated that the black touchstone, the marble and the alabaster that were to be worked, could best be worked by "foreigners", because they have better experience with these materials.[340] Finally, Aerts and De Smet pointed out that "foreign" mates were permitted in towns such as Antwerp, Brussels, Mechelen, and Ghent to name but a few.

---

[336] See also Goudriaan et al. 1996.
[337] Parmentier 1948, p. XV.
[338] Ibidem, pp. 13–15.
[339] This matter concerned inhabitants of Bruges and "foreigners". They also asked for permission to work by can-

dlelight, something that was usually forbidden. See Ibidem, pp. 35–48 for more on this matter.
[340] ... *toutse, abastre ende marbresteene.* Ibidem, p. 35.

The request was turned down in an expansive missive by the magistrates. The reasons given included the guild's regulation to which both gentlemen had sworn to abide to nine years earlier, in 1551, and which was to benefit all the tradesmen in the guild. However, their request would only benefit Joost Aerts and Jan de Smet. Reference was also made to the limitations the guild in Antwerp had imposed whereby only one "foreign" mate was allowed to work, and where the guild contribution was higher than in Bruges. The response then went on to list a large number of stonemasons from Bruges who had worked, in among other places, Antwerp, Sluis and Nieuwpoort and had to pay the guilds of those towns a particular sum for every day they had worked. The regulation was therefore very common within the guild system, in contrast to what the two men had suggested in their request.[341]

This matter reveals that in practice it was not hard for a stonemason to work in another town where there was another guild, the principal consequence being that part of the daily wages had to be made available to the guild in order to allow it to protect its own tradesmen.

The relationship between Van Neurenberg, the town administrations and the trade guilds

In Nijmegen, as in many other towns, there was a regulation on the books stating if someone wished to work a trade or occupation in the town, they had to be a citizen of that town. The same applied to wagoners transporting goods for money in the town's surroundings.[342] Moreover, masters were obliged to pay for their admission to the trade,[343] and they had to have a cuirass that fit them in order to be able to help defend the town. If a potential guild member could not afford the cuirass, then he could negotiate a postponement. However, he had to have the cuirass before he was accepted into the trade. The cuirass could not be sold. In order to check whether everyone abided by the rules, there was an inspection every four years.[344] Furthermore, tradesmen in Nijmegen were prohibited from entering into alliances without the council's knowledge.[345] This regulation was aimed at protecting guild members. The guilds were first and foremost aimed at ensuring citizens of the town the well-organised and honest execution of their trade. In addition to obligations pertaining to the trade in which the masters worked, there were also rules of protocol.[346]

If the influence the guilds had on construction in towns is examined, then it becomes clear that it is primarily the separation of trades that is of importance for determining differences. If a citizen wanted to build a house, he had to go and see various craftsmen. There were no building contractors who could build an entire house, as there are today. Due to the strict separation of trades, construction was a disjointed affair: carpenters, bricklayers and slaters all had their own areas of expertise, from which they were not allowed to deviate. In practice the position of stonemasons in the town of Nijmegen was subordinate to that of carpenters.[347] The social status of stonemasons was lower than that of other craftsmen,[348] but this lower status concerned the smaller stonemasons, not the major players such as Van Neurenberg.

Naturally, the materials trade avoided the guild regulations that applied in towns. There the building trade as a whole was strongly dependent on the supply of building materials and the trade was therefore only subject to regulations that transcended town administration. Stone merchants often concluded agreements with captains, so that they indirectly controlled their own transport.[349] Citizens

---

[341] The conflict nevertheless seems to have been settled to the applicants' advantage. It was decided on 10 September 1561 that the petitioners, due to exceptional considerations, would be allowed to work by candlelight. Ibidem, p. 48.

[342] Krom, Pols 1894, pp. 43, 46-7.

[343] Ibidem, p. 70.

[344] Ibidem, p. 81.

[345] Ibidem, p. 43.

[346] Ibidem, p. 47 and 367.

[347] Meischke 1993, p. 53.

[348] Janse, De Vries 1991, p. 27.

[349] For more on this subject, see Chapter II.

arranged the transport in a town. Traders brought their wares to the unloading dock, after which they were taken over by the town's citizens.

Towns and travelling traders

Towns did have particular delivery channels and were aware of alternate purchasing possibilities. But generally there was no such thing as regular clients. Supply took two different routes and generally two types of product can be discerned: local and foreign products. The former were purchased from local traders and manufacturers. Foreign materials on the other hand were purchased from travelling traders or captains, at markets in other towns or from the source.[350]

Due to Nijmegen's location on the Waal River, it would seem obvious for most of the materials to have been supplied over the Rhine. Although there are some instances of shipments of Baumberger stone being supplied to the town in the sixteenth century, marlstone and lime shipped down the Meuse occur much more frequently in the town's accounts.[351] These materials were purchased in Venlo until 1525 and after that time in Maastricht.[352] The ships were unloaded at Mook on the Meuse, after which wagoners, first from Mook and later from Nijmegen, brought the materials into town, to be stored or immediately processed there.[353]

Instead of using intermediaries, there was personal contact between the trader and the town's representative (read messenger). After the conclusion of the purchase and the transportation of the material, the ships were unloaded at Mook and their cargos inspected. Servaas Boom, who also traded in lime, regularly supplied the marlstone purchased.[354] Large towns such as Nijmegen were better at maintaining contacts with standard traders than smaller towns in the vicinity such as Tiel or Grave; there was a bigger demand, and it was more advantageous to circumvent the distributors and go straight to the source. The cost of a messenger was then negligible. In general, direct trade was more common for the larger towns, while travelling traders played a more important role in the smaller towns.

The role of town craftsmen

In the sixteenth century, Nijmegen had a number of craftsmen who regularly worked for the town. These were craftsmen who took care of the regular work and who only occasionally provided designs for town buildings. Examples include Quirijn Petersz, Claes de Waell and Adam de Stratenmaker (the Paviour). The town did not permanently employ the latter, although his services were regularly used and he was paid per job.[355] The town's accounts of 1540 prove that, in practice, these irregular jobs combined with a good relationship with the town were as valuable as a permanent job. In that year, Adam worked for the town for a total of 241.5 days, which, considering the nature of the work (paving is impossible if there is frost) and sundays, means he worked for the town for a full working year.[356] Adam was paid per day together with his main labourer. The remuneration for both of them amounted to fifteen stivers. In November this figure was twelve stivers, as productivity was lower due to the weather conditions and the shorter days. The 1540 accounts mentions the names of twenty-two men for general work such as diggers, foremen and lime mixers and together they worked a total of 2,729 days and eleven nights for the town, and earned an average of four to five stivers per day.

---

[350] See also De Vries 1994, p. 21.
[351] Kleintjes, Sormani, SR 1527, pp. 28-29.
[352] There are also examples of the town acquiring materials from travelling traders.

[353] SR 1530, p. 211.
[354] SR 1531, p. 282.
[355] SR 1543, p. 211.
[356] SR 1540, pp. 150-153.

Another person who could bank on regular work was Gairt Ketell, "our town carpenter". In 1540, he and his labourers worked a total of 485.5 days for the town, whereby he generally earned some eight to nine stivers per day.[357] However, the term "town carpenter" does not allude to permanent employment. As the example of Coenraad I van Neurenberg "town master mason" of Maastricht shows, the term was an indication of regular work, or of a working relationship, rather than a permanent position.

Willem I van Neurenberg and the Hezel gate in Nijmegen

In 1533, the town's accounts include the entry that Derick Scheymaker had been to Willem van Neurenberg in Maastricht regarding a delivery of blue stone.[358] The stone was shipped in the south and a short time later Derick could be found in Mook receiving it.[359] In the same year, Derick was sent out again to purchase "grey stone".[360] These purchases were made for the construction of the new Hezel gate. When the development of artillery made reinforcing of the ramparts essential, the old gateway tower was demolished. The 74.000 bricks thus provided were partially used for the construction of the new gate, which was then clad in blue stone. Bentheimer sandstone was used for the ornamental parts.[361] Master Quirijn Petersz, who started construction on the new gate on 22 May 1533, supervised the work.[362] The town's accounts show that Willem I van Neurenberg acted as a supplier of worked blocks of stone for the construction of the gate.[363]

An interesting fact is that there was a price difference between the various blocks of stone. One shipment cost ten Brabant guilders per hundred feet of blue stone, whereas another cost eighteen guilders per hundred feet. The conclusion may therefore be made that the stone was supplied in two different phases of processing. One shipment probably consisted of simple blocks, while Van Neurenberg had already turned the other into arch posts, which explains the difference in price.

Other people were also mentioned in connection with the construction of the Hezel gate. In the 1533 accounts there is an entry dedicated to the activities on the new gate. Between 25 May and 16 November a total of twenty-four bricklayers worked on the Hezel gate. Master Quirijn Petersz supervised the work.[364] In 1540, 125.5 feet of stone cross-window frames were purchased from Herman Steenhouwer. The price per foot was three stivers and one-quarter stiver. Twelve and one half blocks of Sichener stone (marlstone) were purchased from Herman for ten stivers per block.[365] Gairt Ketell and his labourers also worked on the Hezel gate in 1540 for a total of forty-five days doing carpentry work.[366] The work was completed in 1540-1542. The Hezel gate was demolished in 1876-1877.[367]

[357] Ibidem, pp. 140-144.
[358] SR 1533, p. 80. The name "Blauwe Steen" was also used for the executioner's block in Nijmegen. Van Schevichaven 1901. p. 28. A similar blue stone is known to have existed in Leiden.
[359] SR 1533, p. 81.
[360] Ibidem.

[361] Gorissen 1956, p. 149.
[362] Ibidem.
[363] SR 1533, p. 99.
[364] Ibidem, pp. 95-96.
[365] SR 1540, p. 157.
[366] Ibidem, pp. 140-144.
[367] See Gorissen 1956, p. 149 and Janssen 1966, p. 91.

The cloth hall: previous history, function and ownership structure

The earliest reference to the cloth hall in Nijmegen dates back to 1382, when a slater worked on the roof for six days.[368] In that year some of the arcades in the hall were given out in hereditary leases to shopkeepers.[369] The cloth hall itself was on the first floor. A 1389 statute stated that no one else was allowed to cut or sell cloth in the Nijmegen area outside the cloth hall, with the exception of the cloth markets, which were held biannually.

It is reasonable to assume that the medieval cloth hall occupied the same location as its sixteenth-century successor. Almost nothing is known of its external appearance though. It is known, however, that at least thirty-one cloth merchants must have existed in fourteenth-century Nijmegen as that is the number of places allocated in the building's main room.[370] In 1410 the cloth hall was definitely located in the exact spot it can be found today (Fig. 35).[371] If, at the close of the fourteenth century spaces on the ground floor had still been leased in perpetuity, they were referred to as "owned" in the

35. Nijmegen, cloth hall with church arch (photograph by author).

fifteenth. The cloth hall's function changed over the years. In the fifteenth century the Lower Rhine cloth trade suffered under competition from Holland, which is the reason why, around 1420, the cloth hall was also used for other purposes. For example, the town received distinguished visitors such as Jacoba of Bavaria in 1422 and Duke Arnold of Gelre in 1440 there.[372] By the sixteenth century, the cloth hall had long since ceased to solely serve the purpose for which it was built, as shown by the list of other functions wich were accomodated there at the time, such as a bottling works, ballroom, town wine house and reception hall. These other activities were probably also the reason why, in spite of a recession in the cloth trade, the town decided to make a major investment in the building of a new cloth hall at the middle of the sixteenth century.

The design and plans for rebuilding

In the fourteenth century the cloth hall consisted of the cellars, the ground floor with an arcade, the first floor and cloth hall and a roof.[373] The 1531 town accounts show that crenellations were removed from the building, presumably due to dilapidation. Nevertheless, these repairs were not sufficient to save the building. In 1533, Willem I van Neurenberg was commissioned to inspect the building's cellars in cooperation with master Quirijn Petersz.[374] It is not surprising that stone trader Van Neuren-

[368] Van Schevichaven 1909, p. 142.
[369] Gorissen 1956, p. 110.
[370] De Heiden 1983, p. 32.
[371] Van Schevichaven 1909, p. 142.
[372] De Heiden 1983, p. 32.

[373] Van Schevichaven 1909, p. 143. The latter also writes that there were lofts.
[374] Weve 1889, p. 8. This cellar probably refers to the spaces underneath the arches on the ground floor.

berg's judgement on the building's condition was unfavourable. In the same year, negotiations took place with him regarding the delivery of stone for the construction of the new hall.[375]

In 1535, Masters Quirijn and Herman helped demolish the old cloth hall's facade. This measure was possibly occasioned by the building's poor condition, as it was not until a year later that a design for the new hall came into being. In 1536, master Claes de Waell was paid for the design he had made for the cloth hall.[376] Claes de Waell was a surveyor and often carried out inspection activities for the town. Furthermore, he was active as a designer and a stonemason for the town.[377] It is possible De Waell also had his own masonry company. In 1539 he made the patterns for the Haarsteegse Gate.[378] His position was similar to that of a town stonemason. In 1552 he was commissioned to enlarge the southern transept of Sint-Stevens Church, to build the western crossing pillars and the adjacent transept pillars including the accompanying pier arches.[379]

In the years after 1536, work took place on the cloth hall, although it was sporadic. It is unlikely that De Waell's design was executed during these years. There are entries for slate work and for a tinsmith,[380] but it does not mean that construction activities were taking place. The large building required constant maintenance and was in such poor shape that repair activities may have taken place in order to enable the building to be used as long as possible. Moreover, Claes de Waell's design has not been preserved. His design may have pertained to the distribution of plots, the measuring of the existing dimensions or to the appearance of the new building. If the data in the town's accounts and the traditional character of the building are taken into account, it may be assumed that the design concerned a rough plan, focussed on plot layout and building volume.

The first unequivocal entry for materials purchasing for the cloth hall dated back to 1540. The actual construction of the cloth hall was contracted to Willem I van Neurenberg.[381] There are no indications that Willem was ultimately responsible for the design. The bill is quite clear and he received no money for a design. After De Waell's design had been made, no new design costs were incurred. An entry in which Willem is paid for making scantlings does occur.[382] However, this entry is only significant with regard to the making of scantlings. If one considers the church arch leading from the market to the churchyard, which clearly has Meuse Valley stylistic characteristics, it cannot be excluded that Van Neurenberg was also responsible for detailing the building. In this case, this work was part of the technical execution of the job and not part of the planning or design phases.

---

[375] Ibidem.

[376] SR 1536, p. 116.

[377] *Claes die Waell totten patronen tmaeken gehadt een boick dobbels pappier, gekost 5 st.* (SR 1539, p. 88); *Van tmeten die plaets aen die Borchport ende oick dair Ffy Grobben huys gestaen heefft, gegeven 18st.* and *ons heren meister Claes lanthmether, van tmeten der armer lueden dack, toegelaeten 1 gl. 4 st.* (SR 1539, p. 91); *Claes die Waell steenhouwer, van te meten den thiirsdiick, durch ontheit onser heren gegeven 1 gl. 4 st.* (SR 1535, p. 55); *Claes die Waell tot een ny maetry tmaeken, gecofft een dennen sparr voir 5 st. Brab., (vz.) 10 stuivers.* (SR 1538, p. 207).

[378] SR 1539, p. 88.

[379] Van Agt 1954, pp. 122-123.

[380] SR 1538, p. 213.

[381] *Soe meister Wilhelm van Noerenborch van onsen heren aengenomen heefft idt gewanthuys van hardden steen te tymmeren, ick* [the steward] *denselven den 6den dach Septembris dairop gesanth 100 rider gl., vz. 250 gl.* SR. 1540, p. 157 and *Meister Wilhelm van Noerenborch in aen te nemen dat gewanthuys te tymmeren, ons heren denselven te vollenste siin teronghen toegeleten 10 rider gl. vz. 25 gulden.* Ibidem, p. 182.

[382] *[…] durch beveelt onser heren meister Wilhelm tot siin breder tmaeken totten gewanthuys uutgericht 3 wagenschotten, tstuck gekost 11 st. Brab. vz 3 gulden 6 stuivers.* Ibidem.

Execution and completion

Van Neurenberg spent a total of eighty-nine days acting as master mason in Nijmegen. He worked in the same manner as he did for the construction of the Carmelite nun's church in Huy. He was responsible for supplying the building materials and for the construction itself. Just like in 1540, Willem I van Neurenberg received 250 guilders from the individual lessees or part owners of the cloth hall. A messenger took the money to Maastricht.[383] This payment was not as odd as it might seem if we take the property structure of the cloth hall into account. Moreover, Willem received five yards of English cloth from the town in this year.[384] A delegation left Nijmegen for Maastricht "on behalf of the cloth hall because of the blue stone".[385] Although this visit seemed to have finalised everything, construction did not start immediately. The organisation was disorganised and it would take another two years before the actual construction of the new cloth hall could start. In 1541, Bernt van Asselborn was sent to Maastricht to ask about the stone.[386] A messenger by the name of Herman was also sent to Master Willem for the same reason.[387] When people arrived to collect the stone, it was not ready yet. Unnecessary costs had been incurred and construction came to a halt.[388]

However, this delay did not prevent Willem from once again receiving the town cloth in 1542.[389] This year also finally saw the arrival of the stone and work took place on the cloth hall.[390] Van Neurenberg received 661.5 guilders for the Namur and Sichener stone.[391] Willem's son (Coenraad II) took this money to Namur to pay for the shipment and the town also paid for this trip.[392] Moreover, Willem spent eighty-nine days in the town in this year in order to supervise work on the building. Among other things, he had wood delivered, probably to build scaffoldings, which was listed separately in the town's accounts. What his other activities entailed is not known exactly. Judging by his remuneration, twenty stivers per day his work was more important than that of the average craftsman. In comparison, Adam the paviour and his labourers, jointly received fifteen stivers per day, the town's permanent carpenter Gairt Ketell only eight to nine stivers, while ordinary labourers had to make do with a wage of four to five stivers per day.

No other construction activities were mentioned in 1543 and 1544, as a result of the war and the temporary closing of the Meuse. In 1545 enormous quantities of building materials were transported to the Sint-Stevens churchyard behind the cloth hall. There may possibly have been a modest yard here or the Sint-Stevens Church still extant yard was used. Not only was work taking place on the cloth hall, but the adjacent Latin School was also being built during these years. This dual construction sometimes makes it difficult to determine which materials were intended for which purpose. In 1545, Willem made his still young son Coenraad responsible for supervising the stone transport. Unloading and transport were not without risk as the loss of a large block of stone into the Meuse during unloading shows. All manner of things could also go wrong during transport. For example, the same entry describes a block of stone having to be abandoned on the heath after the cart carrying it broke down. It goes without saying that additional costs were incurred to have the stone picked up later.

---

[383] Ibidem, p. 118.
[384] Ibidem, p. 120.
[385] Ibidem, p. 135.
[386] SR 1541, p. 11.
[387] Ibidem, p. 12.
[388] Ibidem, p. 200.
[389] SR 1542, p. 95.

[390] Ibidem, p. 117.
[391] Ibidem, p. 118.
[392] Ibidem, pp. 118-119. The same entry also lists other payments in money and goods that were made to Master Willem and his son Coenraad, and payments to captains who transported the Namur stone to the town.

In order to check whether Master Willem had supplied sufficient stone, Master Herman was ordered to measure the 1,220 feet listed. It is clear, however, that at this time building materials were in high demand, partly due to the long and arduous route they had to take to reach the destination. This demand was not merely expressed by the price and the meticulous checking of what had been delivered, but also by their popularity with the local population. After timber, stone and lime had been stolen from the churchyard at night, one Jan van Versen was appointed as a night watchman.

The cloth hall was completed in the years that followed. The church arch was completed in 1551. The part above the arch was covered in pantiles. A local carpenter carried out the carpentry work as the twisted bolsters, typical of Nijmegen and Arnhem, show. Carpenters from Nijmegen made the composite layers of beams and the roof structure and it is highly unlikely that Willem supervised them as well. Overall, construction took a long time and involved countless problems such as those encountered transporting stone down the Meuse. On 30 April 1542, the town of Nijmegen wrote to Liège. The captains Symon Boesse and Krijn van Eijsden had transported Namur stone to Nijmegen and had been forced to pay toll en route in Liège, which was a clear contradiction of the privileges. In the letter, the town requested the reimbursement of the money and that such shipments be allowed to pass toll-free in future.[393] There were also problems with tolls in 1548. On 24 September of that year, Maastricht wrote that the citizens of Nijmegen only had to pay toll over the Emperor's toll (in his capacity as the Duke of Brabant), but not the town toll. Maastricht therefore requested that the nuisance its citizen Coenraad (II) van Neurenberg had been subjected to, be rectified.[394] What exactly this nuisance consisted of and what the exact reason behind this conflict was, remains unknown. However, it is clear that Nijmegen had tried to charge the tolls incurred by its captains in Maastricht to Coenraad II van Neurenberg.

That this reference had to do with the cloth hall is obvious. On 26 March 1564, well over thirty years after Willem I van Neurenberg was first encountered in Nijmegen, Joist Laurens, slater and Henrick van Luyck, paviour bore witness to the mayors, aldermen and council of Nijmegen, that they and Master Gabriell Gossart of Namur, had heard from the council of Nijmegen that the town no longer owed *Wilhem van Nurenborch* anything for the Namur stone delivered for the construction of the cloth hall.[395]

Description of the building

Since the close of the sixteenth century the cloth hall of Nijmegen has changed considerably. The traces of the sixteenth-century cloth hall can still be seen however (Fig. 36).[396] The building no longer served as such at the time. During the alteration the entire building was raised and the church arch was equipped with a gable (Fig. 37). It was around this time that the cloth hall also became privately owned.[397] New gables were constructed and later on, other alterations were carried out whereby the seventeenth-century gables were replaced by cornice fronts. In the 1920s and 1930s a number of plots were restored to their former glory.

Research on site reveals that some of the hall was not renewed around 1540. In contrast to the archival data, the cellars under the cloth hall date back, in part, to before the new construction work undertaken in 1542. The inspection of two cellars proved that these had an irregular structure whereby one cellar bore traces of two construction phases. The cellar was equipped with a candle niche and

[393] De Jong 1960, pp. 39-40.
[394] Ibidem, p. 58.
[395] Ibidem, p. 215.

[396] Weve 1889, p. 9.
[397] Ibidem, p. 10.

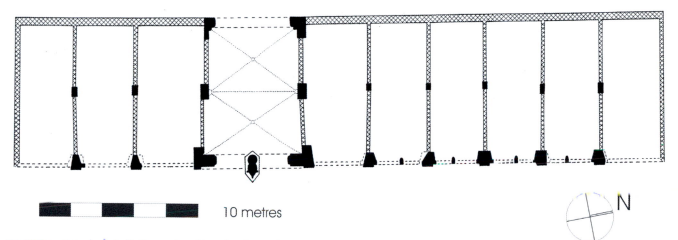

10 metres

36. Nijmegen, cloth hall, floor plan (drawing by author, after Weve 1889).

had bricks that measured twenty-nine to thirty centimetres down the long side, which were not used in Nijmegen after 1500. The cellars examined were barrel vaulted. Willem van Neurenberg was therefore only responsible for the part of the building located above ground. The structure of the sixteenth-century cloth hall was based on an older extant plot structure. On the ground floor blue stone posts were set out approximately 3.5 metres apart, according to an almost square or rectangular floor plan. The height of the blocks of which the columns were composed varied between approximately thirty to approximately forty centimetres. The width of one of the posts measured was approximately fifty centimetres. The posts had bevelled corners, which also indicates that they were, at one time, free-standing.

The placing of free-standing posts created a large open space on the ground floor of which the western side may already have been closed off in the sixteenth century.[398] The space was open on the market side. The market hall was provided with a composite sixteenth-century layer of beams, which is still partially present.

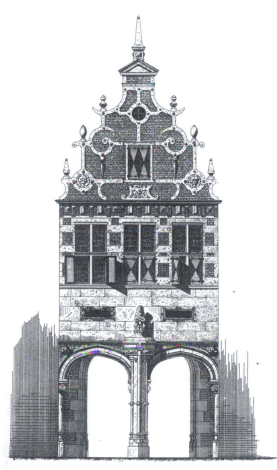

37. Nijmegen, church arch (after Weve 1889).

[398] No blue stone posts could be observed on this side.

The actual cloth hall was on the first floor and probably involved a closed hall, which ran the entire width of the building. The posts on the ground floor continued here and supported a single, large roof over the entire building (Fig. 38). It is not proven whether the building had a single roof at right angles to the church arch as early as the middle of the sixteenth century, or not. It is also unclear whether or not the roof corresponded with its medieval predecessor (Fig. 39). There is a surprising report in the Nijmegen town archive of town architect Duer, who when a building built onto the northwestern corner of the cloth hall was demolished in 1946 saw the remains of a guerite tower. These remnants were however not documented.[399] The observation pertained to a medieval sidewall, which still exists and was built as a brick-faced wall. The note could point to the medieval cloth hall having had a pseudo-inner gallery and guerite towers at each corner.

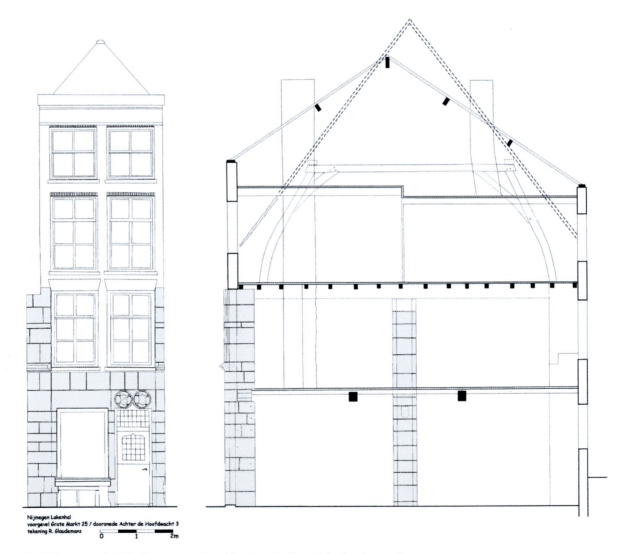

Nijmegen Lakenhal
voorgevel Grote Markt 25 / doorsnede Achter de Hoofdwacht 3
tekening R. Glaudemans
0   1   2m

38. Nijmegen, cloth hall, cross section (drawing by Ronald Glaudemans).

[399] Just as people were arriving to document the remnants the building contractor removed the last of them. Separate note GAN, photography collection.

The place of the cloth hall in architectural history

The cloth hall is an important Gothic building with a few early Renaissance characteristics in
the building's most conspicuous part: the church
arch. This church arch, which offered passage from
the market to the churchyard, has consistently been
viewed as an independent entity in art historical literature. The blue stone substructure dates back to
the Van Neurenberg period (1542-1545). Here is
where the art historical, building historical and
archival history of the building come together and
provide insight into the position the cloth hall and
the church arch occupied in the development of
architecture in the sixteenth century. The cushion
capitals with vine motifs have also been encountered in other places, which were influenced by the
Meuse trade (Fig. 40). The search for parallels soon
leads to the so-called Spanish Government building
in Maastricht (circa 1545). Here medallions can be
found in the spandrel niches, composite balusters
with cushion capitals, decorated with faces and
foliage (Fig. 41).[400] Another example is the Bishop's Palace in Liège, built under Erard de la Marck
(from 1526 onwards).[401] Further north, the same
motifs reoccur in the entrance to the Maarten van
Rossum House in Zaltbommel (1537)[402] and the
(lost) gate of the Baselaars convent in 's-Hertogenbosch (Fig. 42).

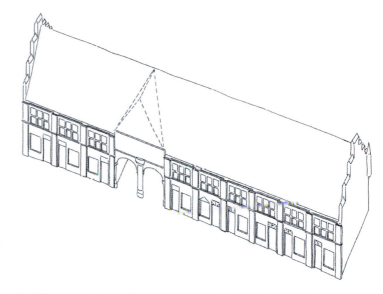

39. Nijmegen, cloth hall, reconstruction (drawing by Ronald Glaudemans).

[400] Timmers, undated.
[401] Erard de la Marck (1472-1538) was a contemporary of
the notary public and abbot Gérard van der Scaeft (circa
1460-1530) and Coenraad I van Neurenberg (circa 1465-
1542). He developed a strong Counter Reformation activity
during his term of office.
[402] Van Tussenbroek 2003, pp. 168-171. Although it has been
assumed for stylistic reasons that the same artist worked in
Zaltbommel, Delden and Arnhem, where other buildings
owned by the Van Rossum family with early Renaissance
characteristics were built (Temminck Groll 1979, Witteveen-
Jansen 1995), totally different material flows operated in
these three instances. The motifs employed also seem to differ. Compared to well-known engravings, Arnhem shows
the strapwork influences of Cornelis Bos. The Utrecht connection seems to have been important here, partly due to
the fact that De Nole also worked in Baumberger stone and
not in marlstone, as far as its known. In Zaltbommel many
more arabesque motifs were used and almost no band- and
strapwork. The materials used, marlstone and Namur stone,
indicate an influence from the Meuse Valley.

40. Nijmegen, cloth hall, capital church arch (photograph by author).

41. Maastricht, so called Spanish Government building, detail (Anonymous Photograph, July 1917, RDMZ, Neg. Nr. 3.085).

42. 's-Hertogenbosch, Gate of the Baselaars Convent, Namur stone and marlstone (Anonymous photograph from around 1920 (Werkarchief Bouwhistorie – Archeologie – Monumenten 's-Hertogenbosch).

The similarities and consistency are striking. Namur stone occurs in Liège, Maastricht, Nijmegen, 's-Hertogenbosch and Zaltbommel, sometimes combined with marlstone. In every case the buildings concerned are Gothic in style, though early Renaissance motifs have been used. In addition, Coenraad I van Neurenberg had formerly frequented Liège and also had contacts with, among others, Gérard van der Scaeft, who had been the notary public of the Prince Bishop of Liège. Moreover, he was responsible for part of the rebuilding of Herkenrode Abbey, which was protected by the aforementioned Prince Bishop. Coenraad traded in Namur stone and marlstone, and had his place of business in Maastricht. His son Willem I van Neurenberg was, without doubt, responsible for the construction of the cloth hall in Nijmegen. But there is more: all the abovementioned buildings bear characteristics of the so-called Liège Renaissance. There are also similarities in the use of materials and they all bear traces of a combination of traditional Gothic and Renaissance motifs. In Maastricht, Nijmegen, 's-Hertogenbosch and Zaltbommel Gothic profiling is combined with Renaissance motifs.

One of the earliest examples of this Meuse Valley Renaissance is the Prince Bishop's palace in Liège (from 1526). The town of Liège's position as an early centre for change in architectural stylistic vision, is also revealed by other examples such as the Hotel de Cortenbach and the organ loft in Liège's Saint-Martin Church. There is a trail that leads north from Liège and parallels the development of trade as discussed earlier.[403] The matter of where these shapes originate has been under discussion for some time. Influences from Spanish books, such as that of Diego de Sagrado, from 1526, can be discerned. The fact that these books were rapidly available in a French version could be an important clue.

In conclusion, if one attempts to contrast the impression outlined above with the traditional notions regarding the stylistic development of Renaissance motifs, one can state that a modest group of buildings can reveal similarities that go beyond mere stylistic aspects. This does not suggest that it was Coenraad I or Willem van Neurenberg who were responsible for the dissemination of Renaissance forms in the north or for the design or construction of the Spanish Government building or the Maarten van Rossum House, although this possibility should not be ruled out. The importance of the materials trade in the dissemination of influences in certain markets should be on the contrary emphasised. The strong emergence of the Meuse trade left an obvious impression on these buildings within a period of just a few years. The precondition for this situation, namely that the merchant and the master mason are one and the same person, was fulfilled, though it was not to last long. Stone merchants soon started supplying ready-made shipments, which patrons in the north had created according to detailed orders and which removed the opportunity to incorporate aspects of the stonemasons' own tradition or stylistic vision in the work.

---

[403] See Timmers 1980, p. 283ff. for more on this subject.

VI. Deliveries for the Old Church in Amsterdam

From the end of the sixteenth century the activities of the Meuse Valley stone merchants would start to focus almost entirely on the north, where Namur stone and Bentheimer sandstone were to become the principal types of stone available in large quantities on the market. However, around 1550, it had not come to this point yet. What became apparent was an increasing concentration on the northern market and decreasing activity in the south. This shift was accompanied by a growing difference in working method. Although in Nijmegen it could still be seen that Willem van Neurenberg acted like a medieval stonemason involved in both the supply of the materials and the actual construction, this state of affairs definitely no longer applied to Amsterdam around 1565. For the raising of the tower of the Old Church, Van Neurenberg and his partner Lambillon were used for only part of the work, namely material deliveries made to order. This practice was entirely in line with what was considered the modern idea of construction organisation.

The raising of the Old Church's tower in Amsterdam

There is a remarkable tie between Sint-Stevens Church in Nijmegen and the Old Church in Amsterdam. Lightning destroyed the tower of the Sint-Stevens Church on 14 February 1566.[404] The documents pertaining to the restoration of the tower contain an entry in which the churchwardens paid Jan Kelffken eight stivers for a drawing of the tower in Amsterdam so that they could copy it to crown the Sint-Stevens Church.[405] The low sum paid suggests his work was purely copying. In any case, it is clear that architectural influences were also disseminated in this manner.[406]

The Old Church is Amsterdam's oldest parish church and it was augmented during the fifteenth and sixteenth centuries with a number of chapels;[407] also, the side aisles were raised. The church's history reveals that parish priest Florentius Egbertz provided an important impetus to the enlargement of the church in the 1550s. The crossing was raised to the height of the middle aisle sometime before 1558, and these years also saw the construction of a chapel dedicated to Mother Mary. During this period the church was a bastion of anti-Protestantism.[408] After parts of the church had been raised in the preceding decades, to the point that a hall church had been created, the church-wardens decided to raise the church tower in 1563. The existing medieval tower, which can still be seen on a 1558 lottery print (Fig. 43), dated back to the fourteenth century. The tower had become too small in comparison to the church itself. Only in 1563 it was actually decided that the tower was to be raised by some thirty-six feet, in order to provide room for the belfry. The church council would finance the cost of the tower and the town council would pay for the crowning spire, which was to go on top of the belfry.[409] The total costs were estimated at 11,200 guilders.

[404] Van Agt 1954, p. 126.

[405] "[...] of the design of the tower in Amsterdam, and of the roof, in order for us to copy it for a roof on our tower [...]". Quote in Philipp 1989, p. 70.

[406] The "crown" would remain until 1590 when it was shot to pieces by Prince Maurits' troops during the siege of the town.

[407] Noach wrote the principal overviews in 1939 and B. Bijtelaar published articles between approximately 1955 and 1980 in *Amstelodamum*. Finally, Wegener Sleeswijk 1970 should also be mentioned. H. Janse was preparing a monograph while this book was being written. See Janse 2004.

[408] Noach 1939, p. 31.

[409] Meischke, etc. 1995, pp. 34-35. GAA, resoluties vroedschap I, f. 252, 252 v.

43. Amsterdam, Old Church, 1558. Anonymous engraving (Koninklijk Oudheidkundig Genootschap, Amsterdam, Inv.Nr. Atlas A'dam, portef. 31E).

Preparations for construction

It is generally assumed that town stonemason Joost Jansz, nicknamed Bilhamer (a millstone sharpening tool), was responsible for the design of the "crown" for the Old Church's tower. The name Bilhamer was first connected to the design of the Old Church's tower in 1646, in the second edition of a 1613 print, published anonymously.[410] Persons mentioned included Joost Jansz Bilhamer, "famous Architect and Sculptor", Reyer Cornelisz, who designed the stone parts and Jelis Jansz van Groningen who drew the wooden structure of the crown (Fig. 44). Bilhamer could have drawn the outside cladding for the latter.[411]

Bilhamer's name was first mentioned when the tower's crown was already eighty years old. Bilhamer himself (1521–1590) had been dead for more than fifty years. He was known as a surveyor and sculptor, but was also active as a building contractor.[412] For example, Marcus Aelberts from 's-Hertogenbosch ordered a large shipment of stone from him destined for the new registry of 's-Hertogen-

---

[410] Meischke 1995, p. 35.
[411] Ibidem, Note 93. Legend on the second print run of the woodcut of the tower from 1646. (The anonymous first printing from 1613 did not bear a legend).

[412] Ibidem, pp. 36–37.

bosch's town hall. The shipment primarily consisted of Bentheimer sandstone window frames, which were prepared by Bilhamer or his workshop in Amsterdam and were then shipped south.[413] In 1581 Bilhamer was working on Amsterdam's civil orphanage where he carried out a range of activities with various labourers. His name occurs both as a carver and stonemason in the accounts.[414]

Besides a mention in 1646 there is another source that suggests that Bilhamer was the designer of the tower. An auction catalogue from 1764 mentions a drawing of the tower of the Old Church signed by Bilhamer.[415] The attribution of the tower is not the most crucial aspect of this information. More important is the fact that people selected a design themselves in Amsterdam and only then started the construction process. This method says a great deal about the position of Van Neurenberg and the other parties involved; the design and execution were increasingly being taken over by the town's construction companies, while the stone merchants now only looked after part of the construction process.

The timber and brick work

After the new crown had been designed and specifications had been made, the job was tendered. Bids were called not just for the stonework, but also for the timber and brickwork. Carpenter Dirck Jacobsz submitted a bid of five thousand guilders. He did not get the commission; Jelis Jansz from Groningen and Jelis Quirynsz won the bid

---

[413] Van Tussenbroek 2001b.
[414] Meischke 1975, p. 137.
[415] Meischke 1995, n. 102; "An extraordinarily long, rolled-up drawing, drawn very artfully and in great detail on parchment, depicting a draft for the construction of an extra beautiful tower in Amsterdam for the Old Church by Joost Janz Bilhamer, Amsterdam town architect". GAA, Ms. Ir. B. de Boer. This drawing may be the same one described as a drawing of a "beautiful tower made by Joost Jansz Bilhamer in the auction of Jacob Marcus" estate. See Koning 1831, p. 203. It is also possible that this drawing was the preparatory drawing for the woodcut.

De Houte Kap van d' Oude Kerks Tooren.

44. Amsterdam, tower of the Old Church, 1613. Anonymous engraving (GAA, Inv.Nr. D 30.167)

for the carpentry work.[416] The work consisted of two parts:[417] one shipment of timber for the belfry in the stone part of the tower, and one shipment for the crown, which would be made entirely of wood. In fact there were two different patrons, namely the church and the town. Due to the fact that two different carpenters worked on two different parts of the tower, it may be assumed that there were two different specifications and tenders too.

Several bricklayers signed up for the brickwork, too. No specification has survived, but the names of some of the building contractors who bid for the job are known. One of them was Jaep Coensz, who was prepared to do the work for 3,200 guilders.[418] However, he was certainly not the only one.[419] Jan Cornelisz from Utrecht bid the sum of 1,850, considerably less than the sum for which Coensz offered to do the job. It is unknown how Coensz arrived at this sum. Cornelisz charged 375 guilders for 360,000 bricks (36 feet x 10,000 bricks), 150 guilders for lime and sand, 1,000 guilders for stone and the estimated bricklaying costs came to 325 guilders. It is clear that Jan Cornelisz was awarded the commission although it is unclear how he circumvented the guild regulations. It is possible that he sub-contracted the work to a bricklayer from Amsterdam,[420] though he may have also temporarily relocated to Amsterdam or may have paid the Amsterdam guild for his activities in the town.

The stonework

Coenraad II van Neurenberg and Pierçon Lambillon were responsible for the delivery of Namur stone. Although information regarding the prior history and the bid process are unknown, the contract and the specifications have survived. The contract for the delivery was concluded in August 1564, whereby it was stipulated that the work had to be finished before May of the following year. The total figure came to 1024 guilders, only twenty-four guilders over the amount budgeted. It is unknown whether Van Neurenberg and Lambillon encountered competition.

Regardless of who was responsible for the design of the structure and the crown of the tower, it is clear that Coenraad II van Neurenberg and Jacob Pierçon Lambillon only supplied material to order. The specifications for the stonework to be supplied provide insight into this process. On 11 August 1564, Pierçon Lambillon agreed to supply stone for the gallery and everything that entailed with the churchwardens of the Parish of Sint-Nicolaas. Pierçons partner Coenraad was not present, and was represented by Pierçon. The best quality Namur stone was requested and the condition was included in the contract that less high-quality blocks would not be used nor purchased. The contract, which also served as the specifications, was structured bottom-to-top, whereby dimensions and other specifications were explicitly listed (Fig. 45).

It started with the tower's niches, which were to be encircled with stone bands. The blocks are not described, but reference is made to scantlings having been given to Lambillon to this end for use at the quarry. The next part concerned the stone for the belfry arches. These stones were to be five feet wide, five feet high, half a foot thick and be one foot square on top. Because these were rather specific forms, the contract featured schematic drawings that provided cross sections of the blocks. Thirdly, reference was made to pillars one and a half feet, four feet and three inches long and sixteen feet high.

[416] He always worked in Groningen and Zwolle. De Vries 1994, p. 121, n. 653. Meischke 1995, p. 35, suggests that he is the same person, known under two different names. Nevertheless, this is not probable; there is only a similarity in first names. The patronymics clearly differ and were the most important way of discerning between people with the same first name if there was no surname in the sixteenth century.
[417] Ibidem.
[418] How this sum was composed is not known.
[419] Ter Gouw 1886, p. 508.
[420] Meischke 1995, p. 35.

These pillars were in fact obelisks intended for the corners of the balustrade. In other words here the specifications deviate from the correct sequence. The obelisks were well over five and a half metres high and can still be discerned on old pictures of the Old Church. The specifications then return to the building's structure. A moulding, half a foot thick, was to be applied to the brickwork, once again according to the scantling provided. The consoles were put on top of this brickwork and they were two feet high, ten inches wide and four and a half feet deep. However, there were a few exceptions: four double consoles were to be supplied for the corners[421] and eight double consoles to be mounted evenly spaced between each other and the corners. In total there were forty-four consoles. A moulding was then applied to the consoles and a scantling had also been made for their shape. The moulding was to be one foot thick and four feet deep, and was to be so wide that each field would come to consist of five pieces. The balusters of the tower gallery would be placed on top of this moulding. These balusters were to be four feet, eight inches in height. Moreover, a number of double balusters had been provided for, which corresponded to the structure of the consoles. Finally, a moulding would be laid on the balusters, which was to be eight inches thick, made according to the scantling.

The finishing of the work

The work was tendered in 1564. The old fourteenth-century tower was retained and used as the core, while thick walls were wrapped around it like a coat. The stonework was supplied in 1565 as agreed. Coenraad van Neurenberg stated on 8 June 1565 that he had received 400 Carolus guilders for blue stone, which included stone he had cut for the church and stone that was yet to be cut. A few months later, on 27 September Pierçon Lambillon declared he had received over six hundred and twenty guilders for the stone supplied for the building of their church. He also declared that no money

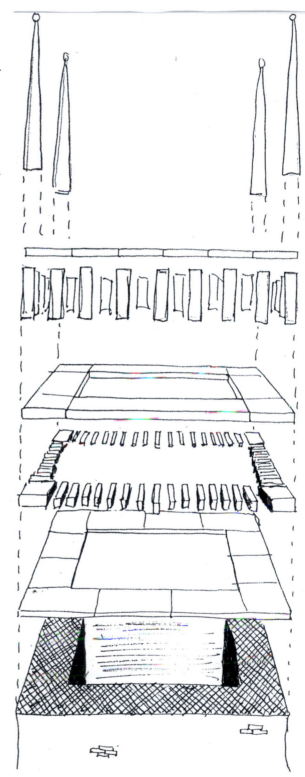

45. Amsterdam, Old Church. Reconstruction of the stone delivery on the basis of the specifications (drawing by author).

[421] The four corner consoles were each counted as four singles. They were one guilder and seventeen stivers each.

46. Amsterdam, Old Church, Receipt of Coenraad II van Neurenberg 1565 (GAA archief van kerken en kloosters, inv.nr. 116).

remained to be claimed, which allows us to conclude that his contribution to the delivery had been completed.[422] Finally, on 22 October 1565 the last payments were made to Coenraad van Neurenberg (Fig. 46).[423] This separate declaration allows the conclusion to be made that, although the building contractors were retained together, they delivered their goods individually, which shows that there was no mutual hierarchy. In fact, it looks as if Lambillon, who seems to have developed contacts in Amsterdam before Van Neurenberg did, asked the latter to take on part of the commission because he could not handle the work on his own.

Yet a year later, in 1566, carpenter Jelis Quirynsz and bricklayer Jan Cornelisz received the sum of twenty guilders for finishing their work on the tower as commissioned by the town.[424] Due to the fact that this payment appears in the treasurer's accounts, it may be assumed that the tower crown had been entirely completed and to the full satisfaction of the town patron. Jelis Jansz van Groningen's role therefore remains somewhat obscure. It is clear that he did not work for the town's administration, but for the church council. Jan Cornelisz' role is also somewhat problematic as his involvement, which deals solely with the stone structure, was led by the church council; it is unclear why he was also mentioned in the town's accounts.

Archaeological evidence

Today, there are few traces of the Van Neurenberg's sixteenth-century stonework remaining (Fig. 47). Research on site revealed that the work was either replaced or disappeared behind the brick casing, which was built in 1735 to stabilise the tower. It is therefore not possible to examine all the parts described in the contract. The only visible Namur stone left can be found in the belfry arches, though only on the inside. In addition to the horizontal parts mentioned in the contract there was also a post made of Namur stone. The dimensions listed in the contract are not in accordance with what was actually delivered. The width of the work is only four instead of approximately five feet. The drawing in the contract, in fact, pertains to a composite of two blocks. The work on the tower is smaller than described in the contract by approximately 20%. Unfortunately, it is impossible to measure the dimensions of other parts of the work, which makes it difficult to say anything meaningful concerning the difference in dimensions. The reference to patterns and scantlings in the contract suggests no risks were taken with dimensioning. The most plausible solution for this discrepancy is that the stone was reworked after being delivered because of a possible calculation mistake made during the preparation of the preliminary specifications.

[422] Noach 1939, pp. 171-172.
[423] Ibidem, p. 172.

[424] Ibidem, 1939, p. 235.

47. Amsterdam, Old Church's tower, circa 1910 (GAA, Inv.Nr. D 29.182).

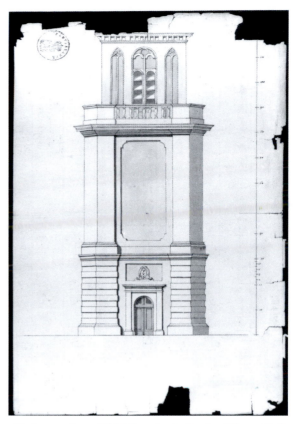

48. Amsterdam, Old Church, design by Sibout Bollard for the stabilisation of the tower, 1735 (GAA, D 45.283).

The tower's exterior may possibly still exist encased in the walls, but is covered by eighteenth-century work and the same applies to the mouldings mentioned in the specifications (Fig. 48). The tower gallery was entirely replaced and now consists of Bentheimer sandstone. The current obelisks are made of iron and are not in accordance with the historic dimensions.

★

Conclusion of Part I

The above material has provided an impression of the Van Neurenberg family until ca. 1570. The family and the company's early history are somewhat obscure. At the point in time that the first descendants appear in the archives they already held distinguished positions. For example, around 1500 Coenraad I was already the master mason of Maastricht and had obtained a high social status. Little is known about his immediate ancestors. Both Coenraad I, and Willem I had a son capable of taking over and expanding their activities. Their patrons were also distinguished, and the quality of the work supplied was such that a particular level of continuity was guaranteed. This early period still showed medieval tendencies in that the supplier of stonework also supplied the design.

Coenraad, Willem and Coenraad II van Neurenberg managed to expand their regionally operating stonemason's workshop into a major company. The specialisation in a type of stone that was much in demand, combined with knowledge of construction and favourable political and economic conditions, were the principal reasons for the expanding and flourishing of the family business. The rare data available on the personal contacts with patrons seem to suggest that the family's descendants made prudent use of the opportunities open to them. Furthermore, the expansion in trade and the expansion of the area in which the company was active, were cleverly accommodated by the further refinement of the delivery options. The way in which merchants presented themselves to the construction industry in the north is also clear: they provided service. Although Van Neurenberg had the skills to act as a master mason, he often did not. The client's word was law and determined the activities for which Van Neurenberg was responsible.

PART II

1570–1609: THE JUMP WEST

VII. Construction at the Start of the Revolt against the Spanish

The years around 1570 are generally considered a transitional period of decline and renewal. The political and religious tensions that had been discernable for years culminated in an outburst, which would signal the start of the Revolt against the Spanish (Fig. 49). The war that followed had a complex course and was to influence large areas of public life and trade. Philip II's reduction of the power of the nobility and the increasingly strong Inquisition, coupled with growing Calvinist sympathies and the rise of the town bureaucracies, caused dissatisfaction. Religion and economic downturn were, however, the principal causes of the widespread dissatisfaction, which encompassed everyone from the nobility to simple craftsmen. The measures Philip II tried to impose through the Duke of Alva were also disastrous for trade; plans from 1569, which did not require permission from the States General, led to resistance. In particular, the *tiende penning*, which amounted to a tax of 10 percent on trade in moveable goods, would be a bitter financial blow to merchants.[425]

49. Maastricht, Spanish Fury 1576, engraving by Frans Hogenberg circa 1590 (GAM).

The Revolt against the Spanish was organised after the first skirmishes and iconoclastic actions in 1566, which heralded the coming separation. The armed resistance against Spanish rule started in 1568, under the leadership of William of Orange. A number of high nobles aligned themselves against the Spanish authorities and were rapidly followed not only by Gent and Antwerp, where Calvinist republics were installed from 1577, but also by most towns in the Northern Low Countries, which saw an allegiance with Orange as a chance to improve their standing. Towards the close of the sixteenth century a front between north and south opened, which underwent considerable changes especially at the start of the war. Trade between north and south was forced to seek new passages to and from enemy territory, with all the dangers and problems this entailed. Only the Prince Bishop's diocese of Liège managed to retain its independent, neutral position during these years. Namur, and also Limburg belonged to the Catholic south, while most of the Van Neurenberg's market lay in the rebellious provinces. Don Juan of Austria, half-brother of Philip II, captured Namur itself in 1577. However, this conflict did not hamper the export of building materials, not even when these were intended for the construction of fortifications and gates. Strong offensives by Alexander Farnese, the Duke of Parma,

---

[425] Groenveld, Schutte 1992, p. 82. The *tiende penning* was largely not implemented but bought off, which nevertheless put pressure on trade. Furthermore, attempts were made in the south to slow price inflation. The *Carolusgulden* had less and less value. Margaretha of Parma wished to freeze builders' wages in order to counter inflation. Only in the early eighties was actual price-fixing implemented in Namur and the surrounding area. Master bricklayers' wages were ten to eleven stivers per day during the summer and eight to nine stivers per day during the winter. Brouwers 1934, pp. 50 and 53.

between 1581 and 1588, and counter offensives by Prince Maurits of Orange, between 1589 and 1606 would regularly change the boundary between north and south until 1609 when a temporary truce was negotiated, which suspended the war for twelve years.

However, the truce had not yet been negotiated and for the time being, the war situation and other factors had great impact on the construction trade. The combined force of these factors would lead to a modernisation of the construction process that had only just started to assert itself when the Revolt broke out.

Changes to the town construction trade during the sixteenth century

After 1570, the Church was definitely no longer the main patron. The towns took over the Church's role slowly, but surely. Only rarely were complex facades ordered at the quarries, so that the development of a new architecture primarily became an urban phenomenon, independent from the trade in construction materials.[426] Simultaneously, at the top of the construction hierarchy, it could be observed that in the world of painters, the 'architect' was conceptualized as an intellectual.[427] The rise of the architect as an independent professional man is to a large extent a product of these times; just like the merchant, sailor or regent, he tried to distinguish and profile himself socially. In the towns the former lodge masters of the fabric lodges, and in some cases also the town master masons, were pioneers in implementing innovation in the building sector. There are multiple examples of such craftsmen, who generally had their own stonemason's workshop, and who are sometimes referred to as town architect or town master mason.[428] This movement first gained attention with figures such as Lieven de Key and Hendrick de Keyser, who, as town master masons, managed to leave their mark on the architecture of their era.

But there were more developments in the town organisation. Various towns founded a town construction company with its own administrative structure (Kampen, Amsterdam, Haarlem, Leiden, etc.), in which the independent and increasingly influential position of the towns was once again expressed. In contrast to the preceding period, it can be ascertained that from the start of the sixteenth century the town's fabric lodge was no longer merely responsible for standard matters such as the maintenance and the construction of bridges, streets and of course fortifications. The towns and their town officials realised buildings, which expressed the town's prestige, and the towns Amsterdam, Haarlem and Leiden in the province of Holland are the best-known examples (Fig. 50). Town fabric lodges were founded. Their representatives did not have to come from the construction trade, though there are examples of people that did,[429] which constitutes a crucial difference with the preceding period. Town masters started to determine the towns' appearance, instead of the travelling master masons who had formerly been contracted to lead major projects. If churches and courts had previously been behind the main architectural innovations, from around 1570 the principal construction activities were buildings for and owned by the towns. Organisationally speaking the town's fabric lodge shared some char-

[426] Meischke 1997, Chapters IV, V and VI. A limiting factor for the ordering of entire facades was the guild regulations. Particularly in smaller towns, where less illustrious stonemasons could be found, town administrators (the potential buyers of prestigious facades) will have more readily provided exemption from these regulations, than those in larger towns. See Kolman 1993, p. 135.

[427] The changes to the design process were also influence by the presence of Italian masters in the Northern Low Countries. See De Jonge 1994, p. 364ff. These changes became apparent as early as the first half of the sixteenth century. Duverger 1964, pp. 181–182.

[428] Kolman 1993, p. 170. Other examples include Jan Darkennes in 's-Hertogenbosch, Joost Jansz Bilhamer in Amsterdam and Lieven De Key in Haarlem.

[429] For example, Jan van Hoppen in Amsterdam or Peter Frans in Antwerp.

acteristics with the medieval church fabric lodge, which, during the fourteenth and fifteenth centuries, left its mark on the architecture of its day; the difference being that now it was without a single binding construction project, but instead had an entire urban planning complex. This shift in patrons necessitated that master masons, craftsmen and building contractors' customer relations moved closer to town administrations than to the church and ecclesiastical institutions.

An important factor in the emancipation of the towns under discussion here was the increase in scale that took place. The population increased strongly at the close of the sixteenth century. Between 1514 and 1622 the population underwent a marked (245%) increase, particularly in the County of Holland. The level of urbanisation was also high.[430] Moreover, there was more money in circulation and financial trading experienced a clear professionalisation.[431] Urban growth was combined with a number of technical and economic innovations, such as the invention of the wood saw mill and the equalisation of a number of currencies. All these factors together ensured that for a number of towns, a more close-knit organisation of construction became feasible. Smaller towns nevertheless continued to work according to the old methods for much longer, and did not have their own fabric lodge.[432]

50. Amsterdam, exchange by Hendrick de Keyser 1608–1611. Engraving in O. Dapper, *Historische Beschryving der stadt Amsterdam etc.* Amsterdam 1663 (GAA, Inv.Nr. N 17509).

Changes in the independent construction trade

As early as the fourteenth century, call for bids took place in the Southern Low Countries. In 1376 the carpentry of the bell cage and the roof of the Belfry in Ghent was tendered. In 1386, the town hall of Nivelles was commissioned after a bidding process.[433] After the decision had been made to build a new town hall in Damme in 1461, a letter was sent to carpenters and stonemasons in various countries and towns, in order to garner the most favourable subscription possible. Town carpenter Ingehelle Baert was sent to Ghent, Brussels, Mechelen and Antwerp with copies of the work, whereby a distinction was made between the carpentry work and the stonework. The later concerned the guild-enforced trade separation.[434] In the same year, the accounts for the Dom in Utrecht mention *verdingen* or tendering, for the first time.[435]

The principle of a (public) procurement process was therefore far from new. However, what we can observe is that the far-reaching sub-division of the construction process, which entailed a professionalisation, encouraged this process. As the sixteenth century progressed, the number of call for bids increased. The construction of the new Schuttersdoelen in Gorinchem in 1589, also involved the public tendering of parts of the structure. Jan Gerritz offered 2,000 guilders for the carpentry. It had been determined that the person who made the offer would receive twenty-five guilders for his offer

430 Groenveld, Schutte 1992, pp. 6–7.
431 De Vries, Van der Woude 1995.
432 Van Tussenbroek 1999c, passim.

433 Janse 1964, p. 26.
434 Devliegher 1965, pp. 148 and 151.
435 Janse 1964, p. 26.

and the drafting of the specifications. Until the middle of the sixteenth century, generally speaking, the craftsman who drafted the specifications was automatically awarded the subsequent commission. However, this practice was slowly disappearing.[436]

The disappearance of this practice creates problems for present-day researchers as the design, specifications and execution became less and less related, which, in turn, makes the attribution of buildings more problematic. More and more often the patron provided the design *before* approaching a building contractor. This state of affairs required more flexibility from the construction industry. At the time, it was primarily the contractor who provided the design in consultation with the patron. The fact that an increasing amount of work was undertaken or accepted in its entirety is directly connected to this shift. A single, all-encompassing concept occurred more often than adding to an existing building, which was the result of smaller building projects being commissioned than during the era that the church was still the main patron. Moreover, town building patrons, in particular, increasingly had an executory body such as the town's fabric lodge with a town carpenter and bricklayer so that the nature of the construction projects not accepted by the own town's fabric lodge became increasingly specialised.

Now that the design and the execution were less directly attuned to one another the necessity for implementing a procurement process for the work increased. Moreover, the checking aspect also played an important role; during the Middle Ages another master mason would assess the work after it had been built, thereby examining the price-quality ratio. From the sixteenth century, patrons perpetuated this process by guaranteeing themselves the lowest subscription. The fact that many construction projects nevertheless ended in arbitration is something else entirely.

One result of the specialisation was that the dissemination of new forms sped up incredibly. Specifications and drawings were made when the work was sent out for bid. Specifications were disseminated, drawings could be perused during the procurement process, and both served as guidelines on the basis of which building contractors could submit the bid for the commission. In this way the majority of the building contractors had access to the design so that, regardless of receiving the commission, they were nevertheless exposed to any possible developments and innovations that might have been incorporated into the design. This practice enabled a large group of people to rapidly perceive, adopt and implement new developments in their own work if the market demanded.

The individual master mason, building contractor and supplier.

Traditional town master masons, such as Coenraad I van Neurenberg in Maastricht, had barely been capable of making their mark on urban construction. Only at the end of the sixteenth century did people, such as Lieven de Key or Hendrick de Keyser, manage to express themselves more clearly. When he was not designing architecture the town master mason occupied himself with maintenance, work on fortifications, bridges, locks, etc. Such commissions were also part of the work for people like De Key and De Keyser, but it was precisely the architectural work that allowed them to distinguish themselves, regardless of their technical capacities. The anonymous nature of most of their work explains why the activities of late-medieval town master masons were not distinguishing nor recognisable.

However, the presence of a town stonemason did not mean that the fabric masters had all their designs and projects executed by this person. They were free to ask masters from outside town for a design, and then to build this design, which was a regular occurrence especially during the first half of the sixteenth century. The more clearly defined the stonemason's position within the official organisation, the more natural it became to ask him for a design. In some cases the stonemason was explic-

---

[436] Ibidem, p. 27.

itly appointed to provide drawings. If a comparison is made between the town master mason and an independent building contractor, then it can be observed that the latter was the most like the medieval master mason. In Van Neurenberg's case this meant that when he acted as a master mason: he was responsible for the design (Averbode, Huy, Nijmegen, Herkenrode); the supply and working of the building material; its transport and the supervision of the work itself. However, all the examples mentioned above are before 1550. After 1550, when he no longer acted as the designer or master mason, the tenor of his activities changed. Stone shipments were then prepared and delivered according to a design made elsewhere (Amsterdam, Sittard, Cologne).

Van Neurenberg as a building contractor, designer or supplier. Shifts in working practice

The working practice of Van Neurenberg and other stone suppliers is actually based on the rise of the stone trade in the fifteenth century. The flexible attitude and availability of stone traders in the construction process constituted the basis of their later success. Formerly, the building contractor as embodied by the Van Neurenberg family, was really an exception. Only major entrepreneurs were capable of realising large projects (Fig. 51). They had the funds to pay the labourers their wages on time, which put a heavy burden on the company's liquid assets as deliveries were generally paid afterwards. Moreover, large projects demanded a great deal of organisational talent, contacts and experience with logistics. The financial risks of a project also had to be shouldered.

Until this point in time, the Van Neurenberg's commissions could be subdivided into three groups. Firstly, there was the supply of stone, which in almost all cases was the catalyst for further activities. Secondly, during the early period activities such as executing work, construction supervision and design work were also done. A third factor may be added to the period currently under discussion. As seen previously, occasionally designs for altars, church buildings, etc. were supplied. However, there is too little data to say anything concerning the family's design work with any great certainty, but the years after 1570 will reveal a few examples of the Van Neurenberg family bearing the responsibility for drafting the specifications. The Van Neurenbergs did not necessarily create the design for the building. The professionalisation and specialisation of the construction trade put an end to a large part of the design and master mason's work that the Van Neurenbergs had previously done. In exchange, their position improved as specialists in the supply of pre-cut Namur stone. The increasing use of technical specifications, on the basis of which building contractors (including the Van Neurenberg family itself) could submit a tender, contributed to the expansion of their activities. In their improved position they capitalised on increasing social changes, resulting in the family's role as an authority in the field of stone.

51.Dordrecht, group of merchants. Anonymous engraving (GAD, Inv.Nr. DI 452 d).

VIII. STONE TRADE BEFORE THE TWELVE YEAR'S TRUCE

The changing stone trade: declining exports from Brabant

The blockade of the Schelde in 1585 terminated the western export route north for stone, which is of great importance to the history of the trade in Namur stone. Nevertheless, the blockade of the Schelde was not the sole cause of the slowing of exports. A conjunction of unfortunate circumstances occasioned the decline. The principal factors besides the blockade of the Schelde were the gradual depletion of the quarries around Brussels and changes in the construction trade in the north. Moreover, Bentheimer sandstone became an increasingly important competitor, a development, which became apparent as early as the fifteenth century.

What was important for the stone trade was to have sufficient contacts to enable the northern patrons to purchase stone in the south. The stone trade had to be able to meet the changing demands of the market. Maintaining the network and capitalising on the shifting market were matters in which the Brabant stone trade could not participate. Although they were physically able to cross the border, the blockade proved an insurmountable obstacle to maintaining exports. There were no suitable alternatives for the transport of stone from the area around Brussels.[437]

The trade from Brabant had always exported its own architecture, which meant that when the north developed its own professional and specialised tradition the trade from the south had no adequate response. The same case applied to traders from Hainaut. The limestone from Hainaut also experienced a strong decline in demand from the north.[438] Although the De Prince family, in particular, controlled an important part of the market during the second quarter of the sixteenth century, they did not manage to maintain their position during the second half of the century.[439] Entrepreneurs from trading areas, which did not have these problems, were able to further expand their position thanks to the disappearance of the trade from Brabant. After all, replacements had to be found for the stone that had formerly been transported over the Schelde and for which there were no suitable alternative routes. There were several candidates, but of primary importance was the stone's suitability for working as both facade cladding and detailing, and moreover its weather resistance. The two types of stone, which met these requirements, were Bentheimer sandstone and Namur stone.

The influence of stone from Germany[440]

The trade in Bentheimer sandstone started to flourish around 1600. Initially traders from Zwolle leased the quarries around Gildehaus for enormous sums from the Count of Bentheim, but later merchants from Holland ousted these traders, which created a monopoly that would continue well into

---

[437] See Duverger 1991. These hindrances do not mean that no more shipments of stone from Brabant reached the north after 1585. The town hall of Bergen op Zoom (1611) was clad in Brabant stone.

[438] See Van Belle 1990 for more on the history of this type of stone.

[439] Meischke 1997, p. 48. The developing relative scarcity of material at the quarries was also a factor and so it seems as if the condition of the quarries also played a role: it is apparent that fifteenth- and sixteenth-century examples of *Ledi-*

aanse stone had larger dimensions; thicknesses up to thirty-five cm. occur. In the seventeenth century these dimensions decreased to a maximum of seventeen to nineteen cm. The fact buyers had to maker do with smaller pieces could indicate an increasing scarcity of stone. Examples include the Begijnhof Church in Brussels and the Hanswijk Church in Mechelen. The more the seventeenth century progressed the lower the quality of the stone became, as has been observed in the Sint-Pieters Church in Leuven.

[440] See Voort 1968 and 1970 en Stenvert 1996.

the eighteenth century (1766). From 1646, the trade in Bentheimer sandstone was run entirely from Holland, which influenced the application of the stone in the west.[441]

The trade in Baumberger or Münster stone did not break through during this period. The period during which this stone was used is conspicuously short, which possibly relates to the fact that the trade in Baumberger stone was never professionalised to the extent that competition with the stone trade could occur. Moreover, Baumberger stone was only marginally suitable for outdoor work, which definitely hindered its popularity.

Finally, the trade in Bückeburger or Obernkirchner sandstone, which was transported to the north of Germany over the Weser and then shipped to market from there, should be mentioned in this context. An interesting example of how contacts between stone suppliers and patrons developed comes from Leiden in the year 1595. Daniel van der Meulen (1554-1600), a merchant from Leiden, lived in Bremen for years before relocating to Leiden in 1591.[442] Van der Meulen, who was originally from Antwerp, had amassed an international network of trading contracts in the Low Countries, Germany, Sweden, Italy, Spain and Portugal as a result of trading in cloth, metal, grain, fruit, fish and skins over the years. He was a member of various companies and had shares in ships that sailed to the East and West Indies, Guinea and São Thomé. He maintained close contacts with a merchant from Middelburg called Balthazar de Moucheron and with Willem Barendsz.[443] Van der Meulen was also politically active, acting as a diplomat and corresponding with, among others, Marnix van Sint-Aldegonde and Louise de Colligny, the Admiral's widow. He spent a number of years living in Bremen, where his brother, Andries van der Meulen, had a trading company. When the Leiden town council decided to give the town hall a new facade, it was Van der Meulen who mentioned Lüder van Bentheim to the magistrates. During these years the stone merchant Van Bentheim from Bremen worked on Bremen's town hall.[444] Van der Meulen made contact and negotiated with Van Bentheim himself.[445] Van der Meulen also maintained contact with Van Bentheim for private reasons. For example, Lüder van Bentheim provided the stone for Van der Meulen's house on the Rapenburg while Johan van Sambeeck, who also lived in Bremen, supplied the timber. This house was built under Haarlem town master mason Lieven de Key, who also made the design for the new facade for the town hall.

The contacts between the Low Countries and Bremen were not limited to this example. As early as 1538, Johann de Buschere from Antwerp went to Bremen and was master mason, alongside his two sons and a number of craftsmen, for the new *Schütting*, the seat of the commercial court. De Buschere, with the help of his fellow countrymen, was responsible for the execution of the building's facade; they returned to Antwerp after 1538.[446] Fortifications builders from Holland were also active in Bremen. Theologians, scientists and students moved to Bremen during the first half of the sixteenth century due to its religious climate, but merchants, craftsmen and master masons also had contacts there, particularly after 1583. It was these wide-ranging contacts that were responsible for the inclusion of a different type of stone in the normal range of products.

Namur stone

Namur stone trade benefited from the decline in the trade from Brabant. Although the economic situation also worsened in the Meuse Valley and the number of building commissions declined, merchants managed to continue trading because the Meuse was hardly blockaded. The traders in Namur

---

[441] Janse, De Vries 1991, p. 16.

[442] Information from Verburgt 1937, passim.

[443] More on the Van der Meulen family in Kooijmans 1997, passim.

[444] Albrecht 1993, in particular pp. 79-83.

[445] Ter Kuile 1938, p. 86.

[446] Schwarzwälder 1997, p. 88.

NIEVVVE
LISTE VAN HET
RECHT VAN LICENTEN,

Datmen voortaen betalen fal voor alle toeghelaten ende
ghepermitteerde VVaeren, ende Coopmanfchappen,
varende naer de landen ghehouden by den Vyant ende
Rebellen, ende die vã daer comé, met declaratie op d'eynde vande Spetien vande verboden Coopmanfchappen,

TOT BRVESSEL,
By Rutgeert Velpius, geſvvoren Boeck-vercooper ende Drucker inden
Gulden Arent by t'Hoff. 1597.

Met Priuilegie van feſ Iaren.

52. Printed *licent* list, published in Brussels, 1597 (GAD, Archief van de gemene Maashandelaars, Inv. No. 877.).

stone seemed to be very capable when it came to capitalising on changes in the northern construction trade. When architectural construction activities decreased, the Namur stone trade had an important compensatory factor. Alongside important architectural creations, land reclamation activities guaranteed a steady stream of buyers. At the close of the sixteenth century, major land reclamation projects required expertise and suitable construction materials.

Between 1584 and 1586, the Meuse was blocked, but these blockades were primarily incidental acts of war and did not have a permanent character such as the blockade of the Schelde. Captains from neutral territories, such as Germany, Liège and Mechelen, the chapter of St. Servaas, and the free domains Elsloo, Eysden and Leuth were not overly hindered in their trading, but they were prohibited from transporting war-related materials. However, this semblance of free trade did not protect them from violence[447] and high toll rates continued to be a source of conflict. On 8 August 1594, the mayor and aldermen of Maastricht declared that Huijbert Coninx, captain and merchant, had complained of unduly high tolls after being received. The administrative councils of Liège, Roermond and Venlo related similar complaints in 1598.[448]

In addition to the much older tolls, the system of *licentgelden* (a tax system introduced by William of Orange to finance war activities) and convoy duties that had been introduced in 1573, played a major role (Fig. 52). Besides the standard land and water tolls, William of Orange introduced this system in Holland and Zeeland as an additional levy on the import and transit trade in order to cover the cost of the war against Alva.[449] The Duke of Parma soon also adopted this system, so that additional levies on transport existed both in the north and the south. The captains and merchants were issued with permits (*licenten*) recognised by both north and south. Convoy and *licent* masters were appointed for every area where import, export and transit duties were due and where inspections were necessary to prevent illicit trade. In principle no products were excluded from trade, which kept the Meuse navigable for captains from both north and south between Liège and Dordrecht.[450] The levies were prescribed in ordinances that listed the rates and regulations with regard to the collection and justification of the monies. In order to prevent fraud these regulations were repeatedly renewed. In 1597 an agreement was reached between the United Provinces aimed at repealing the existing mutual differences in collection.[451]

---

447 Meulleners 1886, p. 104.
448 Knoors 1993, p. 290. See Klein 1965, p. 203 with regard to import and export duties on a number of wartime products.

449 Meulleners 1886, p. 106.
450 Ibidem, p. 107.
451 De Vrankrijker 1969, pp. 38-39.

During the blockade of the Meuse, captains such as Jan Conincx spent their time in Dordrecht with their ships and family, leading to great economic loss.[452] In 1587 trade and also shipping resumed, although it took a number of years for shipping on the river to become safe again. Jan Conincx, who spent the summer of 1590 transporting a shipment south from Holland, spent five weeks waiting at Grave due to low water levels in the river. However, no problems with the authorities are apparent.[453] A few years later, in the spring of 1593, he transported a shipment of Namur stone to Dordrecht for 800 Brabant guilders for Pierre Alard, a merchant in Namur stone, who travelled on board the ship. After unloading in Dordrecht and returning to Liège, Conincx once again transported a shipment of Namur stone; he seems to have specialised in the transport of this material.

Andreas of Austria proclaimed on 19 February 1599 that trade to the United Provinces, be it import, export or transit trade was prohibited;[454] this ban also lasted for three years. Meuse shipping recommenced shortly after the taking of Grave, on 18 September 1602.

Dordrecht as the new centre of trade

Stone trade constituted only a fraction of the total trade on the Meuse. Although there is no real evidence at the moment, fragmentary research has revealed that other products such as coal, iron, copper and cloth were much more important.[455] This impression is confirmed by a 1597 list, which mentions the principal Meuse captains by name.[456] Of the approximately thirty captains and merchants on the list, only two are familiar names from the stone trade, namely Rochet and Van Neurenberg. Nevertheless, the stone trade's subordinate position did not stop Van Neurenberg from using the favourable trading conditions which Dordrecht offered. The staple right on many goods meant that foreign merchants had always been assured of the opportunity of selling their goods and purchasing a return shipment.[457] The wide range of products at the staple market included coal, lime, slate and stone.[458] Countless sources reveal that people travelled to Dordrecht from all over the surrounding area to purchase building materials. All these factors ensured that Dordrecht was an exceptionally favourable place in which to live and work (Fig. 53).

Merchants from Liège and Namur must have had a modest foothold in Dordrecht as early as the fifteenth century. As pointed out earlier, Namur stone was previously used in Dordrecht, a result of the influence of the staple rights. But the reverse situation could also be seen. In 1338 the 'Meuse right' of Dordrecht was decreed, which determined that all ships and cock boats that originated in Germany and that travelled up the Meuse from the sea must sell their goods in Dordrecht.[459] In spite of the extremely favourable legal position the town thus possessed, trade declined slowly in the sixteenth century. Dordrecht was experiencing increasing competition from Amsterdam and particularly Rotterdam, and could no longer maintain its position as the most important trading town in Holland. In order to bring an end to this decline, the town imposed measures that resulted in preparing "the new work" ('Het Nieuwe Werk'), a new harbour area for construction, on land, which had been reclaimed for some time.[460] Attempts to attract traders from elsewhere went well and the town implemented an incentive policy that brought it on par with towns such as Amsterdam, Leiden, Haarlem, Gouda, Delft, Rotterdam and Alkmaar, who were also implementing active incentive policies in order to attract mer-

---

[452] Meulleners 1886, p. 109.
[453] Ibidem, p. 112.
[454] Meulleners 1886, p. 116.
[455] GAD, archief van de gemene Maashandelaars [Archive of common Meuse traders] 15e E-1738, see for example Inv. No.s 265, 849 and 877.

[456] Ibidem, Inv. No. 77.
[457] Van Herwaarden 1996, p. 79.
[458] Ibidem, p. 82.
[459] Ibidem, p. 83.
[460] Lips 1974, p. 197ff.

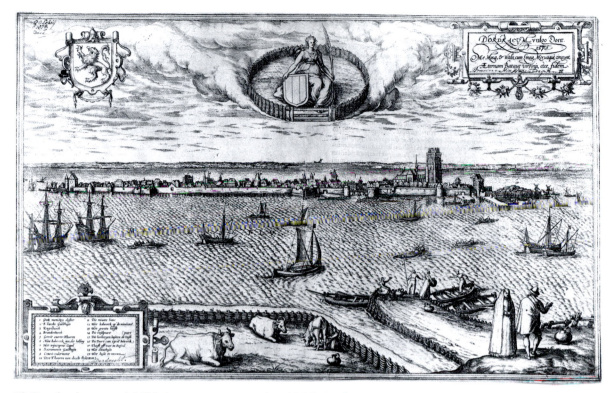

53. Dordrecht around 1600. Anonymous engraving (GAD, Inv.Nr. DI 271).

chants and industry. To this end, they offered donations, patents, monopolies, cheap loans, tax benefits, the use of town facilities, etc.[461] This policy was at its peak during the years 1575-1620, when people from the Southern Low Countries could also benefit from it.[462]

As a result of the factors mentioned above, a large number of merchants from the Meuse Valley permanently relocated to Dordrecht around 1585. Famous merchant family names include De Lairesse, De Geer, Becx, Lambillon, Gerards and Hellinckx.[463] Van Neurenberg was also a member of this group. Another newcomer was Pierçon Lambillon, known in Dordrecht as an iron merchant, but who also traded in Namur stone.[464] This mass relocation to Dordrecht was a logical consequence of the measures taken in Dordrecht and of the strong expansion and modernisation of the coal and iron industry near Liège.[465] However, religious persecution is usually mentioned as the principal reason for the migration of Walloons north; nevertheless, it is not improbable that opportunistic, economic reasons also motivated the move. Relocating to the north was probably due to the fact that it was easier to trade from the north and have the material supplied from the south, than the other way around.

[461] Davids 1995, p. 168.
[462] Ibidem, p. 171.
[463] Klein 1965, p. 67.
[464] Frijhoff 1998, p. 42.

[465] Ibidem, p. 142. During the 1560s Liège coal was marketed in Antwerp for the first time. The coal was partially transported over land, which reflects the strong expansion of the Walloon industry. Thanks to G. Asaert, 12 December 1998 for pointing this fact out. See also Breuer 1969, p. 82.

Historic overview of the trade in Namur stone (1570 - 1609)[466]

A large number of Namur stone deliveries to the Southern, and in particular, the Northern Low Countries are known from the start of the Revolt against the Spanish until the Twelve years' Truce. In 1570, one Michon[467] supplied 5,900 feet of Namur stone for a lock near Steenbergen, a few kilometres northwest of Roosendaal. Four years later, Pieter de Lambillon supplied Namur stone for the town hall in Emden. Lambillon also supplied stone for a number of locks in the Province Zeeland.[468] It is conspicuous that by far the majority of Namur stone deliveries can be attributed to Van Neurenberg, which reinforces the hypothesis that Van Neurenberg nearly had a monopoly on Namur stone during this period.[469] The material was also being used more and more often in the west during this period. An important building was the Vlissingen Gate in Middelburg, which Joris Rochet from Liège executed in Namur stone in 1596.[470] Rochet received 1,070 guilders in three instalments.[471] In 1604, he supplied 550 floor tiles for the flat roof on the Rijnlands House in Leiden.[472] Rochet also worked in Leiden where he supplied stone for the Blue Gate (*Blauwe Poort*).

Around 1600 there were at least six mercantile houses active in the Northern Low Countries specifically focused on Namur stone. At the top of the list was Van Neurenberg, who appears to have occupied the most important position in the Namur stone trade, followed by the merchants Lambillon, Rochet, Misson, Willemot and De Valckenaer. With the exception of De Valckenaer all these families originated in the south.

The growth of the Namur stone trade in the light of the changing economic climate

The Namur stone trade had an aggressive acquisition policy and used outposts and branches to be able to maintain control of the logistics and to keep the distance between themselves and the patron as small as possible. The contacts with the quarry thereby became an internal matter within the company. The patron need not travel any further than Dordrecht, after which the merchant arranged all aspects of the delivery. Not only Van Neurenberg, but also other merchants of Walloon origin, used this tactic which had first been implemented in the 1530s. As soon as an opportunity arose they would semi-permanently relocate to the north, which made Nijmegen the first outpost for the Van Neurenbergs' trade in the 1530s and 1540s.

The traders from Brabant were no longer able to generate demand, and therefore, not surprisingly, the Meuse Valley traders moved north en masse. The south's economic and demographic recession made major new architectural projects with administrative or mercantile scope impossible.[473] The Church initiated most construction activities in the south, but their number could not compete with

---

[466] Data for this overview was largely culled from Slinger 1980, Janse, De Vries 1991 and Meischke 1993-1997.

[467] This person is possibly the same person or a relation of Jan Misson, who supplied Namur stone: in 1535 for the castle in Grave, in 1561 for the town hall in Antwerp and in 1565, together with Van Neurenberg, for the town gate in Bruges.

[468] Vierlingh 1920.

[469] See also Meischke 1997, p. 77.

[470] He is mentioned in the town's accounts.

[471] Meischke suggested that Van Neurenberg could have made the design of the Vlissingse Poort. The gate bore great

similarity to the Blue Gate in Leiden, for which Van Neurenberg drew the specifications. Another option was that the Namur stone merchant Andries de Valckenaer from Middelburg provided the design. Meischke 1997, p. 83.

[472] Janse 1964, p. 61. *550 blaeuwe Naemsche estricken, groot van acht duym int viercant, van Joris Rochet vuytet landt te Luyck, omme gebruyckt ende verbesicht te werden op 't plat comende boven op t comptoir.*

[473] Vlieghe 1998, p. 258. See also Briels 1978.

the construction boom in the north. The continued demand for Namur stone in the north was much higher than in the south because the merchants maintained contact with the patrons. This direct contact was very important because as a result of the war, the States General required permission to import materials.[474] These patrons provided their own permission for importing materials. Naturally, this permission was almost intrinsic to a commission or purchase.

The relocation of a number of Walloon stone merchants to Dordrecht around 1585 seems to have sealed the fate of the Brabant trade. Whether this move, which almost coincided with the blockade of the Schelde, was a conscious coup or not, can hardly be ascertained today. At any rate, it is certain that emigrating from the south provided more benefits than just the religious environment in which the émigrés landed.

---

[474] See, amongst others, Chapter XIII.

IX. THE VAN NEURENBERG FAMILY (1571–1609)

Coenraad II van Neurenberg, continued (approximately 1520 – before October 1595)

Just like his father and grandfather, Coenraad II had managed to further expand the company, with the prestigious delivery of stone for the Old Church in Amsterdam as provisional high point in his career. In 1570 there was a turnaround in activities. In that year Coenraad was sworn in as the Count of Namur's master mason and a year later, he was appointed master of masonry work.[475] In 1570, he was responsible for the rebuilding of part of Namur's town wall after it had been severely damaged by Meuse water. The work was similar to work encountered in Nijmegen, 's-Hertogenbosch and Bruges, primarily for land reclamation and fortification. Coenraad II died in 1595.[476]

It is unknown whether, and to what extent, Coenraad II was involved in the stone trade alongside his activities for the Count of Namur. It is known that during this period, Coenraad III van Neurenberg mostly supplied stone to the north. Coenraad II's involvement as an intermediary between the quarry and the northern buyer seems nevertheless likely.

Coenraad III van Neurenberg (1548 – 2 November 1603)

When Coenraad II entered the employ of the Count of Namur, his son Coenraad III was old enough to continue the business independently. Coenraad III was registered as a citizen of Namur in 1568.[477] His youth was probably spent in Maastricht, which would make him approximately twenty-three when his father entered the Count's employment. Shortly after Coenraad III had relocated to Namur with his father, he married Marie le Bidart, who was probably a member of another stone trading family.[478] They had five children, of which four were born in Namur and one in Dordrecht. Marie le Bidart must have died before 7 November 1597[479] because Coenraad remarried, this time to Margaretha de Swart, who died in March 1613.[480] There were no children from this union. Coenraad died on 2 November 1603, at the approximate age of fifty-five.[481]

Coenraad III worked in Namur for a long time. Various activities and deliveries of stone can be attributed to him. One example is a delivery of 4,000 blocks of Namur stone by the firm in 1577, commissioned by the Spanish king for the fortifications in Arnhem (Fig. 54).[482] Two years earlier he had been to Arnhem to provide stone for a lock. Coenraad, who explicitly called himself the Young Coenraad van Neurenberg and who still lived in Namur at the time, finalised a contract to build a Namur stone lock near the Velper Gate in Arnhem on 3 January 1575. The lock was to be delivered

---

[475] Courtoy 1912, p. 510.

[476] On 20 October 1595, Charles Misson succeeded him as *tailleur de pierre a son art au conté a Namur* [stonecutter according to his art for the Count of Namur]. Brussels, Algemeen Rijksarchief, *Audiëntie* 1235, 'sculptures'.

[477] Courtoy 1912, p. 511.

[478] A few decades later, Thierry le Bidart was a quarry operator.

[479] See also De Bruin/Huisman 1992 and GAD, birth, marriage and death registers in the reading room. The children were 1. Coenraad IV (ca. 1571 – ca. 1635), 2. Willem II (ca. 1575 – ca. 1640), 3. Pieter (ca. 1580 – 29-2-1636), 4. Maria

(ca. 1582 – ?) and 5. Anna (before 1 November 1585 – 19-12-1652). Courtoy 1912, p. 511 also mentions a Jean and an Isabelle. However, he has not explained the origin of this statement and the names do not occur in the Dordrecht sources. They may have possibly died at an early age in Namur. Dordrecht's guild lists include a Daniel Coenraadsz van Neurenberg who became a member in January 1598. He worked as a slater. No more is known about him. See also De Bruijn 1992, p. 69.

[480] Ozinga 1929, p. 151.

[481] Courtoy 1912, p. 511, Note 9.

[482] Classen 1951.

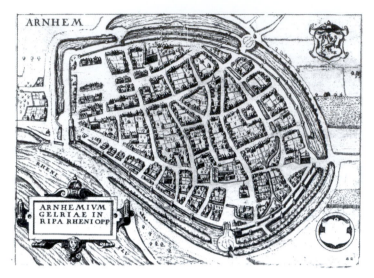

54. Arnhem around 1570. Anonymous engraving, after Guicciardini 1612, Pl. 22 (Universiteitsbibliotheek Utrecht).

ready-made and was to be eighty-five feet long and twelve feet high. He received twenty-three Carolus guilders per hundred feet of stone. The delivery and construction of the lock was undertaken very quickly. Because of the unstable political situation, the vulnerability inherent in fortifications standing unfinished, and the "war season" starting in spring, Coenraad was to deliver the stone before Easter. In passing, a reference is made to Coenraad supplying four hundred tons of the best lime for the fortifications. He was to receive ten stivers per ton. The work was completed in May 1575. Coenraad signed the final bill of 450 Carolus guilders with his signature and his mark, which was very similar to that of his father. A month later, on 30 June, he received a sum of well over 750 guilders for 4,400 feet of Namur stone and 400 tons of lime, including remuneration for toll and transportation costs.[483] In 1578, he entered into negotiations concerning the supply of four or five bridges in Amsterdam.

The exact date Coenraad III 'fled' to Dordrecht is unknown, but his move probably took place in 1584 or 1585.[484] He continued to trade and it seems as if things went well for him. On 3 March 1597 he bought an empty plot of land from Jan Jansz Cocq on Het Nieuwe Werk in Dordrecht, for the sum of eight hundred Carolus guilders. A few months later he purchased another site for 340 guilders.[485] It had been decided that no stonemason's workshops were to be allowed to open on Het Nieuwe Werk, but it is very well possible that he used the site as storage. Almost immediately after the purchase of the plots he had a house built. He owned a yard on the Hoge Nieuwstraat, which ran all the way to the Nieuwe Haven. His house fronted the Hoge Nieuwstraat, while at the back there was a shed and storage space.[486]

From Dordrecht, Coenraad primarily supplied stone to Holland and the west. He was partly responsible for the construction of the church in Willemstad, in 1596, supplied stone for the weigh house in Haarlem and carried out work on the convent church in Etten. Other special deliveries included stone for the town hall in Antwerp. Moreover, Coenraad may possibly have been involved in the construction of Vlissingen town hall.[487]

[483] RAG, Gelderse Rekenkamer, toegang 0012, Inv. No. 7.090. Appendices to the bill of Arnt van Steenler for the years 1574-1577, pertaining to the town of Arnhem's fortifications.
[484] In Dordrecht Coenraad III was a member of the Walloon Church. His youngest daughter, Anna, was baptised there on 1 November 1585.
[485] De Bruijn 1992, p. 70.
[486] Ibidem. In 1604 Coenraad's widow was taxed for no less than seven fireplaces.
[487] Meischke 1997, pp. 74-75.

Coenraad IV van Neurenberg

After Coenraad III, the family tree branched out and his three sons, Coenraad IV, Willem II and Pieter all entered the construction trade. Coenraad IV van Neurenberg was Coenraad III's eldest son. He was born in 1571 in Namur and moved to Dordrecht with his father in the mid-eighties. There he married Marie Avondeaulx, Daniël van Schie's daughter and the widow of David van Asche on 10 August 1594.[488] The pair had two sons, Coenraad V in 1601 and Johan in 1603.[489] Marie died a year later in February 1604, after which Coenraad married Yde Jans.[490] In order to advance and develop himself as a stonemason, Coenraad received the sum of three hundred guilders from his father on 7 November 1598, so he could start "mercantile activities and trading actions".[491] Coenraad IV, whose mother had died in 1597 during his absence, agreed to the execution of her will and testament, which may be connected to his activities.[492]

On 29 May 1601 he purchased a house for 1,575 guilders on Het Nieuwe Werk in Dordrecht; this house may have belonged to his father.[493] Coenraad was also involved with other activities alongside his work as a stone supplier; one such activity was the invention of a dredging machine. This machine worked according to the wheel principle, i.e. a series of buckets affixed to a turning wheel scooped up dredging material. Coenraad's invention could be mounted on a ship. On 25 June 1605 he received a patent for the machine for a period of ten years.[494] The invention of the dredging machine is an important indication of the diversity of his activities. Besides deliveries for architecture, he also spent a considerable portion of his time building locks and foundations in damp soil. In this field he also seems to have had a certain reputation, which is logical considering his father and grandfather's activities. From today's perspective it is hard to determine to what extent this kind of work was the driving force behind the stone trade. Most of the hydraulic-engineering projects were done anonymously and bills and specifications are scarce. Nevertheless, in order to view the architectural deliveries in the correct perspective, these activities should also be considered.

Willem II (approximately 1575 - approximately 1640) and Pieter van Neurenberg (approximately 1576/80 - 29 February 1636)

Willem II van Neurenberg was Coenraad III's second son and brother to Coenraad IV. He was born in Namur around 1575 and died around 1640 in Dordrecht.[495] In 1606 he joined the bricklayer's guild there. He married Marie Wijmoth (Willemot), Jan Wijmoth's daughter. Their first child was baptized in Dordrecht on 24 February 1613. The Wijmoth family of merchants originally came from Liège and had moved to Het Nieuwe Werk in Dordrecht just like the Van Neurenberg family. Willem II would run the company in Dordrecht until his death. His most important work in the first few years of the seventeenth century is the gable on Nijmegen's church arch. This church arch, which had been built as part of the cloth hall by his great-grandfather Willem I, was altered during these years. Later he would receive a number of important commissions and create an extensive personal network.

[488] GAD, Marriage register of the Walloon Church.
[489] Ibidem.
[490] The date of this event is unknown. See Chapter XVI.
[491] De Bruijn 1992, p. 71.
[492] Options include his work in Leiden or Willemstad, or a trip to Namur.

[493] Huisman 1986, p. 41. He paid 200 guilders in cash, 300 in 1602, and 200 every year after that. Huisman based herself on a lost folder on the Van Neurenberg family in the GAD.
[494] Doorman 1940, p. 115.
[495] 20 March 1640 and 4 June 1641 are both mentioned as possible dates.

The third brother's name was Pieter, who was probably born in Namur around 1580. It is interesting to note that although he moved to Dordrecht with his parents at an early age, he returned to Namur in the nineties, probably in order to safeguard the supply of materials to the north after the death of his grandfather Coenraad II. Little is known about Pieter.

In general, the family's stone selling business seems to have been a men's affair. Male family members negotiated contracts and agreements and only occasionally did the women make a brief appearance. However, a woman was permitted to control her husband's company financially in the event of his death. Such practices imply that women must have had knowledge of the workings of the company, and that regular consultation must have taken place between the couple. Unfortunately the inner workings of a marriage are hard to isolate and would require an extensive personal archive. More can be said on the daughters' role in expanding and reinforcing the network and improving the family's social standing. The daughters were used to help forge ties with the (stone) trading families Mercenier and Van Delft, and similar ties are suspected to have existed with the Misson, Lambillon, Wijmoth families and others. For example, Anna van Neurenberg was married to Pieter Ariaensz van Delft, a stone merchant from Amsterdam. The number of ties the Van Neurenberg family had with other families of stonemasons and stone traders also increased due to Van Neurenberg's sons marrying the daughters of families involved in the abovementioned trades. The family's female members played a vital role in this expansion.[496]

Business operations, market and acquisition

Relocating to Dordrecht was an excellent move for the Van Neurenberg family; the group of traders that decided to move north dealt a considerable blow to their competitors from Brabant. They all moved to an area where there was high demand for Namur stone and avoided the religious problems and economic downturn the south experienced. However, ties with the south were not severed, because trade needed to continue. Moreover, several members of the family stayed behind in the south, such as Coenraad II who worked for the Count of Namur and Pieter van Neurenberg, whose presence in the south made organising and controlling the work a great deal easier. The traders who moved to Dordrecht began acting as intermediaries between patrons in the north and the quarries in the south, as they had done when they were travelling traders.[497] The Van Neurenberg family's activities expanded during the period 1570 and 1610. The first references to lime kilns and brickworks date back to the years around 1600.[498]

It is therefore not implausible during this period more attention was paid to hydraulic-engineering works. A factor, which cannot be ignored in the Low Countries during this period (after 1550), was the "Small Ice Age". During the 1560s and 1570s a succession of extremely low temperatures coupled with changes in sea level occurred.[499] Problems with the loss and growth of land led to large-scale enterprises such as land reclamation. Of the total acreage reclaimed in the Northern Low Countries between 1500 and 1815 half was achieved in the period 1590 to 1650.[500] Naturally, these enterprises had consequences for the development of hydraulic-engineering and subsequently also for the stone

[496] De Bruijn 1992, p. 73.
[497] Moreover, Dordrecht became an artistic centre for workshops. These workshops were possibly responsible for the early dissemination of classicist facade ornaments, which started becoming popular from the 1640s onwards. Meischke 1997, pp. 61–65.
[498] Huisman 1986, p. 53, no sources mentioned.
[499] De Vries, Van der Woude 1995, p. 37ff. See also Buisman 1998.
[500] Ibidem, p. 49.

trade. A number of references pertaining to the construction of locks show the extent to which these hydraulic-engineering activities positively influenced the development of the trade in Namur stone. Plenty of examples of Namur stone being used for 'wet' fortifications and quay walls have been enumerated previously.

The expert we have mentioned before, Andries Vierlingh, stated his preference for stone locks instead of wooden ones in his *Tractaet van Dijckagie* (Treatise on Dike Building), though the introduction of stone sometimes experienced formidable resistance. It was much more lucrative for the dike warden to have wooden locks built, as these required much more maintenance.[501] Nevertheless, stone locks were also built. The delivery of Namur stone for the lock near Spaarndam is a good example.[502] The Namur stone was to be measured and made on the basis of the Namur foot.[503] Master Jan Lambillon, a merchant from Namur, accepted the work on 24 July 1567. He supplied the stone for nineteen guilders and ten stivers per hundred feet, with a possible bonus of ten stivers per hundred feet, if he did his job well.

A network of contacts

In contrast to a hundred years earlier, patrons less and less frequently sent out messengers to approach master masons. Posters and printed specifications were now used to publicise an impending commission, indicating a shift in business-related contractual aspects. If, at the start of the sixteenth century, contacts had primarily been personal in nature (Abbot Van der Scaeft, the Abbesses Van Léchy, work for the town of Maastricht), they were now much more professional and contacts occurred primarily through standard business relations. In addition to this professionalisation in contacts with clients, the trade between merchants also became more professional. By joining together they could arrive at agreements that were beneficial to all of them. An exceptional example of this occurred in 1597. On 14 October of that year, the principal Meuse captains concluded an agreement with Philips van Bockhoven, privy councillor to the King in Brussels, that determined the captains no longer had to pay tax on the goods they transported if they agreed to a levy of twenty percent in *licentgelden* for a period of two years. Approximately thirty captains, including Coenraad van Neurenberg and Joris (George) Rochet, signed the contract.[504]

Sources of this importance are rare. The one described above proves that the forming and organisation of a cartel existed, whereby independent traders came together to form an interest group. This point is crucial as it indicates that regular consultations took place between the most important Meuse Valley traders, and that they viewed themselves as a more or less coherent group with joint interests. By acting in this manner they brought to fruition decisive action and managed to achieve trading objectives, thus making the idea that conscious competition existed between merchants from the Meuse Valley and the Schelde basin much more plausible.

---

[501] Vierlingh 1920, pp. XIII-XIII.
[502] Ibidem, pp. 240-248.
[503] Ibidem, p. 247.

[504] GAD, Archief van de gemene Maashandelaars [Archive of the Organised Meuse Merchants], Inv. No. 77.

Family relations

As far as the development of social status and the related family relations are concerned a two-sided image develops. On the one hand the ties with other stonemasons' families remains, whereas on the other the acquisition of commissions became a much more formal affair. In particular the contacts with patrons became less personal. Thanks to source material becoming more extensive at the close of the sixteenth century, a clearer picture emerges of the marriage politics the family implemented. Unfortunately, it is impossible to compare this picture with the image of the preceding period when the names of the female members of the family often remain unknown.

When concerted politics can be discerned in family relations, it can serve as a model with which to explain the cooperation between the Van Neurenberg family and other families. The image archival research provided is very illuminating: almost all the Namur stone trading families were related to one another.[505] A few examples from before 1610 pertaining to the Van Neurenberg family follow: witnesses to the baptism of Coenraad V van Neurenberg on 18 November 1601, included Johan Polyander[506], Jan Jansz van Neurenberg and Marguerite (Marie) van Neurenberg. At the baptism of his younger brother Johan on 6 April 1604, the following names appear: Paulus Pancratius, Robrecht Pietersen and Isabeau Lambinon (Lambillon). When Marie de Riol, daughter of Nicolas de Riol was baptised, the witnesses were Marie van Neurenberg and Johan Wijmoth who was also a member of a stonemasons' family.[507]

The social group that moved to Dordrecht from the Walloon country managed to maintain and expand its position through family and business ties. Mutual marriages, cartels and focused trading politics ensured unprecedented growth for the trading houses, whereby the families were destined to become members of the urban patriciate and would hold prominent positions during the seventeenth century. The period before 1610 can therefore be described as a consolidation of mutual contacts, which must have already existed in the Walloon country. Interconnection with families from other geographic and religious groups, and closer cooperation with northern architects, stonemasons and merchants started to become more noticeable from the 1620s and will therefore be dealt with in Part III.

The professional contacts within their own sector of industry are proved by the fact that several members of the Van Neurenberg family were members of the Dordrecht bricklayers' guild, which included stonemasons. For example, Willem II van Neurenberg joined the guild in 1606, and he was listed as having children.[508] Daniel Coenraedtsz was admitted to the guild in January 1598. He was registered as a slater.[509] It is conspicuous that of the well-known Namur stone merchants who had relocated to Dordrecht, only members of the Van Neurenberg family joined the bricklayers' guild. Perhaps their joining, as opposed to other families, had more to do with the families' specialization because the trade required the working of stone in Dordrecht.

---

[505] Data based on Courtoy 1912, GAD, Waalse Kerk and Nederlands Hervormde Kerk and GAA folders, NA. See also Chapter XVI.
[506] Between 1591 and 1611, Johannes Polyander was the pastor of the Walloon congregation. In 1577 Walloon reformed Protestants had requested their own church and pastor in Dordrecht. The congregation was awarded inde-

pendence and its own church council in 1586. From: Frijhoff 1998, p. 288.
[507] GAD, Baptismal registers of the Waalse Gemeente Dordrecht [Walloon Congregation in Dordrecht].
[508] GAD, Archief van Gilden en Confreriën, Inv. No. 669.
[509] Ibidem.

X. VAN NEURENBERG CONSTRUCTION ACTIVITIES 1570-1612

The Van Neurenberg family's construction activities were continuous (Fig. 55) with stone deliveries taking place throughout the entire period between 1570 and 1609. The deliveries of stone discussed below and for which Van Neurenberg was responsible, are not so important regarding the objects themselves, but all the more important as evidence for the status and position the Van Neurenberg family obtained within the construction trade at the close of the sixteenth century. Examination of the limitations enforced on trade due to the war shows that their position was very difficult. For example, a printed overview of the licence monies (licentgelden) per product dating back to 1597 features the following phrase: "specification of the prohibited and not allowed goods [...] stones of all types for cobblestones, dike work or props or stone for construction".[510] This regulation applied to the exporting of the abovementioned products to areas outside the Republic; importing was much less of a problem, although this also required permission. A number of merchants managed to obtain exemptions from this regulation. As will be discussed below when examining the price development of Namur stone, these licenten constituted an additional taxation. The tolls which had always been a burden on prices, also continued to exist.

Nevertheless, in spite of these drawbacks, the traditional transport along the rivers continued to be used almost exclusively. Exemption for imports was requested and granted. The new situation in the north did therefore influence affairs, but hardly hampered the continuity of the stone merchant's trade.

Activities in Namur: meat hall and town hall

When Coenraad II van Neurenberg entered the service of the Count of Namur as master of masonry, his principal task was to repair and maintain the fortifications. He was also responsible for the reconstruction of the walls after the Meuse caused great damage to them in 1570.[511] Nevertheless, these repairs were not his only task. Although his activities in Namur have not been exhaustively studied in the framework of this book, it is known that Coenraad II was responsible for the construction of a few local government buildings in the town. For example, he worked on the construction of the meat hall, which was built between 1588 and 1590 at the behest of the government in Brussels. Coenraad worked together with Bastien Sion, who was responsible for the woodwork and who held the equivalent position with the Count as Coenraad, but in carpentry.[512] It is unknown who designed the meat hall. The building is one of the first expressions of Renaissance architecture in Namur and has been well preserved. It was restored at the start of the twentieth century. With eleven bays, two storeys set atop quayside cellars and topped by a hipped roof (Fig. 56), the meat hall was built of brick and Namur stone. The latter was used for the plinth, dripstone mouldings, window frames and corners. A contract from 31 October 1587 has been preserved and lists the stonemasons responsible. These included people with names already familiar such as Johan Lambillon and Remy and Jacques Misson.[513]

Another town project in which Coenraad II was involved was the old town hall.[514] Here he once again cooperated with carpenter Bastien Sion. The plans for construction date back to the mid-sixteenth century. In 1572, Van Neurenberg measured the building site and supervised construction.[515]

---

[510] GAD, Archief van de gemene Maashandelaars, Inv. No. 877.
[511] Courtoy 1912, p. 510.
[512] Ibidem. Their salary for these services amounted to 600 livres.

[513] Van de Casteele 1883, p. 169.
[514] Courtoy 1912, p. 508.
[515] Ibidem, p. 510.

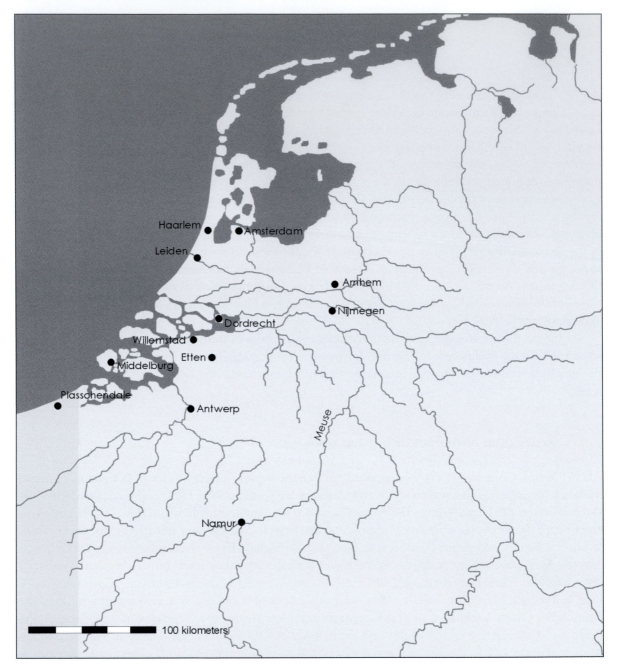

55. The Van Neurenberg family's area of activities between 1570–1610 (drawing by author).

The town hall was demolished in 1826. An old dwawing reveals that it was a building with a roof over its entire length of eight bays and two storeys (Fig. 57). Conclusions with regard to detailing can hardly be based on the scant extant illustrations, although it is conspicuous that the entrance had rustication, which was most probably executed in stone.

Although Van Neurenberg worked on the fortifications, the meat hall and the town hall, he was involved with far more. A very remarkable object on display in the meat hall, which is currently used as an archaeological museum, is a block of Namur stone that bears the Van Neurenberg and Jeanne Dembourg/Demry family crest. The coat of arms is flanked by the date "15 [coat of arms] 7?". The

116

56. Namur, meat hall, built between 1588-1590 (photograph by author).

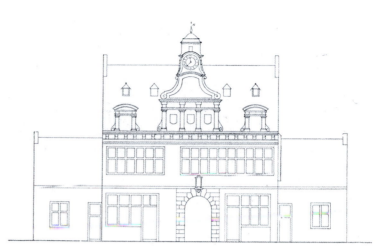

57. Namur, council hall, 1572 - demolished in 1826. Anonymous drawing (Musée Archéologique, Namur).

stone may have served as a lintel or as a chimney frieze. The fact that both families are represented in the coat of arms could indicate that the work had a place in Van Neurenberg's home in Namur, where he moved to in 1571. Unfortunately, there is no further context.[516]

Hydraulic-engineering activities in the west

On 20 October 1592, the mayor, council and aldermen of Amsterdam issued Coenraad III van Neurenberg a permit so that he could import a shipment of stone into the United Provinces tax free: this concerned a shipment of stones Coenraad was supplying to Amsterdam's town *fabricque*. The stone was readied in Namur country at the quarry, and was to be sufficient for the construction of four or five bridges. It was stipulated that Coenraad was not allowed to add stones intended for others, and he was to provide proof of the stones he had already delivered. The stone was for the sole use of the *fabricque*.[517] This end-user declaration says a great deal about standard practices. Obviously, there had been regular attempts to import stone under false pretences for use in projects other than those originally intended.[518]

Two years later, on 20 November 1594, Coenraad once again requested a licence for the supply of stone for the construction of a stone lock and other works in Amsterdam.[519] This line can be continued to Zeeland where he also made deliveries for water works. For example, in 1598 Coenraad III supplied the stonework for a lock in Middelburg's Nieuwe Binnenhaven. The work in the year mentioned was contracted out for 1,250 pounds.[520] If these examples of Van Neurenberg deliveries are seen in conjunction with the hydraulic-engineering projects undertaken by the descendents of the Misson and Lambillon families, they provide an impression of the broad range of activities developed by Namur stone traders.

---

[516] Huart 1935, pp. 43-44.
[517] Japikse 1923, p. 724.
[518] The temptation to do so was large: by being granted exemption from taxes, it was possible to import a relatively cheap product and the difference could amount to approximately 20%. By acting as a distributor it was possible to increase profits further still.

[519] Japikse 1925, p. 337.
[520] Huisman 1986, p. 34, without reference to sources. The costs of the digging work amounted to over 117 pounds, the carpentry 293 pounds and the stone 835 pounds.

Architectural relations in Flanders and Zeeland

If the first delivery occurred in Bruges at the start of the 1560s, it would take another twenty years for Van Neurenberg to supply stone for the repair of Antwerp's town hall, which was originally built between 1560 and 1565. It is remarkable that in the lead-up to construction a competition was announced for which various people supplied designs. In addition to the designer who received the commission, Cornelis Floris de Vriendt, these others included Wouter van der Welsmaer, Willem van den Broek, Lambert van Noort, Hans Vredeman de Vries, Jan Massys, Louis du Foix, Johan du Gardin, Lambert Suavius and Niccolo Scarini.[521] This competition reaffirms the further specialisation of the construction trade. The design and the procurement process were streamlined and the design, bidding and execution were differentiated to a great extent, which meant that the various parts of the construction process were entrusted to different executing parties. This division of work was a new phenomenon.

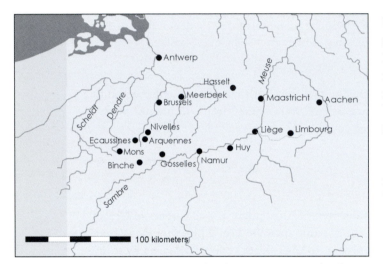

58. Map with quarries where Cornelis Floris went in search of suitable materials for the construction of Antwerp's town hall (drawing by author, after Adriaenssens 1980, p. 129, Fig. 2).

It is unlikely that Coenraad II van Neurenberg played an important role at this stage of construction.[522] However, Cornelis Floris was sent to Limbourg (a place beyond Liège) to purchase red marble (Fig. 58). Blue (crinoid) stone was purchased in Ecaussines, i.e. the Schelde basin close to home. Van Neurenberg does not occur in the list of original stone suppliers.

The new town hall burned in November 1576. Coenraad III van Neurenberg was involved in the repair work, which did not start until 1579. Two years before, Antwerp had fallen to William of Orange who wanted to use the building to store ammunition. The fall of Antwerp in 1585 signalled the end of Protestant rule.

Coenraad III van Neurenberg's contribution to the repair of the town hall in Antwerp consisted of the supply of 640.5 feet of stone from Agimont. Johan Tonnoy from Liège was also involved in this delivery.[523] This delivery probably did not concern carboniferous limestone, as was usually the case; the area near Agimont, under Dinant, on the left bank of the Meuse is known for its rich marble quarries. Red and grey marble is currently still quarried at five sites in the area.[524] The quantity of 640.5 feet is considerable taking into consideration that this figure concerned running feet, which amounts to approximately 180 metres. The interior of the building seems to have been gutted by flame, but the walls survived (Fig. 59).[525]

---

[521] Bevers 1985, p. 8.

[522] The existing literature provides no indication in this matter. The materials delivery was exhaustively examined. See Adriaenssens 1980, passim.

[523] Janse, De Vries 1991, p. 35, based on SAA, privilegekamer 2200, letter from Coenraad van Neurenberg to Insolvente Boedelkamer. And: SAA, Insolvente Boedelkamer 1562.

Johan Tonnoy may possibly be the same person as Jean Tonnon. Many thanks to Herman Janse.

[524] Cnudde 1990, p. 21.

[525] In fact Belgian marble is not really marble but a non-metamorphous limestone. See Adriaenssens 1980, passim for more on the stone deliveries for the town hall in Antwerp.

There were other deliveries during these years. In 1584, Coenraad III van Neurenberg wrote a letter to Peter Timmermans work master of the town of Antwerp, better known as Peter Frans, town master mason.[526] If Peter was not present, stone merchant Johan Tonnoy was to deal with the letter. Van Neurenberg wrote that he had sent the remaining shipment of stone he had promised. The stone was allowed to be unloaded and the captain was to receive thirteen guilders for the shipment. Van Neurenberg would also journey to Antwerp himself. Furthermore, he requested that Johan Tonnoy be informed that the cut stone he had ordered was also underway, and a shipment of uncut stone that was to be subdivided between Tonnoy and Peter Frans was also in transit. Potting compost and even more stone were to follow, but Van Neurenberg would agree on that with him a week later. Finally, he mentioned that a scantling had to be made of the facade of Het Silveren Pant, in order to be able to tender it.[527] This short letter, full of personal trading matters, provides a good impression of a merchant's daily reality. It particularly highlights the logistical aspect of trade. Coordinating trade, transport and processing constituted the core activities for Van Neurenberg.

When examining Zeeland, it is clear that the Meuse Valley traders had been active here for quite some time, primarily when hydraulic-engineering projects were concerned. Nevertheless, Namur stone was also used in architectural projects, such as the town hall in Vlissingen, the facades of which were probably executed entirely, or maybe only clad in Namur stone. The town hall was built between 1594 and 1600 (Fig. 60).[528] Adriaan Bommenee, the eighteenth-century civil and hydraulic-engineer from Veere, indeed wrote in his "testament" on the use of materials in the town hall, "But that in Vlissingen is all made of blue stone. The square work and the decorative work was made of Gotland stone and that stone comes from Norway, it is very soft and had been mostly eaten away by

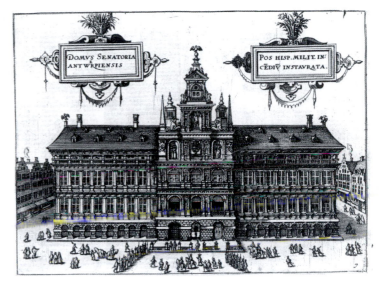

59. Antwerp, town hall by Cornelis Floris 1561-1565. Anonymous engraving, after Guicciardini 1612, Pl. 7 (Universiteitsbibliotheek Utrecht).

60. Vlissingen, town hall. Anonymous engraving, after Guicciardini 1612, Pl. 63 (Universiteitsbibliotheek Utrecht).

526 Lombaerde 1999, p. 240, Note 28. Peter Frans worked as town master mason of Antwerp from ca. 1540 until 1582.

527 Stadsarchief Antwerpen, Insolvente boedelskamer 1562.
528 Meischke 1997, pp. 74-75. Van Grol 1931, pp. 52-53.

the sea air so that it pulled out a few years ago and the same building was repaired with blue stone."[529] With a view to the trading relations between the Northern and Southern Low Countries in this period, it can be assumed that, in spite of the ambiguity of the term "blue stone", this reference concerned Namur stone and not Ecaussines stone.

It is not known who supplied the stone. In the past it has been suggested that this could have been Van Neurenberg and Valckenaer on the basis of Van Neurenberg's involvement in Antwerp town hall.[530] There is hardly more insight into the involvement of Namur stone merchants in the construction of the Vlissingen Gate in Middelburg. This lengthy project was started in 1596. The design for the gate must have been made before 1600 because Meuse Valley trader Joris Rochet supplied a delivery of Namur stone from Dordrecht in that year. He received 1,070 guilders for the shipment in three instalments.[531] The gate was not finished until 1634. Due to the lack of further source material, it is difficult to draw any conclusions on this subject. Rochet is not known to have carried out any design work and as the following chapters will reveal, the design activities of other Namur stone merchants, such as Van Neurenberg, Valckenaer or Misson, is also highly debatable.

Repairs, tiles and tombstones

The pragmatic and varied character of Van Neurenberg's activities recurs throughout the known source material. For example, Coenraad III was involved in the rebuilding of the church in Etten, around 1600; this church had sustained severe fire damage in 1584 from shelling by soldiers from Bergen op Zoom.[532] The spire of the church's tower, the roofs, the wooden barrel vaults and the wall work of the side-aisles, in particular, suffered greatly. Repair activities did not start until 1594. It was Thorn Abbey, which was obliged to provide two-thirds of the upkeep of the church.[533] The three-aisled church was reduced to just the central nave, which was closed off with walls. However, the three choir chapels remained intact. The two side chapels were provided with a facade to the west and the ruined side aisles survived until the eighteenth century.

The notes of the Thorn chapter meeting of 2 January 1604 reveal that the chapter's representatives, including the parish priest of Etten, were arrested at the behest of Coenraad van Neurenberg due to an outstanding claim on the Chapter of Thorn, amounting to 4,000 guilders.[534] This note probably concerns only a stone delivery, as Coenraad was not mentioned as one of the executing parties for the work. He may possibly have been responsible for supplying the tiles, which were re-used during a 1646 alteration.[535]

A number of deliveries to the Old Church in Amsterdam also took place during this period. On 7 October 1603, the expenses ledger of the Old Church in Amsterdam states: "paid to Master Coen Van Neurenberg [...] over 422 guilders".[536] One of the Namur stone doorways can still be found in the tower at the entrance to the ascending stairs. A year later, on 23 March 1604 Willem II van Neurenberg was paid 211.5 guilders for 130 feet of blue cover stone, which cost 32.5 stivers per foot. The stone

[529] Bommenee 1988, p. 161.
[530] Meischke 1997, pp. 74-75.
[531] Ibidem, p. 83.
[532] Kalf 1910, p. 214.
[533] The abbey had owned the tithes of the parish since 1277.
[534] Huisman 1986, p. 40, based on Rijksarchief Limburg, Archief van het kapittel van Thorn. Inventory Number 532.
[535] Kalf 1910, p. 218. The names of the labourers are known from a study carried out in 1644. Master at law Adriaan van Ryen, lawyer in Breda and Johan de Bruyn, steward of the

count's bishopric Thorn in the Barony of Breda, had set up the study with the aim of providing clarity concerning the former shape of the church i.e. before 1584. The bishopric wished to use the information obtained to cut the compulsory costs, which also explains the later payment conflicts in which Van Neurenberg was involved. The bishopric primarily wished to prove that the church had not had an expensive vault, but a cheap beamed loft. From: Habets 1885, k. 146-154.
[536] GAA, PA 378-28, Uitgifteboek Oude Kerk (1581-).

was intended "to be laid on top of the new wall".[537] Such deliveries must have been almost a daily occurrence. Another example, dating back to 18 May 1604, shows Pieter and Coenraad van Neurenberg receiving more than 1,297 guilders for cover stone, door stones and twenty-seven tombstones.[538] On 4 April 1606, Pieter van Neurenberg supplied twenty Namur stone tombstones for fourteen guilders each, and other small articles.[539]

Products such as tiles, doorways, tombstones, etc. usually concerned anonymous work for which the supplier can no longer be traced. Simultaneously, the above confirms that Van Neurenberg's activities were far from limited to architectural projects. As shown by the multitude of activities related here, his trading policy obviously aimed at maximising profit through diversification.

Willem II van Neurenberg and the gable of the church arch in Nijmegen

The Old Church in Amsterdam did not constitute the only building site with which the Van Neurenbergs were connected over several generations; it was also the case in Nijmegen. On 15 November 1604, the town council sent a letter to Dordrecht summoning "Guilliam Conradsz van Neurenberg" to negotiate the purchase of cut stone. This stone was required for the facade *aen de kerckroester*, i.e. the gable on the "church arch" or passageway from the churchyard to the market square underneath the cloth hall, which Willems great-grandfather, Willem I van Neurenberg had erected sixty years earlier. On 7 December, a number of members of the council negotiated with Willem regarding the delivery of a facade to crown the cloth hall's arch and the meeting ended with a signed agreement.[540]

The stone ordered from Van Neurenberg arrived from Dordrecht instead of Namur in May 1605, i.e. within six months, which is remarkable as it implies that the decision was taken to either transport stone worked in Namur via Dordrecht or to cut the stone to size in Dordrecht. The latter is by far the most likely hypothesis. In the former case, the diversion via Dordrecht was in fact unnecessary as the Waal could be reached much sooner, from the Meuse at Heerewaarden, in fact. Furthermore, this route avoided the tolls and saved time. Unloading the stone at Mook was also a much used option in the mid-sixteenth century. However, another factor came in to play. Although the rules pertaining to the issue of plots on Het Nieuwe Werk in Dordrecht stipulated that no stonemasons were to be located there, this rule seems to have been ignored. Increasingly, stone was being worked in the north and the desire to tie merchants to the town may have occasioned a relaxation of the initially strict rules for newcomers to Het Nieuwe Werk.[541] The use of this practice points to a permanent stock of unworked or roughly pre-cut stone intended for fulfilling orders, available in Dordrecht itself.

Cornelis Janssen from Delft, who had been appointed town bricklayer on 31 August 1604, executed the stone placement in Nijmegen.[542] Lambert Lambillon assisted him. This Lambillon, also from Dordrecht, possibly took on the work as a sub-contractor for Van Neurenberg.[543] Lambillon provided the gilding of the date and the painting of both cartouches with legends and a lion. This lion, which was placed atop an existing pillar, was brought by ship, possibly from Dordrecht, or possibly straight from the Walloon country.[544] The work was completed in the summer of 1607.

---

[537] Ibidem.

[538] Ibidem. In total 1,297 guilders. The price per tombstone was 14.5 guilders.

[539] Ibidem.

[540] Van Schevichaven 1909, pp. 206-207.

[541] The possibility that Van Neurenberg had a workshop elsewhere in Dordrecht or sub-contracted the working of the stone should also be taken into account.

[542] Weve 1919, p. 128.

[543] Van Neurenberg employees were also involved in the placement of stone in other projects such as the weigh house in Haarlem and the screen in 's-Hertogenbosch.

[544] Van Schevichaven 1909, p. 207. The cutting of the stone for the vault above the passage from the churchyard to the market square underneath the Cloth hall was tendered on 17 December 1605.

A design already existed when the stone for the facade was ordered from Van Neurenberg. One of the possible suppliers of this design is Master Thomas Singendonck, who was also a town bricklayer. He received 1.5 guilders for the design of the bow.[545] The gable, a scrolled gable, was clearly designed in line with the tradition of Vredeman de Vries' publications. The facade is definitely not unique for its time. Comparable examples can be found at Rijnstraat 41 in Arnhem, in Brouwershaven town hall, in the Rietdijk Gate in Dordrecht and in the Gemeenlands House of Rijnland in Leiden. But not just the scrolled gable as an architectural concept, but also smaller facade elements such as diamond heads and root motifs occur in Van Neurenberg's work in Haarlem and Willemstad, and also in the countless pavement-poles spread around the country, which were made of Namur stone and are classed as anonymous works.

XI. WILLEMSTAD 1596: THE PROTESTANT CHURCH BY COENRAAD III VAN NEURENBERG

The construction history of the Protestant Church in Willemstad is known since the 1920s (Fig. 61).[546] The design and construction of the church was partly done by Coenraad III van Neurenberg, as commissioned by Prince Maurits. Willemstad Church was one of the first Protestant churches to be built in the Low Countries, and is therefore not only interesting from an architectural-historical point of view. Van Neurenberg's role is interesting as he strayed from the norm observed earlier; here Van Neurenberg not only acts as the stone supplier, but also as master mason in line with medieval traditions, which is surprising, but not inexplicable.

Brief history of Willemstad

Willemstad was founded as a bastion against the Spanish. When the Count of Berlaymont, who was loyal to the Republic, captured Steenbergen in 1583, Gaspar van Kinschot was charged with readying Fijnaart's and Ruygenhil's defences. The idea of fortifying the town had existed since forces loyal to the Republic had occupied Klundert. The commission Van Kinschot was given read, "To reinforce Ruygenhil and to wall it with haste."[547] The Ruygenhil polder had been formed over the preceding centuries. Land reclamation started early, but the Elisabeth flood in 1421 caused major setbacks. On 14 November 1563, Jan IV van Glymes, the Marquis of Bergen, decided to reclaim new land outside the dikes of the Ruygenhil. The work was finished in the spring of 1565, after which plots were issued to the new inhabitants of the settlement.

In the year 1584, the village was given to William of Orange as remuneration for the damage to his private property.[548] He personally travelled to the village twice to acquaint himself with the activities. A garrison was stationed there and its name was changed to Willemstad.[549] After the Prince's death on 10 July 1584, his successor Prince Maurits gave Willemstad town privileges on 12 August 1586. In addition to fortifications, a town hall was built. On 8 August 1587 Maurits gave permission to the local administration to withdraw 2,400 guilders in order to cover the costs. At this point in time, nothing had been determined regarding the architect and building contractor. All that is known is that Wouter Aarts from Grave signed a receipt on 14 July 1588 for 600 guilders for erecting the church's spire. Initially the town hall also served as a place of worship,[550] but after 1609 that situation would change (Fig. 62).

[545] It is open to debate whether the sum was high enough for an entirely new design. Weve suggests that Master Cornelis Janssen from Delft might have supplied the facade's design. He is said to also have worked on the houses adjacent to the arch, in order to reinforce them, together with Singendonck. See also Van Schevichaven 1909, p. 207.

[546] Juten 1922, passim and Ozinga 1929, pp. 12-19.
[547] Juten 1922, p. 11. For more on Willemstad see also Van Nispen 1985.
[548] Dane 1950, p. 21.
[549] Ibidem, p. 56.
[550] Ibidem, p. 64.

61. Willemstad, church from the south. Anonymous photograph, July 1928 (RDMZ, Neg.Nr. 9.984).

The church: preparation and design

When issuing the town privileges, Prince Maurits had ordered the repair of all the houses that had been destroyed in the town. He promised the sum of 600 guilders for the church, tower, streets, etc.[551] Nevertheless, planning the church's construction did not start until 1594. On 2 August 1594, Master Adriaan de Muyr, a carpenter from Middelburg, was commissioned to make a model of the

[551] Ozinga, p. 12, Note 5, based on op Gemeentearchief Willemstad, Octrooi van 12-8-1586.

124

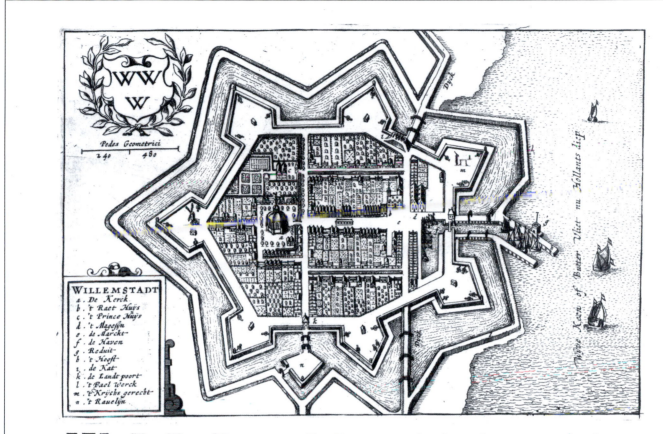

WILLEMSTADT
a . De Kerck
b . 't Raet Huys
c . 't Prince Huys
d . 't Magefyn
e . de Marckt
f . de Haven
g . Reduit
h . 't Hoeft
i . de Kat
k . de Lande poort
l . 't Rael Werck
m . 't Krijchs gerecht
n . 't Rauelijn

WILLEM-STADT.

Gelegen-
heydt.

W ILLEM-STADT leght aen de Roovaert, omtrent het Hollands-diep , in een landeken den Ruygenhil genoemt,dat in 't jaer c I ɔ I ɔ LXIV bedijckt is. Prins Willem van Oranje heeft defe ftadt, om 't uytloopen der vyanden te beletten , gebouwt, en met *Heeren.* fijn naem verciert.Hy had oock 't gebied over de felve , tot erkentenis van fijne groote wel-daden, die hy aen den Staet der vereenighde Nederlanden betoont heeft;'t welck fijne na-komelingen noch hebben, die in hunne tijte-

len Heeren van Willem-ftadt genoemt wor-den. Sy is gefterckt met feven bolwercken , *Stercke.* een ravelijn , en een kat , meeft alle met ge-fchut voorfien. Oock is hier een Kerck,Raet- *Gebouwen.* huys, Marckt , wapen-huys , een huys voor den Prince,en een bequame haven. De locht is hier fwaer , en, om de nabyheydt der zee , niet feer gefont ; 't welck voor eenige jaren fommige burgers van Leyden ondervonden hebben , die daer door hunne gefontheydt verloren.

g 2

62. Willemstad in the seventeenth century. Anonymous engraving (RAB, Kaarten- en prentenverzameling, Inv.Nr. 1456, Neg.Nr. 1604).

125

church.[552] Prince Maurits determined that it was to be a centralised structure, as would be confirmed by a later document.[553] On 19 December 1597 he repeated his wish that the church of Willemstad be built in a round or octagonal shape.[554]

A captain from Middelburg who received five pounds for the transport delivered the model on 25 September 1594.[555] As the design featured eight window frames and a doorway, the model was indeed most probably a centralised structure. Nevertheless, this model was not built without alterations.[556] In accordance with De Muyr's plan, orders concerning the supply of bluestone were placed with Coenraad III van Neurenberg, who was in Antwerp at the time.[557] The size of the order is unknown. De Muyr provided the Middelburg iron measures on which the calculations were based. There must have been two of these measures, of which Van Neurenberg received one, and the town, the other.[558] For the sum of 5,800 guilders Van Neurenberg accepted the order for the stone. He probably drew up the specifications himself.

Besides the stone delivery, the commission consisted of two other elements. First, Van Neurenberg had to adapt the existing design, which essentially meant he made the church even more spacious, and he designed a tower for the church. This change had consequences for the stone to be delivered. It cost an additional 1,933 guilders and eight stivers, "as this temple has now been made wider than the first model, and also a tower has been added by the magistrates."[559] Second, Van Neurenberg was responsible for converting De Muyrs design into specifications for the church's foundations. He was entrusted with this work because he had a certain level of renown as a lock builder and digger.

After the initial design phase, the name De Muyr no longer appears in sources. His basic model served as the point of departure for further developments, of which the addition of a tower was the first step. His services were no longer needed. Andries de Roy, engineer and bricklayer, took over the specifications, scantlings and patterns.[560]

Because of the church's more spacious layout and the addition of the tower, Van Neurenberg brought a second model of the church with him on 11 July 1595. He received one hundred and twenty guilders, a considerable sum, for the effort and artfulness of the model provided.[561] The architectural changes possibly explain the making of the second model.[562] The additions to the original design must have entailed considerable changes, which were also spelled out in the justification of the second instalment of the payment for the job. In the margin reference is made to great changes having been made to the delivery of blue stone for the tower, gate, window frames and other parts.[563]

Van Neurenberg's position in the construction process

When he signed the contract after the initial bid, Van Neurenberg signed as master mason. He was to be responsible for the supervision of the first phase of construction. This nomenclature is remarkable because no descendant of the family had actually worked as a master mason since the construction of the cloth hall in Nijmegen around 1540. It could be said that this exception was only an appar-

---

[552] Juten 1922, p. 12. Unfortunately, he does not state his source. De Muyr had been town carpenter in Middelburg since 1 April 1587.
[553] Dane 1950, p. 116.
[554] See Juten 1922, p. 15 and Ozinga 1929, p. 17.
[555] He received an additional ten stivers for unloading the model and taking it to the town hall. Among the appendices to the original bill is a specification of the costs De Muyr incurred for making the model. Ozinga 1929, p. 14.
[556] Ibidem, pp. 13-14.

[557] Juten 1922, p. 12.
[558] Ibidem.
[559] Juten 1922, p. 13.
[560] Ibidem. He made more detailed designs and received fifty guilders for this.
[561] Ibidem, p. 12.
[562] It cannot be ruled out that it was a conversion of the first model.
[563] Ozinga 1929, p. 14.

ent one, caused by a lack of data, but taking the consistent line into consideration with the activities of the preceding half century, something else seems to have occurred. A constant factor in Van Neurenberg's commissions was that he was always brought in from the outside to provide specialised services which, in particular, the northern construction trade could not provide, namely the supply of stone. Van Neurenberg was therefore repeatedly involved with a more or less independently operating construction company. In Willemstad the opposite occurred; the village, which consisted of little more than a few dozen houses, had few facilities and did not have a well-equipped construction company or a strong guild structure. The situation Van Neurenberg encountered in Willemstad was therefore totally different from that in other towns. Labourers had to be attracted from elsewhere, a fact which provided Van Neurenberg with an opportunity to act as master mason. The lack of facilities, administrative structure and strong trade guilds can be seen as the main reason why Van Neurenberg deviated from normal working methods in Willemstad. His expertise was a good deal more comprehensive than just the supply of stone and in this favourable, exceptional case, his services were gladly accepted.

Laying the foundations

Work started in October 1596 when carpenter, Pieter Cornelissen, surveyed and laid out the building.[564] First, it was necessary to check whether the soil conditions were suitable for building a church, which was accomplished by digging a deep shaft and examining soil samples. The soil samples proved to be suitable and shortly afterwards, a call for bids was announced for the first part of the brickwork according to the specifications. Van Neurenberg received the work when the contract for laying foundations and the brickwork for the church's lower reaches was signed in The Hague on 17 November 1596. Besides Coenraad van Neurenberg, this contract also involved Cornelis Verhoeven, a bricklayer from Rotterdam and Jan Jansz Orguel, a stonemason from Delft. The specifications reiterate the fact that Coenraad van Neurenberg created the pattern for the foundations. The town magistrates approved the payment of 7,500 guilders on 28 November 1596.[565] Five months after signing this contract, the laying of the foundations for the tower was also awarded to Coenraad on 22 April 1597, for the sum of 1,500 guilders.[566] Approval followed on 25 July.

Examination of the specifications for the church's foundations provides an impression of the work Van Neurenberg was to execute (Fig. 63), which concerned the foundations and the brickwork up to the dripstone moulding under the window frames.[567] First, he had to dig a three-foot deep trench;[568] then a nine-foot wide 'bed' had to be laid at the bottom of the trench, on top of which four heavy beech beams, each five inches thick, were to be laid.[569] These beams were to extend over the foundations of the pillars alternating crosswise, where necessary they were fixed to one another using wooden pins and iron nails as Coenraad's pattern prescribed. The building contractor would then lay a second set of five-inch thick beech planks, as wide as the others, on the first set of beams. The actual foundations that were to be made on top of this structure were to be seven feet wide, which consisted of brick where the first layer was embedded in sand and the rest in mortar. The wall was to taper on both sides until it was only five feet thick. The wall would then be further narrowed by a half foot

---

[564] Dane 1950, p. 117, Juten 1922, p. 13.

[565] Juten 1922, p. 13.

[566] Ozinga 1929, p. 16.

[567] The dimensions were based on the Middelburg foot, which was thirty centimetres (twelve inches). Verhoeff 1983, p. 53.

[568] The specifications are not entirely clear on this matter. The reconstruction reveals that the depth of the foundations was approximately three metres or around ten feet.

[569] No information is available on the actual execution of the foundations. Letter F. Sturm, architect BNA, dated 11 December 1998.

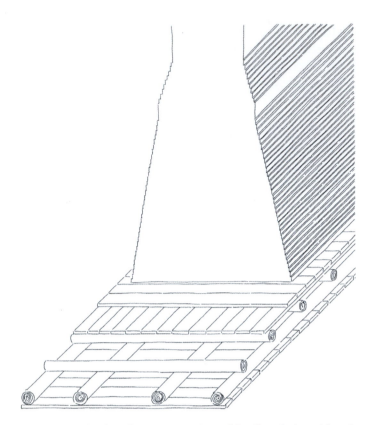

63. Willemstad, Church, reconstruction of the foundations (drawing by Ronald Glaudemans).

until it had reached a height of eight feet. The wall would then be within two feet of threshold level at which the next taper was to be made, with small cuts tapering parts on either side so that at ten feet high the wall would be three feet, two inches wide at threshold level. The diameter of the interior was to be sixty feet, whereby each side would measure 23 or 24 feet corner to corner. A pillar and a buttress was to project from corner of the wall's sides, thus making the pillars part of the foundations.

The foundations were to bear a breastwork 4.5 feet high, which projected above ground level. The wall was to be three feet, two inches thick, the same as at ten feet high. The pillar and buttress were also supposed to be the same thickness at this height. The breastwork was to be made of blue stone on the outside. The brickwork was to be laid in cross bond; with the exception of the bases and the capitals, the columns were to be made of carved brick. The specifications determined that the building contractor would supply the necessary materials he required, with the exception of stone, which had already been the subject of an earlier contract with Van Neurenberg. The building contractor for the foundations was obliged to go and get the blue stone from the ships in Willemstad's harbour.

The building contractor was to start around 1 March 1597 and was to finish at the end of September or mid-October at the latest, under penalty of fifty Carolus guilders for Willemstad's poor.

Standing walls

If the laying of the foundations seems to have been unproblematic, the church's structure progressed slowly, possibly as a result of financial problems. After the magistrates had sent a request to Prince Maurits, he promised them a subsidy of 7,000 guilders on 19 October 1597. This sum was to be paid, in addition to the already allocated rations from tithes and town excises, in three instalments.

Coenraad III van Neurenberg's death on 2 November 1603 caused a setback, too. When he died activities in Willemstad were fully underway, although he was only involved in supplying stone. Another building contractor, Cornelis Verhoeven, had already been contracted for the brickwork on the church. He was also involved in the laying of the foundations and assumed the next part of the work for 2,800 guilders. Later he continued the work on the church with his mates receiving daily wages.[570] From 14 March till 11 October 1602, Verhoeven received 886 guilders, ten stivers and six deniers and during the following summer ninety-seven guilders and nineteen stivers[571] for work on

---

[570] Juten 1922, p. 15.

[571] Ibidem. Furthermore Verhoeven received another 250 guilders.

the walls, which Verhoeven built to considerable height. He purchased 721,000 bricks in three shipments for thirty-five, thirty-eight and forty-two stivers per thousand respectively, and later the building required 141,500 red Leiden bricks for the outside work, which were purchased for three guilders and two stivers per thousand.[572] These bricks can still be recognized in the masonry between the buttresses. Their bright red is in sharp contrast to the greyer stone used for the plinth and buttresses. These activities probably pertained to the wall work up to the second dripstone moulding. Because the workers receiving daily wages were becoming too expensive, attempts were made to tender a bid for the final stage of construction. To this end, the town messenger was sent to Rotterdam, Delft, Gouda and Dordrecht with posters announcing when the work was to be tendered. A captain took a number of posters with him to hang up around Zeeland.[573] Mayor De Coninck travelled to Rotterdam and Delft to urge the bricklayer and the carpenter to finish the specifications for the brick and woodwork for the roof as soon as possible.[574] In November 1603, the patterns and specifications for the tower, church and roof were discussed. Verhoeven from Rotterdam mostly likely prepared the brick specifications and would eventually be awarded the work for 2,900 guilders. Adriaen Dirksz van Brantwijck from Delft was awarded the woodwork, which consisted of the making and delivery of the wooden roof structure, for 8,000 guilders. It is probable that, once again, the person who drew up the specifications ultimately received the commission.[575]

In the accounts for 1600-1605, the agreed 500 pounds for capitals and 400 pounds for column bases were paid to Coenraad III van Neurenberg and his heirs. Later on, Willem II van Neurenberg, Coenraad's son, received an additional 100 pounds.[576]

After the awarding of the commissions to Verhoeven and Brantwijck work continued; however, it was not executed as agreed, which meant that Verhoeven did not receive his 2,900 guilders. He received 1,800 guilders at the start of the activities and of the remaining 1,100 guilders he received only 452.15, the reason given being that the tower and other work had not been finished, which led to conflict between Verhoeven and the magistrates.[577] However, Verhoeven felt that he had a right to the full sum because of problems in the subsoil, of which "the honourable gentlemen had been repeatedly warned". In other words he put the blame on the magistrates, who, according to Verhoeven, were well aware of the fact that the subsoil was too soft to build a tower on. These soil conditions can be indeed seen as the principal reason for the tower remaining incomplete.[578] The subsidence of the tower is clear from the manner in which the brickwork sags.

Finishing the work

After the roof's timberwork had been commissioned to Adriaen Dirksz for 8,000 guilders, slating started on 11 April 1605. Gerrit Mertens, who was born in Maastricht, but who lived in Dordrecht, executed the slate work. For the sum of 38 guilders Claes Jansz, blacksmith of the town of Delft, supplied a cross, which was erected on the small dome-shaped tower. The Delft coppersmith Aert Thonisz received thirty-five guilders for making the weathercock and Wynant Jansz from Amsterdam supplied the bell above the church for which he received 472 guilders. Cornelis Egelos installed some new windowpanes in the tower, and Segher Krynen from The Hague provided seven new windowpanes and its coat of arms. The latter were gifts from Prince Maurits, the States General, the States of Hol-

---

[572] Ibidem.
[573] Juten 1922, pp. 15-16.
[574] Ibidem, p. 16. ... op t spoedichste de bestecke van de metselrye ende van thoutwerck van de cappe gereed te maken.

[575] Ibidem.
[576] Ozinga 1929, p. 17.
[577] Ibidem.
[578] Ibidem, Note 2.

land, Zeeland and Utrecht to the administration of the Ruygenhil and Heyninge polders. Jacob Olivier from Delft designed the pulpit and the magistrates' bench and Joost Hendriksz from Dordrecht and cabinetmaker Joris Adriaensz from The Hague made them. Finally, at the close of 1609 the town hall's clock was transferred to the church.

The many craftsmen involved in the finishing of the church primarily originated from Delft and Dordrecht, which was no coincidence. The two principal building contractors involved in the project, Coenraad van Neurenberg and Cornelis Verhoeven, came from Dordrecht and Delft. Unfortunately, the names of these craftsmen do not appear in relation to other sites and it is therefore unclear whether they cooperated more regularly with Van Neurenberg or Verhoeven. What can be ascertained is that, here too, craftsmen were consistently brought in from elsewhere because of the lack of specialists in Willemstad itself. Simultaneously, the distribution of posters announcing a call for bids for the work provides some insight into the main centres in the construction trade, i.e. which towns people looked to and where they expected to find good building contractors.

The church, its construction and its influence

The sources have already revealed that the tower was not built to the intended height in an attempt to avoiding subsidence. This sinking can also have played a role in the fact that the church has a wooden vault instead of a stone one. Buttresses have been built on the outside of the church, which indicates that a stone vault was part of the plan. Brick columns have been built in the interior, on which the vault was originally to have been supported. The wooden vault that was finally built features crossed tie beams.[579]

Carpenter Adriaen Dircksz of Delft provided Willemstad's church roof and timberwork.[580] He must have been relatively young when he worked there. In 1618 he wrote an estimate of the costs for repairing the timberwork in the council house in Delft.[581] A 1629 reference to his name is very interesting. At the start of the construction of the church in Maassluis, which was a centralised structure, he travelled to Amsterdam with his son Dirc Adriaensz to make a drawing of the Noorder Church, also a centralised structure.[582] It can be cautiously stated that Adriaen Dircksz must have had a certain reputation when it came to building roofs for centralised structures. It is natural to assume that for the roof structure in Willemstad he must have studied and perhaps measured an example. It would be interesting to locate this example, as this structure would be the first centralised structure in the Northern Low Countries.[583] For Adriaen, the commission in Willemstad must have been unusual. Building a round, wooden dome, a vault and a roof structure was less than common. Although the church's old roof went up in flames in 1950, it is fortunate that a surveyor's drawing has been conserved so that it is still possible to gain insight into the roof structure used in Willemstad (Fig. 64).[584]

---

[579] Janse 1989, p. 275 does not show tie beams. Ozinga has already pointed this problem out and he too considered the problem of soft sub soil.

[580] Adriaen Dircksz also appears to have been referred to as Den Elger. See Meischke 1997, p. 72.

[581] Ibidem.

[582] See also Terwen 1967, pp. 147-148.

[583] A comparison of roof structures between the Willemstad Church and that of the Noorder Church in Amsterdam led nowhere.

[584] There is little discussion on whether this survey was based on the original roof structure. The church was refurbished in 1789, but the roof structure does not seem to have been replaced at that time. Ozinga saw the roof and was of the opinion that on the basis of the profiling it must still be original, due to the detailing of the pedestal. Moreover, the 1789 specifications do not list the renewal of the roof. Ozinga 1929, p. 18. Old depictions, such as that by Pronk, also indicate that the dome and roof were the original form.

The structure proves to be very unusual. The roof in Willemstad uses a method of construction, which would be more likely found in Southern Limburg or the Meuse Valley than by the Hollands Diep. The cross section was a 6.5 metre high circle segment on a floor plan nearly eighteen metres wide. It has four trusses, which cross one another. Two link beams have been pinned into the diagonal truss posts.[585] It is conspicuous that there is a post roof with the overlying roof plate. Post roofs occur a great deal more in Limburg and in the Southern Low Countries generally, while they are hardly seen in the west.[586] Furthermore, the roof in Willemstad has link beam trusses and a ridge truss, comprising five posts altogether. These link beam trusses are actually foreign elements, which are generally only found in the southeast of the Low Countries. Concentrations of link beam trusses have indeed been found in Nijmegen, 's-Hertogenbosch, the Bishopric of Münster, which is part of the Rhine land, and the entire Meuse Valley area.[587]

This information, and the well-known methods of carpenter Adriaen Dircsz in Maassluis, indicate a possible example of a centralised structure roof in the Meuse Valley or the Rhine land. After all, an existing structural solution was used for the roof's timberwork.

Finally, the church's window frames warrant mention here. These were made of Namur stone. They are stone cross windows just like the ones common in the Meuse Valley, and it is natural to assume that the stone trader designed them.

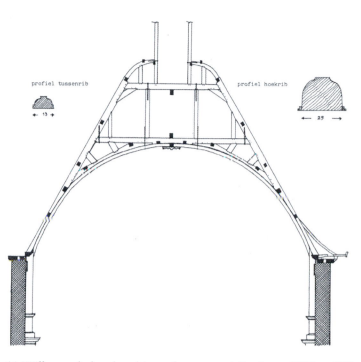

64. Willemstad, the church's roof structure (after Janse 1989, p. 275, Fig. 543).

Conclusion

It is particularly difficult to make a definitive statement concerning the sources for the church in Willemstad. The centralised church had been known here for some time through the architectural treatise of Serlio (Book V), and after the Willemstad Church had been built, a considerable number of centralised structures were realised in the Northern Low Countries including structures in Amsterdam, IJzendijke, Maassluis, Leiden and Middelburg. Centralised structures also once stood in Haarlem, Ghent, Antwerp and Oudenaarde.[588] However, little more is known of these churches, other than the fact that they were built and later demolished. Comparative research on the basis of structural solutions, the use of materials and the master masons involved must for the moment be excluded.

---

[585] Janse 1989, p. 275.
[586] Typical Meuse Valley accents: Janse 1989, II, 5, p. 235ff.

[587] Boekwijt and Van Drunen 1996, p. 22.
[588] Snaet 1999, passim.

The question of the designer of Willemstad Church remains problematic. Although there are a number of names attached to the project, these most probably concern the drafting of specifications and the detailing of existing plans. The earliest design phase can be associated with De Muyr, who made a model. Coenraad III van Neurenberg's role as designer is also problematic. Although he was responsible for widening the church and adding a tower to the existing design, it cannot be ascertained to what extent these additions concerned personal input.

XII. HAARLEM: THE CONSTRUCTION OF THE WEIGH HOUSE

In Haarlem, where a new weigh house was erected at the close of the sixteenth century, Coenraad III returned to his normal role of stone supplier and the actual construction was left to town craftsmen. Haarlem, which in contrast to Willemstad had its own town construction company, carried out as much of the work as possible on its own. The town's position regarding the materials supplier and building contractor was therefore more independent than had been the case in Willemstad.

Haarlem's fabric lodge during the second half of the sixteenth century

During the course of the sixteenth century, the Haarlem town building lodge developed, as it did in other towns in the Northern Low Countries, into an official body with its own administration, which means that during the second half of the sixteenth century all the elements for a true town fabric lodge were already present. However, it was only after the major fire of 1576 that the town construction trade received such an impetus that one could actually refer to an official construction company.[589] In 1581, Willem Diericxsz den Abt was appointed town stonemason and Pieter Pietersz town carpenter.[590] The wages connected to these positions then rose rapidly. If in 1570 the fabric lodge masters still received twenty guilders per year, by 1581 this sum had already risen to sixty guilders. In 1590, fabric lodge masters Willem Maertsz and Ysbrant Hageman received two hundred guilders, a figure which later increased by one hundred guilders.[591]

The number and size of the construction projects the town undertook during this period also increased considerably.[592] This quantitative increase not only illustrates the town's economic growth and prosperity, but also how important the town council considered public works to be. This impression can also be gained from other towns. Towns were increasingly profiling themselves as independent strongholds with their own prestige and history, which was closely related to the rise of the mercantile class.[593] The town administrators, all members of the bourgeoisie, handled the town's protection, its preservation and growth, which were related to the maintenance of Public Works. Salomon de Bray noted in the introduction to his *Architectura Moderna* that a good administration should also pay attention to roads and water. In addition to the works themselves, this care for the town was also expressed in the architecture the town administration built. In order to express the identity of the town, buildings should actually be recognisable as municipal buildings. The town had an increasing need for representative architecture provided with a concrete iconography. Coats of arms, allegories of good government and functional depictions constituted the architectural arsenal with which a town could express itself. When these factors were coupled with suitable scale, presence and a prominent location in the urban vista, they combined to make a town recognisable through its architecture. In Haarlem a similar policy can be observed in the construction of the meat hall, the transformation of the town hall and the construction of the weigh house. The appointment of Lieven de Key would formalise this policy. His idiosyncratic designs would leave a mark on Haarlem's public buildings built between approximately 1595 and 1625.

[589] Eisler 1914, pp. 249–250.
[590] Ibidem, p. 250.
[591] Ibidem.

[592] Meischke 1993, p. 57.
[593] Kooijmans 1995, p. 26.

Town master mason Lieven de Key

Lieven de Key was a descendant of an old stonemasons' family from Ghent. He was born around 1560 and remained there until after his father's death in 1584. Due to political and religious upheaval De Key then left for London, where he married Katelyne de Caluwe who was also from Ghent.[594] Between the end of 1590 and October 1591 he relocated to Haarlem where he was first mentioned as town stonemason on 28 October 1591.[595] Whether this employment was also the immediate reason for travelling to Haarlem or whether other motives played their part is unknown. On 3 July 1593 however, the town permanently employed De Key.[596] In addition to a daily wage of twenty stivers in the summer and eighteen stivers in the winter, he received an annual stipend of seventy-two pounds (432 guilders) and a house.[597] De Key had a prominent position in the town fabric lodge. Until his death in 1627, he would be involved in a large number of buildings and projects in the town. Furthermore, he had his own stonemasons' workshop, which supplied orders from third parties.[598]

From the beginning of his appointment De Key was involved in a considerable number of projects in the town such as the Sint-Jorisdoelen (1591/92), the Sint-Jans Gate (1593), the gable of the baptismal chapel of the Sint-Bavo Church (1594) and the meat hall (1603). However, he also had patrons beyond Haarlem. For example, in 1610 and 1613 work took place in Utrecht on a lock that De Key designed. In 1625, De Key was a member of the arbitration commission as an agent concerning the construction of the Catharijne Gate in Utrecht, which will be examined in more detail in Part III of this study.[599]

The sources and the influences underlying De Key's architectural creations are not clearly traceable. Factors involved include his origins in Ghent, with his unclear education, his move to London, which appears to have played an important role and major architectural developments during this time. Because De Key worked in a broad context, little can be said with regard to his oeuvre with any certainty. Attributions on the basis of purely stylistic characteristics are disputable, which renders the impression of De Key somewhat vague, particularly regarding his employment with the town as opposed to his being paid for individual designs. Moreover, his activities can not be limited to a single type; just like Claes de Wael from Nijmegen, Marcus Aelberts from 's-Hertogenbosch or Joost Jansz from Amsterdam he acted in various capacities. He took commissions as a designer and stonemason, but also as an inspector of other people's work and as a materials supplier of stone in particular. De Key purchased building materials in Leiden, among other places[600] and he was also a distributor (or town buyer), who supplied Namur stone and Bentheimer sandstone to order. In 1611 he supplied Bentheimer and blue stone to the dike board Rijnland for a lock in Spaarndam. In 1613 he received eighty-five pounds and one stiver for a journey to The Hague, the tendering of blue stone and a trip to the Lek (river) to purchase good stone, all of which was for the reinforcement of the sea dike near the house of Ter Hart.[601]

This role of stone trader leads to the question whether one should view De Key as a competitor of the Van Neurenbergs or as a colleague. The answer seems relatively simple. Lieven de Key was strongly embedded in the Haarlem town construction company due to his position as Haarlem's town stonemason. Furthermore, he was primarily active as a master mason in the region of Holland; he definitely did not maintain a multi-regional work area, purchasing stone in the Meuse Valley or any

[594] Van der Blom 1995, pp. 10-11.
[595] Ibidem, p. 12.
[596] Quoted in Meischke 1993, p. 57.
[597] Eisler 1914, p. 251.
[598] See Van der Blom 1995, pp. 10-16. The suggestion has been made that a lot of work he supplied from here was

actually made by his brothers Michiel and Guillaume. However, almost nothing is known of the existence of these brothers or of the work they are supposed to have made.
[599] Meischke 1993, p. 58.
[600] Eisler 1914, p. 252.
[601] Meischke 1993, p. 58.

other area where stone was found. It is therefore natural to assume that when De Key was responsible for a stone delivery he merely acted as a distributor. The circles from which he acquired his material should be sought through merchants such as Van Neurenberg. Such a system is also the most obvious for the trade in Bentheimer sandstone. In that sense, these activities are more or less extensions of one another.

The construction of the weigh house in Haarlem and Coenraad III van Neurenberg's role

The weigh house in Haarlem is one of the few still extant buildings for which Coenraad III van Neurenberg supplied stone (Fig. 65). There are few doubts concerning his stone deliveries, but the question of who designed the weigh house has led to a great deal of discussion. Coenraad III van Neurenberg was in Haarlem on 22 June and from 8 to 11 July 1595 to negotiate the delivery of stone for the town hall's steps and for the yet to be built weigh house.[602] The town hall was undergoing radical alterations during these years and the town purchased an unknown quantity of Namur stone from Coenraad for a staircase.[603] The new weigh house was to be built where the town had purchased a house earlier that year at the Spaarne.[604] The design must have been completed by this date as a definite order must have been made during the negotiations with Van Neurenberg.

At the start of 1597, the house was demolished and in June of that year Coenraad received the first payment of 3,000 pounds for stone. Presumably he had scantlings and patterns at his disposal at this point in time, to cut the stone to size.[605] Many details are known concerning the construction process. On 31 August 1597, the town fabric lodge's accounts state that Lieven de Key and his staff have worked on the new weigh house.[606] These activities probably consisted of laying the foundations. Simultaneously, preparations for the rest of the construction process were taking place. Lieven de Key supplied a block of Obernkirchner stone for consoles under the crossbeams.[607] Oak and pine, lime and cement were purchased. The timber was possibly partly used for the foundations, but it cannot be ruled out that beams and the roof were also under construction. For example, on 16 November 1597 town master carpenter Pieter Pietersz was mentioned in the accounts, where he worked for five days on the weigh house with a team of woodcutters.

The foundation laying activities made good progress, and this meant the first stone could be laid in September. Cornelis Bartholomeusz, the foreman who delivered the building materials to the site, received ten pounds and ten shillings. He had advanced this money to pay for drink upon the laying of the first stone.[608] In December another shipment of Namur stone arrived.[609] Cornelis Bartholomeusz received money for lard with which to grease the sleds, to transport a shipment of stone a short distance from where it was unloaded to the construction site.[610] In early January 1598 the stone-

[602] On 11 July 1595, Coenraad continued on to Willemstad with the model for the church there. He obviously went straight to Willemstad from Haarlem (possibly via Dordrecht).
[603] Japikse 1926, p. 335.
[604] Roding 1993, p. 441.
[605] It seems impossible for Coenraad to have supplied the stone uncut, which will become clear when the conflict is described below. In general, deliveries were only paid for once the material had actually arrived.
[606] Roding 1993, p. 442.
[607] Ibidem: block bockenberger steen (Bückeburger or Obernkirchner), for making the consoles under the beams.
[608] Ibidem.
[609] Roding mentions 16,000 items. This entry should probably read 16,000 feet.
[610] Roding suggests that because Cornelis Bartholomeusz received money for lard for the sleds shortly after Christmas 1597 it means the cold had arrived. However, at the time, sleds were not just used when it had snowed, but were a general mode of heavy transport. Moreover, there had already been frost in November and December. The weather turned unpredictable after Christmas. Buisman 2000, p. 178.

65. Haarlem, weigh house. Photograph by G.Th. Delemarre, September 1959 (RDMZ, Neg.Nr. 57.241).

masons were paid for overtime, which may indicate that work continued over Christmas. This work concerned the possible additional cutting of the stone supplied or the placing of the stone in the work. In March it was primarily the carpenters who were at work, perhaps having started on the second layer of beams. The weather then took a turn for the worse. Two tarpaulins covered the work, which could be removed again a short time later after which work intensified.[611] On 16 August, the roof must have been nearly finished.[612] In the autumn of 1598, Olivier Cokelen, the town paviour, was at work around the building.

The last payments pertaining to the weigh house took place in February 1599, but it is unlikely that work was still taking place at this time. Although the work seemed to be concluded, Coenraad III van Neurenberg was still mentioned in November 1599. A conflict had arisen surrounding the last payment for the stone he supplied. The town objected to paying the entire sum agreed upon because a particular quantity of stone had not been or had been incorrectly worked, thus forcing Haarlem to recruit stonemasons to work the stone there. The town wished to charge these additional expenses to Van Neurenberg. This conflict clearly reveals that the agreement between Van Neurenberg and the town stated that Coenraad was to supply the stone in a worked form. Lieven de Key was therefore not responsible for working the stone. At most he was involved in adaptation, which the conflict illustrates. Incorporating the stone into the work was a task for the town's craftsmen and involved its bricklayers and stonemasons.

The attribution

The weigh house in Haarlem was clearly custom made. The floor plan is irregular and tailor made for the plot on which the building stands (Fig. 66). The foot measure used for the weigh house's construction was the Haarlem foot, which is 28.7 centimetres.[613] A question that arises is whether the use of the Haarlem foot provides any clues as to the identity of the weigh house's designer. Willemstad's Church used the Middelburg foot although Coenraad van Neurenberg's partial responsibility for the design cannot be excluded. The foot measure used for the Old Church in Amsterdam was the same as the Amsterdam foot and the measure used for the Blue Gate in Leiden was the same as the Rijnland foot.[614] It seems obvious that patrons determined which measures were to be used to standardize all the elements. Moreover, there is an inherent checking aspect involved: unequivocal measurements better enable a patron to check whether he has received what he ordered. Furthermore, it greatly reduces the risk of confusion.

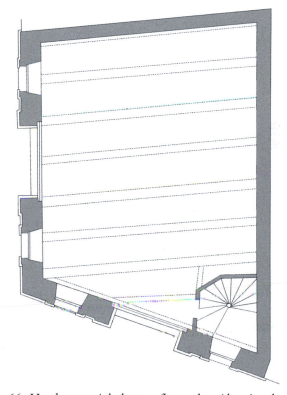

66. Haarlem, weigh house, floor plan (drawing by Ronald Glaudemans after Roding 1993, p. 451, Fig. 3).

[611] Roding 1993, p. 442.
[612] See De Vries 1994, pp. 120-121 or Nagel 1996, pp. 120-139 concerning this tradition.

[613] Roding 1993, p. 444 wrongly bases herself on a foot measure of 29 centimetres.
[614] The foot measure used was generally imposed by the patron and sheds little light on the origin or identity of the designer.

The use of the Haarlem foot does not answer the question of who designed the weigh house. The organisation of the construction trade is crucial to this discussion. Various possibilities have been mentioned in the past, including in addition to Lieven de Key, primarily Willem Thybault and Cornelis Cornelisz. Roding proposed the latter two were due to an item on the treasurer's accounts of a payment for the design of three patterns for this town weigh house.[615] Thybault received six pounds (thirty-six guilders) and Cornelisz eighteen pounds (108 guilders). The payment took place around October 1596, a year and a half after Van Neurenberg had come to Haarlem to negotiate the delivery of stone. The sums are high enough to have paid for a new, original design.[616] The item is unequivocal, although the meaning of the terms *bewerpen* (designing) and *patronen* (patterns) is open to discussion. Due to the fact that these terms are open to multiple interpretations, it is possible to defend that these concern neat perspective drawings in colour, for example for a patron, i.e. presentation drawings. The fact that payment occurred almost a year and a half after the negotiations with Van Neurenberg happened can, on the one hand, be seen as an indication that it does indeed concern something other than a design. However, it often took a long time before local authorities paid their bills, a problem we have encountered several times already when discussing of Van Neurenberg's stone deliveries.

The hypothesis that Coenraad III van Neurenberg was responsible for the design is highly improbable.[617] The same applies to carpenter Pieter Pietersz. There are no indications that either of them designed weigh house. Although the existing literature assumes that Coenraad III van Neurenberg regularly acted as a designing master mason and stonemason, this contention is far from certain. Attribution takes place on the basis of the name connected to the specifications, which does not prove that either person was the designing party. Lieven de Key is then the only one remaining. De Key has recently been put forward again as the weigh house's designer, in line with a assertion that has existed since the nineteenth century.[618] The proof is based on a number of nineteenth-century drawings of the weigh house, which have been retained. On the basis of the reconstructed design scheme and the foot measure used, which remained the same in spite of changing dimensions, Kiem concluded that these drawings were copies of the original design variants. This assertion is not improbable and research reveals how the design could have come into being. However, it does not prove that these design variants are actually De Key's and not someone else. For the time being, Cornelisz and Thybault remain the most probable candidates for the design.[619]

The supply of stone for the weigh house in Haarlem provides an additional impression of Van Neurenberg's work process, allowing a parallel to be drawn with the delivery for the Old Church in Amsterdam. The question why Namur stone cladding was opted for in Haarlem can be answered in several different ways. Initially, one may wonder why specifically stone was selected, which probably related to the building's function. In particular the piers on the ground floor were vulnerable spots, which would suffer a great deal from the weigh house's use. Furthermore, it was obviously a town building and so prestige also played a role.

---

[615] Roding 1993, p. 441.
[616] They are not as low as earlier authors have tried to suggest. See also Kiem 1996.
[617] Roding 1993, p. 452.
[618] Kiem 1996. In this article on the weigh house of Haarlem, Karl Kiem tries to provide the proof that Lieven De

Key was indeed the designer in emulation of earlier authors such Galland, Eisler and Weissmann.
[619] See also Miedema 1980, in particular pp. 80-81 and Mc Gee 1991.

XIII. THE BLUE GATE IN LEIDEN (1599-1610)

Just like the Reformed Church in Willemstad and the weigh house in Haarlem, the history of the construction of the Blue Gate in Leiden is largely known.[620] Nevertheless, it is useful to trace the building history again. The building is one of the earliest surviving commissions of the young Coenraad IV van Neurenberg. Trained in his father's business, he was well versed in new developments in military architecture from an early age. Moreover, fortification building was a sector that demanded its practitioners keep abreast of the latest developments. Nevertheless, it is questionable whether young Coenraad could apply his knowledge of fortifications in practice. Although he was clearly involved in the renewal of the old Lopsen Gate in Leiden, it is impossible to determine to what extent he was actually responsible for the innovations this gate entailed.

The construction trade in Leiden around the year 1600

During the final years of the sixteenth century the town of Leiden grew quickly. Immigrants from the south relocated there, sometimes via a detour, and the manufacture of cloth increased strongly after the fall of Antwerp.[621] This flourishing is echoed by the development of Leiden's town building lodge. During these years the town had a town bricklayer, a town carpenter and a town stonemason. The official position of town stonemason was introduced in Leiden before Amsterdam or Haarlem.[622] The town building yard was also a professional company early in its existence. In 1553, the town purchased a piece of land on the site of what is currently Rapenburg 114. A shed was built there and a narrow canal bound the site where small vessels could (un)load materials and tools directly on site. At the close of the sixteenth century the town took over the care of bridges and streets and started to involve itself in the new construction of rampart walls, refuse collection etc.[623] In 1603, a new town workshop was laid out which was equipped with a saw mill. In 1612, the construction of a new town carpentry yard and accompanying tied house began on the Galgewater.[624]

The first town stonemason was Claes Cornelisz van Es. He was possibly the son of stonemason Cornelis Claesz, who restored the sacrament house of Leeuwenhorst monastery near Leiden in 1549. Town stonemason Claes Cornelisz entered the town's employ in 1578.[625] In 1592, his wages were increased to twenty stivers per day, which means he earned the same salary as Haarlem's town stonemason, Lieven de Key.[626] Claes Cornelisz from Leiden probably served the town of Leiden as stonemason until his death in 1612, so in 1608 he was still fulfilling his duties.[627] On 20 January 1620, eight years after his death, Pieter Pietersz de Neyn succeeded Cornelisz. De Neyn had worked at the stone cutting workshop before and was married to the widow of Willem Claesz van Es who had died

[620] Van Oerle 1975, pp. 344-347.

[621] Kooijmans 1995, p. 25.

[622] Ter Kuile 1938, p. 84 and Meischke 1997, p. 75.

[623] De Baar, Barendregt, Suurmond-van Leeuwen 1986, p. 8.

[624] Ibidem, p. 9.

[625] Ibidem.

[626] As early as 1578, the name Van Es also appears in the construction trade in Dordrecht, which was the year that Cornelis Jansz van Es joined the bricklayers' guild. His sons can also be found on the list of members of the Dordrecht bricklayers' guild. For example, Cornelis Cornelisz van Es joined the guild in June 1604. A year later in 1605 Jan Cornelisz van Es also became a member and in 1611 Teunis Cornelisz van Es. GAD, archief van Gilden en Confreriën; archief van het metselaarsgilde. Inv. nr. 669. The list runs from 1576, "scraped together with great effort from old documents which have now perished and been lost forever" (*met moeijte bij een versamelt uit de oude documenten die nu voor vergaen en eeuige verloren syn*).

[627] Ter Kuile 1938, p. 85.

in 1616, or stated more succinctly his predecessor's daughter-in-law. She was the daughter of Hendrick Cornelisz van Bilderbeeck, the town bricklayer.[628] Between 30 December 1624 and 22 January 1632, De Neyn was not employed as a stonemason nor was he active as one. It is believed that during these years he was active as a painter.[629]

Town stonemason Claes Cornelisz van Es

The town stonemason was primarily responsible for supplying the designs for the town and stonemasonry necessary for the designs. An example of such a delivery is the purchase of 400 feet of "white stone" in the year 1590, for the White Gate.[630] The stone was purchased from Frederick Ryckens in The Hague, probably in an unworked form.[631] Nevertheless, the work that the town administration commissioned during the town stonemason's period cannot necessarily be attributed to Claes Cornelisz van Es and Pieter Pietersz de Neyn. Because, as Ter Kuile and Meischke have already described, the services of Haarlem's Lieven de Key were also used.[632] The most well known example of his service is the construction of the town hall (Fig. 67).

67. Leiden, town hall. Anonymous drawing, around 1600 (GAL, Inv.Nr. P.V. 16.772).

On 8 January 1594, it was decided that Lieven de Key and a number of other master stone-masons were to be summoned and asked to make a design for the new town hall.[633] In August of the same year Lieven de Key had definitively been selected. De Key was responsible for making the designs, the patterns, but also the scantlings Bremen stone merchant, Lüder van Bentheim, used for the stone-masonry.[634] However, Van Bentheim was given a certain amount of leeway when it came to the details.

[628] Meischke 1997, p. 79.
[629] Ter Kuile 1938, p. 85.
[630] Probably Bentheimer sandstone.
[631] Ter Kuile 1938, p. 85.
[632] Meischke 1997, p. 77.

[633] Ter Kuile 1938, p. 85.
[634] The stone for the town hall is Obernkirchener or Bücke-burger sandstone; in spite of the stonemason in question having the confusing name 'Van Bentheim'.

Although Van Es had also made a design for the new facade of the town hall, he was passed over by his employer in favour of his colleague from Haarlem. He was, however, involved in the actual construction. On 24 August 1596, Cornelisz received two ship loads of sandstone from Bremen. Although stone supplier Lüder van Bentheim sent along two labourers in 1597, Cornelisz was involved in the construction as a coordinator supervising the building activities. It is unknown whether he had his own workshop.[635] This state of affairs was no exception. Lieven de Key was also responsible for the design of another construction commission, namely, the Gemeenlands House of Rijnland in Leiden.[636]

Coenraad IV van Neurenberg and Leiden

There are several options for the way in which Coenraad may have come into contact with Leiden's town administration. Van Neurenberg had fame and a large location in Dordrecht. Furthermore, in Haarlem he was responsible for the supply of stone for the weigh house. Due to the fact that that Coenraad had been to Haarlem several times it would have been natural for him to meet Lieven de Key. This supposition does not determine how particular contacts were exactly made, but the following will reveal how small the circle of important stonemasons and traders actually was. The same has been ascertained for the Willemstad Church where Coenraad III had contact with Adriaan de Muyr from Middelburg.

Another activity in Leiden reveals that Van Neurenberg tried to get the most from the situation. On the last page of the specifications for the Blue Gate, which is discussed below, there is a note which states that the town of Leiden notified the States General that, in order to reinforce and improve the town, it purchased and imported approximately 6,000 feet of Namur stone from Mr. Coenraad van Neurenberg.[637] The note states that Coenraad generally supplies sound work[638] and on 14 May 1602, the States General granted approval for the import of the stone.[639] This delivery once again underlines that the contacts Van Neurenberg maintained with a town such as Leiden were far from limited to architectural ones.

The Blue Gate

Contrary to the view in existing literature, Leiden's Blue Gate does not seem to have been built anew around 1600. In fact, the available data point more in the direction of an alteration and modernisation of the Lopsen or Oude Rijnsburger Gate, which dated back to approximately 1355 (Fig. 68).[640] The rare images of the old and new gate reveal a remarkable similarity. For example, the new gate retained the round towers on the inside of the gate, which had become an archaic feature in fortification building by 1600. The activities were limited to the beautification and modernisation of the gatehouse, with the probable retention of the medieval core during this process.[641]

---

[635] Albrecht 1997, p. 71. The two labourers Van Bentheim sent were Albert and Hans Rotvelt. p. 72.

[636] Meischke 1997, p. 57. He received 75 pounds for this work.

[637] SAL, Verhuring en Bestedingsboek C fol 217, 10 March 1603. Inv. No. 1384, c. 1599-1606, 30 November. Last page of the specifications. ... *de quantiteyt van omtrent vi m voeten blaeuwen naemschen steen.*

[638] Ibidem. [...] *alsoe Meester Coenraad gewoonlick zijn tot vorderingen van deugelijke wercken.*

[639] Ibidem. [...] *den blaeuwen steen* [...] *gevoert in deze landen zullen mogen doen brengen.*

[640] Lambrechtsen-Van Essen 1994, p. 23.

[641] A small archaeological observation exists which dates back to sewer work carried out in the 1980s. Only a very small part of the foundations were exposed at this time. The gate has never been excavated and there is no floor plan available. Friendly notification by Maarten Dolmans, Leiden Municipal Archaeologist, 4 September 1998.

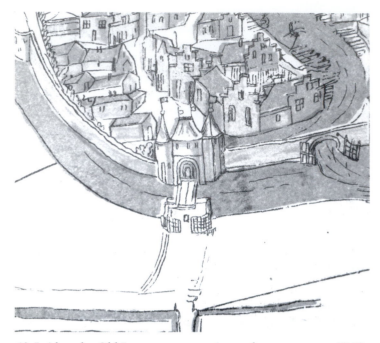

68. Leiden, the Old Lopsen gate on a sixteenth-century map (GAL, inv. nr. P.V. 951, 1a).

DE BLAEUWE POORT   C. Hagen fecit.

69. Leiden, Blue Gate from the landside. Engraving by Chr. Hagen, 1675 (GAL, Inv.Nr. P.V. 8-3202).

The gate was strategically located and after the 1574 siege it had been equipped with a half bastion with a half moon-shaped bridge in front of it. A few years later it was decided that the gatehouse also needed to be modernised. This building was to replace the old gate and was to join with the existing wall houses. Walls encircled the bastion in front of it.[642] After Coenraad van Neurenberg the younger had made a pattern for the new gate, the construction of the gate was left to Cornelis Egbertsz, the town carpenter. Jan Ottensz van Seyst succeeded him in 1604. Jacob Dircksz supervised the brickwork and Hendrick Cornelisz van Bilderbeeck succeeded him in 1603.

Mayor Johan van Gael's son laid the first stone on 26 August 1602. The demolition of the old medieval tower, probably the centrally located main mass of the old gate, had started in March of that year. A cartographical source from 1675 shows that the two round medieval towers on either side of the main building were retained in the new gate (Fig. 69). The laying of the first stone for the new gate should therefore not be taken literally. It was a symbolic laying, more to indicate the start of the activities than actually being the first stone of a new building.[643] In May timber had been transported to the site in order to build dams to dry out the site pit. In July and August the demolition of the old work was completed and new foundations were laid.

Taking on stone work

The stonework was tendered and executed separately. The specifications, most probably made by Van Neurenberg, provided for "good, blue genuine Namur stone". Coenraad's design, which consisted of the specifications, floor plan and patterns, was available for perusal at the town hall. Those that had submitted bids could consult the plans and determine the price they wished to charge for supplying and placing the work.[644] In total there were four bids submitted. The people who submitted tenders were:

[642] Van Oerle 1975, p. 344 makes the following cryptic statement on this matter: "The town was entered across the axially projected bridge through a gate in the walls, via the site of the old bastion now made virtually symmetrical, through the main gate" (*Over de nu axiaal geprojecteerde brug kwam men*

door een poort in de ommuring, via het terrein van het oude, nu nagenoeg symmetrisch gemaakte bastion, door de hoofdpoort de stad binnen).
[643] De Vries 1994a, Chapter 3.3.
[644] Van Oerle 1975, p. 344.

Mr. Coenraad van Neurenberg, for 11,000 guilders
Andries de Valckenier from Middelburg, for 13,500, 13,000 and 12,800 guilders
Cornelis Roelandtsz from Delft, for 9,900 guilders
Jeroen Gerytz, from Leiden, for 11,000 guilders

The original call for bids on 10 March 1603 offered 7,000 guilders for the work. No one intended to undertake it for such a low sum, so this amount was raised by a hundred guilders at a time, until it reached 8,000. Still no one was interested. Because the figure kept growing, thereby increasing the town's costs, the sum was now raised ten guilders at a time until it reached 9,000 guilders. Still no one wanted the job. The next series of price increases were five guilders a time and continued until eventually one of those present thought the sum so reasonable that he was prepared to supply the prescribed work for that figure.[645] It was Cornelis Roelandtsz from Delft who raised his hand and took the job on for the sum of 9,900 guilders. The incremental increases stopped and those present were polled to see if anyone else was willing to undertake the work for the same figure. Obviously someone did, as Cornelis Roelandtsz was obliged to drop his price and ultimately undertook the work for 9,700 guilders.[646]

Cornelis was received at the town hall the following morning with his guarantors Joris Rochet, a merchant from Dordrecht who also acted as supplier for the stone, and Jeroen Gerytz, the fourth person to have put in an offer. The guarantees were to give the local administrators the guarantee that Cornelis would indeed supply the work for the agreed sum and that the work would be of good quality. Jeroen Gerytz promised to provide credentials within eight days. A citizen of Leiden who was known as reliable, was his guarantor. On 15 March the mayors, aldermen and councillors of the town of Dordrecht stated that Joris Rochet was known as an honest merchant who owned immovable property and who, to the full satisfaction of the district water authority, had supplied blue stone for the lock in the Alblasserwaard. Bailiff, mayors and aldermen of Delft declared that Cornelis Roelandtsz was the son-in-law of the former town master bricklayer and had, in 1600 and 1602, supplied the hard stone work for the new ammunitions dump and for the Hoornbridge in Rijswijk to their full satisfaction. Rochet may have been the actual supplier of the stone in this instance too.

The delivery

The total value of the stone was 4,000 guilders and Rochet was to receive this sum. He had the stone readied for transport at the quarry, which was relatively simple. In July 1603, the town administration asked the States General for permission to import Namur stone free of import duties, which was granted by an act dated 24 July 1603.

The stone was supplied in two shipments. The first, which amounted to eleven feet and ten inches, arrived before March 1604. The rest was delivered before the end of June 1604. The town provided the transport of the stone to the site. The stone probably remained on the town's dock for some time because the carpenter was still building the scaffolding outside the Rijnsburger Gate, which was where the stone was to go in 1605.

The building contractor had more responsibility than just supplying the stone. For example, he had to make two professionals available when necessary to help place the blocks. These two were to receive wages amounting to twenty-two stivers per working day, which indicates that they were not foremen, but specialised staff. The building contractor's salary came in four instalments.

---

[645] Ibidem, pp. 344-345.

[646] Ibidem, p. 345.

The town paid Rochet and not Cornelis Roelandtsz. On 20 March 1605, he received 1,200 guilders and on 16 April another 1,225 guilders. The money was for the first deliveries of blue stone and sixty-five days' wages.[647] On 23 May 1606 Rochet received his last instalment amounting to 1,425 guilders, which means that in total he had received 3,850 guilders. Around this time problems began developing at the construction site. Although work continued on cutting the stone to size, the original building contractor Cornelis Roelandtsz was no longer involved. He had handed the work over to Joris Rochet, who failed to finish the work for the agreed sum.[648] Joris Rochet submitted a request for an additional 3,000 guilders referring to the long duration of the work, the heavier and more expensive execution, and the more experienced and more expensive staff necessary for the placement at the construction site; all of which had cost more than anticipated.

A committee was formed on 27 October 1608 to assess the request, which included, alongside a number of municipal representatives, town master carpenter Jan Ottensz van Seyst, town stonemason Claes Cornelisz van Es and town bricklayer Hendrick van Bilderbeeck. Thanks to their personal involvement in the construction of the new gate they were able to adequately assess the situation. The judgement was that the work had been made larger and had been executed to a more technically skilled level than described in the specifications. The town masters stated that they assumed that if Van Neurenberg had been the building contractor he would have also executed the work better.[649] The improvements primarily concerned the anchoring and the delivery of new globes, which had proved too small in comparison to the work. In the end, the additional work was determined to be worth 1,800 guilders, which was further increased by two hundred guilders when the town took over the remaining stone.

Town stonemason Claes Cornelisz van Es' role was comparable to his role during the construction of the town hall. It was his task to take care of a large part of the construction. He supervised the placement by his own staff assisted by two of Rochet's labourers. Simultaneously he also coordinated the work and maintained contact with Rochet in Dordrecht.[650]

The speed with which the stonework was finished determined the construction's progress. Stone had to be anchored and incorporated into the brick wall. Incidentally, it was possible for this work to be done at a later time. But as seen in the case in Sittard, the delay would incur additional costs, increase the difficulties and augment the risks to the building.

Work began on the facades in 1607. A carpenter had made temporary wooden supports for the construction of the vaults a year earlier and in 1607 he started making the roof, which was placed between 23 January and 6 February 1610. In July he was still working on the gate's loft. The bricklayer finished work on 19 July 1610.

The stonework was finished earlier on 28 September 1609. Van Bilderbeeck, Van Seyst and Rochet came to measure and deliver the stonework. In March 1610 the lead was brought to the site and in August the slates were delivered.

The specifications

The specification for the stonework for the Blue Gate in Leiden is a unique document (Fig. 70). It consists of seven printed pages and is the oldest Dutch example of a printed specification made with the intention of circulating it among building contractors. Building contractors from various towns actually used the document during the bid process.

---

[647] The stone/labour ratio is unknown.
[648] It is disputable whether the transfer was a matter of incapacity or a business deal.

[649] Van Oerle 1975, p. 347: [...] *voor zeker houden, dat zo hij, van Noerenberch, aannemer waer geweest, hij 't werc nieuwers naer zo rijckelicken ende onbecrompen en zoude hebben vollevert.*
[650] Ibidem.

De Burgermeesterey ende
Regierders der stadt Ley-
dey iy Hollant, Willey opt
Volgende bestec, mitsgaders
dey gront ende de patrooney
daer bay gemaect, ende opt
Raedthuys der Voorschre-
bey Stede berustende, al
Waer de zelbe elc eeney, des begeerende, zulley Wer-
dey Vertoont, bestedey tWerckey bay het hard steen-
Werc bay der Voorschrebey Stede Reynsburger
poorte, ende dat bay goedey blacuWey onberbalsch-
tey, ofte onberispelickey Naemschey steey, zoWaer,
dick, diep, ende hooch, als hier naer Volcht, gestelt
by Rijnlantsche Voetey, daer bay de tWaelf makey
eey roede, duymey ende greyney naer beloop bay diey.
Om tWelc naerder te Verstaey, is eey halbey Voet
berdeelt aey zijy zes duymey, ooc eendeels aey greyney, optey cant hier beneffens gestelt.

Eerst is tgantsche Werc iy zijney gront opter
aerdey, breet tey Oostey zessenbijstich Voetey, tey
Westey tWeenderticg Voetey, Vier duymey de
Zuyt-Vleugel zessentWintich Voetey: de Noort-
Vleugel xxij. Voetey: de Zuytzijde, mitsgaders de
Noortzijde, elc xxiij. Voetey, bj duymey

De poortey, zo buytey als binney, Wijt tiey Voetey, Vier duymey: hoocg het recht-staende, elf Voetey, tiey duymey: Daer op geslagey eey boocg bay

A   eey

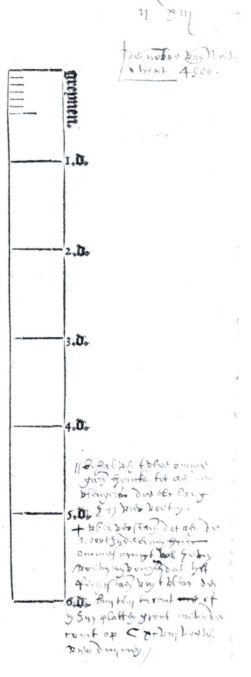

70. Leiden, Blue Gate. First page of the printed specifications for the stonework (GAL, Sa.2, nr. 1384).

The question of who authored the specifications for the Blue Gate is crucial. It seems to have been Coenraad IV van Neurenberg. The sources refer to a statement that states Coenraad devised and drew the pattern for the gate.[651] The problem with the term pattern is that it can be used to refer to both the total design and working drawings, which belong to the specifications.[652] Furthermore, there is the fact that only the specifications remain, which deal with the stonework and activities Van Neurenberg could execute. The same situation applies to other projects. The specifications for Averbode, Zutphen, Amsterdam and Willemstad all only pertain to Van Neurenberg's activities.

Questioning whether Van Neurenberg is also responsible for drafting the timber specifications is the next logical step and to this inquiry a negative response can be given with almost complete certainty; many examples are extant of carpenters drafting timber specifications.[653] The material, the techniques and the terminology are so different that drafting timber specifications demands great specialisation, which Van Neurenberg almost certainly did not possess. It can virtually be ruled out that he was responsible for drafting these specifications. After all, if the drawing up of a stone specification and of a timber specification was done by two separate specialists, then this means that the specification stage of the preparations lies beyond the design stage. In other words: the flat design is turned into a technical description, which can be executed by someone other than the designer.

In the Blue Gate's case there is therefore no certainty concerning the question whether Van Neurenberg was the designer or not. Meischke has pointed out the possibility that Coenraad might also have been responsible for the design of the Vlissingen Gate in Middelburg, because of parallels with Leiden.[654] On the basis of the above argument this supposition seems hard to prove. It is far from certain that Van Neurenberg was responsible for the making of architectural designs and so, attributions on the basis of suppositions such as these are exceedingly uncertain.[655]

Although there is nothing left in Leiden of the Blue Gate bar its name, it is nevertheless possible to gain an impression of the building thanks to the stone specification and a number of iconographical sources. The specifications start with the description of the gate's floor plan. It then deals with the width and height of the gate and details the various stone parts. The text also refers to drawings intended to clarify the description. Unfortunately, these drawings are not extant. The result is that not all the descriptions are clear enough to enable a full reconstruction of the Blue Gate. The floor plan has a few unclear aspects, but other parts can be reconstructed, like the pilasters described in the specifications. The structural elements listed: plinth, base, pilaster pieces and capital provide insight into the ratios used.

The stipulations enclosed in the specifications also deserve attention. For example, with regard to the delivery it was determined that the town would bear the cost of unloading the stone. The town could reject qualitatively unsound stones or badly worked ones, and the building contractor would then have to supply new ones. If this supply did not take place on time, the town would do so at the building contractor's expense.[656] As far as the schedule was concerned, it was later stipulated that the building contractor would be exempt from prosecution if he could prove that the work lay ready in the quarry and had no deficiencies, but circumstances hampered traffic on the Meuse. This note undoubtedly has to do with the blockade of the Meuse in 1599-1602. Merchants could not guarantee their own unhampered passage, and so the delivery of material could be prevented through no fault of their own.

---

[651] Ibidem, p. 344.
[652] Haslinghuis-Janse 1997, p. 348.
[653] Janse 1989, p. 333ff.
[654] Meischke 1997, p. 83.
[655] Ibidem, p. 78.

[656] SAL, Verhuring en Bestedingsboek C fol 217: [...] *ende zo hy zulx niet tijts genouch en dede, dat de Gecommitteerden alhier gelijcke andere stucken zullen doen behouwen, tot coste ende last vanden aennemer, ten eynde twerck, ter zaecke van dien, niet en werde verhindert, of verachtert.*

Approximately twenty years after the construction of the Blue Gate, Leiden was expanded westwards and the gate ended up within the new walls and lost its function. It was demolished in 1735. There are a small number of known depictions (Fig. 71),[657] but no design drawings or surveys remain. The only contemporary drawing is the specifications drawing of the gate's small tower, which will not be dealt with here. The Blue Gate's sandstone reliefs are all that remain of the edifice and can currently be seen in Museum de Lakenhal.[658]

★

Conclusion Part II

The construction trade underwent extensive change during the period 1570-1610, in particular with regard to the organisation of construction projects. In contrast with the situation at the start of the sixteenth century, the various building trades and activities were subdivided even further. The emergence of the town fabric lodges can be seen as one of the principal factors. The independent companies, stonemasons, carpenters, etc., were increasingly employed as specialists, while the town

71. Leiden, Blue Gate from the landside. Engraving by Abraham Rademaker, early eighteenth century. Detail (GAL, Inv.Nr. P.V. 9-3202).

administration organised the project itself. This specialisation is also expressed in the organisation of the design and the bidding process, and in the use of specifications and drawings.[659] The old medieval system, which relied on the survey and estimation of the executed work by peers, disappeared, to be replaced by a bidding process, where the patron attempted to secure in advance the negotiation of the best price. Only in the case of very serious conflicts did arbitration occur during or after the construction process.

Research into the activities of the Van Neurenberg family confirms this impression. Moreover, the research reveals that the Meuse Valley, the family's ancestral home, managed to realise its aim of supplying stone to the west of the Northern Low Countries. The changes in the construction trade, and the weakening of the stone trade in Brabant, contributed to the flourishing of the Namur stone trade. Additional factors included the increasing demand for Namur stone from the hydraulic-engineering sector and the cartel building of the Meuse captains. This group of at least thirty merchants was tightly organised and maintained professional and personal contacts from their base in Dordrecht. The contacts between traders found in sources were not coincidental, but are the result of conscious marriage and trading policies. These policies contributed to the fact that the Namur stone traders, and in a larger context the Meuse captains managed to create a unified front, which allowed them to get a foothold in Dordrecht. The market was then expanded west from there.

---

[657] Huisman 1986, p. 43. Besides *De kwakzalvers* [the quacks] by Gerard Dou, Pelinck 1949 mentions a copper engraving by C. Hagen from 1675 and an engraving by J. Hennebo from 1668, a drawing by Van de Velde in the GAL and a painting by Van Beerstraten in the Rijksmuseum.

[658] Pelinck 1949, pp. 119-122.
[659] See Van den Heuvel 1991 and Gerritsen 1997 for the use of drawings in the construction process.

Part III

1609–1650: The Era of Major Commissions

XIV. THE REPUBLIC AFTER 1609

Continuing expansion

The decision by a number of Meuse Valley trading families to relocate to Holland in 1585 proved to be a prudent move. Holland was on the brink of what would later be referred to as the Golden Age, an era of unparalleled wealth and prosperity which offered countless opportunities for an ambitious, specialised mercantile house with the right contacts. The growth and modernisation of society, which had started in the sixteenth century, continued in the seventeenth. The population of the Northern Low Countries increased from approximately 1.2 million around 1550 to approximately 1.9 million in 1650 under the influence of the immigration from the south and the flourishing economy.[660] In less than a century, Amsterdam's appearance underwent drastic changes. The population rose from 60,000 to 200,000, building heights increased, the town's size tripled. The land reclamation, which started in the sixteenth century, reached its zenith during the first half of the seventeenth century thanks to, among other things, technical innovations and the use of windmills. The more the population grew, the more the demand for food and utility crops intensified. Reclaimed land, therefore, provided good returns for the increasing amount of money circulating after 1600.[661] Simultaneously, industrialisation expanded. Industrial windmills which, until approximately 1550 had primarily been concentrated in Flemish towns such as Ghent, Bruges and Antwerp, were now used in Holland.[662]

Another consequence of the growing population was the expansion of the town, which took place numerous times during the seventeenth century. The extensions of Amsterdam are famous, but Leiden, Utrecht and Haarlem also underwent expansion.[663] Holland's high level of urbanisation, which increased from 44% to 62% between 1520 and 1670, was partly responsible for this expansion.[664] Other parts of the Northern Low Countries were also experiencing growth, although in a much more gradual manner.[665] The economic boom of the Northern Low Countries was expressed in countless ways. The founding of the *Verenigde Oostindische Compagnie* (Dutch East India Company), the V.O.C. in 1602 and the Amsterdam exchange in 1611 are a few examples of this expression (Fig. 72). Increasing production capacity, the relatively calm national politics and Holland's favourable location enabled the country to capitalise on the expanding international demand for products. Dutch trade fared well due to the fact that its foreign competitors were often riddled with internal strife.[666]

72. Amsterdam, exchange designed by Hendrick de Keyser. Painting by painter/architect Philips Vingboons, 1634 (GAA, Inv.Nr. D 36780 – N 11211).

The increasing specialisation in the construction trade, also applied to other sectors of industry. For example, herring fishing had become an independent industry during the sixteenth century and in 1612 whaling became one. The Committee for industrial fisheries had been set up in 1567 as an interest group to defend the fishing industry's

[660] Groenveld, Schutte 1992, p. 103.
[661] De Vries, Van der Woude 1995.
[662] Jurgens 2000, pp. 202-203.
[663] Taverne 1978, pp. 117-398.

[664] Groenveld, Schutte 1992, p. 104.
[665] Ibidem, p. 105.
[666] Ibidem, pp. 109-110.

interests.[667] Agriculture and livestock farming were also specialising. Farmers were starting to concentrate on lucrative utility crops and livestock farming, whilst less profitable activities were outsourced. These secondary activities subsequently developed into independent trades, a process which started in the sixteenth century and would continue until after 1670. Seventeenth-century industry reveals the start of a flow of goods from the towns to rural areas.[668] Although the internationalisation of trade was on the rise, old local structures were still maintained. The guilds did not lose their status until the end of the eighteenth century and immigrants who moved north during the sixteenth century could expect to become members of a guild.[669]

Leiden and Haarlem were the principal industrial centres besides Amsterdam. As far as shipbuilding was concerned Rotterdam, Edam and Hoorn were also of importance. However, their position as shipbuilding towns decreased in the first half of the seventeenth century as the Zaan region became predominant.

The export area expanded dramatically as a result of this intensification of trading contacts. Many cases concerned transhipment goods or goods in transit, but simultaneously there was an increase in foreign industrial activity. The export of national products increased and, as a result, Dutch merchants started relocating abroad for longer or shorter periods of time in order to set up a business or a branch.[670] In addition to overseas trading posts, which were systematically visited by V.O.C. ships from the start of the seventeenth century, Scandinavia and the Baltic were of great importance. For example, an average of 60% of all ships that passed the straights between Sweden and Denmark, the Sound, between 1580 and 1670 were of Dutch provenance. During the years 1611-1620 this percentage actually increased to 70%.[671]

The Twelve Years Truce (1609-1621) was of great significance to the development of this international trade. During this period of calm the foundations for the economic prosperity of the seventeenth century were laid. Although there were internal conflicts within the Republic, Prince Maurits attempted to increase unity between the states.[672] After 1621 the war abroad was resumed. Increased levies were implemented along the major rivers, which made trade with the south more difficult.[673] Although Spinola captured Breda in 1625 the tide was turning and the fortunes of war smiled upon the Dutch. Prince Maurits' successor, his half-brother Frederik Hendrik, achieved a number of impressive victories such as the captures of 's-Hertogenbosch (1629), Venlo, Roermond and Maastricht (1632). A pivotal portion of the battle was naval. Although Dunkirk raiders won major victories between 1626 and 1633, countless victories by the Republic counterbalanced these defeats, such as Piet Hein's taking of the Spanish bullion armada in 1628, which filled the Prince's war coffers and financed his building fund.

Construction during the seventeenth century: the town building lodge

The development outlined in Part II of this study regarding the town building lodge continued in the period after 1609. A long line of town master masons, town carpenters and town bricklayers would begin to dominate construction during the seventeenth century. The most well-known names were Hendrick de Keyser, Cornelis II Danckerts, Hendrik Staets and Daniël Stalpaert in Amsterdam, Arent van 's-Gravesande (Leiden and Middelburg), Willem van der Helm (Leiden), Claes Jeremiasz Persoons (Rotterdam), to name a few.[674]

---

667 Ibidem, pp. 112-113.
668 Ibidem, p. 111.
669 GAD, Archief van gilden en confrerieën, archief van het metselaarsgilde [Archive of guilds and confraternities, archive of the bricklayer's guild].
670 Well-known examples are the Trip and De Geer families. See Klein 1965 and Lindblad 1995 passim.

671 Groenveld, Schutte 1992, pp. 117-118.
672 Ibidem, pp. 214-215.
673 Ibidem, p. 216.
674 Vermeulen 1938, passim. See Van Essen 2000 for more on Stalpaert.

The town craftsmen were employed for longer periods of time and depending on their contract they also carried out commissions for third parties. An essential element of their activities is that they were the principal group to implement architectural innovations. The town stonemasons combined technical and structural knowledge with aesthetically innovative designs. Simultaneously, the separation of trades continued, at least as far as it was functional. The guilds, which determined who would design buildings, seem to have played only a minimal role in the west of the Northern Low Countries during the seventeenth century. This lack of involvement led to carpenters like Staets also designing entire buildings, which is clearly shown by the *Kroniek van Staets*.[675] Willem van der Helm also supplied complete designs. Simultaneously however, the separation between the trades continued to exist; for example, when Staets and De Keyser straightened the old Amsterdam town hall in 1601 or when they built the new armoury hall in 1605, they both represented their individual trades only.[676] In contrast to the preceding century, when stone merchant was, still more or less, synonymous with master mason and designer, the town fabric lodge's masters had now entirely assumed the latter two positions. The town fabric lodge masters did not solely occupy themselves with town construction activities; their influence reached a great deal further as they were also active in ecclesiastic and private architecture.

Their influence had major consequences for the stone trade: in contrast to prior practices, contact between the merchant and the actual patron diminished. Instead it was now important to have good contacts with the town craftsmen, who coordinated construction. The town stonemasons now had a larger say in the purchase of stone. They acted as experts par excellence who also controlled materials purchases. As seen earlier, Lieven de Key had his own stone company; the same applied to Joost Jansz Bilhamer and Hendrick de Keyser in Amsterdam.[677] Later in the seventeenth century a ban would be issued against town masters having their own trading company in combination with their public position.

Other principals and builders. Court and architects

In addition to changes in the organisation of the municipal building, changes also occurred in the society's class system. Moreover, with the demise of the clergy a new elite developed, emerging from the class of merchants and guild masters. At the start of the sixteenth century, members of the Van Neurenberg family were higher on the social ladder than the average stonemason. Their social superiority was seen in their business activities: they employed other people; they had financial power, which enabled them to pre-finance activities; they had contacts among the highest circles in society; and their services garnered high remuneration. The family's position eventually enabled it to join the ranks of the urban upper class or elite. In the seventeenth century merchants often swapped their trading activities in favour of public administration tasks (which could be a financial boon) whilst family members overtook their trading interests, often using the former's money.[678] This tendency will become apparent when the later descendants of the Van Neurenberg family eventually left the stone trade.

For the time being however, it was not only the merchants' social status, which changed, but also the patrons' social status as well. One of the most conspicuous changes concerns the position of the court of Nassau. There was a long period during which the court in the Northern Low Countries

---

[675] Meischke 1994, pp. 104–106.
[676] Ibidem, pp. 102–104.

[677] See Van Tussenbroek 2001b, pp. 467–469 for more on Bilhamer's stone trade.
[678] Groenveld, Schutte 1992, p. 143.

had no court culture. This situation changed under Frederik Hendrik, who was partly educated at the French court. The construction projects he ordered included the prestigious palaces Ter Nieuburg and Honselaarsdijk. It is in these palaces, which many famous builders and architects built, where French influences first appeared.[679] After Hendrick de Keyser and Lieven de Key's generation, a new series of master masons came to the forefront, of which Pieter Post and Jacob van Campen are the most well-known.[680] The principal architectural designers did not have roots in the construction trade. Painters or designers with a background in painting increasingly supplied architectural designs,[681] which, in certain cases, entailed the actual builders converting the design drawings into stone and timber specifications. This approach was already anticipated at the close of the sixteenth century. However, this impression is not unequivocal. Pieter Post drafted his own specifications, although he had also been trained as a painter.[682] The separation of designer and executing party also occurs in aristocratic and civil construction projects.[683]

The construction organisation

The engagement of a painter-designer or a separation between design and execution cannot immediately be explained as a major change to the construction trade. The shifts the trade underwent were subtle. Various activities and methods of organisation continued to co-exist for decades, which were dependent on the construction project, the patron and the designers, master masons and building contractors involved.

The town fabric lodges made use of the private sector when needed.[684] The same applied for the increasing group of independent patrons, who also turned to the private sector for their design and construction projects. Essential for an independent entrepreneur was the position he managed to occupy within the network of patrons. For example, in the stone trade it was important to be able to guarantee a continuous supply of materials. The Van Neurenberg family solved this problem by having a continuous presence on the southern market that purchased bulk shipments of Namur stone and marble for them. By manoeuvring themselves into the right position they managed to maintain the demand for stone here. The more important the potential patron was, the more attractive the contract became. Various merchants employed this principle, which resulted in the concentration of a number of merchants in Amsterdam. The importance of the relationship with designers needs no explanation. A good example are the two facades Claes Ariaens supplied for Pieter Jansz Sweelinck in 1641 on the Rokin (Oude Turfmarkt) at No. 145-147. Claes was to arrange for the manufacture of the stone parts required for both facades, which had been designed by Philips Vingboons.[685] Vingboons drew and calculated the parts down to the smallest detail.[686] To what extent Master Claes was a mere link in the entire process is proven by a part of the contract, which stipulates that he was to make the work in such a

---

[679] Ottenheym 1997, pp. 105-106.
[680] Terwen, Ottenheym 1993 and Ottenheym 1995.
[681] Concerning painter architects: Ottenheym 1999b. There are also sixteenth-century examples of painters supplying architectural designs, such as Lanceloot Blondeel or Jan van Scorel.
[682] An example of a design and specification by Pieter Post is the water gate in Willemstad. Willem van der Helm also combined designs and specifications, as was the case with the Morspoort in Leiden.
[683] The aristocracy, which was losing ground, tried to maintain its status in the seventeenth century and did so by embel-

lishing, converting and adapting their family castles. Furthermore, we see a tendency among the wealthy patriciate to move to their country seats. Initially these were just rooms on estate farms, but quite soon a demand developed for proper country homes or *buitens*, which became expressions of the latest architectural developments. Olde Meierink 1997, pp. 146-148.
[684] See Sander-Berke 1995, Chapter III.
[685] Ottenheym 1989, p. 82.
[686] GAA NA 423-351 and NA 424-400. Not. J. Jacobs. 11 October 1641. See also Van Dillen 1974, pp. 317-319.

way that there would be no unclear points for a master carpenter or master bricklayer, and that their work was to suffer no delays as a consequence of his inaccuracies. If this contingency should occur, then Claes himself would have to cover the expense.[687]

It should be clear that contact between patron and stone supplier generally came about through the designer. The patron was, more often than not, an outsider in the construction trade, and an architect or building contractor would coordinate his construction project. It was therefore important for independent stonemasons to maintain good relations with this emerging group of architects. By the same token, architects would prefer to cooperate with craftsmen and merchants who could realise their designs in the best way possible, and so the quality of the supplied parts definitely played a role.

Constructional practice and architectural theory

From the sixteenth century on the influence of architecture and construction theories also increased along with construction practice. During the seventeenth century architectural theorists had little to do with actual construction practice as opposed to the sixteenth century, when there was still a direct link between theory and practice. Charles De Beste was an example of this direct link.[688] De Beste was a master mason who occupied a prominent position in the Bruges bricklayers' and stonemasons' guild.[689] Book Five of his treatise *De Architectura* from 1599 deals with *architectura* in emulation of Coecke van Aelst. In the spirit of Vitruvius, building materials and the selection of the healthiest sites for homes are discussed.[690] De Beste combined architectural-theoretical considerations with practical problems, such as how one should prepare *Arduyn* (cut stone) to make a stone bridge open in the middle.[691] Although the manuscript was, for the most part, based on existing architectural treatises, De Beste's text has a strong practical side. The influence of theoretical works on craftsmen's daily practice should not be overestimated; most craftsmen were occupied with matters that required little theoretical grounding, such as the supply of materials, bricklaying and carpentry.[692]

Fortifications builder and mathematician Simon Stevin did not involve himself with construction theory. He paid attention to construction techniques based on a theoretical, and not immediately practical, interest. And so practice and theory diverged. Typical of these developments are the considerations of Isaac Beeckman, another theoretician, who founded the *Collegium mechanicum* in Rotterdam in 1626, but dissolved it again after approximately ten years. The *Collegium* was aimed at gaining insight into the workings of physics, and to provide new technological solutions or try to solve everyday conundrums. Among other things, the *Collegium* consisted of a surveyor, a merchant, a mill builder, a carpenter and a silk weaver. However, Beeckman himself soon became sceptical, "While people discussed one after the other matter, I thought to myself: We are now discussing mills, in which we have no practical knowledge; how can we then do something good in this field [...] unless we take on solely this activity and work on it diligently for years? Because if we want to help the smiths, the carpenters, the bricklayers, etc. it will be a labour without end and we cannot do it perfectly."[693]

---

[687] Van Dillen 1974, p. 318. An example from 1649 proves that such compensations were occassionally claimed. On 25 June of that year, Romeyn de Hoge protested against a stonemason who had not stuck to the design when carrying out the facade work for his house Het Wapen van Hamburg. Van Dillen 1974, p. 531.

[688] For more on De Beste, see Van den Heuvel 1994, pp. 65-93 and Van den Heuvel 1995, pp. 11-24.

[689] Van den Heuvel 1995, p. 12.

[690] Ibidem, p. 15.

[691] Ibidem, pp. 16-7.

[692] Ibidem, p. 20.

[693] Quoted in Van den Heuvel 1994, p. 8.

Beeckman's comments provide a clear illustration of the problems, but everyone did not support his view. Simon Stevin, for example, had already written on technical matters such as mortar compositions or stucco, but his outsider status is also noticeable. The intellectual objective to integrate architecture into a theoretical system, invariably encounters practical problems. The lack of detailed practical knowledge of all crafts did not, however, stop Stevin from seeking and finding practical solutions for certain problems, such as those in the field of hydraulic-engineering or house building.[694]

At the close of the seventeenth century architectural theory was also gaining importance. In his *Algemeenen Huysbouw* Willem Goeree (1635-1711) presented God as a great master mason.[695] Because houses, neighbourhoods and towns were not created at the same time as the world, God appointed man as His sub-master mason. The following quote reveals the potential moral accountability for which master masons could be held, "A certain merchant in Amsterdam whose servant had made one of his servant girls pregnant, wished to send the child immediately as an apprentice to the master mason, because he had built their bedrooms too close together."[696] So the master mason was also blamed for the servant girl becoming pregnant, because he had built their rooms in too close a proximity. Perhaps Goeree overestimated the power of earthly master masons in this case. However, he was simultaneously very critical of contemporary as well as of older architecture. He was also critical of the manner in which this architecture had been written about in the past, "Very little has been written concerning general house building and almost too much on the five orders."[697] He also appealed to Amsterdam's administrators not only to enrich the town with new works, but also to carefully maintain the existing buildings. He also entreated them to not just have an eye for the beautiful buildings, but also to remember the less prestigious ones, just like Salomon de Bray had done.[698] Apparently such exhortations were necessary. Goeree also dealt with the characteristics of a good house. He emphasised climate control, layout, light and smoke extraction. He was very critical of houses from the past. Their layout made him wonder "whether people had their eyes in their neck or their sense in their elbows" as the houses had no courtyards.

One may wonder to what extent treatises such as that of Stevin or Goeree actually influenced construction practices in the Low Countries. The influence of treatises has been ascertained with regard to innovation in architecture and the dissemination of examples. Changes to building practices under the influence of such works were however, an entirely different matter. These books seem to have primarily been intended for dilettantes and were not to be used as practical manuals. The same actually applies to the stonemason's trade. There is scant evidence that these texts caused any actual changes. It is only indirectly that their influence can be felt in stonemasons' practice: it penetrated chiefly through the changing design principles.

The design process

Design developed from an activity integrated into the construction process into a separate specialisation. People like Lieven de Key and Hendrick de Keyser were still rooted in sixteenth-century tradition and were, in many cases, responsible for both the architectural design and the stonemasonry. When important seventeenth-century design commissions are examined, it turns out that these increas-

---

[694] Ibidem, p. 8.
[695] Van den Heuvel 1997, p. 161, note 36. From: W. Goeree, *d'Algemeene Bouwkunde. Volgens d'Antyke en Hedendaagse manier* [General architecture. According to methods both contemporary and from Classical Antiquity]. Amsterdam, 1681, p. 4.

[696] Ibidem, p. 166.
[697] Ibidem, p. 154.
[698] Ibidem, p. 164.

ingly ended up in the hands of painter-architects or master masons, stonemasons, etc. who subsequently did not execute the construction. Due to specific demand from the towns and patrons, a differentiation occurred in the constructing trade, complete with drawings, specifications and partial commissions.

However, there is a change in the design principles used. The Italian influences, which arrived in the Low Countries in the sixteenth century, were initially applied without necessarily understanding the context.[699] However, the more Palladio, Scamozzi and other people's theories became common practice, the more the influence of theoretically grounded designers increased.[700] The influences of Vredeman de Vries and Coecke van Aelst characterised design at the end of the sixteenth century. Primarily ARCHITECTURA, oder der Bauung der Antiquen auss dem Vitruvius by Vredeman de Vries, which was published in 1577, offered a large number of variations for facade compositions and was also used a great deal by sculptors and architects.[701] This increasing influence of printed examples on architectural design resulted in a certain amount of theorising, which was expressed by the publication of theoretical books on the application of column orders such as those of Bosboom and Vermaarsch.[702]

However, it was the immediate referral to classical authors that led to a stricter application of the classical architectural canon. The study of Vitruvius, in particular, took off and had a noticeable influence on a number of structures.[703] This change was possible because from the mid-sixteenth century the influence of painters, fortifications builders, sculptors, engineers and others had increased. Specifically painters would determine the upper echelon of architects during the seventeenth century, as evidenced by the success of De Bray, Post, Van Campen and Vingboons. They created a new architecture in the Northern Low Countries through the strict application of classical orders, ratio and measurement systems. The painters' background demanded that they be aware of the rules of classical architecture in order to incorporate it into their paintings. But it was not only the application of classical Vitruvian design principles that was important, knowledge of surveying, strength calculation, etc. was also essential.[704]

The previous discussion makes it clear that the descendants of the Van Neurenberg family cannot be placed within the theoretical architects' tradition. Originating in the stone and stonemasons' trade, their services remained limited to the supply of stone according to other people's designs. During the construction process they appear in the capacity of suppliers and merchants, as in their cooperation with De Keyser or Van Delft, or as an independent supplier, as was seen at Honselaarsdijk castle and the rood screen in 's-Hertogenbosch.

---

[699] Stenvert 1999, passim.
[700] Ottenheym 1997b, p. 18ff.
[701] Gerritsen 1997, pp. 41-46.

[702] Ibidem, p. 46.
[703] Ottenheym 1997a, passim.
[704] Van den Heuvel 1997, passim.

XV. Materials Trade: Blue and Yellow Stone, Red and Grey Marble

Anyone who did business in commerce and moneymaking moved to Holland or more specifically, to Amsterdam, and the stone trade was no exception. Stone from the Meuse Valley and Germany could be found on the Amsterdam staple market as could Swedish tiles, English alabaster and Italian marble. Merchants from Amsterdam constituted the core of the import and export of stone. It is therefore not surprising that Namur stone merchants, who had been located in Dordrecht since 1585, moved to Amsterdam and made contacts with merchants there. In order to ensure a continuing excellent competitive position it was necessary to become involved in the centre of world trade. Nevertheless, the hegemony was less natural than the fast rise of Namur stone in the sixteenth century. The position of Namur stone traders and of sandstone merchants was clearly demarcated.

German stone in Amsterdam

The Northern Low Countries did not restrict themselves to one kind of stone exclusively, but naturally used a wide variety of types: apart from the blue Namur stone and the yellow German sandstone, for instance, there was red Weser stone or Sollingen stone.[705] In the sixteenth and seventeenth century the Hooptal, near Holzminden on the Weser, was already characterised by dozens of quarries.[706] The majority of the quarrying concerned locally applied slates, for which the stone, due to its layering, was eminently suitable.[707] Nevertheless the stone was also used for construction. The image we have of the quarrying of this red sandstone is a traditional historical one, and once again indicates what every stone delivery entailed before the stone reached its destination.[708] One of the Sollingen stone industry's products (not to be confused with red sandstone from the Main area) was tile. Around 1600 the stone trade already stretched along the Weser from Holzminden to Bremen and further. The chronicler Merian in his description of Braunschweig and Lüneburg wrote in 1654 that "foreign, faraway places such as Holland and Denmark" could also share the rich stone harvest of Solling stone.[709]

Most of the stone coming from Germany during this period originated from Bentheim or Obernkirchen. The enormous growth of the use of German sandstone during the seventeenth century can partially be explained by the search for alternatives to the stone trade from Brabant, which had dwindled. In looking for alternatives, a regular supply had to be guaranteed. During the sixteenth century the individual stone merchants from Bentheim did not have the financial power to build up large stocks. At most they had buffers to cope with drops in supply brought on by low water levels or ice.[710] Operational booms were directly linked to construction projects in the Northern Low Countries.[711] The constantly increasing demand at the start of the seventeenth century had a demonstrable effect on the way the Count of Bentheim leased the quarries. Previously the Count issued leases to several lessees, but that now changed and the count leased all the quarries to a single lessee.[712] The payment of the lease fees also changed. Joost Krull the younger from Zwolle, who was the only lessee in 1616 paid his lease with eleven barrels of butter; a decade later payment in coin was exacted and the "stone trading companies" paid thousands and sometimes tens of thousands of guilders per year.

---

[705] Czypull, Mitzkat 1998, passim.
[706] Tacke 1941, p. 141.
[707] Tacke 1939, passim.
[708] Tacke 1941, p. 146.

[709] Ibidem, p. 151.
[710] Voort 1970, p. 2.
[711] Ibidem.
[712] Ibidem, pp. 2-3.

The trade from Germany to the west was obviously the principal trading flow for the area around Bentheim. But Bremen and the areas located upstream along the Weser near Obernkirchen and the Bückebergen were equally important source areas. The trade to Holland ran through two channels: first there was the Bentheimer and Gildehauser trade, which ran via the staple market town of Zwolle. Secondly there was the North Sea trade from Holland, which was in direct contact with Bremen. The value placed on the lease rights can be seen in the fierce conflict that occurred concerning the sole right to be allowed to operate and export Bentheimer sandstone. For example, Johann Gottfried van Beveren, a quarry operator in Bentheim opened two quarries between 1669 and 1670. The Count of Bentheim permitted quarry masters to quarry sandstone for their own use, but not for independent trade. Count Ernst Willem consequently took steps to stop this infringement; he used military force to end operations and imprisoned the stonecutters working in the quarry. Van Beveren resisted and brought the manner before the Imperial high court in Speyer, which found him not guilty and so operations could resume.

After the lease had been granted to a single person at the start of the seventeenth century, a situation developed in which the Dutch operators started controlling trade and exports to the west increased. For the most part the Count of Bentheim's officials did not involve themselves with the trade. Even the Bentheim dimensioning, which had previously been applied to all stone industry products, had to go. A 1650 memo by the Bentheim official Maximilian van Offenberg includes the comment that the breaking wages at the quarry and the transport costs for the material to the North had always been settled in the same dimensioning. One Berckelius, probably a Dutch lessee, had however managed to change this rule. Using his agents and through "bad practices" he replaced the traditional dimensioning with the Rhineland measure.[713] This devious change added fourteen to fifteen percent for the lessee. Nothing came of Offenberg's attempt to reintroduce the old measure.

Amsterdam as a staple market

The more the town and, subsequently, the trade increased the more Amsterdam's importance as a stone trading and processing town grew. The west exerted a strong pull on the German sandstone trade, but the trade in Meuse Valley stone did not escape Amsterdam's influence either. Amsterdam was both a staple town and a creative centre and, as far as the blue stone trade was concerned, was destined to overtake Dordrecht. A good example of its central role in the stone trade and stonemasonry was Hendrick de Keyser's practice; although the town employed him, he received a large number of private commissions as a sculptor.[714] He was also the centre of a network of stonemasons. In a few instances he cooperated with Van Neurenberg and with the Ariaens Van Delft family of stonemasons, who, as will be detailed below, were soon to be related to the Van Neurenbergs. Smaller towns, that did not have their own town stonemason, such as Hoorn, sought out De Keyser, which also expanded Amsterdam's influence.

Partly thanks to De Keyser's work, Amsterdam remained an important centre for creativity. Work carried out in the private sector, in workshops or at the town masonry workshop became well-known, which in turn generated more business. Rich merchants, a growing number of which lived in the town, were the principal clients beside the town administration. The brickwork used in their homes was usually applied in combination with stone, which was generally sandstone. Nevertheless, stone from

---

[713] Ibidem, p. 14. ... *het breekloon op de kuyllen en het voerloon, na Northorn is altyt betaelt geweest nae de kuylmate, die voor honderden van jaeren int gebruyck geweest, en tot Gildehuys nog kan werden gezien. Welcke olde steen maete Berckelius met assistentie van zijn factoren alhier door quade practycken en abusive praemissen heeft weeten in Rijnlantsche maete te veranderen.*

[714] Meischke 1995, p. 52.

73. Amsterdam, Oudezijds Voorburgwal 127, designed by Hendrick de Keyser (after De Bray 1631, pl. nr. XXXIII).

the Meuse Valley was also shipped to the town in bulk shipments. This material was not only used for tombstones, plinths, curbs and gutters, but also for decorative elements and facades. An example of this use is the home the jeweller, Hans van Wely, had built in 1611 on the Oudezijds Voorburgwal 127 (Fig. 73). This house was said to have been "above the usual kind of civil architecture", because of the expensive materials used, consisting as they did of blue stone with marble inlays and black touch-stone.[715] The facade may have possibly been prepared at the quarry in the Meuse Valley after a design by Hendrick de Keyser.

The same situation appears later in the seventeenth century: a bisection of stone use and processing (German sandstone/Meuse Valley limestone) where the stone from the Meuse Valley occupied a secondary place. An agreement, which involved all of the town's stone buyers, reveals the extent to which the trade between the buyers of blue and yellow stone was separated. On 4 and 18 November 1634 all stone buyers and stonemasons of Amsterdam declared to Klaas Jansz Ruitenburgh, collector of the taxes, that they would to list all stone, lime and lead to the tax masters of the rough wares.[716] The sandstone buyers listed were: Maurits Jacobsz, Cornelis Sijbrantsz, Leenert Albertsz, wid. Heinrick Dircksz, Adriaan Jansz Baij, Jan Davidsz, Lijsbeth Danckerts, Heinrick Thomasz, Joost Cornelisz, Jan Matijsz, the widow of Barent de Vries, Jacob Huygen, Heijnrick Gerritsz, Huybert Roelantsz, Wiggert Holleslooth, Heijnrick Danckerts, Heynrick Willemsz Dommer and Ysbrandt Holleslooth.[717]

Blue stone buyers mentioned were Dirck van Delft, Pieter (Ariaensz) van Delft, Claes Claesz van Medemblick, Jan van der Sluijs, Jan van Dalen and Master Pieter de Keyser. The distinction between both trading areas and the people involved in the stone trade was therefore a contemporary dis-

---

[715] Ibidem and De Bray 1631, p. 19. The latter states that the house *is boven de gewoonlijcken aert van Burgerlijcke Gebouwen, gantsch uyt-steeckende, en gheheel kostelijck, en seer gheciert met alle maniere van uytgehouwen wercken: En is 't Voorhier en daer met Marbre en Toets-steene tafelen en platen ingeleyt is.*

[716] GAA, NA 728-499/501. Not. P. Carels.

[717] Stonemasons for Bentheimer sandstone were: Aris Claesz, Jan Caspersz (crossed out), Pieter Jansz, Jan Jansz and Cornelis Dircksz, Philips Roelants, Jan Claesz, Huijbert de Keijser,

Pieter Pietersz, Jan Cornelisz at brewery van 't Roohart, mr. Pieter Rogiersz at Nieuwezijds Arm, Arent Gerritsz, mr. Albert on the Prinsengracht near the Leliesluis, master Elbert Croesz on the Prinsengracht opposite the *huiszittenhuis*, Adriaen Jelles, Roelof Rithorst, Laurens Jacobsz behind the Cathuisers, Heije Olfertsz, Jan IJder, Jan van Gronsvelt, the widow of Gerrit Egbertsz on the corner of the Egelantierstraat, Jan Dirksz van Assensteegh, Jannetje Haes on the Verwersgracht. GAA, 1623 4/18-11. NA 728, 499/501. Not. P. Carels.

tinction. The group of sandstone buyers was three times the size of that of the Namur stone merchants: six blue stone traders versus eighteen sandstone merchants. Nevertheless, there also seem to have been stonemasons who worked both types of stone, although the two types remained separate within the business. On 16 January 1642 two witnesses made a statement pertaining to apprenticing a boy to stonemason Jeronimus Fonteyn on the Singel in Amsterdam. The apprentice would work in the *witte winckel* (white shop) for two years and then two more years in the *blauwe winckel* (blue shop).[718] On 28 April 1650, Hendrick de Keyser jr. declared that Gerrit Sillen had worked for him for two years and had learned the art of working the *wit steenwerck* (white stonework).[719] On 25 April 1671, Willem van Bredero and Pieter de Keyser started a *wittesteenhouwerij* (white stone workshop) together. Furthermore, Van Bredero is said to have planned a *blaeuwesteenhouwerij* (blue stone workshop) too.[720]

Namur stone

Moving to the Namur stone trade as it developed during the first half of the seventeenth century, two remarkable phenomena can be seen in this trade. First there is the tendency in the north for stonemasons and merchants, who had no roots in the south, to enter into the trade in Namur stone. This development can for the most part be ascribed to the fact that Walloon families in the north entered into family relations with people from outside their circle. Also active in the same trade, families such as the Van Delfts or De Keysers provided attractive marriage partners, thereby further entangling the trade in Namur stone and mutual stonemasonry activities.

A second trend concerns the merchants who originated in the south. Their relocation north and the increasingly strong ties there led them to develop more along the lines of their erstwhile competitors. In this context it is useful to also examine the Walloon family Wijmoth, who moved from Dordrecht to Leiden, and further developed as a family of stone merchants. During the 1650s Willem Wijmoth supplied Bentheim sandstone for the Bibliotheca Tysiana in Leiden[721] and he was responsible for the construction of a number of houses on the Rapenburg. Furthermore, he supplied large quantities of stone to the town.[722] In 1657, he cooperated with Pieter Post on the weigh house in Leiden.[723] Wijmoth also worked together with Arent van 's Gravesande and Willem van der Helm. In addition to his trade in Bentheim sandstone, Wijmoth also continued to the trade in blue stone.[724]

Blue stone remained the Van Neurenberg family's principal trading product. The trade in this type of stone continued to be sufficiently profitable to continue providing deliveries throughout the first half of the seventeenth century. The example of Captain Jan Conincx, who specialised in the transport of this material to the exclusion of all others in the 1590s, as discussed in Part II, amply illustrates how lucrative the trade in Namur stone was. In 1615 he left his floating home and owned a house in Elsloo, whilst simultaneously owning a large warehouse in Dordrecht for his trade in Namur stone.[725] His sons Michiel and Dirk captained his ships between Liège and Dordrecht, and occasionally temporary captains were used. He also had two agents, Pieter Franssen[726] and Jan van Slingerlandt, who travelled to Amsterdam and elsewhere for his business.[727]

[718] Van Dillen 1974, p. 333. The boy would earn a guilder a week during the first year. The differences between the various types of stone should be taken into account here.
[719] Ibidem, p. 553, No. 1095.
[720] Ibidem, pp. 834-836, No. 1758.
[721] Meischke 1997, p. 412.
[722] Lunsingh Scheurleer 1988, IIIa, pp. 220-227.

[723] Terwen, Ottenheym 1993, pp. 186-190.
[724] In 1642, Joan van Neurenberg was a witness at Wijmoth's wedding. Ibidem, pp. 94-95.
[725] Meulleners 1886, p. 120.
[726] From Venlo. Not to be confused with master Peter Frans from Antwerp.
[727] Meulleners 1886, p. 120.

Overview of operations 1609-1650

One of the most important constant factors for the Namur stone trade, occurring from the Twelve Years' Truce and after, was transport over water. References to transport over land, not including the small distance from the site at which the stone was unloaded to the construction site, are extremely rare. If one examines the list of land transports between Liège and 's-Hertogenbosch, dating back to 24 June 1637, then it becomes apparent that the sums for *land licenten* received in times of war in the "Meijerij" of 's-Hertogenbosch pertained to iron, nails, pantiles, pots, alum, wire, copper, slates, sheeting and canvas.[728] Due to the stone's weight it was, as it had always been, transported over water.[729]

Constant problems for the merchants were the taxes and the continuous checks on the Meuse southwards. Permission needed to be obtained from the States General for the export of the stone. However, this permission did not constitute a real obstruction to trade. In the years after 1609, the year the Twelve Years' Truce was declared, the Namur stone trade was stable. Deliveries were made during almost every year. Pieter van Neurenberg, for example, supplied blue stone for the weigh house in Hoorn as a subcontractor for Hendrick de Keyser. A few years later, in 1613, Coenraad IV van Neurenberg was active in Middelburg, where, among other things, he was involved in an alteration and the supply of a blue stone lower front for the town hall.[730] In 1615, Willem II van Neurenberg supplied stone for the curbs and mouldings of the town hall in Leerdam. In Dordrecht Namur stone was also used in this time. During the years 1616-1618 work took place on the Groothoofdse Gate concerning the town side of the building, which was executed in brick and Namur stone and can still be seen today (Fig. 74). Gilles Huppe, a stonemason from Liège, who had had the House with the Heads built in Dordrecht shortly before, is said to have participated in this project.[731] In 1619, Coenraad IV van Neurenberg supplied stone from Dordrecht for a lock in Plasschendaele in Flanders and for the Jesuit Church in Antwerp.[732] The lock is said to have incorporated 2,000 feet of Namur stone, which cost 2,675 guilders and thirteen stivers, including shipping. The delivery for the Jesuit Church probably concerned a delivery of marble, which was transported to Antwerp via Dordrecht.[733]

At the same time as these deliveries, the ties with Hendrick de Keyser were consolidated. Both blue stone merchants, Van Neurenberg and De Keyser, continued to seek each other for jobs. De Keyser stated on 8 April 1619 that in 1616 he had excavated the Old Inn near Nieuwersluis in order

74. Dordrecht, the Groothoofdse Gate, circa 1750. Water colour by P.C. la Fargue. (GAD, inv.nr. DI 928).

[728] GAD, Archief van de gemeene Maashandelaars [Archive of the Organised Meuse Merchants], Inv. No. 427.

[729] Various plans were drawn up for the creation of canals in order to improve accessibility. For example, there was a plan in 1608 to dig a canal between Zaltbommel and Culemborg. In the Southern Low Countries there were also plans to connect the Schelde and the Rhine. These were however never realised. De Vries, Van der Woude 1995, p. 53.

[730] Unger 1932, p. 11.

[731] Meischke 1997, pp. 80–81.

[732] GAD, ORA 1619 Inv. No. 760. Fol 30vs and 31.

[733] GAA, 1619, 8 April NA 435-194 and NA 461-116, not. P. Matijsz.

to install a salt pan for salt trader Willem van Royen. De Keyser had made drawings of a new type of salt pan, as indicated by a master from Alkmaar. Willem van Neurenberg had forwarded these drawings, due to mediation, to Liège to have the salt pans made there. When the people in Liège failed to understand the drawings, patron Willem van Royen journeyed to Liège himself.[734]

Namur stone continued to occupy a special place in the trade. As mentioned previously, the stone usually does not occur on toll lists. If it is encountered, then sometimes deviant rates applied and a distinction is made between worked and unworked stone. The 1619 Urmond toll account stated that Namur stone and other goods that were not listed separately were allowed to be taxed at half or at most two-thirds the level of similar goods, such as coal, lime, marlstone or slates. This special treatment was because merchants and captains had lodged complaints stating that Urmond's toll charge on Namur stone was too high. In order to facilitate trade, the Lord of Urmond decided to impose a lower tax.[735]

Such reductions in charges will undoubtedly have been realised because the Meuse Valley traders managed to organise themselves into a tight-knit group. To what extent influential patrons in the north added their voices is unknown. However, it is a fact that the Namur stone trade could bask in the interest of a number of serious patrons. During the following years, Namur stone was regularly selected for the facade cladding and other parts of ambitious architectural projects. For instance, between 1621 and 1625 Willem II van Neurenberg supplied worked stone for the Catharijne Gate in Utrecht and around 1630 he was involved in large deliveries of marble and blue stone for Frederik Hendrik's Honselaarsdijk castle.

A witness statement dates back to 11 June 1630. On this date Willem stated that Mathijs Willems, a captain from Zaltbommel, had transported Namur stone to Laurens Sweijs, just like Willem had previously delivered, which concerned a shipment of forty-five boats, with a value of thousands of guilders.[736] A few weeks later, on 3 July, Coenraad IV van Neurenberg declared, for the same Meuse captain from Zaltbommel, that he had also seen a shipment of stones for Laurens Sweijs'.[737] The stones were of good quality, which was normal for stone from Namur County. Van Neurenberg stated that he had supplied this type of stone for thirty years, which was used for the lower front of the town hall in Middelburg, the gate on Pieter Koerte's house there and for the last eight to ten years also in Vlissingen, for the Big Lock. This lock had incorporated some 15,000 feet and he, together with Lijn Hermansz, his partner, had supplied over 17,000 feet of stone for a lock, a bridge and for four sluices in Plasschendaele near Oostende.[738] In 1634 Willem II supplied 3,075 floor tiles for the church in Sommelsdijk.[739] On 31 March 1635 the Hospital paid Pieter van Delft's wife, Anna van Neurenberg 300 guilders for the pillars of the hospital's office gallery.[740]

Although these enormous quantities paint a rosy picture of the trade, problems regularly occurred. Dordrecht captain Teunis Jansz declared on 9 June 1635 that blue stone merchant Pieter van Delft had agreed in early April that captains Huijbrecht Dircksz de Baas and Jan Jansz Kelck would take a shipment of blue stone to Amsterdam for him. The shipment was intended for the gentlemen of the V.O.C.,

---

[734]Van Royen was related to De Keyser and a merchant who traded in commodities including salt. See GAA, NA 461-115 concerning the patent for the salt pan, and NA 348-99, not. W. Cluyt, concerning the purchase of the old inn.

[735] *Namuijr steen ende andere coopmanschappen die hier niet en sijn gespecificeert, sullen naer advenant van de bovengedachte goederen in haere qualiteijt ofte weerden aengeslaegen en vertolt worden, maer alsoo het sulx is, dat sijn Doorlt. veel claechten heeft vernomen, dat de coopluijden, ende schippers sooals sij menen sich beswaert vinden, ende te hooge belast, soo heeft sijn Doorlt. als een lieffhebber van de gemeene negotie gehegt, ende verclaert, dat de licent- ende tolmeesters, tot op naerder order, niet meer en sullen nemen dan de*

helft, ofte een weijnigh meer, maer niet hooger als de tweederte parten, scheldende aen de voorn. coopluijden en captains bij discretie quit ontrent eenderde part... See Knoors 1993, p. 286.

[736] GAA, NA 724-235. not. P. Carels. In 1620 Sweijs supplied the altar for the Trefoldigheds Church of Christianstad, for Christian IV of Denmark, possibly from Hendrick de Keyser's workshop. Sweijs often mediated between De Keyser and Christian IV. See Roding 1991, p. 94.

[737] GAA, NA 724-288.

[738] Ibidem.

[739] Slinger 1980, p. 51.

[740] GAA, PA, 342-1191-91.

possibly for the construction of a fort abroad. Captain Kelck stayed in Dordrecht eight days longer than Huijbrecht, which was the immediate cause of the conflict. Van Delft had received his stone too late and therefore wished the defaulting captain to reimburse him. The latter listed waiting for a number of chair makers who had to journey from Geertruidenberg as the reason for his delay.[741] They had been detained by a storm. The consequence of the delay was that the stones arrived too late in Amsterdam.[742]

Another problem occurred in 1640. On 25 June of that year Pieter van Delft, a blue stone merchant, permitted his wife Anna van Neurenberg to demand payment from Gilles van der Eggen, alderman in Utrecht, for the blue stones Anna had sold and supplied to him.[743] On 1 November of that year, bricklayer Jan Theunisz declared that, at Anna van Neurenberg's request, he had been to see her approximately six years earlier with his cousin Rutger Harmansz. At that point in time, Rutger had been charged with a commission for Van der Eggen. Rutger had ordered a considerable shipment of thresholds and flagstones, which had been made and shipped to Utrecht, at his patron's behest for use in the patron's house near the Dom Church. Gilles van der Eggen's brother-in-law, a soap maker from Amsterdam, witnessed the sale.[744] The exact nature of the conflict is not elucidated, but it can, however, be ascertained that Gilles probably did not want to pay afterwards or denied that he purchased stone from Pieter van Delft. Such trivial difficulties were commonplace.

Belgian marble

The importance of 'Belgian' marble only attained substantial form around 1600, particularly in regard to the Van Neurenbergs. The Southern Low Countries and the Prince-Bishopric of Liège were the principal marble suppliers to the Northern Low Countries, and their wide variety and quality of types was remarkable. There are roughly three main colours of 'Belgian' marble: red, black and grey. Contrary to popular belief, various colours, shades and tints could be found in the same place.[745] The red and grey variants in particular are closely related and are both found alongside one another in the same reef (Fig. 75).[746]

In addition to the related red and grey marble, there is also black marble. Dinant was the centre of the deep black limestone quarrying.[747] Namur stone was also used as black marble in the past, which then concerned the top layer of a bank, where the limestone was most pure. The thickness of these layers was limited. Sources refer to a number of quarries, such as Limbourg, Rance and Agimont.[748] Other places mentioned include Saint-Remy near Rochefort, Vinalmont, Mazy-Golzinne, Longpré, etc. The well-known Tournai stone from further west was also referred to as black marble in the past.[749]

---

[741] Probably to make repairs to the 'chair' on which the stone was to rest during transport.

[742] GAA, NA 520-114 and NA 554-151. not. Ja. Westfrisius.

[743] GAA, NA 524-27. not. Ja. Westfrisius.

[744] GAA, NA 1282-64, not. H. Schaeff. Bricklayer Jan Theunisz himself worked for Van der Eggen for seven or eight weeks. Witnesses to Theunisz' statement in 1640 were the stonemasons Frans Zeynte van Nijvel and Jaques Matijn.

[745] Cnudde 1990, p. 25.

[746] In the past the red types of marble were also referred to as 'Rouges des Flandres' [Flemish Reds]. See Groessens 1981, passim. On red marbles in particular pp. 243-247. The stone is found primarily in the areas of Rance, Philippeville, Rochefort and Durbuy, and a little further east near Limbourg.

[747] Courajod 1901, passim.

[748] Janse, De Vries 1991, pp. 14-15.

[749] See Westerman 1998 for more on Tournai stone. More details on Tournai stone: Nys 1993.

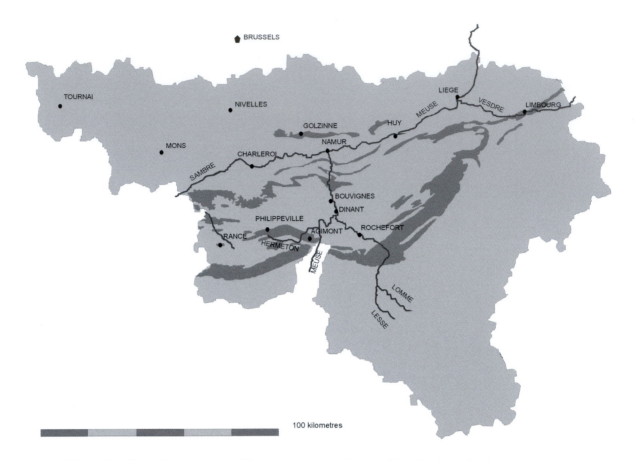

75. Just like carboniferous limestone, marble occurs over a wide area (drawing by author).

Just like Namur stone, Hainaut stone and other types of stone, Belgian marble has its own operation and usage history, particularly regarding its export.[750] Material and written sources reveal that the quarrying and sale of coloured marble did not expand until the start of the sixteenth century, which does not imply that earlier applications are unknown, but these were local in character and cannot be attributed to a constant flow of trade from the quarries in any way.

On the other hand, black marble had been an important export product for some time. Written proof of its quarrying and operation dates back to the thirteenth century.[751] Examples of sepulchral monuments dating back to the fourteenth and fifteenth century incorporated black marble from Dinant,[752] which explains the presence of someone like Hubert Lambillon from Namur at Claus Sluter's workshop in Dijon.[753] This *ouvrier tailleur de marbre* worked with Sluter in 1397-1398 on the bottom part of Philip the Bold's tomb, which was executed in marble and alabaster. Sepulchral monuments in particular, which were sometimes inlaid with copper, another Dinant speciality, were an important early export product. The stone was worked in the immediate vicinity of the quarries. There were also a large number of specialised craftsmen from the north working in Paris, which provided an important impetus to the material's application.[754] It is known that black marble was applied at court in works

[750] For its quarrying and processing see Van Tussenbroek 2001a.
[751] Groessens 1994, p. 84.
[752] Ibidem, p. 76.
[753] Courtoy 1946, p. 24.
[754] Groessens 1994, p. 76.

for Philip the Bold, John the Fearless, Charles IV and Philip the Good. The black marble industry there-fore already had an extensive history by the time red marble was first applied.[755] From the sixteenth century the new styles stimulated the demand for black marble. Initially the material was primarily used for sepulchral monuments in combination with English alabaster or white limestone from Avesnes. Slowly, it was also being applied architecturally to the detriment of the more traditional types of stone, which had been used in parallel until that point in time.[756]

Southern applications (workshops)

In contrast to, for example, Italy, where marble was often used as facade cladding, this was hard-ly the case in the Low Countries. Causes for it not being used have to do with building traditions, the available stocks, transport and marble's costliness. But another more important reason can primarily be attributed to the fact that marble rapidly loses its lustre due to weathering. With a few exceptions, it was applied predominantly indoors in objects such as tomb sculptures. The manufacture of such items took place near the quarry and was done by workshops with a long history of stonemasonry. One such example of this manufacture is the production of baptismal fonts, many of which have been con-served.[757] Production increased during the fifteenth and sixteenth centuries and a large number of baptismal fonts were exported, primarily from Namur.[758]

Jean de Loyers from Dinant was one such black marble worker. When Dinant's economy revived after the plundering in 1466 the stone industry as well as the export of floor tiles and sepulchral mon-uments increased dramatically. At the start of the century, it was the Nonons who left their mark on the export market.[759] In the mid-sixteenth century Jean de Loyers was one of the leading manufac-turers. On 14 March 1556, Loyers signed a contract with Pierre de Salmier, Lord of Brumagne and a descendant of a Dinant family of patricians, who had made a fortune as copper smiths. Pierre de Sal-mier ordered a tomb for the Franciscan Church in Bergen/ Mons. Jean de Loyers was to use a good piece of Dinant marble without veining or other impurities, nine feet long and five wide to make the figures according to the pattern the Lord of Brumagne had supplied. The contract does not explicitly specify whether Jean was to do the work himself or to have it done. The cost of working the stone was included in the cost price agreed in the contract.[760]

Dinant continued to be an export centre for black marble. The *tombiers*, tomb makers, were perhaps the oldest and most important group of craftsmen. The material had continued to be popular in Paris throughout the sixteenth century.[761] Merchant Jean Noël and stonemason Nicolas Duchesnoy supplied a tombstone to master sculptor François Lheureux and master sculptor and painter Jean Autrot 10 June 1586. Noël had married Guillaume I Wespin's widow, Jaqueline le Febvre, in 1575, which made Noël stepfather to the sculptors Jean and Nicolas Wespin. Both had left for Italy at a young age[762] as a result of Noël's short temper and subsequent beatings.[763] The third brother, Guillaume II

---

[755] There are also examples in the Northern Low Coun-tries. Groessens 1997, p. 69.

[756] Think for example of rood screens, altars, etc. in Lede stone, marlstone, Namur stone, Baumberger stone, etc.

[757] For example at Sint-Stevens Church in Nijmegen, the Sint-Joris Church in Amersfoort and the Nederlands Her-vormde Church in Baarn.

[758] See Courtoy 1925, pp. 59-62.

[759] For more on this family see Chapter III.

[760] The delivery term was set at a maximum of one year. Transport and the installing of the piece were on De Loyers'

account and at his risk. The price agreed was 170 Carolus guilders. Twenty guilders were to be paid in advance, the rest in four instalments: when the stone was cut from the quar-ry and it had started to be worked, then three months later, then again three months later and finally when the tomb had been made according to the design and installed to full satisfaction. Courtoy 1929, pp. 61-62.

[761] Vanaise 1966, pp. 8-9.

[762] See Devigne 1920.

[763] Courtoy 1920, p. 220.

Wespin, worked as a quarry master. Together with Guillaume, Noël supplied two hundred feet each of black and coloured marble for the Paris market in accordance with a contract dated 8 December 1600.[764] In 1604, Wespin cooperated with Nicolas Duchesnoy on a delivery for the Duke of Lotharingen's chapel in Verdun.[765]

Wespin had a flourishing company, which was also important for the market in the Northern Low Countries. Not only did he trade in stone from the quarries around Dinant, he also traded in red or grey veined marble from the quarries in Saint-Remy and Agimont – Gochenée. He managed to bind clients, such as Jacques Matthijsz, a trader from Delft, to him, with lifetime agreements for the supply of materials. The price Matthijsz was to pay was the same as that paid by two other Wespin clients, namely Coenraad IV van Neurenberg and Thierry Bidart.[766] Bidart was a Namur sculptor and was probably Van Neurenberg's uncle or cousin because Coenraad's mother's maiden name was Marie le Bidart.

The circle of clients primarily consisted of the church, the court and the aristocracy, with the church holding the predominant position. Sixteenth-century churches in the Southern Low Countries used a lot of traditional materials such as white limestone combined with Namur stone, but there was a shift at the close of that century with marble being used architecturally more and more often. A good example is the Jesuit Carolus Borromaeus Church in Antwerp, for which Coenraad IV van Neurenberg delivered materials from Dordrecht in 1619.[767] Another example is the Saint-Loup Church in Namur where the interior is a combination of red and black marble with a carved marlstone barrel vault.[768] If the work of sculptor-architect Lucas Faydherbe from Mechelen is examined this shift also becomes apparent. Faydherbe (1617-1697) used various materials in his work and his sculptures include sandstone, Carrara marble, terracotta, ivory, black marble, red marble and stone from Avesnes.[769] He also used marble in his architecture. For example, a specification for the construction of the Onze Lieve Vrouwe of Leliëndaal Church in Mechelen dated 2 July 1662 refers to the quality of stone used in the Jesuit Church in Namur when discussing black marble parts.[770] Stucco and a painted imitation of red marble were selected for the *contrepilasters* above the entablature. Faydherbe maintained contacts with marble suppliers from Namur. When, in 1648, he became embroiled in a conflict with his patron Elisabeth Danesin concerning his saint Joseph's altar (she was of the opinion that the quality was below par) he tried to prove that the material was of the best possible quality, using the statement provided by stone merchant Jean Duchesne from Namur.[771] Problems also occurred during the construction of the high altar in the Sint-Rombout Cathedral in Mechelen concerning the purchase of the materials. Faydherbe had been commissioned to build a new screen on 21 October 1664 and a new high altar on 19 January 1665. On 16 September 1666, however, he was still busy with preparations and with the purchase of the materials. The trouble with marble acquisitions was war-related, as the material had become very rare and (therefore) expensive.[772]

---

[764] Vanaise 1966, p. 10.

[765] Ibidem, p. 14.

[766] Courtoy 1920, p. 227.

[767] Huyssens made the church's design and also designed the Jesuit churches in Maastricht and Namur. It is unknown whether he maintained personal contact with Van Neurenberg. Plantenga 1926, p. 89ff.

[768] See Genicot 1991 for more on this matter.

[769] De Nijn 1997, catalogue section.

[770] De Jonge, De Vos et.al., 1997, p. 84.

[771] Duchesne stated that the stone he supplied *est pierre de touche, et du fin que se peut trouver comme aussy de celle qu'il est accoustume delivrer, est quil ait livré pour les ouvrages est autels le plus ouvrieux de ces pays, et nommement aux peres Jesuites de Bruxelles, Anvers, Bruges, Duinkercke et de ceste ville* [Mechelen]. See Van Riet 1996, in particular pp. 210-219 for the court documents. Jean Duchesne was from a family of *marbriers* [marble workers] who were active in Namur throughout the seventeenth century. Jacquet-Ladrier 1999, pp. 89-90.

[772] De Jonge 1997, p. 112.

Over the course of the seventeenth century a market once again developed in the south, as did an increase in artistic endeavours with personages such as Rubens, De Nole and Van Mildert. This revival also seems to have provided an impulse to the stone industry in Namur and around 1650 there were a large number of stonemasons and sculptors active in the town.[773] The same applies to Liège and Dinant.[774]

Luxury products and overseas trade

The wealthier the north became, the more the demand for marble increased. Dutch merchants in Northern Italy developed the trading activities that expressed this point.[775] Primarily during the second half of the seventeenth century, Amsterdam had grown to become a very important centre for the trade in Carrara marble. So important in fact that an English traveller visiting Amsterdam in 1701 wrote: *There are such vast Magazines in Amsterdam, that a Man would think [...] there were Quarries of marble near the City Gates.*[776] This comment also concerns certain types of Belgian marble.

At the start of the seventeenth century, the use of Italian marble was irrevocably tied to the name Hendrick de Keyser. De Keyser is considered the first to have used Italian marble for sculptural purposes.[777] Although he initially worked in the softer stone alabaster, which came from England, in 1612 he declared, "Nobody in this country so far works in marble," except for himself.[778] De Keyser's earliest known work in Carrara marble dates back to 1608 and is a portrait bust. Although he still supplied an alabaster sculpture for the screen in the Sint-Jans Church of 's-Hertogenbosch during these years, it is clear that he was increasingly using marble (e.g. the funerary monument for Elisabeth Morgan in Delft, 1611 and the tomb of William of Orange) (Fig. 76). De Keyser's son-in-law Nicolas Stone, and his sons Pieter and Hendrick Jr. worked in marble. A patent that Hendrick de Keyser submitted to the States General in 1612 for the invention of fake marble also reveals the shift in the use of materials.[779]

The use of Belgian marble in the Northern Low Countries has been known for some time.[780] This use also increased during the seventeenth century, alternating periodically with the use of alabaster. On 28 September 1617, François Stiesep, who was originally from Nottingham and now lived in Leiden, declared that he had purchased twenty-one blocks of alabaster in Staffordshire in June. The seller was Christoffel Greeffs. Stiesep had purchased the blocks at the behest of Pieter van Delft. Fifteen blocks were already finished at the time the sale was concluded. The men agreed that the entire delivery would be made in August.[781]

With Amsterdam as its centre of trade, Belgian marble and Namur stone were traded far and wide. On 23 September 1623, Gerrit Sijmonsz, a timber buyer (probably active in the Baltic), declared before the notary public that at Willem van Neurenberg's request the government of Brandenburg in Königsberg had commissioned him to buy a shipment of red, black and white marble. This shipment was to be used for a sculpture. Commissioned by Jan Filippijn, master stonemason of Königsberg, Sij-

[773] The Duchesne family was a good example. Courtoy 1938, p. 286.

[774] For example, the De Hontoir family of sculptors, who were from Namur, were active in Liège during the second half of the seventeenth and the early eighteenth century. Yernaux 1952, passim.

[775] More general information on this subject: Engels 1995.

[776] Scholten 1993, p. 197.

[777] Ibidem, p. 199.

[778] Kossmann 1929, p. 287.

[779] Ibidem, pp. 199-201. See also Van Tussenbroek 2001a.

[780] For example, Jan Coninx from Venlo travelled from Liège to Dordrecht in 1593 with a shipment of Namur stone, "granite" and marble. See Thurlings 1945, pp. 66-67.

[781] GAA, NA 279-218. not. Fr. van Banchem. Hendrick de Keyser and Pieter Carels were witnesses.

76. Delft, New Church. Funerary monument for William of Orange by Hendrick de Keyser. (after De Bray 1631, pl. nr. XXXIX)

monsz had ordered red, black and white marble from Van Neurenberg. In August 1623 Sijmonsz purchased the stone from Van Neurenberg, loaded it aboard three ships and shipped it to Königsberg.[782] A year and a half later, on 4 February 1625, Gerrit Sijmonsz once again appeared before the notary public.[783] He declared, at the behest of Willem van Neurenberg and Pieter Ariaensz of Delft, that Adriaen Vlack de Jonge had purchased approximately 2,500 feet of black and red marble from Van Neurenberg (in the presence of Van Delft and Sijmonsz) in September 1623. The stone had been delivered and shipped to Königsberg and so Sijmonsz declared that Vlack had indeed received his order.

The origin of the Vlack's order is another matter entirely. Normally, an order was prepared and supplied to the patron. Vlack's order was however originally intended for Anthony Moens. He represented the King of Poland and purchased stone from Van Neurenberg in Jan Fillippijn's name, in a similar way as Sijmonsz. Van Neurenberg and Van Delft had, in the meantime, become in-laws, which might explain why they were so closely involved in each other's business. Van Neurenberg sent the stone ordered by Moens to Amsterdam. Once the stone had arrived there, it was Van Delft who offered the stone to Moens. It had been agreed that Moens would pay immediately upon delivery. However, due to a lack of commission Moens refused to do so. Van Delft thereupon decided, in consultation with Van Neurenberg, to store the stone. Later some of the stone was sold to Adriaen Vlack.[784] Moens later confirmed that it had been agreed that he would pay for the stone immediately. However, the following problem arose: Moens' patron had not given him any money and he would therefore have to advance the money himself. Because he was not inclined to pay it himself, when offered the stone, Moens said that he would be willing to receive it and send it to Königsberg, but Willem van Neurenberg would then have to wait for payment until the money arrived. Van Neurenberg then decided to keep the stone, which terminated the sale.[785]

Such problems were part of the daily occurrences in the stone trade. In that sense there is little distinction between marble and ordinary stone. The stone measurer and the excises inspector saw it in those terms. When on 16 August 1624 the sworn stone measurer Arent Arentsz was questioned at Laurens Sweijs' behest, he declared he had measured six blocks of marble for Willem van Neurenberg on 22 June 1621.[786] The stone was not entirely unblemished, but Arents stated that he had not subtracted more for cracks and dents than he would have done for other types of stone, such as Bremer or Bentheimer stone. A few decades later, the point of view put forward by Amsterdam's city administration was slightly different; the rate for measuring stone varied widely for the various types of stone in 1656. Having marble, alabaster and black touchstone measured was three times as expensive as measuring other types of stone.[787]

---

[782] GAA, NA 691-421 (13). Not. J. Warnaerts. Van Neurenberg seems to have acted as distributor for the white (= Italian) marble.

[783] GAA, NA 691 B-1256 (47).

[784] Moens confirmed the story at Willem van Neurenberg's request. GAA, NA 691 B-1257.

[785] Ibidem. The above does not list all known marble exports. For example, Pieter Ariaensz van Delft exported an epitaph in 1633 for the merchant Johan Füchting from Lübeck. (Scholten 1993, n. 26.). Along the Baltic coastline in the Hanse towns there are a number of examples of the work of Dutch stone suppliers, sculptors, etc. Works that come to mind are those of the Van Steenwinkels, the marble gallery on the Frederiksborg and the construction activities of traders from the Republic who moved to Scandinavia for extended periods of time. Laurens Sweijs also supplied stone for the Frederiksborg. See Slothouwer 1924 and Roding 1991.

[786] GAA, NA 691 B - 889 (2). Not. J. Warnaerts.

[787] Scholten 1993, p. 207.

The organisation of independent stone trade in Amsterdam

Both the Amsterdam town masonry yard and various independent companies were involved in processing marble (Fig. 77). The Van Delft family also had its own workshop and even a stone saw, which could be either wind- or horse-powered as Van Delft had purchased miller Willem Claasz Kindt's mill, stone saw, tools, a boat and half a house. The mill was used to polish floor tiles.[788] Such industrialisation can also be seen at Willem de Gooijer's marble mill.[789] In his 1687 travel journal, the Swedish architect Nicodemus Tessin provides an extensive description. De Gooijer had "the best marble mill for the sawing and polishing, which he is privileged to run only." The mill powered no less than fourteen saws that were controlled by a single man. "At the same time 200 marble tiles [...] are being polished by 60 other men who walk around there."[790]

Although the town building lodge managed to leave a strong impression on construction in towns, it was to a large extent dependent on independent entrepreneurs for execution and materials. Because they were active in a vulnerable sector, they were forced to defend their position as well as possible. On 18 April 1642, Pieter van Delft, Pieter de Keyser, Eijlart Krouse, Claes Arentsz, Willem de Keyser, Jeronimus Fonteyn and Willem van Delft, all Amsterdam citizens and stonemasons, concluded an agreement regarding their labourers.[791] They agreed to pay their staff no more than twenty-four stivers in summer and eighteen stivers during the winter. If a labourer were to work for another master without his master's permission he would have to pay a fifty-guilder fine to the poor. It was agreed that they would not execute *hoopwerk* in Bentheimer stone, although they would in other types of stone.[792] The witnesses were Adriaen Pietersz van Delft and Isaack Stevens, a labourer in the Kloveniersdoelen.[793]

77. Amsterdam, town stonemason's workshop between the Herengracht and Keizersgracht, to the north of the Leidsegracht. Drawing by G. Braat, 1652 (GAA, Inv.Nr. E 5943).

[788] Van Dillen 1974, p. 673, No. 1432. The mill was located on the Singelsloot level with the Bullebaksluis.
[789] This mill was located on the Prinsengracht.
[790] See Scholten 1993, p. 208.
[791] GAA, NA 992-15-117 and NA 994-43v. Not. J. Bosch.

[792] The term *hoopwerk* might refer to bulk shipments. This agreement may have had to do with the fact that all those mentioned were blue stone buyers.
[793] GAA, NA 992-15-119. Notaris J. Bosch.

The merchants and stonemasons mentioned had considerable stocks. For example, it took Pieter Ariaensz van Delft a great deal of effort to move stone buyer Hendrik Gerritsz's stock off the land Van Delft purchased from him in 1633. On 30 April he made his first payment on the condition that Gerritsz would tidy up the property. Gerritsz agreed, but on condition that Pieter van Delft first tidied up the facade, which he had placed on Hendrik's plot before May.[794] This facade obviously got in the way of Gerritsz tidying up his own materials.

In addition to the purchase of Brouwersgracht Nos. 120 and 122, Van Delft had on 23 March sold a house with a polishing mill at Brouwersgracht No. 130/134. Here too the stocks caused problems for him. Pieter de Keyser purchased the building. The parties had agreed that De Keyser would take over all the stocks in the atelier and on the dock from Van Delft. The stones were to be valued to this end. On 1 May, De Keyser had accepted the house, mill and the stones, and had started selling stone without the valuation having taken place. On 23 May 1633, Van Delft urged Pieter de Keyser to stop selling his former stocks.[795]

Stonemasons could be found in various parts of the town. The Brouwersgracht was one of the principal places (Fig. 78). In addition to Pieter van Delft, Pieter de Keyser and Hendrik Gerritsz (van Eijck), this street also housed the town stonemasonry yard of Jan van Dalen (from 1617 to 1660), Thomas Gerritsz de Keyser (from 1623 to 1635), his cousin the painter and blue stone seller, Thomas Hendriksz de Keyser (from 1640 to 1654), Huijbert Thomasz de Keyser, the architect Hendrick de Keyser's cousin, brother of Pieter (from 1652 to 1665), Claes Claesz van Medemblick, Elbert Croese,

78. Amsterdam, Brouwersgracht. Anonymous photograph from around 1900 (GAA, Inv.Nr. D 23.250).

---

[794] GAA, NA 543B-37. 4 May 1633. Not. J. Westfrisius.   [795] GAA, NA 543. Not. J. Westfrisius. 23 May 1633.

Jan Foppe de Graaf, Jacob Kidt, Barend Kronenburg and others.[796] Other places in town where stone-masons were located included the eastern side of the Prinsengracht (from the Leliesluis to the church-yard behind the academy), from the Heiligewegs Gate to the Reguliers Gate and from the Amstelbrug (bridge) to well past the bake house.[797]

The stocks the various stonemasons had lying around their workshops, especially the more established and wealthy ones, could sometimes be considerable. Many different types of stone and states of processing could be found there. For example, the inventory of the stocks, furniture and household effects in the property of Willem Pietersz van Delft, stone buyer, dated 7 and 8 January 1650 listed the following items: in the shop: 1,700 8 inch blue stones squared, 80 15 inch white stones Italian, 324 8 inch white Italian polished and squared, 100 8 inch blue stones polished, 220 8 inch grey Swedish stones, 14 stone crowns, 360 white Italian *voetstenen*, 32 8 inch white Italian stones, 500 small 12 inch grey Swedish stones, 58 10 inch blue [stones], 880 10 inch grey stones, 1,540 10 inch blue stones, 177 blue *voetstenen*, 358 Italian rough voetstenen, 660 blue ones, 280 grey ones, 760 Swedish ones, 1,400 10 inch Italian *rouw* stones, 140 grey ones, 520 10 inch blue ones, 864 white Italian ones, 496 10 inch white Italian stones, a large brick, 400 white Italian stones, 539 12 inch white Italian, 168 blue ones, 150 white Italian ones, 80 15 inch white ones, 250 12 inch white, 138 white ones. The courtyard held: 637 5 inch blue stones, 500 7 inch blue stones, 15 *waterbakstenen*, 481 blue stones, 341 grey stones, 700 red Swedish stones, 216 10 inch grey stones, 230 12 inch blue, 5 small *waterstenen*, 47 *waterstenen*, 72 grey Swedish, 28 grey Swedish, 376 blue stones, 335 white stones, 189 8 inch Swedish red stones, 60 rough grey stones. The cellar housed another 159 8 inch Italian and 200 white stones. The atelier 451 8 inch white Italian stones, 58 10 inch white Italian stones, 768 white stones, 40 Italian voetstenen, 100 grey stones, 30 15 inch grey stones, a stone saw, 550 iron weights. Outside the front door in the street there could be found another 440 feet of thresholds, 30 1.5 foot wide thresholds, 111 thick thresholds, 130 thin thresholds, another 117 + 100 + 34 + 40 +34 + 30 + 33 the same, 36 single benches, 28 double ones, 5 water troughs, 18 blue stones from/of 3 to a tomb, 24 1.5 foot Swedish stones, a total of 17 10 foot tombstones. On a lot outside the Heiligewegs gate and in the house there could be found one 11.5 foot long and 3.5 foot wide tombstone, together with another 14 tombstones, 30 benches, 15 stepstones, 22 blue double consoles plus another 18.[798]

In another instance, the inventory of stone buyer Dirck van Delft the Younger – dated 5 September 1653 – similarly shows huge quantities of stock. The list includes: tombstones, flagstones, white stones, white rough stones, blue stones, red stones, Swedish stones, thresholds, pump troughs, mortars, but also two horses, a saddle, a stable, tools, drills and a jack for moving heavy stones. His household effects included a painting of a small ship by the painter Vroom, two portraits, two white marble busts on pedestals, a marble bust of Erasmus, four marble inkwells and two marble salt cellars.[799] A seemingly endless list enumerates the stones once owned by this Van Delft, who lived on the Leliegracht. The stones were stored on the Prinsengracht and Leliegracht, at various places on the ramparts and at his home. The total value of his, truly enormous, stocks amounted to 30,000 guilders (Fig. 79).[800]

---

[796] Information supplied by Ruud Koopman. With thanks.
[797] GAA, Vroedschap 5025-12-160. 31 January 1623.
[798] GAA, Desolate Boedels 5072-355-93. 7 and 8 January 1650.

[799] GAA, NA 1812-821. Not. A. Eggericx. 5 September 1653.
[800] GAA, NA 2822-90. Not. H. Westfrisius. 1 December 1656.

79. Amsterdam, Leliegracht. Photograph by J.M. Arsath Ro'is, 1976 (GAA, Inv.Nr. C 16.376).

Conclusion

During the seventeenth century the trade in Namur stone was consolidated and expanded, becoming more or less an independent branch of the construction trade. This independence was primarily expressed by the manner in which a division was created in Amsterdam between sandstone and blue stone buyers. Just as had been the case in preceding periods, the stone trade was closely tied to patrons, quarry operators, building contractors, architects and other people active in the construction trade. The principal difference is, however, that during the first half of the seventeenth century there is a clear intertwining of trading families from the Meuse Valley with those in Holland. Two good examples of this intermingling are on the one hand, the merging of the Van Neurenberg family with Ariaensz van Delft in Amsterdam, and on the other, the shift of the Wijmoth family's activities to Leiden. The trade in marble became a substantial part of the activities of the stone merchants under discussion.

XVI. Dynastic Development from Dordrecht to Amsterdam: Intertwining Trading Contacts

Coenraad IV van Neurenberg (1571 – approximately 1635)

As more becomes known about the family's history it becomes possible to place a number of phenomena into the wider context of seventeenth-century society. For example, a number of crafts-men, merchants and traders managed to climb the social ladder thanks to thoroughly considered trad-ing politics. But there were different routes to attaining this goal. It could be achieved through the acquisition of wealth and through favourable marriages. Furthermore, good education or an official career also played a considerable role.[801]

Over the course of the seventeenth century official careers often gained priority over actual trading activities. The accumulated wealth of the Van Neurenberg family, for example, eventually became the basis for the family's disappearance from the stone trade. People who had originally been traders joined the patricians and their trading activities slowly shifted into the background. It was not that the family left trading entirely behind, but such tasks were transferred to other family members so that the financial gains remained, and at the same time advantages could be reaped from the official positions they fulfilled. These were often even more lucrative than the original activity and so combining tasks provided the perfect opportunity to increase the capital already amassed.[802] Contacts with tax officials could ensure that checks were carried out by contacts they knew. Furthermore, there were great advan-tages to be had in building public works.[803] The context for such a shift towards the patriciate natu-rally had to be favourable. A generation with several active merchants who had good contacts outside the personal network guaranteed the continued existence of lucrative activities if one of the descen-dants should opt to involve himself in official administrative duties.

Coenraad IV van Neurenberg, who appeared in the previous part in connection with the Blue Gate in Leiden, was born in 1571 in Namur and married in Dordrecht in 1594 to Marie Avondeaulx van Schie, who bore him two sons, Coenraad V (1601) and Johan (1603). His wife died a year after the birth of their second son, after which Coenraad, at an unknown date, married Yde Jans. From 1607 he could regularly be found in 's-Hertogenbosch. During the winter of 1607-1608 he sold large ship-ments of Meuse Valley coal to the town,[804] which may possibly have been done in the guise of a dis-tributor. He made no other known coal deliveries. He was, however, also in 's-Hertogenbosch for other activities. So frequently, in fact, that on 31 March 1608 he was made a burgher of the town.[805] Two years later, in June 1610, the churchwardens of the Sint Jan asked him to draw up a cost calculation for the construction of a new rood screen for the church, which would tie him to the town for some time.[806]

In addition to his activities in 's-Hertogenbosch, Coenraad IV maintained his contacts with Dordrecht where he probably continued to live until well into the twenties. However, just like his brother Willem he would also increasingly focus on Amsterdam, which resulted in the now widowed Coenraad announcing his intention to marry Judith Dermelle van Nieuwelle (Nivelles), on 2 January 1627. Until that point in time he lived in Dordrecht. At the time of the announcement, Judith Der-

---

[801] Prak 1985, among other things Chapter 5.1.
[802] Such developments are known to have happened in vari-ous trading families, including the Van Neurenbergs. Van Deursen 1991, p. 190, Kooijmans 1997, passim.
[803] Van Deursen 1991, pp. 190-191.

[804] Van Zuijlen 1866, p. 1178. *1256 gangen colen, als Lieve Reynders ende Coenraerdt van Norenberch, hier hadde liggende.*
[805] Van Zuijlen 1866, p. 1175. *Item Coenraert Coenraerts van Norenberch, geboren tot Namen.*
[806] See Chapter XVII.

melle was fifty-three years old, making her three years younger than Coenraad. She lived on the Boomstraat in Amsterdam.[807] This marriage did not last long either. An inventory of Judith Dermelle's possessions was drawn up on 1 May 1633, which took place soon after her funeral. The inventory lists clothing (no valuation) in a black suitcase, a white, square chest, a white jewellery box and a white chest, which had been brought down from the loft for the inventory.[808] A few months later, on 12 August, Coenraad collected some of his belongings, which concerned, among other things, a number of bonds and the marriage contract. The fact that Coenraad explicitly came to collect things allows one to conclude that the couple each kept their own homes.[809]

The image of Coenraad that emerges from various sources is fragmentary and varied. He is known to have traded in coal, Namur stone and marble. Furthermore, he was active as a hydraulic engineer and he received a patent for his dredging machine. Unfortunately, it is not known when he died, nor is there insight into the other activities in which he may have been involved. However, the above information does reveal that the core of the family's network had partially shifted to Amsterdam.

Willem II van Neurenberg (approximately 1575 - approximately 1640)

Coenraad's brother, Willem II van Neurenberg, was born in Namur around 1575 and moved to Dordrecht with his parents at an early age. He married Marie Willemot, probably in Dordrecht, shortly after 1610.[810] She was the daughter of Jan Willemot, a Liège stone merchant, who had also relocated to Dordecht around 1585 just like the Van Neurenbergs. Willem's wife Marie was baptised in Dordrecht on 11 March 1587, with Coenraad III van Neurenberg and his wife Marie le Bidart as witnesses.[811]

Willem II continued his father's business from the family home. After the death of his father, Coenraad III, in 1603, and Coenraad's widow (his second wife Margaretha de Swart), in March 1613, Willem II purchased his brothers' and sisters' shares of the inheritance in the house so that he owned it.[812] Things were going well, both personally and professionally; his son Johan who was born in 1613, followed by Coenraad (1615), Willem (1619) and daughter Beatrix (1623). In 1616 and 1620, Willem owned plots Nos. 7 and 8 on the Hoge Nieuwstraat, which stretched to the Nieuwe Haven. At that time plot No. 7 had a house on it and plot No. 8 had a shed.[813] Although Willem retained his base of operations in Dordrecht, he was slowly gaining a foothold in Amsterdam, just like his brother Coen-

---

[807] GAA, NA DTB 431-540.

[808] GAA, NA, 562-11. Not. J. Westfrisius. The inventory was drawn up at the request of blue stone buyer Pieter Ariaensz van Delft. This episode took place in her living room in the house De Witte Pauw onto the Leliegracht, the same canal along which the Van Delft family lived. Coenraad and Judith were not married in community of property. NA, 708-1. Not. P. Carels.

[809] Daniel Wery and Jan Mareijn acted as witnesses. It concerned a bond payable by Pieter and Willem van Neurenberg, dated 26 July 1608, worth 1000 guilders, written in French. Furthermore, there was a bond payable by Coenraad, worth 550 guilders, dated 1 April 1627 and a bond payable by Pieter Jansz Reaal, worth 250 guilders, dated 19 April 1633. The last item mentioned is the marriage contract of 1 January 1627 that had been drawn up by notary public P. Carels.

[810] Their first child Johan was born on 24 February 1613.

[811] GAD, Klapper Waalse kerk, p. 143.

[812] Huisman p. 54. On 21 March 1621 he purchased his sisters' shares and he probably also purchased his brother Pieter's share before 1624. In 1624 he purchased his brother Coenraad's share.

[813] Huisman states that her source is a folder on the Van Neurenberg family in the GAD. This folder has been lost. In 1626, just No. 7 was mentioned in connection with Willem's name. Huisman suggests that this is because he had to buy out his brothers and sisters and therefore sold No. 8. However, in 1633 plots No. 7, 8 and 9 are in his name, so at most he may have mortgaged No. 8. In this year he is said to have had a new house built on plots No. 7 and 8. No. 9 was used as a shed and workshop.

raad. On 31 July 1623, Willem purchased a lot from Grietje Jans and Willem Barentsz Hartman on the western side of the Keizersgracht, now number 122.[814] Hendrik Trip inhabited the later house on the plot on the Keizersgracht. It was therefore not their home. It should probably be viewed as an investment intended for rental purposes.[815]

Just like his brother Coenraad IV, Willem II van Neurenberg was part of the wealthy upper level of society. J.M. Montias has made a plausible case for the supposition that Willem III van Neurenberg stayed in Amsterdam in 1638 as an apprentice to Rembrandt van Rhijn, and purchased prints for himself and possibly for his father. At the auction of the former possessions of the late Jan Basse, in March 1637, Willem listed his address as living with Schelte Dirricxsz in the Molsteeg. At the auction of the former property of the late Gommer Spranger, in February 1638, Willem was staying adjacent to the brewery 't Lam, on the Singel near the Koningsplein. It is remarkable that Willem did not stay with family, but in a boarding house. Willem attended auctions in order to buy prints. Jan Basse, an artist and dealer, and Gommer Spranger, a major merchant and painter Bartholomaeus Spranger's cousin, both had interesting collections which attracted prominent buyers. These buyers included Rembrandt van Rhijn, jeweller Davidt ter Haer and Willem III van Neurenberg. It was Van Rhijn who at Basse's auction purchased a total of 133 guilders and two stivers worth of prints. The auctioneer Daniel Jansz van Beuningen's notes reveal that Van Rhijn sold some prints even before he had paid for them to people including Willem van Neurenberg.[816]

Van Rhijn possibly purchased the prints at Van Neurenberg's request or consultation took place concerning them. It is certain that this was the case at the Spranger sale; Van Rhijn, Van Neurenberg and Samuel Smijters all purchased a copper plate by Albrecht Dürer. Prints of these plates were also auctioned, whereby the buyers did not bid for prints of their own plates. Willem van Neurenberg acquired the original plate of Dürers *Dream of the Doctor* for eighteen guilders.[817] For two guilders and two stivers Van Neurenberg acquired twelve prints other prints of which Smijters had purchased the original and also a dozen prints, of which Van Rhijn had purchased the original. When eight dozen prints of the *Dream of the Doctor*, the original plate Willem now owned, were auctioned he refrained from bidding. Everything points to an agreement having been made as to who was to bid on which lot.[818] Incidentally, Van Neurenberg was not one of those bidding most at the auction. That was the role of Rembrandt van Rhijn and Cornelis Danckerts, the publisher of the *Architectura Moderna*. The third most important bidder was Abraham Alewijn (1607-1679), who was a cloth merchant on the Warmoesstraat.[819]

Although such data on the personal life and interests of the protagonists in this study is rare, it does supply invaluable information on the social group Willem and his family were a part of. When this social circle is taken into consideration along with the family relations and the trading contacts with Hendrick de Keyser, for example, a view of Van Neurenberg as part of the economic and artistic elite emerges.

When Willem II van Neurenberg's widow sold the house and plot on the Keizersgracht in December 1643, Hendrik Trip oversaw the matter.[820] The buyer was Aeltje Danckerts, the widow of Jacob Valcksz. Witnesses to the sale were her brother Cornelis Danckerts, surveyor, town bricklayer and

---

[814] With thanks to Ruud Koopman. The plot, that at the time was probably still uninhabited, was 17.5 feet wide and 150 feet deep. It bordered on Hans Claesz's land at the northern and rear side, and at the southern side it bordered on the land of the seller Grietje Jans. GAA, KW 43-226. Simultaneously, at Willem van Neurenberg's request sixty-one year old merchant Evert van Duijren, and fifty-eight year old stone buyer Dirck Hendricksz, declared that the account was real and written by Laurens Pietersz van Sweijs. Sweijs

has already been encountered earlier. GAA, NA 691-380 (34v). not. J. Warnaerts.

[815] Van Eeghen 1985, p. 65. The Scheltes mentioned was Schelte Dirck Sr., who also made purchases at the auction.

[816] Ibidem.

[817] Ibidem.

[818] Montias 2002, 144-149.

[819] Van Eeghen 1985, p. 68, No. 14.

[820] GAA, NA 992-60. not. Ja. Bosch.

the father-in-law of Laurens Sweijs (and Claes Ariaens van Delft) with who Van Neurenberg had regularly done business and Arent Remmingh, her cousin.[821] Even this personal transaction involved the construction sector's elite.

Pieter van Neurenberg (approximately 1576/80 - 29 February 1636)

In contrast to Coenraad IV and Willem II, Pieter van Neurenberg did not base himself in Dordrecht or Amsterdam. He was born around 1580 in Namur and moved north with his parents. He probably moved back to Namur quite early to guarantee business continuity after Coenraad II's death sometime before 20 October 1595. In 1601, his name appeared in the Namur municipal income tax register.[822] In 1618, he was the godfather during a baptism on 12 August at the Saint-Jean Church in Namur.[823] In 1601 he married Anne d'Harscamp, thereby joining an important family of master smiths and ironworkers. Pieter fathered at least two children. The merchant, captain of a militia, and a member of the town authority of Namur in 1626, died on 29 February 1636.[824]

Pieter clearly spent the better part of his active life in Namur. He only travelled north occasionally. For example, in 1606 he arranged matters pertaining to the stone deliveries for the Protestant Church in Willemstad for his deceased father.[825] On 6 June 1612 Pieter sold his shares in the V.O.C., for six hundred guilders to Elias Trip. The accompanying deed refers to Pieter as a merchant from Dordrecht.[826]

Due to his base in Namur, it was natural for him to deal with the deliveries and orders of his brothers Coenraad IV and Willem II. However, the lack of a personal or family archive makes the internal structure of family activities difficult to reconstruct. But proof of the above hypothesis can be found in 1614. On 9 October 1614 Pieter, then an inhabitant of Namur, concluded a contract in Dinant with Gilles van Maasniel and his father-in-law Hubert Misson for the delivery of a years' worth of tombstones to Van Neurenberg. The stone was to be loaded onto ships in Bouvignes. The order was without doubt intended for the Dutch market.[827] Here we see Pieter purchasing the contents of an entire quarry, as it were, to provide his brothers in the north with material.

The network widens

Upon the death of her husband, the widow often took over the responsibility for the company and continued operating under her own name, which was even the case after the death of Coenraad III. In Willemstad Coenraad III naturally was no longer mentioned as a merchant, but neither were his sons Coenraad IV or Willem II, although they were active in the stone trade at the time. Instead it is Margaretha de Swart whose name appears as stone seller.[828] The death of the husband was, therefore, a legitimate reason for the wife to become involved in the stone trade. In that sense, the wife had a more prominent role than may at first be apparent. Coenraad III's daughters, Anna and Maria, did not marry indiscriminately. Take for instance Anna van Neurenberg, whose case provides clear indications of the ulterior motives on which marriage policy was based.

---

[821] Ibidem. The agreement stated that the purchase price of 15,260 guilders did not include the gold leather and stove in the house.
[822] Courtoy 1912, p. 511.
[823] Ibidem.
[824] Ibidem, p. 512.

[825] Huisman 1986, No. 122. The contract dates back to 27 May 1606. See also Ozinga 1929.
[826] Ibidem, p. 63. See Klein 1965 for more on the relationship between Van Neurenberg and Trip.
[827] Courtoy 1920, pp. 236-237.
[828] Ozinga 1929, p. 151.

Anna van Neurenberg and Pieter Ariaensz van Delft

Anna van Neurenberg was one of Coenraad III van Neurenberg and Marie le Bidart's daughters.[829] She was baptised in Dordrecht on 1 November 1585.[830] She married Jaques Saverij in Dordrecht, and with him had a son, Mathijs.[831] She was, however, soon widowed. On 28 May 1616, when she was thirty, she provided notification of her intention to marry Pieter Ariaensz van Delft from Amsterdam.[832] The attestation of the Walloon Church concerning Anna van Neurenberg followed a month later, on 27 June 1616. Anna, now the wife of Pieter van Delft, was transferred from Dordrecht to Amsterdam in the Walloon Church's register.[833]

Anna and Pieter had six children together: Coenraad, Adriaan, Pieter[834], Gilles, Daniel and Maria.[835] Coenraad (1617-1653) would also enter the stone trade. In November 1635, Anna and Pieter reviewed their marriage contract. At that point in time they were living on the Brouwersgracht and still had their health. The review indicates the existence of a number of children and children from previous marriages or liaisons. Pieter already had two children with Mayke Steenwinckel: Willem and Neeltje. The nine children were given advances on their inheritances totalling 5,300 guilders in cash. Willem and Neeltje were to receive five hundred guilders upon Pieter's death. Mathijs, Anna's son, was to receive eight hundred guilders.[836] Daughter Maria was to be given Anna's clothes, jewellery and trinkets, while she would also receive the inheritance plus five hundred guilders with her five brothers. Maria probably died early. When Anna and Pieter, the first healthy, the latter ailing drew up their testament on Sunday 10 February 1647 at seven 'o clock at night, she was no longer mentioned.[837] Five years later, on 19 December 1652, Anna van Neurenberg was buried at the West Church.[838] Pieter died in 1657.[839]

When they announced their intention to marry, Pieter was already well-known as a blue stone buyer. He was one of Adriaen van Delft's four sons active as a stonemason and stone merchant. Of the four brothers, Pieter seems to have occupied the most prominent position. However, this statement should be qualified by the fact that the brothers often cooperated. The eldest, Claes, born around 1573, was in Deventer in 1612/1613 in connection with the raising of the Lebuïnus tower. He had set up a partnership with Hendrick de Keyser in order to carry out this work. After six months of preparation, De Keyser took on the work in December in cooperation with his partner Claes Ariaensz van Delft, with work starting immediately. De Keyser's master labourer (and executing party) was Herman Ariaensz (van Delft).[840] Claes was involved in a delivery of stone for a lock, which was built by the towns Arnhem and Nijmegen in 1612 in Elden. He was also responsible for the previously mentioned delivery of stonework for the houses designed by Philips Vingboons on the Oude Turfmarkt 145/147, in 1641.[841] He supplied a funerary monument for the Maria Church in Lübeck commissioned by Johan Füchting (Fig. 80).

[829] She is listed in the register of births of the Walloon Church in Dordrecht on 1 November 1585.
[830] GAD, Doopboek N.H. Gemeente.
[831] GAA, NA 502-76. Not. J. Westfrisius.
[832] GAA, DTB 763 46. Pieter survived his wife Mayke Steenwinckel. He lived in the Ververije, next door to the Glashuis. He already had children from his first marriage, of whom Willem (20 March 1614 - 1661/1662) would also become active as a stonemason. On 21 October 1608, Pieter, then twenty-nine years old, announced his intention to marry Mayke Steenwinkel Willemsdr, of Antwerp, who was twenty-one years old. DTB 413-304.
[833] GAA, PA 201-46. A. Attestaties Waalse kerk.

[834] GAA, DTB 6-4. Pieter Jr. was baptised in the Old Church and the witnesses were his uncle Pieter van Neurenberg and Marijtje Cornelis. Pieter was born on 3 February 1622.
[835] GAA, NA 502-76.
[836] This distribution may illustrate status relations between the families. Anna was possibly better born than Pieter van Delft, judging by the higher sum to be paid to her son. Another option is that the figure is higher because it contains part of the property of her first husband.
[837] GAA, NA 1661-51. Not. P. de Bary.
[838] GAA, DTB 1100 B-116.
[839] Pieter died between 8 May 1656 and 27 June 1657.
[840] Meischke 1994, p. 113.
[841] Ibidem, p. 118.

80. Lübeck, Maria Church, funerary monument for Johann Füchting, 1633 (Anonymous photograph, 1970 (Denkmalamt Lübeck).

81. Nijmegen, weigh house 1612 (Anonymous photograph, RDMZ, Neg.Nr. 179.212).

In 1614, the youngest brothers Herman and Dirk were inducted into the Amsterdam guild as stonemasons. Dirk seems to have specialised in trading in marble floors. In 1632 he supplied an Italian floor to Joan Huydecooper for a new room behind his house on the Lauriergracht. A year later, he supplied the floors for Frederik Hendrik's Palace ter Nieuburg and later for the Amsterdam municipal orphanage.[842] He also shipped stone to Copenhagen and Calmar. In 1648 Dirk was responsible for supplying a mantelpiece for the house at Rapenburg 34 in Leiden, for Daniel van Ceulen. The blue stone seller Willem Wijmoth, carpenter Jacob Dircxz van Banheyningen and stonemason Henrick Jansz Mausen assessed the mantelpiece. They measured it and declared that it in no way corresponded to the Ionic order in which the capitals and bases had been made.[843]

Pieter van Delft has left the most traces of his existence. His date of birth is unknown, but he was probably born around 1580. He was initially married to Mayke Steenwinckel from Antwerp, daughter of Willem, and related to the famous master masons family Van Steenwinckel. The son and heir, Louwrens, worked on the town hall of Emden from 1578 on; Hans the Elder, his son, worked as royal architect for Christian IV of Denmark from 1582 on. Hans died in 1601.[844] The family continued to work primarily in the north.

---

[842] Ibidem, p. 119. In 1638 he also supplied 140 Dinant blue tombstones and sixty Liège blue tombstones to the churchwardens of Wormer. Each tombstone cost twelve guilders and ten stivers.

[843] Lunsingh Scheurleer 1990, pp. 140-141 and 162. The conflict remained unresolved, Van Delft refused to take the work back or improve it.
[844] See Roding 1991, pp. 27 and 30.

Pieter van Delft's activities remained concentrated around Amsterdam. In 1610, he had his own business.[845] Between 1611 and 1629 his name occurs in the archive of the Old Church in Amsterdam as being responsible for, among other things, the construction of the office of the *Huiszittenmeesters* (a type of alms organisation) (1611). Furthermore, he worked on the sexton's house, supplied tombstones and stone.[846] From early in his career he was already active outside town. For example, Pieter supplied the sandstone stonemasonry work for the new weigh house in Nijmegen in 1612 (Fig. 81).[847] As mentioned earlier he made deliveries as far away as Lübeck,[848] but most of his activities were limited to Amsterdam. In June 1622 he was paid for the blue stone he supplied for the St. Luciensteeg 25 house.[849] On 13 August 1625, Pieter received 187 guilders and four stivers for the delivery of an 'Italian floor'.[850] On 22 November 1632, he received 1,775 guilders for blue thresholds, flagstones, pillars and other hard stones, for the boys' gallery of the Civil Orphanage. On 15 January 1633 he received another three hundred guilders.[851]

His involvement in alterations to the Civil Orphanage also provides interesting information. Besides supplying stonework for the boys' gallery, which Pieter de Keyser probably built, he also supplied stonework for the girls' courtyard in 1634. Pieter was the only stone supplier directly involved in the construction of the boys' gallery in the northern and western wings.[852] For the southern wing of the girls' gallery stone was also purchased from him. Jacob van Campen designed the girls' wing and received three hundred guilders for his designs on 13 November 1634.[853] The sandstone for the building work was purchased in Zwolle. The first mention dates back to 1 December 1633 and notations continue through 1634, concerning a total of fifteen shipments. The orphanage purchased the stone directly and it was then worked under Pieter van Delft's supervision according to Jacob van Campen's plans. In addition to working the stone, Pieter was also responsible for supplying flagstones and he purchased blocks of stone (probably additional sandstone) from Pieter de Keyser and Hannus Hartjes.[854]

The cooperation with Van Campen occurs again during the construction of the Theatre, which was built at the Orphanage's request in 1637. Here too, Van Campen was the designer and Pieter van Delft is the only stone supplier mentioned in the accounts.[855]

The similarity between Van Neurenberg and Pieter van Delft is clear: together with his three brothers he held a position as a stone trader, which can easily be compared to that of Coenraad IV, Willem II and Pieter van Neurenberg. These peers, with their close ties, thanks to the marriage of Anna van Neurenberg and Pieter van Delft, cooperated at the epicentre of artistic development and at the source of the rapidly emerging marble trade. The multiple examples of cooperation with Hendrick de Keyser and the trade with Scandinavia are remarkable. The choice of Pieter van Delft as a marriage partner for Anna van Neurenberg, and vice versa, is an obvious one within the context. There was more at stake than merely personal happiness; the interests of two important companies would be jointly supported in future.

Furthermore, individual motive played a part. When Anna van Neurenberg remarried she not only took the family trading politics into account, but would also have considered her son Mathijs Saverij's future. He was only three when his father died. Anna's new marriage also secured his future; Mathijs joined her in Amsterdam and eventually became a merchant in all kinds of goods. In 1641 he

[845] Meischke 1994, p. 117.
[846] Between 1614 and 1640, Pieter supplied approximately 650 tombstones for the Old Church. Unpublished article by Ruud Koopman.
[847] Meischke 1994, pp. 118-119.
[848] Lunsingh Scheurleer 1990, p. 141, n. 143.
[849] Meischke 1975, p. 154.

[850] Ibidem, p. 155.
[851] Ibidem, p. 178.
[852] Ibidem, pp. 180-182. More details can be found in these pages.
[853] Ibidem, p. 183.
[854] Ibidem, p. 181.
[855] Meischke 1994, p. 119.

married Susanne Neering and in 1668 Elisabeth Lambillon from Dordrecht. One article he traded in was Italian marble. For example, on 12 August 1654 he sold four Italian marble columns, approximately five metres long, to Lambert de Hontoire in Liège, with Laurens de Maen from Maastricht's permission.[856]

Analysis of the composition of the Dordrecht network: allied families

Anna van Neurenberg's marriage to Pieter van Delft was only one of the pillars supporting the network of contacts. If the contacts in Dordrecht are examined, then it becomes clear that there were multiple personal or family ties. Examining the marriage register and the list of baptismal witnesses reveals the personal relations between the Van Neurenberg family and other prominent merchants in Dordrecht. These contacts often originate in the Walloon country. For practical reasons family names, which are known from Meuse Valley trade, like the Van Neurenbergs were traced first. The related families provided cooperation and extensive networks of trading contacts, but simultaneously they could constitute a link to patrons and new markets. When Willem II van Neurenberg married Marie Wijmoth at the start of the seventeenth century it was clearly an economically motivated marriage.

The name *Wijmoth* first occurred as a stone supplier for the Bibliotheca Thysiana in Leiden in 1655. Particularly in the seventeenth century they appear as stone suppliers in Leiden. Both Wijmoth and Willem van Neurenberg acted as witnesses to the baptism of Nicolas d'Emmeri or Damery's children in 1621 and 1624 in Dordrecht.[857] Johan Lambillon was also there.[858] In 1624, Marie Wijmoth, Willem II van Neurenberg's wife was also a witness at the baptism of Hubert Duer Jr. Duer was possibly related to Joris Duer who, at that time, was the town stonemason of 's-Hertogenbosch and a supplier of stone.[859] Lambert Lambillon was also one of the witnesses. The same combination of people occurs at Gille Gilles' baptism on 9 January 1602, where Pieter Lambillon and Willem Wijmoth were witnesses. In addition to the relations between Wijmoth and Lambillon, there are also ties between the Trip and Polyander families who will later re-occur in relation to the Van Neurenbergs.

The Lambillons maintained personal contacts with the Van Neurenbergs, which seem to have been older and closer than those with the Wijmoths. As seen above, cooperation between the two families occurred in 1555 for the delivery of tombstones for the Old Church in Amsterdam by Coenraad II and Jacob Pierçon Lambillon. The kind of familial relationship the two families had during this period has not been clarified; however, it can not be ruled out that Coenraad and Jacob were in fact in-laws. Professional cooperation between both families also occurred in sources pertaining to the gable of the church arch in Nijmegen.

In addition to the relationships with the Wijmoths, interesting interconnections can also be seen with the Lambillons. The baptisms of Lambert Lambillon's children between 1623 and 1632 feature Jacob Trip and Henri de Geer, important Wallloon merchants, as witnesses. At the baptisms of Pieter Lambillon's children between 1599 and 1611, Elias Trip, Johan de Geer (Gerre), Louis de Geer, Coenraad van Neurenberg and [?] Wijmoth appeared as witnesses.[860] And, if we examine the witnesses at the baptisms of the Van Neurenberg children then, here too, the familiar names Wijmoth, Trip and Lambillon occur. Marie van Neurenberg, Coenraad III's daughter, had married Charles le Mercenier before 1618, while Johan van Neurenberg, Willem II's son, married Elisabeth, Jacob Trip's daughter around 1635. The contacts made in Dordrecht proved to be important for the shift to Amsterdam. The socio-geographic position was directly related to these relationships.

---

[856] The price per 17.5 foot pillar was 456 *rijksdaalders*. GAA, NA 1702-295. not. P. de Bary, 12 August 1654.

[857] Damery was undoubtedly a close relation of Van Neurenberg. Coenraad's grandmother's surname was Demry, which probably makes the Damery mentioned here a cousin.

[858] GAD. Klapper Waalse Kerk.

[859] Ibidem. See Mosmans 1031, pp. 330, 444 and 449, and Van Drunen 1977, p. 211.

[860] GAD, Klapper Waalse kerk.

The network expands

The two most important families with whom the Van Neurenbergs entered into relations and who were not active in the stone trade were the Trip and De Geer families. Primarily active in the iron trade, with considerable markets and their own industrial sites in Scandinavia, they represented an important link towards the expansion and broadening of the Van Neurenberg's own activities. Both the De Geer and Trip families were also initially located in Dordrecht. The De Geers originated in Liège, the Trips in Zaltbommel. These families also relocated to Amsterdam after some time.

Louis de Geer (1587-1652) was born in Liège and baptised on 17 November 1587. His father, also called Louis, decided to relocate to Dordrecht in 1596. In 1615, the young Louis moved to Amsterdam to continue his deceased father's business. His trading activities were closely connected to those of Elias and Jacob Trip, in-laws, who had set up major copper trading activities with Sweden. De Geer also started to work this trade and quickly managed to capture a leading role. His role was even more conspicuous in the emerging iron trade. There, De Geer provided investment, infrastructure and the market for the product. He led an enormous conglomerate of production sites. The Swedish crown enabled De Geer to lease land and mines. Specialised labourers and supervisory staff were brought in from the Republic and the Spanish Low Countries in order to guarantee production and leadership.[861] With the major staple market in Amsterdam and Sweden at war, the profit opportunities for De Geer were enormous. In 1627, he relocated to Sweden in name, both in Stockholm and Norrköping, but his actual domicile remained Amsterdam, although he had impressive homes built in Sweden, after designs and using materials and craftsmen he imported from Holland.[862]

De Geer's conspicuous business success was not isolated. The Trip family and in particular Jacob and Elias, developed business activities in Sweden just like De Geer. Active in countless branches of trade they also managed to develop into a respected trading family from their bases in Tiel, Zaltbommel and Dordrecht. Their relocation to Amsterdam led to them also becoming very wealthy due to favourable economic conditions, good contacts and a strong entrepreneurial spirit throughout the family. One of the characteristics of these families is that they, although specialised, attempted to spread risks as much as possible. For example, Trip was active in the iron trade, but the family also made money trading in grain, cloth, and had shares in the V.O.C. The same phenomenon occurred with regard to the Van Neurenberg family's activities. First of all, they benefited from ongoing building activities: trade in Namur stone generated by hydraulic engineering and facing stonework. Furthermore, as discussed above the trade in Belgian marble increased rapidly after 1600, both in the Republic and in the Baltic. During this period the family also began manufacturing brick. Johan van Neurenberg, Coenraad IV's second son, moved to the water meadows outside Dordrecht and worked as a brick maker.[863] Furthermore, alliances were entered into with other sectors of industry, including the Trip family.

In the wake of the Trip and De Geer families, Coenraad IV van Neurenberg also became active in Denmark. An open letter dated 19 May 1622 declared that Johan de Willem and Abraham de la Haye, citizens of Copenhagen, and Coenraad van Neurenberg and their company were given exclusive rights to start a limekiln in Skåne near Malmö. No one else was allowed to set up or use a factory on crown land within a ten-mile radius of the place they were going to start; they were given this right for twelve years. The entrepreneurs had the sole right and moreover the privilege that if they found other stone suitable for construction, they were permitted to use that, too. The sale of products was unrestricted. They could supply to both the home and export markets. The king of Denmark would

---

861 Lindblad 1995, pp. 78-79.
862 Ibidem, p. 79 and Noldus 1999, passim.

863 Huisman 1986, p. 53. Huisman does not support this comment.. Lips 1974, p. 274 states that later Dordrecht stepped gables were made of yellow stones fired at the brickworks of Mr Neurenberg near the Weeskinderendijk.

82. The Van Neurenberg family's area of activities between 1610 and 1650 (drawing by author).

receive two percent of the proceeds. The entrepreneurs were obliged to justify themselves annually to the auditor's office regarding the amount of money they made and what they sold to whom.[864] Deliveries of marble to the King of Poland and the Elector of Brandenburg can be viewed in the light of international trading contacts. Not only was their own trading policy a pillar supporting their success, but also the fact that so many international merchants and patrons went to Amsterdam to do business.

---

[864] Roding 1991, p. 149.

The family's activities in the field of limekilns in Scandinavia and brickyards along the river in Dordrecht should be viewed in a broader context. It was not coincidental that they also expanded their activities in this direction; the limestone was pre-eminently suitable for burning into lime thanks to the high percentage of lime and bitumen it contained. However, what is more important is that general tendencies such as an increase in scale, specialisation and risk spreading, combined with trading alliances with other merchants also apply to the Van Neurenberg family.

The marketing process reveals the interrelationships between merchants, which were also very important for purchasing policy. Hubert Misson, a member of an important stone trading family that cooperated with the Van Neurenbergs, supplied large quantities of stone to the Van Neurenberg family together with his son-in-law Thierry le Bidart, who was an uncle or cousin of Coenraad IV et al. The Van Neurenbergs exported the material and cleverly used their personal contacts in the Republic with Hendrick de Keyser and the Van Delft family. In this way they managed to utilise a widespread network, which reached from the quarry in Namur as far as the Baltic (fig. 82).

XVII. WORKING FOR THE CHURCH: THE SCREEN IN 'S-HERTOGENBOSCH

The screen of the Sint-Jans Church in 's-Hertogenbosch (Fig. 83)

The more political developments further undermined Antwerp's position as a trading metropolis, the more Amsterdam's importance as an export centre (harbour) increased. Examples of marble deliveries to foreign buyers include those for Christian IV of Denmark's Frederiksborg Castle, with which Hans van Steenwinckel was involved.[865] The painter Pieter Isaacsz also supplied a marble floor in 1618. The floor probably originated with Hendrick de Keyser and was therefore supplied via Amsterdam.[866] Whether this floor also contained 'Belgian' marble is unknown. However, the delivery of a four-colour floor, namely white, red, black and grey, curiously polished and cut straight, which stone buyer Gerrit Bouwensz from The Hague supplied to Frederik III of Denmark in 1658, contained Belgian marble.[867]

83. 's-Hertogenbosch, The Sint-Jans Church in from the southeast. Photograph by Martien Coppens, circa 1940 (Werkarchief Bouwhistorie – Archeologie – Monumenten 's-Hertogenbosch).

---

[865] Weilbach 1923, p. 36.
[866] Fock 1998, p. 194.

[867] Ibidem. The price of this floor amounted to 1,193 guilders and eight stivers.

The names that occur most in the marble trade are descendants of the Misson, Van Neurenberg, De Keyser, Ariaens van Delft families, together with relatively unknown merchants such as Jacques Matthijsz, Thierry le Bidart, etc. However, it was primarily the Van Neurenberg, De Keyser and Van Delft families who dominated the marble trade in the Republic. They did not have a monopoly, but their leading role is borne out by their major representation in the trade. It is not surprising that the Van Neurenberg family also became involved in the marble trade and tried to capture a position in this rapidly expanding market. A famous example of the application of red and black marble supplied at the start of the seventeenth century by Van Neurenberg, is the rood screen in 's-Hertogenbosch (Fig. 84).[868] Over the past one hundred and twenty-five years a great deal has been written concerning this

84. 's-Hertogenbosch, The screen of the Sint-Jans Church. Photograph by A. Schull, before 1866 (RDMZ, Neg.Nr. 14.087).

190

screen. Many authors, including Buschman (1918), Mosmans (1931), Neurdenberg (1938), Steppe (1952), Avery (1969) and Westermann (1993) discussed, among other things, what role Coenraad IV van Neurenberg exactly played in the manufacture of the screen. The role of stone trader proves to have often been confused with that of designer, sculptor and stonemason. Both Buschman (1918) and Avery (1969), for instance, erroneously see Van Neurenberg's as the sculptor's hand in this screen.[869]

Prior history

The Sint-Jans Church's first screen incurred considerable damage during the sixteenth century. It did not emerge unscathed from the Iconoclasm of 1566, and was subsequently destroyed by the fire in the crossing tower in 1584, whereby part of the falling masonry hit the screen.[870] The repair of the damaged church took quite some time and only in 1610 did the construction of a new screen start. In the framework of the Counter Reformation the screen gained priority over the essential work on the organ, the ostensory and the west tower.[871]

The statement by a number of authors that the design for the new screen was made by Coenraad IV van Neurenberg cannot be proven. What can, more or less, be ascertained is how the choice of design was made. Once the decision had been made to build a new screen, the churchwardens oriented themselves by viewing a number of screens in the Southern Low Countries. The example for the new screen was sought in Antwerp. The screen of the Onze Lieve Vrouwe Church, which had been entirely renewed after the taking of the town in 1585, was based on those in the Sint-Jans Church in Ghent and that of Kamerijk/Cambrai.[872] The Antwerp screen consisted of a gallery with a railing supported by three round arches and was decorated with sculptured reliefs and statues. Jacob Anthonis supplied two patterns in 1594, based on another pattern of the screen, which dated back to 1589.[873] Ultimately, it was Rafael vanden Broecke (Paludanus) who was responsible for the construction of this screen. Work started in 1597 and, as far as the architecture was concerned, was completed in late 1599. Robert and Hans de Nole then made the sculptural work.[874] In addition to black and red marble, English alabaster was also used for the sculptures.

The Antwerp screen served as an example for the one in 's-Hertogenbosch. The church council decided to have two drawings made of the screen, which probably concerns design variants for the new screen and not just copies. Two designs were made: one of a screen with five archways, another, which followed the Antwerp example more closely, with three archways. It is unknown who was responsible for these designs. Unfortunately, it is also unknown who was responsible for the delivery of materials in Antwerp. With a view to his other materials deliveries in this town, Coenraad van Neurenberg cannot be excluded as a possible responsible party. His other deliveries would also have constituted a good reason for the 's-Hertogenbosch church council to contact him. Unfortunately no further details are known, which makes it impossible to make any further statements on the matter.

[868] See, among others, Buschman 1918, Neurdenburg 1938, Avery 1969, Steppe 1952, pp. 279-286 and Westermann 1993.
[869] The sale of the screen in 1869 to the South Kensington Museum in London (now the Victoria and Albert Museum), was one of the principal reasons Victor de Stuers wrote his famous article, which appeared in the Gids *Holland op zijn smalst* [Holland at its most petty]. De Stuers 1873.

[870] Mosmans 1931, p. 436.
[871] Westermann 1993, p. 389.
[872] Steppe 1952, pp. 274-275, n. 34.
[873] Ibidem.
[874] Ibidem, p. 277.

85. 's-Hertogenbosch, rood screen, rear end. Drawing by Pieter Saenredam, 1632. (Collection Musée Lyonnais des Arts Décoratifs, Lyon).

The most prestigious design, with five archways, had a projected cost of thirteen thousand guilders. Although the specifications are still extant, they were not executed. As far as the use of materials is concerned, this screen deviated little from the screen finally realised, which had three archways. Black *toutsteene* was prescribed for the plinth above the church floor, well polished and framed. The floor was to be laid of red marble and white alabaster. A line of black touchstone was to be laid between every arch, which was to be two feet wide. Ten black stone pedestals were to be placed on the floor inlaid with red Rance or Agimont marble, depending on where the best quality was to be found. For the other parts, the abovementioned stone types determined the rest of the materials used (Fig. 85).[875]

Execution

As early as 1608, Coenraad IV van Neurenberg had obtained citizenship in 's-Hertogenbosch without having to pay for it, which may possibly have been done to partially cover outstanding invoices.[876] What Coenraad's activities in 's-Hertogenbosch between 1608 and 1610 entailed, and whether he was actually present in the town is unknown. However, in June 1610 the church council asked him to calculate the costs of both designs for the new screen. Van Neurenberg did as they asked. After assessing his calculations, the church council decided to enter into a contract with him on 13 December 1610 for the delivery of a screen in accordance with the second design. The contract was signed eight days later on 21 December. In his book on choir screens in the Low Countries J.-K. Steppe wrote that Van Neurenberg's role was more of a practical than of a purely artistic nature.[877] He only acted in the capacity of building contractor, exactly as he did for other commissions.[878]

---

[875] See Buschman 1918, pp. 30-32 for the details.
[876] Mosmans 1931, p. 437. It is doubtful that he received citizenship with a view to possibly carrying out work. It is unknown whether he himself worked as a stonemason. There was no need to be a guild member, for which citizenship was a prerequisite if you were a merchant or building contractor. Compare to Meischke 2000, p. 119.
[877] Steppe 1952, pp. 280-281.
[878] Ibidem. See also Van Neurdenberg 1948, p. 93ff.

Additional conditions were set after Van Neurenberg had concluded the contract in December 1610. The parts not covered by the agreement would be paid for additionally.[879] Early in 1611 the fabric masters decided what the iconography of the screen would be. This wish was announced to the town administration, which would ultimately bear the costs and which, in general, agreed with the choices made.[880] These sculptures resulted in a cost overrun of many thousands of guilders, above and beyond the first estimate of 11,000 guilders.[881]

According to the schedule the work was to be finished by 24 June 1613 or earlier if possible'.[882] As mentioned above, the town financed the project, which relied on sometimes highly remarkable contributions. For instance, the wife of baker Herman van Buegen was owed a number of years' worth of payment for bread from Elisabeth van Brecht. The outstanding amount was paid off in small amounts until a(n) (unknown) sum remained, which seemed irretrievable. The baker's wife, who had given up all hope of being paid the balance, angrily wrote to Elisabeth van Drecht on 8 March 1612 that she had decided to donate the outstanding amount to the sexton of the Sint- Jans Church for the construction of the screen.[883] On 18 November 1611 it was decided that people would be sent out around town to collect donations for the screen.

Work for the screen was executed on site, "in the lodge."[884] Several "engineers" or "masters" were involved in the construction; unfortunately they are not named.[885] In the year 1611/1612, "the labourers working on the screen in the Sint-Jans Church" received ten guilders.[886] Work on the screen was completed in 1613 and after completion, the labourers left town on 28 September.[887]

The sculpture on the screen

The labourers that most probably made the sculpture are different from the ones who created the architectural elements of the screen. Past literature has also paid ample attention to this fact. Nevertheless it is important to consider the materials the sculptors used to create their work. On 27 January 1611, the church's fabric lodge masters issued a statement on the sculpture to be created. At that point in time there were already various white alabaster sculptures and figures or stories carved.[888] The choice of sculptures had therefore already been made. The report once again emphasises that Coenraad van Neurenberg was also the contractor for the sculptures. However, it does not mean that he actually made the sculptures himself. This point of view is no longer logical with all the knowledge of Van Neurenberg's activities and business methods now available.[889] He turned to others for the execution of the reliefs and sculptures. The best-known sculptor who participated was Hendrick de Keyser. Whether the original intention was for De Keyser to supply all the sculptural work is unknown. Once it became known in Amsterdam that the master had agreed to "carve a saint John's statue from marble for the church in 's-Hertogenbosch, to be used there in the church for idolatry" the work was brought to a halt (Fig. 86).[890] The town reprimanded De Keyser and his (soon to be) son-in-law and master

[879] Buschman 1918, pp. 33-34.
[880] Steppe 1952, p. 281.
[881] Mosmans 1931, p. 439. The figure of 11,000 guilders was mentioned at the trial that took place later. See Buschman 1918, pp. 34-35.
[882] Ibidem, p. 437.
[883] Ibidem, pp. 437-438.
[884] Van Zuylen 1866, p. 1212. See also Van Neurdenberg 1938, p. 39.

[885] Van Zuijlen 1866, p. 1212.
[886] Van Zuijlen 1866, p. 1205.
[887] Upon departure the labourers got the money they had paid in beer tax back from the town, which amounted to over 336 guilders. Van Zuijlen 1866, p. 1212.
[888] Buschman 1918, p. 33.
[889] Bergé 1990, Cat. No. 179, writes that Van Neurenberg was responsible for the sculpture and reliefs.
[890] Kannegieter 1942, pp. 110-111.

86. 's-Hertogenbosch, rood screen. Alabaster statue of saint John by Hendrick de Keyser, 1611 (Collection Victoria & Albert Museum, London, photograph by author).

labourer Nicolas Stone probably finished the work.[891] Previous authors have pointed out that several other hands can be discerned in the sculptural work, and it can be added that several types of material were also used. There are differences detectable in the alabaster. For example, De Keyser's sculpture has a red grain while the smaller sculptures are much greyer.

Whatever the case may be, the context of the provenance is clear and can be immediately linked to the Van Neurenberg family's (personal) network.[892] Steppe then concluded that the screen was a product of cooperation between masters from the Southern and Northern Low Countries.[893] Taking the development of Van Neurenberg's activities into account, as well as the changes in the construction trade during this period, this position can no longer be maintained. Referring to Van Neurenberg as a southern master is erroneous. Furthermore, it is doubtful whether he can be referred to as a sculptor at all. His other activities, his position in the building trade, the pragmatic trading activities and the lack of an own oeuvre all contradict this idea.

This point of view also makes Elisabeth Van Neurdenburg's hypothesis from 1938, that the churchwardens themselves sought a sculptor's workshop, less likely.[894] The report dated 27 January 1611 lists Van Neurenberg as responsible for contracting the entire screen. Coenraad maintained personal contacts with Hendrick de Keyser and so the choice of De Keyser was obvious after Van Neurenberg had been commissioned to deliver the screen.[895] The context of the origin of the work in 's-Hertogenbosch can therefore be directly linked to Van Neurenberg's network.[896]

The aftermath

The financial aftermath of the delivery led church archivist Jan Mosmans to state that Van Neurenberg was difficult and enjoyed legal battles.[897] He was known for his temperament and for

[891] Neurdenberg 1938, p. 43. Stone lived in the Low Countries until 1615 when he married De Keyser's daughter and moved to London.
[892] See Steppe 1952, pp. 284-285.
[893] Steppe 1952, p. 285.
[894] Van Neurdenburg 1938, p. 42.

[895] Stone is said to have worked at the fabric lodge in 's-Hertogenbosch. A few years later, he worked for Van Steenwinckel on Frederiksborg Castle. See also Van Neurdenburg 1930, p. 130.
[896] See Steppe 1952, pp. 284-285.
[897] Mosmans 1931, p. 437.

smuggling.[898] Nevertheless, a merchant's existence during the seventeenth century, particularly where payment was concerned, was not an easy one; slow payment was commonplace and the waiting could go on for many years. On the one hand, this delay could be attributed to the imbalance between the patron's low income and excess expenditure. On the other hand, the building contractors raised prices, which completed the vicious circle. Slow payment was one of the root causes. A seventeenth-century pamphleteer said that if he had taken a job for five thousand guilders and the patron were to pay within ten days, he would gladly make do with three thousand instead.[899] The margins were therefore particularly large. But then again, so were the risks. The supplier usually pre-financed material deliveries entirely, and then had to wait years for his interest-free reimbursement.

Coenraad IV van Neurenberg tried to avoid the wait. On 8 May 1614 he was present in 's-Hertogenbosch, where he met the town's representatives and negotiated with the churchwardens. The town incurred twenty-eight guilders for costs and wine.[900] On 15 September of the same year there was a similar meeting, but no agreement was reached.[901] A court case duly followed. The conflict primarily centred on the sculpture, which had only been specified after the contract had been concluded. This later specification constituted additional work, and in order to determine this cost the sculptors Jeronimus Duquesnoy and Hans van Mildert from Brussels and Antwerp were summoned to 's-Hertogenbosch as witnesses in June 1615.[902]

On 9 May 1616, the Council of Brabant ordered the town to pay Coenraad IV van Neurenberg six thousand guilders.[903] In 1618 there was the obligation to pay 700 guilders.[904] This sum was part of a new claim of 2,101 guilders. According to Hezenmans it was genuinely a struggle for the fabric lodge masters to pay Van Neurenberg's bill. For example, they were said to have sold a prestigious property on the Kerkstraat to this end.[905]

Other marble deliveries in 's-Hertogenbosch

The choice of marble for the screen in 's-Hertogenbosch was no exception. Marble was also employed in the Sint-Jans Church in the ostensory, the funeral monument for Bishop Masius and the high altar. Coenraad van Neurenberg's involvement does seem to have ended, which can possibly be ascribed to the fact that the finalisation of the screen transaction was so problematic. However, the demand for marble continued to exist. The Sacrament's Chapel in the Sint-Jans Church was executed in black marble (Namur stone) and alabaster between 1613 and 1616. Jacques Mattijsz, now referred to as Jacob Mathijssen van Wenen, supplied the stone once again.[906] Just like Van Neurenberg he bought from Wespin in Dinant, which shows how small the circle of merchants must have been. Although Jacques Mattijsz is referred to as a sculptor in sources, he did not make the sculptures for the ostensory. A sculptor from Dinant, Jean Thonon, is a more likely candidate; in 1615 he promised to supply twelve alabaster figures, which he was to make in 's-Hertogenbosch.[907] Jacques Matthijsz supplied the

[898] Ibidem. Reference to Coenraad as a smuggler will have concerned the *convooien* and *licentsgelden* on the Meuse. The statement was based on a newspaper article by J.H. [This may possibly have been J. Hezenmans] in the *Provinciale Courant van 's-Hertogenbosch* dated 18 February 1879 and cannot be verified.

[899] Van Deursen 1991, p. 210.

[900] Van Zuijlen 1866, p. 1216.

[901] Buschman 1918, p. 9.

[902] Ibidem and Van Zuijlen 1866, p. 1222.

[903] Buschman 1918, pp. 34-35 and Van Zuijlen 1866, pp. 1221, 1223, 1228 and 1234.

[904] Van Zuijlen 1866, p. 1246.

[905] Hezenmans 1866, p. 256.

[906] Bergé 1990, p. 440, Bergé 1991, p. 99. Bergé calls Jacques Matthijsz an unknown sculptor. However, he seems to have been more of a materials merchant and building contractor like Van Neurenberg. Jean Thonnon did the actual carving work. See Van Tussenbroek 2001a.

[907] Courtoy 1920, pp. 239-241.

alabaster. The sculptures were to be 2.5 feet high. Each sculpture was worth sixteen florins. Thonon is also known for the former screen of the Sint-Peters Church in Boxtel.[908] Matthijs' role here seems to have been more like that of Van Neurenberg, who acted as material supplier, coordinator and building contractor.

Hans van Mildert supplied the church's high altar, which was renewed a few years later.[909] Van Mildert, who had acted as referee during the court case between the fabric lodge masters of 's-Hertogenbosch and Van Neurenberg, visited supplier Brigand in Namur on 5 September 1619 looking for six stones *pour dresser une table d'autel pour situer en l'eglise St. Jean à Boilduc*.[910] A few months later, Van Mildert agreed with Brigand that the latter would supply two columns made of red marble. Erasmus Quellinus supplied six capitals, made of alabaster. The finalisation of this commission is a history in itself.[911]

The funerary monument for Bishop Masius was also executed in marble around 1614. This expensive material was consistently preferred to others, which leads us to think that its choice must have been justified by the particular context in which it was used. Conspiciously, types of stone which were previously commonly used for religious sculpture, such as white Brabant limestone, marlstone and stone from Avesnes, were now being replaced by black and coloured 'Belgian' marble and English alabaster. It was precisely the 'Catholic' south where the use of these materials boomed, due to the nature of the church furniture desired in this area. The Jesuit churches of Antwerp and Namur, but also the Scherpenheuvel Church built by the Archdukes as a response to the Reformation in the north, are eye-catching due to the exuberant use of materials in their decoration. Sexton Sweerts' polemics and the impression the screen would later make on visitors from the Protestant north reveal to what extent the avantgarde of the Counter-Reformation, as sponsored by the Archdukes and the Jesuits, coloured the construction of the screen in 's-Hertogenbosch.[912]

Belgian marble occurs less in the ecclesiastical context in the north, which was primarily to do with the concept of a church as a hall for preaching. The building was 'only' the house of the Word and not the house of God as it was for Catholics. The low demand for Belgian marble intended for Protestant churches was due, to a large extent, to differences in liturgy. Items of furniture such as altars, historically often executed in marble, were lacking in Protestant churches. The use of red marble from Limbourg for the pulpit of the North Church in Amsterdam proves that marble itself was not objected to. Red and black marble was indeed employed in the organ and the choir screen of the New Church in Amsterdam (1650). Black marble tombstones also occur, as shown by the 9 October 1614 shipment, which Pieter van Neurenberg ordered from Gilles van Maasniel and his father-in-law Hubert Misson.[913] Furthermore, marble is used conspicuously in funerary monuments. These mausoleums, which were sometimes set up on the spot where the high altar usually stood, were often very ornate: see, for instance, the funerary monument for William of Orange or those of various Dutch maritime heroes.

---

[908] Staal, Berends 1976, p. 5.
[909] Mosmans 1931, p. 441ff.
[910] Ibidem, p. 443.

[911] Ibidem, p. 446.
[912] Westermann 1993, pp. 393-394.
[913] Courtoy 1920, pp. 236-237. See Chapter XVI.

XVIII. CONSTRUCTION FOR THE TOWN

The weigh house in Hoorn

The stimulating effect of the truce was not just visible in Counter Reformation circles. Trade in the Republic expanded dramatically as a result of the relatively stable situation and this stability resulted in a strong increase in the number of urban construction commissions, cooperation between building contractors and internationalisation. These aspects can all be seen in the weigh house in Hoorn, which was rebuilt in 1609 (Fig. 87). Little is known about the original weigh house. It may possibly have been a wooden building on the same site as the current one, though perhaps somewhat smaller. It was probably a nearly square structure, one storey tall.[914] In 1559 this weigh house was enlarged and renewed. The public bidding process was used for this project. After the town administration had approved the plan by master mason Floris Dircxsz of Hoorn, the call for bids was posted on the doors of the churches and town gates of Haarlem, Alkmaar, Amsterdam, Hoorn and Enkhuizen. Four copies were made of the specifications and three were distributed for perusal in Alkmaar, Hoorn and Enkhuizen. The fourth copy was for the steward. Symon Pietersz master carpenter of Hoorn carried out the work. The new weigh house had five sets of scales, but little is known about the building's exterior.[915]

87. Hoorn, weigh house, 1608. (Anonymous photograph, circa 1900, RDMZ, Neg. Nr. 15.500).

[914] See Dröge 1991, p. 2 for more on this predecessor.   [915] Ibidem, p. 3.

On 13 January 1602, the States of Holland and West-Friesland awarded Hoorn the weigh house and weighing rights. This gift was intended as a thank you for the town's contribution to the naval battle of the Zuiderzee. This transition of ownership explains the renewal at the start of the seventeenth century. Although the building was not even fifty years' old, the town decided to adapt it to meet its needs. As early as 15 January 1608, the town bought the house on the northern side of the existing weigh house, with the intention of demolishing it. This lot would then provide the necessary space to enlarge the existing weigh house[916] and make the building more the centre of the square.[917] Moreover, this lot provided room to move the building's footprint backwards, creating room for scales on the pavement. On 8 May 1608, the corporation decided to definitely build the new weigh house and they determined that the old building was to remain in use for as long as possible.[918] The corporation turned to Hendrick de Keyser for the design and within a month he received the sum of well over thirty-two guilders for making "various designs and patterns". De Keyser travelled to Hoorn twice. It is doubtful whether the first contact between the town and De Keyser only occurred after the decision of 8 May. Earlier examples, such as the weigh house in Haarlem and the Blue Gate in Leiden, have shown how much preparation and consultation took place with regard to the design, specifications and bidding, before actually issuing the order for the delivery of stone. In May 1609 the old building was finally demolished.[919]

On 2 June 1608, within a month of the decision being made to acquire the necessary materials, the town administration issued approval to the mayors to have the stone prepared.[920] The work was tendered to Hendrick de Keyser.[921] The price agreed amounted to eighteen stivers per foot for most of the work and De Keyser would supply the stone before the coming May.

Although the old building had been demolished in May 1609, the terms in the contract had been rather ample. The preparatory activities had not advanced sufficiently by May 1609 for the stonework order to be placed, although a start had been made. There were two reasons for this delay. The first concerned the design of the new weigh house. Although the main lines were already known in the spring of 1608, adjustments were made for details when ordering stone. An important adjustment was the height of the first storey. After the magistrates had reconsidered the matter they concluded that it was to be built higher, undoubtedly with a view to its use. In order to allow this plan to go ahead, Mayor Willem Pietersz Crap was sent to Amsterdam on 7 September 1609 to confer with Hendrick de Keyser concerning the adaptation. They wished to confer with De Keyser "whether the second square could be raised one, two or three feet without hindering the shape of the work,"[922] which confirms that De Keyser was responsible for the weigh house's design. To what extent he was seen as the architect is proved by the fact that people did not wish to violate the copyright of his work and consulted him when changes to the building were desired. Incidentally, it is questionable to what degree adaptation of the design was still possible at this stage. The commission to make the stonework had been issued the preceding year and so there was a high chance of the work for the first storey already having been completed.

---

[916] Ibidem, p. 4.
[917] Also see Kiem 1996, p. 83.
[918] Dröge 1991, p. 4. Kiem 1996, p. 88. *Ter saecke vande Waege geleijc in deliberatie is goetgevonden datmen de oude Waege zal laten staen, ende preparatie maecken van materialen tot een nieuwe Waege.* From: Stadsarchief Hoorn, Resolutieboek van Burgemeesteren, 8 May 1608. Inv. No. 103.

[919] Ibidem.
[920] Kerkmeyer 1911, pp. 235-246.
[921] *Hendrik de Keyser Ingenieur wonende tot Amsterdam* [Hendrik de Keyser, engineer living in Amsterdam]. Ibidem, p. 237.
[922] Kiem 1996, p. 88. On the basis of the proportional system he devised, Kiem assumes that De Keyser did not grant permission to do so.

Problems with stone itself constituted the second reason why the stone could not be placed into the work in May 1609: it had not been finished yet. Not only the design, but also the delivery of the stone was De Keyser's task. However, De Keyser had not acquired his material directly from the quarry. To meet this end he turned to distribution, in this case Willem and Pieter van Neurenberg. On 13 June 1609, thirty-three guilders were paid for the transport of blue stone to Hoorn via Dordrecht.[923] A source dated 7 September, and 17 and 18 November 1609 proves the Van Neurenbergs involvement. In this Pieter Jansz Livorno, fabric lodge master of the town of Hoorn declared that he had measured a dormer window on the new weigh house in the presence of Hendrick de Keyser and Willem and Pieter van Neurenberg, in order to be able to determine the total sum to be paid to De Keyser.[924]

The total delivery amounted to 6,483.26 feet. The agreed price per foot was eighteen stivers and so the total figure amounted to 5,834 guilders and fourteen stivers. Together with the other work this delivery was paid to De Keyser in instalments.[925] De Keyser or his studio also made the sculpture of a unicorn in a niche in the weigh house; for this sculpture he received the sum of 150 guilders.[926] The sculpture was gilt. There is no trace of direct payments being made to the Van Neurenbergs and so it must be concluded that they worked as sub-contractors for De Keyser. In the context of stone deliveries, this is a natural arrangement.

The weigh house in Hoorn is not the only example of Namur stone applied in the town. The town hall and the Statencollege, which dates back to 1632, were clad in this material, so that a number of representative buildings around the market were provided with this valuable and recognisable facade cladding.[927] Furthermore, the weigh house was not the only project in which Hendrick de Keyser was involved in Hoorn. D. Velius' chronicle of Hoorn states the following for the year 1601, "The epitaph of Dr Pieter Hogerbeets was erected in the church: it was very beautifully carved by Master Hendrick de Keyser."[928] Dr Hogerbeets died treating plague sufferers, which led the mayors to decide that he should be honoured with a beautiful funerary monument at the town's expense.[929] The town's accounts list several payments to De Keyser for his services. Furthermore, the facade and the nave of the East Church (1615) are attributed to him, although without archival evidence.[930]

Alterations to the town hall in Middelburg

In 1613, Coenraad IV was involved in alterations to the entrance to Middelburg town hall when it was moved from the Noordstraat to the Markt. Some data suggest that parts of the old entrance were reused. The new entrance was entirely Gothic in style, which was remarkable – but not exceptional – for the start of the seventeenth century.[931] The reason for this retention of style was the possible reuse of a number of elements of the (not yet so old) previous entrance on the Noordstraat.

[923] Dröge 1991, p. 19.
[924] Kiem's supposition 1996, p. 87 is disputable. He writes: *Am 7. September 1609 war der Neubau dann so weit fertiggestellt, daß die Natursteinarbeiten aufgemessen werden konnten.* The measuring of the stone however pertains to the delivery. It was normal for a town official to carry out a check after a shipment of stones had been delivered. Generally this check was done prior to the stones' placement. Placing the stone, therefore, took place after the stone had been measured, which was much more efficient.
[925] The first payment took place on 29 June 1609 (2,588.50 guilders), the second on 29 September 1609 (800 guilders), the third on 16 December 1609 (1,500 guilders) and the last on 1 February 1610 (912.90 guilders).

[926] Van Neurdenburg 1930, p. 110.
[927] Kiem 1996, pp. 81–82. The Statencollege, diagonally across from the weigh house, was provided with new cladding in 1908. See Kramer 1985, p. 26.
[928] Quoted in Van Neurdenburg 1930, p. 103.
[929] Ibidem, p. 104. The monument has been lost.
[930] Kiem 1996, p. 88, n. 294. Hendrick de Keyser was paid thirty-two guilders and two stivers for *verscheijdene uijtwerpen ende patronen* [various designs and patterns] in 1608.
[931] There are more examples of Gothic style in the seventeenth century, such as the tower of the New Church in Amsterdam.

Bricklayer Daniël Carlier did the actual work on the entrance for the sum of 102 pounds.[932] Coenraad IV van Neurenberg supplied the Namur stone placed in the facade.[933] He is said to have collaborated with stonemason Esaias Schaep on this project.[934] As seems to have been typical for Coenraad, the payment of this transaction also was problematic. Due to "faults and misdeliveries" Coenraad had twenty pounds deducted "based on the statements of neutral labourers," which the town administration of Middelburg had appointed as arbitration committee.[935] The facade disappeared in 1756.

Construction overseas: São Thomé (1621)

The enormous expansion of the Republic's colonies, as well as those of Spain, Portugal, etc. led to major construction activities in these areas. Although local building materials were used in a large number of cases, materials from Europe were nevertheless sometimes chosen, which concerned not only brick or stone for construction, but also tombstones, which can be found all over. European materials were primarily selected for local government buildings.[936] For example, at the close of the 1620s an Obernkirchner sandstone gate for the citadel was ordered from Batavia. It was shipped in 1629, but the ship, the Batavia, ran aground off the Australian coast and sank. In 1632, another gate was shipped, which was present in the citadel until the nineteenth century. In 1636 a shipment of blue stone sheets was sent to Batavia, ostensibly intended for the new church; however, they ended up being used for the governor's palace. It is unknown who supplied these shipments of stone.[937]

Although there is only one example, it is known that the Van Neurenberg family also supplied material to the colonies. On 16 September 1621, Willem II van Neurenberg sought permission from the States General to be allowed to export stone to São Thomé, an island off the coast of West Africa, near Gabon. At that point in time, São Thomé was held by Portugal. Willem had taken on the delivery during the Twelve Years' Truce and it concerned "blue worked stone". However, he had not managed to finish and supply the work during the Truce and so he sought permission to be allowed to send the shipment now. An additional argument Willem mentioned was that the contract stipulated that he could only claim the outstanding accounts once the entire delivery had been made. He therefore requested a "passport for the transport of the prescribed remaining stonework to São Thomé".

The States General gave Willem permission to export the stone on 4 October. The condition set for this delivery was the usual one, i.e. Willem was obliged to use "permitted passage of inland guards". Officers were present on these passages who would check the goods to be exported, "the same as every other merchant and captain who used to trade in enemy countries does." The intended purpose of this delivery is unknown. It is quite likely that Portuguese merchants active in Amsterdam arranged the commission.

---

[932] Unger 1932, p. 11.
[933] He received 166 pounds.
[934] Kesteloo VIII, 1, p. 57.
[935] Ibidem.
[936] Pohle 2000, p. 50

[937] Pohle 1999, p. 242. The gate in the citadel was walled in, renewed in the eighteenth century and demolished during the nineteenth century along with the rest of the citadel. The stones from the Batavia were salvaged in the twentieth century and are currently on display at the Western Australian Maritime Museum in Fremantle. See also Pohle 2000 and Bergers 2000.

1620-1625: The Catharijne gate in Utrecht

A commission closer to home was the Catharijne gate in Utrecht. This gate was one of the better-known construction projects in which Willem II van Neurenberg participated (Fig. 88). The gate, designed by Paulus Moreelse, was built between 1621 and 1625. Moreelse was primarily known as a painter. In addition to the Catharijne gate, he has also formerly been credited with designing the town hall in Vlissingen, although there is much less proof available in this case.[938]

88. Utrecht, Catharijne Gate, Elevation from the side of the town by M. Kocken 1844. (Het Utrechts Archief, inv.nr. TA DC 5.32 (a), neg.nr. C 19-116).

The first mention of the gate being renewed occurs on 29 May 1620.[939] After the decision was taken on 7 September concerning the exact positioning of the gate, permission was given on 21 September to have "models" of the new gate created. The corporation's resolution of 16 October 1621 states that they have seen the model and the earthworks of the Catherijne gate. Simultaneously it was decided that Mayor Cornelis van de Poll and Paulus Moreelse would issue a statement in consultation with merchants of Dordrecht to provide information on the stone to be supplied. The intention was to have a public call for bids for the stone delivery, but the statement explicitly states that merchants will be approached individually and not as a group, "so that they have no knowledge of the others and it may stay more secret."[940] The decision to tender the work to merchants from Dordrecht leads to the conclusion that it had already been decided to use Namur stone. If sandstone had been chosen it would

---

[938] Vermeulen. Handboek II, pp. 283-285.

[939] GAU, Stadsarchief II, 121. Resoluties van de Vroedschap.
Thanks to Koen Ottenheym.

[940] Ozinga 1931, p. 19.

201

have been much more logical to go to Amsterdam or Zwolle. A resolution dated 21 November proves that the delivery of the stone was awarded to Willem II van Neurenberg. The price agreed was seventeen stivers per foot, but if Van Neurenberg was to supply "very beautiful" stone, i.e. stone from higher layers in a bank, which was much finer and had fewer impurities, the price would be 17.5 stivers.[941]

In the spring of 1622 preparations were made for construction.[942] A year later, on 7 April 1623, a loan was issued for the financing of the gate's construction, which must have been well under way at the time. Nevertheless, it was once again the financial situation that led to conflict. On 9 August 1624 the corporation received a request from Toussin du Tour, stonemason and one of Van Neurenberg's labourers. Looking at other deliveries where the stone supplier sent a labourer to place the work helps explain his presence there. Toussin requested additional wages, which provides a glimpse into Van Neurenberg's internal business structure. As had been the case in Huy, Haarlem and Nijmegen, there was also a labourer from the company charged with the on site execution in Utrecht.

On 1 November, the corporation received a similar request, this time from Moreelse. A few weeks later a secret commission was set up to deliberate Moreelse's request. Van Neurenberg was paid 1,200 guilders on 31 January 1625 and Moreelse's case continued. There was a meeting on 25 April where a report was given on the findings of the "architect masters of Haarlem and Leiden, Lieven de Key and Hendrik Cornelisz van Bilderbeeck". These two personally viewed the work in Utrecht in order to be able to pass judgment on it. They provided a brief recapitulation of the activities of the past three years, such as cutting the hard stone at the quarry, laying the foundations and the actual construction of the gate. Moreelse gave daily orders, ascertained that the stone supplied was made competently, eventually had the faults repaired, etc.

Both masters arrived at the conclusion that other masters with more experience in the construction trade than Moreelse would have been satisfied with five hundred guilders per year or even less, if they had been employed to realise such a gate building.[943] This remuneration would then total 2,000 guilders for the four years Moreelse had worked. At the request of Utrecht's corporation, Lieven de Key and Hendrick van Bilderbeeck provided a relatively good insight into a building master's income when working for a town. In addition to the construction of the gate they also indicated what reasonable wages would be for a master in charge of all town construction. Their conclusion was that Moreelse's demand was somewhat high.[944]

Nevertheless, they did not have the last word. During the reading of the report Moreelse had been asked to leave the room. After it had been read aloud, he returned and the report was read again, now however without mentioning the names of the masters from Haarlem and Leiden. Moreelse stated that he did not agree with the arbitration and wished to have his own experts provide their opinion. He put forward Hendrick de Keyser and Cornelis Danckerts, the town stonemason and town bricklayer of Amsterdam, good acquaintances of Van Neurenberg. The corporation's resolutions reveal that the sums, and in particular the difference between the sums in question, were small. After the matter was discussed with Moreelse again on 9 June and 9 August, the corporation decided to pay Moreelse 2,100 guilders. He had asked for 2,400 guilders, but the corporation was of the opinion that due to his declining health he should first finish the job before receiving the remaining 300 guilders.[945] It therefore remains to be seen to what extent Danckerts and De Keyser's arbitration was instrumental in raising the price. Naturally, Moreelse put people forward who, as he hoped, would say favourable things about him and who would look after his interests properly.

---

[941] Ibidem.
[942] Resolutions dated 11 March and 29 April.
[943] *... alleenlick gebruyckt soude worden gelyck die* [Moreelse] *gebruyckt es totte voorsz. poort, dat hy wel soude tevreden syn met vijffhonderd gulden 's jaars, jae oock met minder.* Ozinga 1931, p. 21.

[944] Resolution 25 April 1625. Ozinga 1931, pp. 20-21.
[945] Ibidem, p. 22. However, Moreelse did not die until March 1638.
[946] V.d. Berg 1979, pp. 100-102.

Van Neurenberg's involvement in the work on the Catharijne gate can to a certain degree be compared to that on the Blue Gate in Leiden, the main difference being that Willem II van Neurenberg was not responsible for drafting the specifications in Utrecht. The specifications were drawn up within the town building organisation, after which the bidding took place. On 14 August 1626, the corporation's resolutions reveal that a committee, which included Moreelse and stonemason Robbert Petersz, measured the stone supplied. On 15 May 1627 a payment to Van Neurenberg is mentioned.

Other deliveries

A smaller delivery of material can be found in Leerdam. Here Willem II van Neurenberg supplied stone for the curbs and mouldings of the council house in 1615. This project was probably an adaptation to the existing building which needed to look more like a council house. Nevertheless, another building replaced this building shortly afterwards. In 1631, the town administration of Leerdam decided to have a new council house built.[946]

Willem van Neurenberg also supplied stone for the rebuilding of the church in Sommelsdijk in 1632.[947] One of his sons, Willem, wrote a letter on behalf of his father to the magistrates of Sommelsdijk on 25 March 1638, in which he requested the payment of 1,060 guilders and three stivers. The reason given was that the family was in need of money[948] regarding payment for stone delivered in October 1634. Willem also requested remuneration for the 2.5 years of accumulated interest, which the magistrates owed him beginning in October 1635. If the magistrates were incapable of paying, he requested that they at least pay the interest as quickly as possible. Van Neurenberg had supplied materials for repair activities.[949]

---

[947] Huisman, based on Gemeentearchief Middelharnis, Inv. No. 95, various church matters Sommelsdijk. Folder of specifications for the rebuilding of the church in 1632.
[948] It seems improbable for the family to have actually been low on funds. It is however possible that as a result of many pre-financing activities they might have had a temporary liquidity problem, which made them emphasize the need for payment.
[949] Huisman 1986, p. 59.

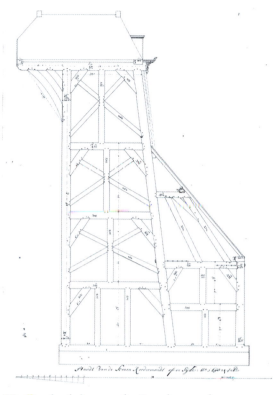

89a. Dordrecht's crane, the Roodermondt, anonymous drawing, made on 24 February 1698 (GAD).

89b. Dordrecht's crane, the Roodermondt, anonymous photograph. Late nineteenth century (GAD, Inv.Nr. GPV M 5381).

On 11 April 1640, Willem II van Neurenberg supplied a tombstone with the coat of arms of the water control authority Delflanden. A bill is known to exist for a tombstone decorated with the coats of arms of the high authorities of Delfland in the service of the lock in Vlaardingen. The tombstone was seven feet long and three wide, and the coats of arms and names on it were made according to the patterns supplied. The tombstone cost 150 guilders. three guilders and eighteen stivers were charged for transport from Dordrecht to Vlaardingen and for the use of the crane (Fig. 89). The tombstone was unloaded on 31 March 1640. Additional costs were incurred for Van Neurenberg's labourer who had been sent down there for the day, for the unloading of the tombstone and for extra efforts. Marija Mijlius (Wijmoth), housewife of Willem van Neurenberg signed the bill.[950]

[950] Wildeman 1902, pp. 309–310.

XIX. Construction at Court and the Family's Withdrawal from the Stone Trade

Construction for the court

In comparison to the Southern Low Countries, the court in the north played a modest role during the seventeenth century as far as construction was concerned. In contrast to the Archdukes of the south, Prince Maurits and Prince Frederik Hendrik did not have their own construction crews or court architects until 1634.[951] Projects such as the Maurits House in Willemstad in 1623 made use of the town masters.[952] Although some names occur regularly within the context of court construction, such as Adriaen Willeboortsz Spierinxhouck, a stonemason from Delft, or carpenter Willem Arentsz van Salen from The Hague, little indicates that these people were part of a court organisation. Florentine architect Constantino de Servi, active at the Binnenhof in 1615, cannot really be considered a court architect either.[953]

Only after Maurits' death, in 1625, would this situation more or less change under Frederik Hendrik. Construction received more attention, which, to a large extent, had to do with Frederik Hendrik's personal interest. In 1631, there was an architect and from 1634 on the "architect of his Highness' buildings", Simon de la Vallée, was one of the royal household.[954] Also after Maurits' death, the carpenter Willem Arentsz van Salen was appointed fabric lodge master of the prince's buildings in 1626. These are the first signs of tighter organisation, while the number of construction projects under princely supervision increased considerably. For example, plans were developed for House Honselaarsdijk near Naaldwijk, House Ter Nieuburg near Rijswijk and the houses in IJsselstein, Zuylenstein and Buren. The court's records echo this structured approach.[955]

From the 1630s onwards, a number of figures emerge who had, more or less, started to occupy permanent positions in the court's construction organisation. For example, Arent van 's-Gravesande was involved in the construction of Honselaarsdijk from 1631. He was paid for the drawings and models supplied. A year later, he occurs again in connection with House Ter Nieuburg, where he led the construction project. Under Frederik Hendrik people such as Adriaen Willeboortsz Spierinxhouck started to become permanent fixtures in the construction organisation. From 1634, the prince actually employed Simon de la Vallée as his architect.[956] In 1645, Pieter Post began in a similar position.

Frederik Hendrik's construction projects were very important for innovation in architecture in the Northern Low Countries. Frederik Hendrik, who had spent part of his youth in France, was personally interested in architecture, which is exemplified by the fact that he continued to be involved in the construction of his palaces even while campaigning. The introduction of new architectural ideas, in particular the layout of palaces, can partially be attributed to him. In the prince's entourage it was primarily Constantijn Huygens and Jacob van Campen who wished to realise the classical ideal in contemporary architecture through the correct application of the classic rules.[957]

---

[951] Meischke 1997, p. 85.
[952] Meischke 1984.
[953] De Vos 1999, p. 200.
[954] Ibidem, p. 204.

[955] Ibidem.
[956] Ibidem, p. 205.
[957] Ottenheym 1997a.

Breda[958]

Before the order for stone for Honselaarsdijk was to be placed, Willem van Neurenberg was responsible for another delivery of stone to the Nassau family, employed for the alterations to the Palace in Breda in 1621. This palace, which had undergone extensive remodelling during the sixteenth century, was again adapted and altered on a number of occasions during the seventeenth century.[959] Willem van Neurenberg concluded an agreement for the delivery of stone with the prince's controller and stonemason. The agreement with the stonemason is of particular interest, if the fact that Prince Maurits did not really have his own construction organisation is taken into account. The designation of the stonemason as "controller" should not be seen as proof of the existence of a permanent "architect" or "builder" on the prince's staff, i.e. an official, but rather as a sign that the stonemason concerned had been authorised to fulfil a number of official or organisational tasks for the duration of his contract. The most obvious person for Van Neurenberg to have had contact with was indeed the stonemason Adriaen Willeboortsz Spierinxhouck from Delft.

Willem van Neurenberg supplied a few samples of blue stone for quality checking purposes before stone was actually ordered from him. There are few examples of this practice, but this does not rule out that it was also used on other occasions. It was common practice to first demand samples before actually doing business in other sectors of industry such as, for example, the gemstone trade.[960] The sample Van Neurenberg supplied concerned most probably mouldings.[961] The samples were approved, as the accounts list 1,800 blue and grey flagstones of eleven inches and another 150 similar stones of fifteen inches.[962] It is remarkable that the price of the pieces of stone is the same, regardless of their size. They both cost twenty pounds for one hundred units. The price was therefore primarily determined by its processing and not by its volume.

Finally, Willem van Neurenberg also supplied a shipment of marlstone. He was to supply 101 feet of moulded threshold stone for a gallery in the palace's gardens, for sixteen shillings per foot. This shipment's price amounted to eighty pounds and sixteen shillings. The total price of the delivery equalled 472 pounds. During the years 1620–1621, the castle complex's gardens were indeed embellished under Balthasar Baldi, the Head of the Prince's Household. Prince Maurits had the garden improved with a gallery and a separate aviary with two arcades. Melchior van Harbach supervised construction.[963]

House Honselaarsdijk

House Honselaarsdijk near Naaldwijk was built a few years later during a very short period of time, at least if one takes into account its size (Fig. 90). The construction campaign lasted from 1621 until 1647, and the craftsmen and designers involved were the elite of the construction trade.[964] Together with House Ter Nieuburg, Honselaarsdijk was one of the most imposing buildings of its day, and can be considered a trendsetting example for later palaces in Holland. Just like other early examples of seventeenth-century Classicism, such as the Coymans House in Amsterdam, House ten Bosch in

---

[958] The following is based on ARA, Nassause Domeinraad, Inv. No. 8414, Rentmeester N.N.'s bill for the year 1621, 1 deel.fol. Cxci v° en fol. Cxcij. Thanks to Annemie De Vos.
[959] Van Wezel 1999 does not list construction activities during the years mentioned.
[960] Gelderblom 2000, p. 128.
[961] The fifteen inch one was worth eight shillings per foot, the eleven inch one, four shillings. A total of twenty-four shillings worth of samples were supplied.

[962] The eleven inch stone cost twenty pounds per one hundred stones, which amounted to 360 pounds for 1,800 stones. The fifteen inch stone also cost twenty pounds per hundred stones, which amounted to thirty pounds. It is remarkable that here, the work determined the price of stone. The quantity of material was not a determining factor for the price.
[963] De Vos 2000.
[964] See Ottenheym 1997c.

Maarssen and the Huygens House in The Hague, Jacob van Campen also played an important role at Honselaarsdijk. Although he was not involved in the construction or design phase from the start, he was responsible for the design of the pediment and parts of the interior.[965]

The use of materials at Honselaarsdijk was commensurate with the building's status. For example, large quantities of marble were delivered during the 1620s. Marble is a logical choice for representative architecture and was already seen as important in Classical Antiquity. At that time, the use of particular types of stone was limited to those in a position of power. For example, only the emperor was allowed interment in a porphyry sarcophagus. For people of lower status, it was seen as unsuitable to use anything other than white marble for funerary use.[966] This differentiation of use also occurred during the seventeenth century under the influence of Vitruvius and other authors from Classical Antiquity, and Renaissance treatises. Excessive use of expensive materials was quickly seen as proof

90. Honselaarsdijk Palace, built between 1621-1647. Engraving by C. Elandts, circa 1680 (Landbouw Hogeschool Wageningen, Spr. 01.1032.10).

of poor taste and the quality of architecture was judged by the correct use of proportions and ratios, rather than by looking at number of ornaments and expensive materials. As Constantijn Huygens put it, "Many types of marble and much gold decorates your odd shed/ that is proliferation on the outside and indoors even worse."[967] Obviously this criticism did not apply to Frederik Hendrik. As the sovereign prince he was allowed to use large quantities of the most expensive materials on his buildings. Displays of great wealth were suitable for his status.

The specifications of Frederik Hendrik's various palaces published by Slothouwer provide a good impression of the use of marble. In Honselaarsdijk's case it was primarily Willem II van Neurenberg who was responsible for the delivery of large quantities of Belgian marble. In 1625, he received 1,100 pounds for three pairs of marble posts for Honselaarsdijk palace.[968] These six posts were possibly intended for the columned portico of the central pavilion on which work was taking place during these years. Unfortunately, it is not known whether the columns were made of red, grey or black marble.

However, the columns were not Van Neurenberg's only delivery for the palace. A later item in the accounts proves that Van Neurenberg's contribution was far more substantial. In 1631, he received over 8,000 pounds for marble and blue stonework, supplied for mantelpieces, floors, mouldings and other purposes in 1626, 1627, 1628, 1629, 1630 and 1631.[969] In addition to the delivery by Van Neuren-

[965] Ottenheym 1995, p. 174.
[966] Jongste 1995, p. 109.
[967] *Veel marmers en veel gouds verçiert uw mal getimmer/Dat buyten wildsangh is, en binnenwerckx noch slimmer.* Worp Part 5, p. 25.
[968] Slothouwer 1946, p. 261: ... *betaelt aen Guillaum van Nore burch mr. steenhouwer, ende cooper tot Dordrecht, de somme van elff hondert ponden artois, voor drie paer marbere posten, bij hem aen Sijn Vorstel. Gen. huijs te Honselerdijck gelevert.*

[969] Ibidem, p. 262, ... *betaelt aen Guillaume van Norenb., coopman van steen ende mr. steenhouwer te Dordrecht de somme van acht duijsent veertienden ponden tien schellingen artois, over soo veele den selven van Sijne Furst. Doorluchticheijt, was competerende, over marber ende hartsteenwerck bij hem aen schoorsteenmantels vloeren, lijsten &c aent gebou vant huijs te Honsholredijck inde jaren XVIC sessentwintich XVIC seventwintich XVIC achtentwintich XVIC negentwintich, XVIC dertich ende XVIC eenendertich gelevert.*

berg, the accounts also provide an impression of the amounts Van Neurenberg had to pre-finance and the terms this financing entailed. The stone mentioned was used to build the east, north and west wing of the palace, under construction during these years.[970] The enormous quantities of stone, both marble and ordinary Namur stone, were used for various purposes. Mantelpieces and floors for the interior have been mentioned, but there were also mouldings and associated items for the exterior.

With these deliveries Van Neurenberg's role on the Honselaarsdijk site came to an end, although they were not the last ones. Other suppliers occur in the sources, which possibly indicates a slow shift in the stone trade. This underscores the lack of a personal archive. It is only possible to speculate on the reasons for the end of Van Neurenberg's involvement. The other merchants' activities make it probable that Willem, who was approximately fifty-five years old, was slowly withdrawing from the trade, but there is no certainty on this matter.

Another factor should also be taken into account. It has already been concluded that northern merchants increasingly controlled the stone trade as the seventeenth century progressed. Merchants such as Jacob Matthijsz from Delft are good examples of this. The importance of a merchant's ties to the south decreased, which opened up the market to others and allowed the newcomers to profile themselves as distributors. For Van Neurenberg it will have been a combination of factors that played a role in the decrease of his importance as a materials supplier. The family had already accumulated a considerable fortune, which they had started investing during the first decade of the seventeenth century. So the necessity of amassing even more capital had disappeared. Furthermore, there were ties with traders in the north so that they could still indirectly benefit from the flourishing of the trade. Finally, the sandstone trade was becoming more and more important to Dutch merchants, and luxury products such as white marble were increasingly imported from Italy.

91. Rijswijk, Huis ter Nieuburch. Drawing by Jan de Bisschop, (after Slothouwer 1946, p. 131, nr. 44).

Ter Nieuburch near Rijswijk

Honselaarsdijk Palace was not yet completed in 1631. Nevertheless, as early as 1630 Frederik Hendrik commissioned a new country palace. Ter Nieuburg near Rijswijk was primarily intended as a private residence (Fig. 91). The palace consisted of a main pavilion and two residential pavilions, mutually connected by galleries.[971] It is unknown who was responsible for the design, but it is generally assumed that there were French influences. The involvement of Simon de la Vallée, the future court architect, cannot be excluded.

In much the same way as at Honselaarsdijk, large quantities of marble were purchased for the construction of Ter Nieuburch. Van Neurenberg's role in these deliveries cannot be demonstrated, as his name does not occur on the list of stone suppliers. However, as the accounts are unspecified, it can no longer be ascertained who the supplier of the material was. Van Neurenberg's involvement, therefore, seems likely. In 1632, Naaldwijk's steward was reimbursed for the expenses he incurred for the transport of the stone materials that arrived from Dordrecht.[972]

[970] Meischke, Ottenheym 1992, p. 120.
[971] Slothouwer 1946, p. 89ff., Olde Meierink 1996, p. 148 and Ottenheym 1997c.
[972] Slothouwer 1946, p. 291.

Other merchants were, however, also involved; in 1633 Jan Michielsz, master stonemason from The Hague was paid for the delivery of a very refined white and black marble mantelpiece.[973] Pieter de Keyser, son of Hendrick de Keyser, who was already responsible for the delivery of ordinary stonework, also supplied two marble mantelpieces, one white and black and one red and white.[974] Furthermore, Dirck Ariaensz van Delft from Amsterdam, Coenraad IV, Willem II and Pieter's brother in-law's brother are mentioned as suppliers of marble and blue floors. The marble floors consisted of red, black and white marble, white and black marble, and white, black and yellow marble.[975] Hendrick Nijsius supplied a few black marble capitals and bases for the marble pilasters in the entrance hall.[976] Philips Roelansz, master stonemason from Amsterdam, supplied two marble mantelpieces in red, black and white marble, one in black and red marble with mouldings, a white and blue cut marble floor, and a white, blue and red Swedish stone floor for the eastern gallery.[977] Other suppliers included Jan Janssen de Vos, master stonemason from Haarlem, who supplied sixty-three black and yellow marble tiles. There was also the anonymous delivery of two large marble columns with capitals and bases around ten feet high, which were located in the downstairs room by the stairs, under the marble arches.[978] The outside of the palace was largely clad in Bentheimer sandstone.[979]

Although Van Neurenberg does not occur directly in the above, a number of people appear who were part of his network. In particular Dirck Ariaensz van Delft and Pieter de Keyser are directly linked to Van Neurenberg. Moreover, Willem II van Neurenberg's involvement was to be expected. Although the accounts pertaining to this matter are scant, there is mention of marble supplied via Dordrecht. If we add this information to the fact that Willem II was one of the principal marble suppliers for the construction of Honselaarsdijk, then it may be supposed that he also played a role at Ter Nieuburg.

The family's withdrawal from the stone trade

During the seventeenth century it was not uncommon for successful merchants to leave their business to others and primarily focus on administrative tasks. These administrative positions were often even more lucrative than their original activities, primarily because it was common for administrators to make decisions and implement measures that would be most favourable to their trade. In 1965 Klein already pointed out that close family ties between the principal Dutch merchants' families made a strong contribution to the monopoly-like atmosphere on the Dutch staple market.[980] The fact that these families had representatives in the administration strongly contributed to this effect.

To what extent the families were allied to one another and how far their activities overlapped can once again be read from the relationship between the Van Neurenbergs Trips and other families that were also active in the stone trade. For example, at the close of the seventeenth century Peter Lambillon, together with Steven and Louis de Geer, purchased shares in the peat company owned by Adriaen Trip, near Wildervank for the purpose of digging peat.[981] Earlier examples of economic cooperation between Trip and Van Neurenberg can be found at the end of the sixteenth century. For the benefit of the textile industry Jacob Trip and Johan van Neurenberg[982] founded the first fulling mill in Dordrecht.[983] There was also a relationship between Jacob Trip and Johan I van Neurenberg, Willem II's

[973] Ibidem, p. 292.
[974] Ibidem. Once again it cannot be ruled out that De Keyser acquired his marble from Van Neurenberg, if prior deliveries are taken into account.
[975] Ibidem, pp. 293, 296, 297. Fock 1998, n. 82 states that that even more marble floors were delivered to Ter Nieuburg, which Slothouwer did not publish. Sellers in this case were Pieter Ockers and Willem II van Neurenberg.
[976] Slothouwer 1946.

[977] Ibidem, p. 297.
[978] Ibidem, p. 298.
[979] Slothouwer 1946, p. 303.
[980] Klein 1965, p. 16.
[981] Ibidem, p. 54.
[982] This person could be the son of Coenraad III, Jean, who was born in Namur and whom Courtoy mentions. Nothing more is known about him.
[983] Klein 1965, p. 84.

son. After Trip had been kicked out of his brothers Louis and Hendrik's company, Johan I was one of the referees brought in to pass judgment on the financial settlement of the case.[984] Johan also joined with Hendrick and Samuel Trip in a textile manufacturing company.[985] The company exported cloth to Bordeaux and Sweden, but was also active in the export of iron to England. Johan van Neurenberg was also involved in salt mining.[986] Finally, the otherwise unknown Jacob van Neurenberg was active as an importer of Liège iron to Dordrecht.[987]

The family's administrative activities were developed even further after the brothers Coenraad IV, Willem II and Pieter van Neurenberg had died circa 1640. Johan I van Neurenberg, Willem II's eldest son, continued to live in the family home at the Nieuwe Haven in Dordrecht and expanded the house in 1651 by purchasing the adjacent building. Johan ran the business from this home. On 21 July 1634 he married Elisabeth Trip, Jacob Trip and Margaretha de Geer's daughter, at the Walloon Church.[988]

Johan I combined business and a number of administrative tasks: he was advisor to the city council in 1650 and 1651; and alderman in 1654, 1655, 1662, 1663 and 1673. In 1646 and 1648 he was a member of the Council of Eight (*Achtraad*), while on 17 September 1685, he was appointed to the Council of Forty (*Veertigraad*) by the *stadtholder*. From 1650 on, he was a member of the Council of Elder (*Oudraad*) and in 1673, 1674, 1680, 1681 and 1685 he served as mayor.[989] In addition to the aforementioned interests and involvement in the cloth, salt and iron trade, Johan was also involved in the trade in linseed and paper, and he had shares in transportation.[990] Johan van Neurenberg died on 6 November 1687. Much less is known of the trading and administrative activities of his brothers or cousins.

Johan's second eldest son, also called Johan (II), inherited his father's house and was also active as an administrator. On 25 September 1674, he married his neighbour Adriana de Sont, Pieter de Sont and Margaretha Trip's daughter. On 24 June 1693 he received his doctorate from the legal faculty at Utrecht University, which was undoubtedly related to his administrative tasks (Fig. 92).[991] As doctor at law he had more influence, which is also an indication of the importance Van Neurenberg placed on his administrative tasks. In 1692-1693 and 1700-1701, he was alderman of Dordrecht, from 1689 until 1692 he was treasurer of repairs, and from 1693 until 1696 he was treasurer of the *groot comptoir*. In 1695 he was a member of the Council of Forty and 1698 of the Council of Eight. From 1691 on Johan was a member of the Council of Elder, and between 1694 and 1718 he was active as mayor for several terms. As if that was not enough, several times he was a member of the Zeeland admiralty and

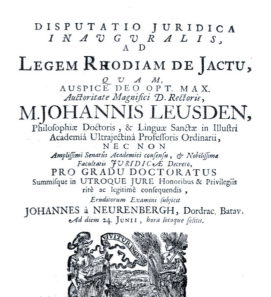

DISPUTATIO JURIDICA
INAUGURALIS,
AD
LEGEM RHODIAM DE JACTU,
QUAM,
AUSPICE DEO OPT. MAX.
Auctoritate Magnifici D. Rectoris,
M. JOHANNIS LEUSDEN,
Philofophiæ Doctoris, & Linguæ Sanctæ in Illuftri
Academiâ Ultrajectinâ Profefforis Ordinarii,
NEC NON
*Ampliffimi Senatûs Academici confenfu, & Nobiliffimæ
Facultatis JURIDICÆ Decreto,*
PRO GRADU DOCTORATUS
Summifque in UTROQUE JURE Honoribus & Privilegiis
ritè ac legitimè confequendis ,
Eruditorum Examini fubjicit
JOHANNES à NEURENBERGH, Dordrac. Batav.
Ad diem 24 JUNII, *hora locoque folitis.*

TRAJECTI ad RHENUM,
Ex Officinâ FRANCISCI HALMA, Academiæ
Typographi, cIↃ IↃc xcIII.

92. Title page of Johan II van Neurenberg's legal thesis, of 24 June 1693. (Universiteitsbibliotheek Utrecht).

984 Ibidem, p. 101.
985 Ibidem, p. 103.
986 Ibidem, p. 116.
987 Ibidem, p. 437.
988 In 1666, Johan, Johanna de Geer's brother-in-law, acted as advisor to her and to her children, who were minors. She was Hendrik Trip's widow. Van Eeghen 1983, p. 109.

989 De Bruijn 1992, p. 77.
990 Ibidem.
991 Van Neurenbergh 1693.

between 1694 and 1708 he was head of orphanages four times, each time for two years.[992] Such shifts from trade to administration were not limited to the Van Neurenberg family. Other families with a similar background also made this shift.[993]

The major emphasis on administrative functions did not mean that Van Neurenberg no longer had any business interests. He founded several fulling mills in Dordrecht with his cousin from Amsterdam, Jacob Trip. Johan II died on 1 May 1724. His son, another Johan (III), was baptised on 17 July 1697 in the Walloon Church in Dordrecht. In the same way that the stone trade was passed from father to son during the sixteenth century, the administrative tasks were passed on in the seventeenth century. Johan III occupied important posts in the Dordrecht town administration, just as his only child, Johan IV, who was baptised on 15 February 1721, did. He also became a member of several councils and would also become Mayor; he was probably not active in the trade.[994]

Johan III's property was sizeable and to a large extent based on the family assets, which had been amassed during the sixteenth and seventeenth centuries. His wealth enabled him in 1729 to have his parental home converted into a modern home, which suited Johan's status and met contemporary requirements (Fig. 93). The stairwell featured a stuccoed ceiling bearing the coat of arms of Johan III van Neurenberg and his wife Rebecca Jacoba van der Voort, whom he had married on 19 May 1720. The centre of the ceiling features a depiction of *Prudentia* (prudence). The iconography of the house's main room refers to the family's mercantile past. Adriaan van der Burgh, a painter from Dordrecht painted the chimneypiece. On it stands a woman crowned with a ship that personifies trade. Signs of trading, such as ledgers, letters and writing paraphernalia, surround her. The god of trade, Mercury, stands to one side of her, leaning over her protectively. Depictions of Peace and Security, both preconditions for flourishing trade, can be found above both doors to the room. In addition to the house in Dordrecht, Johan III also owned a country house called Wielborg, on the Zuidendijk near Dordrecht. The country house was converted into the Dubbeldam cemetery in 1873.[995]

Johan III's son, Johan IV, (15 February 1721 - 17 October 1792) continued the new family tradition of administration, definitively abandoning the trade which had helped the Van Neurenbergs flourish. His son, Johan Mattheus (12 July 1755 - 24 September 1781) also followed in his father's footsteps. No other children reached adulthood. After Johan IV's death his widow, Johanna Reepmaker, inherited the house on the Nieuwe Haven. At that point in time, the house was valued at 20,000 guilders. In her will, Johanna nominates her sister and brother's children as heirs, thereby bringing to an end the history of the trading house of Van Neurenberg. Johanna died on 18 February 1809 at her home on the Nieuwe Haven.

---

[992] De Bruijn 1992, p. 77.
[993] Klein 1965, Prak 1986, Kooijmans 1997.

[994] De Bruijn 1992, p. 78.
[995] Ibidem, p. 90.

93. Dordrecht, Nieuwe Haven 29. Anonymous design, circa 1729 (Museum Mr. Simon van Gijn Dordrecht).

CONCLUSION

This study has not really introduced the reader to the Van Neurenberg family: who they were, what their characters were like, which passions drove them; time has hidden all these things. Then again, it was not our intention to write a personal history, and more importantly, the source material did not allow it. What it did allow was providing insight into the development of the family's Namur stone trade between 1500 and 1650 and the organisation of the work. Prosopographic research allowed the family's position to be catalogued and a major part of their personal and professional network (which in some cases overlaps) to be documented. Interdisciplinary research, the combination of data from buildings, archives and literature enabled the shaping of a diverse cultural-historical and sociological framework within which the family's professional activities could be highlighted.

The family's personal and professional networks are closely intertwined, as was the norm for mercantile families in the early modern era. Analysis of birth, marriage and death registers, notary publics' archives and contracts revealed how the family was part of a partially self-composed network of stone trading and master masons' families. The Lambillon, Wijmoth, Misson, Bidart and Van Delft families were part of the Van Neurenberg family's network and were simultaneously independently active in the stone trade. Cooperative projects, which express both the personal and professional aspects, are encountered on a regular basis. Furthermore, there was also a more professionally oriented network that had several aspects. For example, a network of Meuse merchants can be distinguished, which was a merchant community with common interests that also profiled itself as such, but which seems to have had little influence on the personal network or construction activities. Another network, which was also professional in nature, was that of the patrons and other people involved in construction; through contacts with people such as Hendrick de Keyser, the family indirectly acquired commissions, for example from the town of Hoorn. Such contacts were also established the other way. The commission for making the screen of the Sint-Jans Church in 's-Hertogenbosch by Hendrick de Keyser originated from building contractor Coenraad IV van Neurenberg. Such alliances dramatically increased buyer potential. Moreover, this network generated new commissions once contact had been made. By using reputation, availability and in some cases even seniority, these contacts were used to acquire follow-up commissions. Examples of this networking are the family's activities in Nijmegen over a period of over seventy years and the double deliveries for the towns of Haarlem and Leiden.

The composition of the 1624 arbitration committee in Utrecht proved how close these contacts were and how closely intertwined the elite of the construction sector, to which the family belonged, really was. Paulus Moreelse, after whose design Van Neurenberg supplied stone, was assessed by Hendrick de Keyser (with whom Coenraad IV and Pieter Van Neurenberg worked), Lieven de Key (whom Coenraad III had encountered in Haarlem), Cornelis Danckerts (whose sister bought Willem II van Neureberg's house on the Keizersgracht in Amsterdam and to whom he was distantly related through his sister Anna) and Hendrick van Bilderbeeck (whose position in Leiden had involved him in the construction of the Blue Gate, for which Coenraad IV Van Neurenberg had supplied the specifications). Such direct or indirect contacts are also known to have existed with traders such as Laurens Sweijs (Danckerts' son-in-law) and a large number of stone trading families, such as the Wijmoths, Missons, Lambillons, Le Bidarts, Rochets, etc.

There was also a micro-network active within the family, although the term hierarchy perhaps best describes it within this context. Other studies have clarified how family hierarchy operated during the sixteenth and seventeenth centuries.[996] Fathers generally had the most important say in mat-

---

[996] Kooijmans 1997, passim.

ters. Upon his death his widow would assume his position as head of the family and of the family business, although the eldest son, depending on his age, generally took care of the father's executive tasks. Insufficient source material means that the existence of such a distribution within the Van Neurenberg family is hard to determine. Regarding the last few active generations, the brothers Coenraad IV, Willem II and Pieter we know more; although the relationship between Coenraad and Willem remains somewhat obscure, for example, Willem and not Coenraad obtained the parental home in Dordrecht, while younger brother Pieter was employed as the family's agent in order to guarantee a continuous flow of stone from the Southern Low Countries.

The flow of goods: costs and benefits

The picture of the family's trading seems remarkably coherent. Nevertheless, the source material has dwindled away through time; therefore, the family's history is not based on the analysis of successive years of the company archive such as ledgers and registers, which leads to considerable problems particularly where questions of a quantitative nature are concerned. The amount of stone supplied per year cannot be reconstructed on the basis of the available data, and neither can the developments within the flow of goods. However, the problems go much further than just the quantitative level. The data available on trade, dimensions and dimensioning of the material supplied do not allow for conclusions. Moreover it proved impossible to examine materials provision at the quarry itself further because of the organisation of quarrying. Although a general impression of the state of affairs at the quarry has been provided and a few examples of stone that Van Neurenberg purchased from the quarry owner have been discussed, it is unknown to what extent the family itself was involved in stone quarrying. Some phrases could lead to the impression that their involvement was very unlikely, as the 1540 example in which the town of Nijmegen "had made" Willem I van Neurenberg "buy" (*doen koepen*) Namur stone. Later examples of purchasing stone from the quarry are also known. For the time being at least, there is no indication of them having their own quarry operation.

In addition to the lacunae with regard to stone supply from the quarry, there is insufficient data available to be able to make statements concerning pricing or profit margins and their development. These primarily economic-historical research questions pertain to the lease and operation costs at the quarry, and the transport and taxes on shipments. These aspects should be subjected to closer scrutiny within the framework of a separate study, thereby also examining methods of working the stone and dimensioning in order to be able to make quantitative statements. Materials costs, quarrying costs, processing costs, transport, taxes and profit margins determined the price of a piece of stone in the north. A large number of these aspects are, however, still too unspecified or occur in such a large variety of nuances that they make statements with regard to price development impossible. Concrete figures on the economy of the sixteenth and seventeenth centuries are required in order to be able to prove such changes.[997] An attempt could be made to reverse engineer the problem and to examine the price paid for stone in the north, which should then also take the distance between quarry and construction site, the dimensions and the processing into account. However, what constitutes an insurmountable problem is that the intended profit margins are unknown. Statements from the seventeenth century indicating that a substantial percentage (a few dozen per cent) would be subtracted from the price if payment was speedy make it impossible to draw up a reliable prediction graph for the costs and benefits on the basis of a relatively small number of deliveries.

---

[997] The data from the Van Neurenberg family's practice are too incidental in nature to allow such conclusions to be made.

The differences between the deliveries themselves are also too great. In 1561 for example, Jan Misson charged 12.5 stivers per foot for the plinth of Antwerp town hall and 15.50 stivers per foot for stone intended for the first storey, in 1564 Coenraad II van Neurenberg charged 7.33 stivers per foot for the town hall in Sittard, and Jan Lambillon in 1567 charged 3.9 stivers per foot for a lock in Spaarndam. In 1608, the stone for the weigh house in Hoorn cost 18 stivers per foot, stone for a lock built near Plasschendaele in 1619 cost 26.75 stivers per foot and stone for the Catharijne Gate in Utrecht cost 17.5 stivers per foot in 1621. Missing data on the exact detailing and processing of the stone are the greatest hindrance to making statements here. However, it is clear that there was a large difference in hierarchy and processing of the stone applied. As became apparent from the examples of the Hezel gate in Nijmegen and the stones for the gallery in Breda, differences in processing were a crucial part of pricing, which led to pieces of stone of varying thickness nevertheless having the same price in Breda.[998]

If the general price of stone is discussed then statements such as the following by Jan van Houter, master stonemason in Amsterdam are very useful. In 1661 he stated, at Philips Vingboons' request, that during the time he had been a master in Amsterdam, a foot of ordinary Bentheimer stone had always cost seventeen stivers.[999]

In summary it can be stated that the source material has enabled statements to be made with regard to the general development of the Meuse trade and specifically the Namur stone trade. In particular, the trading organisation and the manner in which seventeenth-century merchants managed to acquire a structural position during the sixteenth century have emerged from this study. Further, micro-economic questions require detailed and specialised research in the area of origin.

Political, economic and other factors

The changes in the construction sector and the political circumstances, which can help explain some of the changes to the Meuse Valley's competitive position regarding other areas, had a great impact on the family's activities. Rapid demographic expansion was accompanied by explosive price development and lagging wage increases. These factors resulted in economic (and social) decline for a large group of salaried labourers. Only a select group of entrepreneurs and merchants managed to use the changes to their advantage, like the Van Neurenberg family.[1000] To what extent a favourable financial and socio-economic point of departure was an advantage at the start of the sixteenth century is not included in this study. It is however a fact that the family's younger descendants were able to take over the family business, which provided them with an existing network and structures so that setbacks, which would have ruined newcomers, had less effect on them.

Major shifts in trading circumstances and politics were matters on which individual merchants had almost no influence. By cooperating with other merchants, an individual could try to defend himself against unfavourable developments and could attempt to capitalise on the changing market so that his position, balanced between supply and demand, remained favourable. During the sixteenth century a number of exceptionally advantageous changes occurred from which the Van Neurenberg family benefited. While until the sixteenth century the Namur stone trade had primarily been a local affair, during the following period a situation developed in which merchants managed to gain a strong foothold in the north. Under the influence of the improvement of iron, expanding industry and new political circumstances, direct trade between the Northern Low Countries and the Meuse Valley developed. Venlo losing its position as staple town was crucial to this development.

[998] See also Thurlings 1945, pp. 47-48.
[999] Van Dillen 1974, p. 696, No. 1477.
[1000] Blondé 1986, p. XVI.

215

This desire for expansion from the Meuse Valley was supplemented by the increasing demand for stone from the north. Under the influence of demographic developments, construction commissions and the setting up of town fabric positions show a discernable increase in construction activity, particularly in the urban context. Furthermore, at the beginning the stone trade was principally concentrated in Antwerp. From around 1540, increasingly strong ties developed between the town on the Schelde and Amsterdam, whereby both towns had their own specialities. Antwerp was primarily a town of industry and export, while Amsterdam was more focused on agriculture, fisheries, etc. Both towns were important to the construction materials trade.

A number of these specialities shifted north from Antwerp due to the separation of the Southern and Northern Low Countries. The international trade with the Baltic and the Mediterranean started to concentrate around Amsterdam, while regional trade was also centred on that city. After the fall of Antwerp in 1585 and the closing of the Schelde, the international stone trade became entirely Amsterdam based, which had important consequences for the national stone trade; the relations between the Meuse Valley, Brabant/Hainault and Bentheim, as the principal production areas for stone, changed drastically. The trade from Brabant and Hainault, which for its export was entirely dependent on transport down the Schelde, almost came to a standstill. At the same time, a group of Meuse Valley stone merchants decided to permanently relocate to the newly founded Dutch Republic. These merchants had basically had a fixed share of the northern market for several decades. Economic, religious and personal considerations, combined with the favourable pre-conditions in the north, moved them to emigrate en masse without cutting their ties with the south. This decision proved beneficial for the Meuse Valley traders' competitive position; the void created by the disappearance of the Brabant and Hainault trade could be effortlessly filled by expanding existing activities. Moreover, due to the relocation to the north the merchants were not cut off from their patrons and managed to obtain licences for importing stone from the Meuse Valley. The negative impact of war was therefore relatively limited for this group.

Their main competition came from the County of Bentheim in Germany. Bentheimer sandstone had been quarried here for some time, but quarry operations were professionalised around 1600. As a result traders from Holland became involved in this trade and ultimately they would lease the quarries from the Count of Bentheim for an extended period of time. These 'Dutch' quarries would eventually be of great importance to the manner in which stone was worked in Holland and for the material's application in the west. By doing as much as possible itself, the Dutch construction trade managed to slowly free itself from foreign stonemasons' traditions and to develop its own architecture.

Construction organisation and innovation in styles: the stone supplier's role

Naturally, the development of a specific architectural style, not dominated by the materials trade, did not happen automatically. One of the causes of the independence of the construction sector was the rise of the town fabric lodges. The more the sixteenth-century towns became patrons for construction projects, the more the institutionalisation of town construction increased; the town administration appointed a fabric lodge master and sometimes there was a separate administration for the construction trade. In various towns such as Amsterdam, Leiden and Haarlem, town officials responsible for the masonry, brickwork or carpentry were introduced quite rapidly. These people were to leave their mark on town construction.

One of the most important consequences of this development was that master masons were no longer 'imported' from elsewhere. The towns attempted to do as much of the work as they could and only called on outsiders if the situation forced them to do so. As far as the materials trade was concerned, this development hardly constituted a change. However, the fact that historically stone merchants had also acted as master masons, entailed a narrowing of the scope of activities for this group, which could be observed in the Van Neurenberg family's practice around 1550. The major difference with the preceding period was not so much a change in the activities themselves, but that from then on the family was forced to specialise. With the exception of the disappearance of their work as master masons; everything stayed the same. In other words, the scope of the family's activities became more limited; others now dictated the design of the stone supplied. Patrons imposed the organisation of construction, including the design, so that the stone suppliers' control of the construction process increasingly became smaller. In the Van Neurenberg family's practice proof of this decrease occurs time and again. Only in Willemstad was Coenraad III still active as a master mason, which was because this small village that had only just been awarded town rights and there was no construction company. During the seventeenth century, the construction trade became further subdivided. The role of specialist was not only expressed in the stone supplier's work, but also in the designer's work. There was often a separation between design and specifications, while someone else executed the work.

A constant factor well into the seventeenth century was the composition of the group of stone suppliers; families from the Meuse Valley had historically dominated the trade in stone such as Namur stone, marlstone and Belgian marble. This situation had undergone almost no change until ca. 1585, when a group of traders relocated to Dordrecht. The families were closely connected through their origins, but also by strong mutual family ties, which meant that a strong network was transported north in its entirety. The research has revealed that it took several decades before this group started focusing on their new surroundings as far as trading and marriage matters were concerned. A good example of this was Anna van Neurenberg's second marriage. After first having been married to Jaques Saverij, who was originally from Maastricht, she married the Amsterdam stone trader and building contractor Pieter van Delft in 1616. Other families such as the Wijmoths for example, left the familiar circle in Dordrecht around this time. Simultaneously, professional ties developed during these years between, for example, Van Neurenberg and De Keyser, which indicate that the Meuse Valley traders were starting to look outside their own circle for other alliances.

For the time being, the family's business centred on distribution between the quarry in the south and the buyers in the north. Although no extensive research was carried out into this topic, it is known that Pieter van Neurenberg purchased stone from quarry operators for the northern market.

Over the course of the sixteenth century and the first half of the seventeenth, the stone trade became a matter of logistics. Stone was purchased in the south while the design was dictated from the north. Examples of this practice include the Old Church tower in Amsterdam, the weigh house in Hoorn, the Catharijne Gate in Utrecht and Frederik Hendrik's palaces. The processing of the material still took place in the south at the quarry for the time being. Various contracts show how the material was processed at the quarry and then shipped north readymade. The responsibility for this processing lay with the merchant, because he entered into the contract with the patron. In practice the building contractor generally also subcontracted the work, as shown in the example of the screen in 's-Hertogenbosch. On the basis of the source material, no watertight conclusions can be drawn concerning who carried out the processing, which can have differed from case to case. A clue which points in this direction is the fact that some agreements included a clause which obliged the stone seller to send a number of craftsmen to place the stone so that they could make any necessary alterations to the stone. For example, in the case of the screen of the Sint-Jans Church in 's Hertogenbosch and the Catharijne Gate in Utrecht the stone was reworked on site.

It cannot be assumed that the situation remained static. In 1585 it was still prohibited to run a stonemason's workshop on Het Nieuwe Werk in Dordrecht; nevertheless, a few years later there were strong clues that stone was being worked there. In Amsterdam there was also a similar development. During the sixteenth century the town largely acquired worked stone from elsewhere, while during the seventeenth century there was a flourishing stonemasons' trade in the town. Dozens of larger and smaller stonemasons' workshops and stone cutting works existed; stone was acquired from the Meuse Valley, Bentheim and the Mediterranean and worked in the town. The dependence on outside sources had been completely reversed within half a century and became a situation in which the New Dutch Republic, to a large extent, took over the processing of stone.

Conclusions

As mentioned at the beginning of this study, the stone trade encompassed three main aspects: the logistic-economic aspect (transport and trade), the material aspect (material and processing) and the cultural-historical aspect (design, networks, etc.). All three changed during the period under discussion. The question is to what extent this change has to do with the exceptional position of stone as a trading product. The material's origin definitely influenced trading contacts between the Meuse Valley and the Northern Low Countries and should therefore also be viewed in this context. In other words: the application of Meuse Valley stone on this scale would have been impossible without structural trading contacts and the opportunity to have these contacts between both regions. The product therefore cannot be viewed in isolation, but is rooted in a much broader flow of trade, which, furthermore, concerns a product that, in contrast to many others, was almost entirely dependent on transport over water. Lists of land-based transport reveal a large variety of products, but do not include stone. It was Namur stone's high weight, which prevented it from being transported over land, with a few exceptions. These specific geographic and material-tied factors ensured that the development of the trade in Namur stone was strongly dependent on macro-economic aspects in conjunction with political developments. The expansion of the Meuse Valley as an export region, the change in political situation and the rescinding of Venlo's staple rights explain Namur stone's presence on the northern market.

The material aspects also offer an explanation for the success. The stone from the Meuse Valley was eminently suitable for a broad range of applications, from decorative to utilitarian. Namur stone occurs as the cladding of fortress and quay walls, as tombstones, tiles, columns, capitals, facing stones, window frames, dripstone mouldings, etc. It is this broad range of applications, which enabled the traders to focus on an attractive market rife with potential buyers. Less frequently applied types of stone, such as marlstone, have a much more limited target group and market, which meant that it was much less lucrative for traders to enter this market, particularly at a trans-regional level. The opportunities for working stone seem to have expanded during the sixteenth century as a result of the improvement in iron making. This aspect can also have contributed to Namur stone's success, although caution is advised.[1001] Changes in surface treatment were examined as part of this study and those in the north proved to correspond with those in the Meuse Valley. A similar development has also been observed in Hainault. These similarities suggest that the stone was, to a large extent, worked and finished in the south. Only in the seventeenth century did this parallel development seemingly cease, and the working of stone in the north increased.

The cultural-historical aspect concerns the organisation of the construction trade and the people, families, etc. involved in the Namur stone trade. In addition to the right prerequisites for trade, the community of merchants involved in trade on the Meuse, in general, and in Namur stone and related products, in particular, was quite homogenous. This group's composition, the way in which it operated on the market, composed its network and functioned were important for the success of Namur stone on the northern market. This personal organisation of trade, the human aspect regarding the interplay of supply and demand was of great importance to the continuity of the Namur stone trade. The Van Neurenberg family managed to claim part of the trade as their own and maintain their position for a very long period thanks to marriages, trading politics, contacts with other traders, alliances, repute, etc. It is virtually impossible to distinguish between the family's personal and professional networks, because these were very closely related. Their personal network served their professional one, which was, however, more than just a means of making money.[1002]

[1001] In Germany, differences in processing have been found in relatively small areas. Further research is required before general statements can be made concerning the Meuse Valley and Dutch situation. See Hochkirchen 1990.

[1002] See Kooijmans 1997 for more on these aspects of personal networks.

Insight into factors that played a role in the stone supply from the Meuse Valley to the Northern Low Countries arises from this combination of various aspects of the materials trade. The Van Neurenberg family, together with other families, managed to maintain their position as market leaders for a long time thanks to their presence or the creation of the right pre-conditions at various levels and the correct amount of flexibility for capitalising on changes in the construction trade in the north. Political and industrial history thereby explain the presence of the Van Neurenberg family on the northern market. Furthermore, the organisation of the construction trade explains the inner workings of the family's actual activities. The family's personal network, finally, provides reasons for the trade successes and the family's long association in the same sector of industry.

The competitive relations between the various stone producing areas are the last item to warrant mention here. Here all the previously mentioned aspects return. The Van Neurenberg family's position within the relations between these areas is clear; as representatives of the Meuse Valley stone trade, where the family possessed ties, which it could not easily acquire elsewhere, the family was bound to this area. At the point in time that another area no longer had access to the market, which was particularly the case for the Brabant trade from the second half of the sixteenth century on, the family managed to relocate to a strategic location and make use of its competitors' weaknesses. Once again, the political and economic factors were actually determining for the trading context within which the family operated.

Epilogue

The disappearance of the Van Neurenberg family from the stone trade did not constitute the end of the trade in Namur stone. In the west, Namur stone continued to be a desirable product. In 1668, Namur stone was purchased for the plinth of the Amsterdam Change. Reference was subsequently made to the Saint-Loup Church in Namur. For the sills of the round Lutheran Church in Amsterdam, Namur stone was used around 1670.[1003] But also in Maastricht, for example, a lively trade in this type of stone continued. From the end of the sixteenth century there was a gradual concentration of members from the construction trade in the Stokstraat area.[1004] There is the noteworthy example of stonemason and stone merchant Steven Matto, who was originally from Seilles and who moved to the house he had purchased, Het Reepken (Stokstraat 26-28) in 1622. The expansion of Matto's property reveals that a stonemason could also achieve great prosperity in Maastricht. During the years until his death in 1656, he purchased a number of houses in the Stokstraat area. Matto's son, also called Steven (1644-1680), provided his parental home, which was now called Den Steenen Bergh (the Stone Mountain), with a rich new facade in 1669.[1005] Matto must have also owned property in Namur and Liège. Other stonemasons had also relocated to the Stokstraat area and these relocations would continue well into the nineteenth century.[1006]

The developments that had taken place in the west slowly became commonplace in Maastricht, too. Paradoxically Namur stone was now used in Maastricht according to the classicist ideas current in Holland. Earlier architectural ideas had been exported north from the south, but it was now Holland, in particular, which became known as an exporter of architectural concepts, even in the Meuse Valley. Naturally, the most famous example of this is Pieter Post's town hall in Maastricht (Fig. 94). The

---

[1003] Kindly suggested by Pieter Vlaardingerbroek.
[1004] Essers 1973, p. 191.

[1005] Ibidem, p. 192.
[1006] Janse, De Vries 1991, p. 36.

94. Maastricht town hall by architect Pieter Post (1659-1664). Anonymous Photograph (GAM).

decision to construct this building had been made in 1655.[1007] Between 1659 and 1664 a new town hall, entirely clad in Namur stone, was built in the middle of the market square. The building committee appointed Philippe d'Ardenne as stonemason responsible for the execution of the design on 4 November 1658. D'Ardenne was born around 1620 and became a Maastricht citizen in 1660. After completing the town hall he continued to work for the town, where he was employed to do maintenance work on the fortifications, among other things. After the French attack of 1672 he worked on a wall along the Meuse and he was responsible for the repair to the Meuse bridge,[1008] which made him a distant successor to Coenraad I van Neurenberg, who had carried out similar work for the town at the start of the sixteenth century.

Our study started with Andries Vierlingh's complaint concerning the unreliability of labourers, who proved to be rather lazy in practice and generally did very little correctly. Now the end of the book has been reached, it is time to recall a similar complaint by Constantijn Huygens. The construction of his house on the Plein in The Hague moved him to write the following in 1639: "As without mentioning the unpleasantness to the nose and eyes, an exceptionally unpleasant entertainment, I must – to the fatherland's shame – and even primarily for The Hague admit that nowhere in the world exists a barbarian and inhuman people that can be more trying to the patience of good citizens than our labourers: lazier than sleeping disease and slower than syrup, yes so notoriously slow, untruthful and disgracefully sloth-like, that someone without the requisite stoic defences against this nightmare may be considered unsuitable and incapable of building in this day and age."[1009]

In the sixteenth century, it was a man from the construction trade itself who complained; in the seventeenth century the complaints came from respected citizens such as Huygens. And although these complaints are naturally somewhat arbitrary, they do illustrate the shift that had taken place in the construction trade over the past hundred years: the nature of the complaint about the labourers had not changed, but the social class of the person complaining had. It is this shift that typifies the construction trade. During the sixteenth century it was primarily the stonemasons, craftsmen and builders from the medieval tradition who determined the appearance of Dutch architecture, which was very different in the seventeenth century. Thanks to the emancipation of the construction trade in the Northern Low Countries, stonemasons and stone traders had been forced to resign themselves to the sole role of materials suppliers. The town official or painter-architect had replaced the master mason com-

---

[1007] Terwen, Ottenheym 1993, pp. 176-182.
[1008] He died in 1699. See Ottenheym 1986, p. 150.
[1009] Blom, Bruin, Ottenheym 1999, p. 21.

ing in from outside, who had ruled the construction site for a long time. The increasing specialisation had led to a limitation of the traditional master mason and stone supplier's field of activities. Whether this change was actually an improvement for the work on the construction site, its organisation and progress remains to be seen. Building was and continued to be a process rife with mistakes and misunderstandings. As seen above, the Van Neurenberg family was no exception to this situation, which sometimes resulted in lengthy court cases. That after well over three hundred and fifty years, attention is still being paid to their activities is not so much due to this aftermath, but to the large area over which their activities extended and the durability of the buildings they helped create. It is these matters that, much more than the complaints made concerning them, still spark our imagination.

BIBLIOGRAPHY

- Adriaenssens, R., 'Sur l'hôtel de ville d'Anvers et les apports des carrières wallones dans son edification'. In: *Bulletin de la Commission des Monuments et des Sites* 9 (1980), pp. 125-141.
- Agt, J.J.F.W. van, 'De Sint Stevenskerk te Nijmegen'. In: *Bulletin KNOB* (1954), pp. 97-131.
- Albrecht, S., *Das Bremer Rathaus im Zeichen städtischer Selbstdarstellung vor dem 30-jährigen Krieg*. Marburg 1993.
- Albrecht, S., 'Eine Fassade geht auf Reisen...'. In: *Bremen und die Niederlande*. Jahrbuch 1995/1996. Bremen 1997, pp. 69-73.
- Anderson, F., E. Groessens, 'The Black Altars of Nehallennia'. In: *Oudheidkundige mededelingen uit het Rijksmuseum van oudheden te Leiden* 76 (1996), pp. 129-137.
- Ansorge, J., H. Schäfer, 'Die Konsolen des Rostocker Franziskanerklosters St. Katharinen'. In: *Wismarer Studien zur Archäologie und Geschichte* 4 (1994), pp. 18-28.
- Arends, G.J., *Sluizen en Stuwen: de ontwikkeling van de sluis- en stuwbouw in Nederland tot 1940*. Bouwtechniek in Nederland 5. Delft 1994.
- Avery, Ch., 'The Rood-loft from Hertogenbosch'. In: *The Victoria & Albert Yearbook* 1969.

- Baar, P.J.M. de, L. Barendregt, H. Suurmond-van Leeuwen, *Stadstimmerwerf, stadshulpwerf, stadswerf*. Leiden 1986.
- Bakker, G., T. Hoekstra (ed.), *Het Stenen Geheugen; 25 jaar archeologie en bouwhistorie in Utrecht*. Utrecht 1997.
- Bauduin, H., 'Bronnen voor de geschiedenis van de Limburgse Maashandel'. In: *De Maasgouw* 81 (1962), pp. 117-121.
- Bavay, G., 'Du lit au délit. Relations entre l'agencement architectural et le travail en carrière (le cas du calcaire carbonifère dans le bassin hainuyer)'. In: *Actes du VIe colloque international de glyptographie de Samoëns*, 5-10 juilliet 1988. [Braine-le-Château] 1989, pp. 11-33.
- Beelaerts van Blokland, W.A., 'Alexander Pasqualini, bouwmeester van het kasteel te Buren en andere sloten, krijgs- en vestingbouwkundige van naam'. In: *Bijdragen en mededeelingen Gelre* 34 (1931), pp. 155-168.
- Belle, J.-L. van, *L'Industrie de la pierre en Wallonie (XVIe et XVIIIe siècles)*. Gembloux 1976.
- Belle, J.-L. van, 'Aspects économiques et sociaux de l'exploitation d'une carrière namuroise à la fin du XVIIe siècle'. In: *Annales de la société archéologique de Namur* LXIII (1983) 1, pp. 96-113.
- Belle, J.-L. van, *Les maîtres de carrière d'Arquennes sous l'ancien régime; un métier. Des hommes*. S.i. 1990.
- Belle, J.-L. van, *Nouveau dictionnaire des signes lapidaires - Belgique et Nord de la France*. Louvain-la-Neuve 1994.
- Berends, G., 'Sint-Servaaskerk te Maastricht: de geschiedenis van het gebouw naar de bronnen tot het midden van de vorige eeuw'. Unpublished, without year.
- Berends, G., 'Maateenheden'. In: *Restauratievademecum* 1996/38-6. RVblad 01-1   01-12.
- Berg, B. van den, 'Kerkelijke bouwprojecten van de bouwmeesters uit de Keldermans-familie'. In: Van Mosselveld 1987, pp. 61-87.
- Berg, R. v.d., *Leerdam in de gouden eeuw*. Ameide 1979.
- Bergé, W., 'Het voormalige hoogaltaar in de Sint Jan'. In: Koldeweij 1990, pp. 439-463.
- Bergé, W., 'Nieuwe gegevens betreffende de meubilering van het koor der Sint Jan te 's-Hertogenbosch tussen 1610-1620'. In: *Jaarboek monumentenzorg 1991*. Zwolle etc. 1991, pp. 96-113.
- Bergers, H., 'Fragment eines für die Waterpoort der Zitadelle von Batavia bestimmten Steinportals'. In: Kastler, Lüpkes 2000, 50.
- Berns, J.L., *Rechtsbronnen der stad Harderwijk*. Werken der vereeniging tot uitgave der bronnen van het oude vaderlandsche recht, eerste reeks, VIII. 's-Gravenhage 1886.

223

- Bers, G., C. Doose (ed.), *Der italienische Architekt Alessandro Pasqualini (1493-1559) und die Renaissance am Niederrhein.* Jülich 1994.
- Bers, G., C. Doose (ed.), *Der italienische Architekt Alessandro Pasqualini (1493-1559) und die Stadt als Idealplan.* Jülich 1999.
- Bevers, H., *Das Rathaus von Antwerpen (1561-1565): Architektur und Figurenprogramm.* Hildesheim etc. 1985.
- Beylen, J. van, *Schepen van de Nederlanden: van de late Middeleeuwen tot het einde van de 17e eeuw.* Amsterdam 1970.
- Binding, G., *Baubetrieb im Mittelalter.* Darmstadt 1993.
- Bloemink, W., H.A.J. Roetert Steenbruggen, 'De Noordenbergtoren'. In: *Deventer Jaarboek 1991,* pp. 35-55.
- Blom, F.R.E., H.G. Bruin, K.A. Ottenheym, *Domus. Het huis van Constantijn Huygens in Den Haag.* Zutphen 1999.
- Blom, A. van der, *Lieven de Key, Haarlems stadsbouwmeester. Een Vlaamse emigrant en zijn rijke nalatenschap.* Haarlem 1995.
- Blondé, B., *De sociale structuren en economische dynamiek van 's-Hertogenbosch (1500-1550).* Licentiaatsverhandeling. Leuven 1986.
- Boekwijt, H., A. van Drunen, 'Het middeleeuwse tussenbalkjuk opnieuw beschouwd' In: *Monumenten en bouwhistorie. Jaarboek Monumentenzorg 1996.* Zwolle etc. 1996, pp. 19-28.
- Bollen M. et al., *Abdij Herkenrode: voorstudie van de rehabilitatie van de voormalige abdij in haar geheel en het 16e eeuwse abdisverblijf in het bijzonder als klooster voor de Reguliere Kanunnikessen van het H. Graf.* Studiegroep Haaldewijn. Rapport. Hasselt 1977.
- Bolly, J.-J., 'A propos des marques du château de Modave: réflexion sur les signes lapidaires de la région Mosane aux XVIe et XVIIe siècles'. In: *Actas del V coloquio internacional de gliptografía* (1 volumen). [Pontevedra] 1986, pp. 383-391.
- Bom, J.A.L., 'Natuursteen bij historische bouwwerken'. In: *Bulletin KNOB* (1950), pp. 161-186.
- Bommenee, A., *Het 'testament' van Adriaan Bommenee; praktijkervaringen van een Veerse bouw- en waterbouwkundige uit de 18e eeuw.* Middelburg 1988.
- Boonstra, J. (ed.), *Soo vele heerlijcke gebouwen: van Palladio tot Vingboons.* Amsterdam 1997.
- Bosman, Th.E.A. et al., *Leven met het verleden; gedenkboek honderd jaar 'Oud-Dordrecht'.* Dordrecht 1992.
- Bos-Rops, J.A.M.Y., M. Bruggeman, *Archiefwijzer; handleiding voor het gebruik van archieven in Nederland.* Muiderberg 1987.
- Bouttier, M., *Cathedrales: les batisseurs.* Cahors 1991.
- Bracker, J. (Hrsg.), *Bauen nach der Natur - Palladio: die Erben Palladios in Nordeuropa.* Ostfildern 1997.
- Bray, S. de, *Architectura Moderna ofte Bouwinge van onse tyt.* Amsterdam 1631.
- Bree, G.W.G. van, *Inventaris van de oude archieven van de stad Roermond (1259-1796).* Roermond 1989.
- *Bremisches Jahrbuch,* Bd. 16. Bremen 1892.
- Breuer, H., *Die Maas als Schiffahrtweg.* Wiesbaden 1969.
- Briels, J., *De Zuidnederlandse immigratie 1572-1630.* Haarlem 1978.
- Brinkman, E. (ed.), *Hollands Classicisme in de zeventiende-eeuwse schilderkunst.* Rotterdam etc. 1999.
- Brouwers, D., 'Une ordonnance de Magistrat de Namur sur les prix et les salaires en 1588'. In: *Namurcum* XI (1934) 4, pp. 49-55.
- Bruijn, C.M. de, J. Huisman, 'Het huis Nieuwe Haven 29 en zijn bewoners tot 1864'. In: Bosman et al. 1992, pp. 67-102.
- Buisman, J., *Duizend jaar weer, wind en water in de lage landen.* Part III 1450-1575. Franeker 1998 and part IV 1575-1675. Franeker 2000.
- Buschman, P., 'Het oksaal van 's-Hertogenbosch'. In: *Onze Kunst* 17, (1918) 34, pp. 1-35.
- Bijtelaar, B., 'Het snijderskoor en het vrouwenkoor van de Oude Kerk'. In: *Amstelodamum* 54, (1962), pp. 49-81.

- Carmiggelt, A., T.J. Hoekstra, M.C. van Trierum, D.J. de Vries (ed.), *Rotterdam Papers 10*. A Contribution to Medieval and Post-Medieval Archaeology and History of Building. Rotterdam 1999.
- Casteele, D. van de, 'Archives d'anciens monuments namurois'. In: *Annales de la Société Archéologique de Namur* XVI (1883) 1.
- Chevalier, A., 'Inventaire des marques de tailleurs de pierre en l'église Saint-Jaques de Liège'. In: *Bulletin de l'Institut archéologique liégeois* LXXXIV (1972), pp. 63-72.
- Classen, W., 'Baunachrichten aus den Klevischen Zollakten'. In: *Duesseldorfer Jahrbuch* 45 (1951), pp. 136-146.
- Clifton-Taylor, A., A.S. Ireson, *English Stone Building*. 2nd ed. London 1994.
- Cnudde, C., J.-J. Harotin, J.-P. Majot, *Pierres et Marbres de Wallonie / Stenen en marmers van Wallonië*. Brussel 1987.
- Colart, A., *Les corporations de Namur*. Namur 1941.
- Comanne, J., 'Les traces d'outils dans la sculpture décorative et les pierres en oeuvre dans la vallée de la Meuse du XIIe à la fin du XVIe s.'. In: *Actes du VIIIe Colloque International de Glyptographie d'Hoepertingen EUREGIO*. Braine-le-Chateau 1992, pp. 393-403.
- Courajod, L., 'L'Exportation des pierres noires de Dinant. Saint Wulfran d'Abbeville'. In: *Leçons professées à l'école du Louvre*. T. II. 1901. Dix-huitième leçon, 7 Mai 1890, pp. 605-615.
- Courtoy, M.F., 'Les de Nurenberg architectes des XVIe et XVIIe siècle'. In: *Wallonia* 20 (1912), pp. 508-512.
- Courtoy, F., 'Les arts industriels à Dinant au début du dix-septième siècle'. In: *Annales de la soc. arch. de Namur* 34 (1920), pp. 217-253.
- Courtoy, F., 'Ateliers de sculpture wallonne'. In: *Namurcum* II (1925) 4, pp. 59-62.
- Courtoy, F., 'Jean de Loyers, tombier dinantais'. In: *Namurcum* VI (1929) 4, pp. 61-63.
- Courtoy, F., *L'architecture civile dans le Namurois aux XVIIe et XVIIIe siècle*. Brussel 1936.
- Courtoy, F., 'Les Duchesne, tailleurs de pierre et marbriers namurois'. In: *Annales de la société archéologique de Namur* XLIII (1938) 2, pp. 285-295.
- Courtoy, F., 'Le travail et le commerce de la pierre à Namur avant 1500'. In: *Namurcum* XXI (1946) 2, pp. 17-29.
- Courtoy, F., 'Les Nonon, marbriers dinantais'. In: *Namurcum* 26 (1952), pp. 24-27.
- Crèvecoeur, R., 'De toepassing van verf op natuursteen'. In: Sarrazin 1999, pp. 135-139.
- Czyppull, B., J. Mitzkat, *Über Land und Stein; Kulturlandschaft Weserbergland - Vom Sollingsandstein geprägt*. Holzminden 1998.

- D.-H., M.M., 'Bentheimer steen voor de Sint-Maartenskerk te Tiel'. In: *Bijdragen en mededelingen Gelre* LX (1961), p. 142.
- Dam, J.D. van, *Nederlandse Tegels*. 2nd ed. Amsterdam etc. 1991.
- Dane, K., *Willemstad; historisch overzicht van stad en polder*. Klundert 1950.
- Davids, K., 'Beginning Entrepreneurs and Municipal Governments in Holland at the Time of the Dutch Republic'. In: Lesger, Noordegraaf 1995, pp. 167-183.
- Denslagen, W.F., A. de Vries, *Kleur op historische gebouwen*. 's-Gravenhage 1984.
- Denslagen, W.F. et al. (ed.), *Bouwkunst; studies in vriendschap voor Kees Peeters*. Amsterdam 1993.
- Deursen, A.Th. van, *Mensen van klein vermogen. Het kopergeld van de Gouden Eeuw*. 2nd ed. Amsterdam 1992.
- Devigne, M., 'Les frères Jean, Guillaume et Nicolas de Wespin. Dits Tabaguet et tabachetti, sculpteurs Dinantais (XVIe et XVIIe siècles)'. In: *Annales de la Société royale d'Archeologie de Bruxelles* 29 (1920), pp. 97-135, and idem 31 (1922), pp. 5-22.
- Devliegher, L., 'De bouw van het stadhuis te Damme 1464-1467'. In: *Bulletin KNOB* 17 (1964) col. 159-166.
- Devliegher, L., 'De bouwrekeningen van het stadhuis te Damme 1461-1470'. In: *Handelingen van het 'Société d'Emulation' te Brugge* 102 (1965), pp. 134-202.

- Dezutter, W.P., M. Goetinck (ed.), *Tentoonstelling op en om de bouwwerf: ambachtswezen - oud gereedschap.* Brugge 1975.
- Dezutter, W.P., M. Goetinck, 'De verering van de H. Eligius, de H. Jozef en de Vier Gekroonden'. In: De Zutter, Goetinck 1975, pp. 97–111.
- Dickhaut, M.F.A., *Documentatieverslag 18 (mei-juli 1987) Restauratie Sint-Servaaskerk te Maastricht.* RDMZ Zeist 1987.
- Dijn, G. De et al., *Herkenrode 800 jaar.* Tentoonstellingscatalogus. Hasselt 1982.
- Dillen, J. G. van, *Bronnen tot de geschiedenis van het bedrijfsleven en het gildewezen van Amsterdam.* III. 1633-1672. 's-Gravenhage 1974.
- Diversen, *De Stevenskerk.* Nijmegen 1969.
- Diversen, Rapport Europees Centrum voor Restauratietechnieken, *Voormalige abdij Herkenrode.* Nota's uit 'Bouwen door de eeuwen heen in Vlaanderen'. 6n 1 (A-Ha) Provincie Limburg, Arrondissement, pp. 434-453. Hasselt.
- Diversen, *Bouwen aan Bouwgeschiedenis; recent onderzoek naar de bouwchronologie van de Antwerpse Onze-Lieve-Vrouwekathedraal.* Antwerpen 1994.
- Doorman, G., *Octrooien voor uitvindingen in de Nederlanden uit de 16e - 18e eeuw: met besprekingen van enkele onderwerpen uit de geschiedenis der techniek.* Den Haag 1940.
- Doperé, F., 'Evolutie van de bouwwerf van de gotische Onze-Lieve-Vrouwekathedraal te Antwerpen op basis van de studie van de steenhouwtechnieken en van de steenmerken'. In: Diversen 1994, pp. 29-57.
- Doperé, F., 'L'extraction, la taille et la mise en oeuvre du calcaire grésieux de Gobertange au Moyen Age'. In: *Bulletin de la Commission Royale des Monuments, sites et fouilles* 16.1. 1997/1998, pp. 45-96.
- Doppler, P., *Schepenbrieven van het Kapittel van St. Servaas te Maastricht.* III, 1470-1686. Maastricht 1910.
- Driessen, M., 'Heeft Limburg ook steenhouwersmerken?'. In: *Actes du VIIIe Colloque International de Glyptographie d'Hoepertingen EUREGIO.* Braine-le-Chateau 1992, pp. 217-221.
- Dröge, J.F., *De Waag aan het Rode Steen te Hoorn. Anno 1609.* Rapport bouwhistorisch onderzoek. Leiden 1991.
- Drunen, A. van, 'Het Kruithuis van 's-Hertogenbosch'. In: *Bulletin KNOB* 76 (1977), pp. 200-215.
- Duverger, E., 'Antwerpen en de Noordelijke Nederlanden'. In: Roy 1991, pp. 40-49.
- Duverger, J., 'De architect Filips Lammekens ca., 1493-1548)'. In: Van der Wijck et al. 1964, pp. 181-189.

- Eeghen, I.H. van, 'De familie Trip en het Trippenhuis'. In: Meischke, Reeser 1983, pp. 27-127.
- Eeghen, I.H. van, 'Rembrandt en de veilingen: (Titus van Rijn, Clement de Jonghe en Samuel Smijters)'. In: *Amstelodamum* 77 (1985), pp. 54-69.
- Eisler, M., *Die Geschichte eines holländischen Stadtbildes (Kunst und Kultur).* 's-Gravenhage 1914.
- Engels, M.C., 'Dutch Traders in Liverno at the Beginning of the Seventeenth Century. The Company of Joris Jansen and Bernard van den Broecke'. In: Lesger, Noordegraaf 1995, pp. 63-76.
- Ennen, L., 'Das Rathausportal zu Köln'. In: *Zeitschrift für bildende Kunst* XI (1876), pp. 282-286.
- Essen, M.C., 'Daniel Stalpaert (1615-1676) stadsarchitect van Amsterdam en de Amsterdamse stadsfabriek in de periode van 1647 tot 1676'. In: *Bulletin KNOB* 99 (2000), pp. 101-121.
- Essers, M.C., *Stokstraatgebied Maastricht: een renovatieproces in historisch perspectief.* Maastricht 1973.
- Eversen, J.M.H., *Alphabetische lijst der magistraatsleden van Maastricht.* Typoscript. Studiezaal gemeentearchief Maastricht.

- Fock, C. Willemijn, 'Werkelijkheid of schijn. Het beeld van het Hollandse interieur in de zeventiende-eeuwse genreschilderkunst'. In: *Oud Holland* 112 (1998) 4, pp. 187-247.
- Friederich, K., *Die Steinbearbeitung in ihrer Entwicklung vom 11. bis zum 18. Jahrhundert.* Augsburg 1988. Reprint.
- Frijhoff, W., et al. (ed.), *Geschiedenis van Dordrecht van 1572 tot 1813.* Hilversum 1998.

- Gee, Julie L. Mc, *Cornelis Cornelisz. van Haarlem (1562-1638)*. Nieuwkoop 1991.
- Gelderblom, A.J. (ed.), *'k Wil rijmen wat ik bouw: twee eeuwen topografische poëzie*. Amsterdam 1994.
- Gelderblom, O.C., *Zuid-Nederlandse kooplieden en de opkomst van de Amsterdamse staple market (1578-1630)*. Utrecht 2000.
- Genicot, L.F. et al., *Les Jésuites a Namur 1610-1773; mélanges d'histoire et d'art publiés à l'occasion des anniversaires ignatiens*. Namur 1991.
- Gerits, T.J., 'Het refugiehuis van Averbode te Maastricht'. In: *Maasgouw* 84 (1965), pp. 33-42.
- Gerits, T.J., 'Bouwstoffen voor de kerkelijke kunstgeschiedenis van Balen-Neet'. In: *Taxandria* 39 (1967), pp. 141-163.
- Germain, J., 'Les carrières et le travail de la pierre dans le Namurois (XVIIe–XVIIIe S.)'. In: *Dialectologie en Wallonie* (Cahiers de l'Institut de linguistique de Louvain) T. 7, nr. 3-4 (1981), pp. 201-239.
- Gerritsen, E., 'De architectuurtekening in de 17de eeuw'. In: Boonstra 1997, pp. 40-61.
- Gerritsen, E., *Architectuurtekeningen. De tekening in de zeventiende-eeuwse ontwerp- en bouwpraktijk in de Noordelijke Nederlanden*. Utrecht 2004.
- Geurts, J.H.J., *'Onsser stadt in sulken gedranghe': Maastricht tussen Brabant en het rijk 1500-1550*. Nijmegen 1993.
- Ghislain, J.-C., 'Essai d'identification des cuves baptismales romanes et gothiques du musée d'art religieux et d'art Mosan'. In: *Les amis du musée d'art religieux et d'art Mosan: bulletin trimestriel* September 1984, nr. 13, pp. 4-15.
- Glaudemans, R., 'Verborgen vakwerk. Bouwhistorische inventarisatie in de binnenstad van Maaseik'. In: Carmiggelt et al. 1999, pp. 77-90.
- Glaudemans, R., G. van Tussenbroek, *The Swamp Dragon. Eight hundred years of 's-Hertogenbosch fortress*. Zwolle etc. 1999.
- Glißmann, O., 'Literaturbericht zum Werk des Wilhelm Vernukken'. In: *Architektur, Kunst- und Kulturgeschichte in Nord- und West-Deutschland* Juli 1998, 8 Jhr. Bnd. 8, pp. 70-87.
- Goossens, D., *Inleiding tot de geologie en geomorfologie van België*. 2e dr. Enschede 1984.
- Gorissen, F., *Stede-atlas van Nijmegen*. Brugge 1956.
- Goudriaan, K. et al., *De Gilden in Gouda*. Gouda etc. 1996.
- Gouw, J. ter, *Geschiedenis van Amsterdam*. Amsterdam 1886.
- Grauwels, J., *Kroniek van Hasselt (1078-1914); grepen uit het dagelijks leven*. Hasselt 1982.
- Groenveld, S., G.J. Schutte, *Nederlands verleden in vogelvlucht; de nieuwe tijd: 1500 tot 1813*. Leiden etc. 1992.
- Groessens, E., 'L'industrie du marbre en Belgique'. In: *Mém. Inst. géol. Univ. Louvain* XXXI (1981), pp. 219-253.
- Groessens, E., 'L'exploitation et l'emploi du marbre noir de Dinant sous l'Ancien Régime'. In: *119e congr. nat. soc. hist. scient.* Amiens (1994). 3e coll. Carrières et construction, pp. 73-87.
- Groessens, E., 'Le marbre noir'. In: *Boiseries et Marbres sculptés en Namurois*. Namur 1997, pp. 67-74.
- Grol, H.G. van, *De geschiedenis der Oude Havens van Vlissingen alsmede de invloed van Oranje op hare verdere ontwikkeling*. Vlissingen 1931.
- Großmann, G. U., *Einführung in die historische Bauforschung*. Darmstadt 1993.
- Großmann, G.U. (ed.), *Historisches Bauwesen, Material und Technik*. Jahrbuch für Hausforschung Band 42, Marburg 1994.
- Guicciardijn, L. [Guicciardini], *Beschryvinghe van alle de Nederlanden anderssins ghenoemt Neder-Duytslandt*. Amsterdam 1612.

- Haans, F.A.C., 'Gisbert Schairt, de succesvolle carrière van een Zaltbommelse bouwmeester (ca. 1380-1452)'. In: *Monumenten tussen de Voorn en Loevestein*. Zaltbommel 1989, pp. 50-88.
- Habets, J., 'Over den toestand van eenige kerkgebouwen uit den omtrek van Breda in het jaar 1644'. In: *Tijdschrift voor Noord-Brabantse geschiedenis, taal- en letterkunde* II (1885), nr. 15, 1 mei 1885. pp. 146-154.

- Haslinghuis, E.J., H. Janse, *Bouwkundige termen. Verklarend woordenboek van de westerse architectuur- en bouwhistorie.* Leiden 1997.
- Heer, E. de (ed.), *Bouwen in Nederland: vijfentwintig opstellen over Nederlandse architectuur opgedragen aan Prof. ir. J.J. Terwen.* Leids Kunsthistorisch Jaarboek 1984. Delft 1985.
- Heiden, H. de, *Een wandeling langs Nijmeegse monumenten.* Nijmegen 1983.
- Heiningen, H. van, *Tussen Maas en Waal: 650 jaar geschiedenis van mensen en water.* Zutphen 1972.
- Hermans, T., 'Materiaal en personeel bij het onderhoudswerk van slot Loevestein in de 14de, 15de en 16de eeuw'. In: *Monumenten en bouwhistorie. Jaarboek Monumentenzorg 1996.* Zwolle etc. 1996, pp. 211-219.
- Herwaarden, J. van, et al. (ed.), *Geschiedenis van Dordrecht tot 1572.* Hilversum 1996.
- Heuvel, Ch. van den, *'Papiere Bolwercken'. De introductie van de Italiaanse stede- en vestingbouw in de Nederlanden (1540-1609) en het gebruik van tekeningen.* Alphen a.d. Rijn 1991.
- Heuvel, Ch. van den, 'Simon Stevins Huysbou' en het onvoltooide Nederlandse architectuurtractaat. De praktijk van het bouwen als wetenschap'. In: *Bulletin KNOB* 93 (1994), pp. 1-18.
- Heuvel, Ch. van den, 'De Architectura (1599) van Charles De Beste; een onbekend architectuurtractaat van een Brugse bouwmeester'. In: *Handelingen van het genootschap voor geschiedenis.* 131 (1994) 1-3, pp. 65-93.
- Heuvel, Ch. van den, 'De Architectura (1599) van Charles De Beste, het vitruvianisme in de Nederlanden in de zestiende eeuw'. In: *Bulletin KNOB* 94 (1995), pp. 11-23.
- Heuvel, Ch. van den, 'Willem Goeree (1635-1711) en de ontwikkeling van een algemene architectuurtheorie in de Nederlanden'. In: *Bulletin KNOB* 96 (1997), pp. 154-176.
- Heuvel, N.H.L. van den, *De ambachtsgilden van 's-Hertogenbosch vóór 1629; rechtsbronnen van het bedrijfsleven en het gildewezen.* Eerste stuk. werken der Vereeniging tot uitgaaf der bronnen van het oudvaderlandsche recht. Derde reeks, nr. 13. Utrecht 1946.
- Heuvel, N.H.L. van den, *De ambachtsgilden van 's-Hertogenbosch voor 1629.* 's-Hertogenbosch, without year.
- Heijden, P.-J. van der, H. Molhuysen, *Kroniek van 's-Hertogenbosch; acht eeuwen stadsgeschiedenis.* 's-Hertogenbosch 1981.
- Hezenmans, J.C.A., *De St. Jans-kerk te 's Hertogenbosch.* 's Hertogenbosch 1866.
- Hochkirchen, D., *Mittelalterliche Steinbearbeitung und die unfertige Kapitelle des Speyerer Domes.* Köln 1990.
- Hoekstra, T., 'Vredenburg; de bouw van en het leven op een zestiende eeuwse citadel (1529-1532)'. In: Bakker, Hoekstra 1997, pp. 112-143.
- Hoof, M.C.J.C. van, E.A.T.M. Schreuder en B.J. Slot, (ed.), *De archieven van de Nassause Domeinraad 1581-1811 met retroacta vanaf de dertiende eeuw.* Algemeen Rijksarchief, Den Haag 1997.
- Houtte, J.A. van, 'Le tonlieu de Lith et le Commerce sur la Meuse de 1551 à 1701. Resultats d'une Recherche Collective'. In: *Economische geschiedenis van Belgie. Behandeling van de bronnen en problematiek* (1972), pp. 297-309.
- Huart, A., 'Décoration héraldique du XVIe siècle'. In: *Namurcum* XII (1935) 1, pp. 43-44.
- Huisken, J., et al. *Jacob van Campen. Het klassieke ideaal in de Gouden Eeuw.* Amsterdam 1995.
- Huisman, H., *Het steenhouwersgeslacht Neurenberg en de donkere Belgische steen.* Doctoraalscriptie. Leiden 1986.
- Huysmans, A., *Cornelis Floris 1514-1575: beeldhouwer, architect, ontwerper.* Brussel 1996.

- Israel, J.I., *Nederland als centrum van de wereldhandel 1585-1740.* Franeker 1991.
- Iterson, A. van, 'L'exploitation de la carrière de marbre Saint-Remy au XVIIIe siècle'. In: *Namurcum* 2 (1964), pp. 17-30.

- Jacquet-Ladrier, F. (ed.), *Dictionnaire biographique namurois.* Namur 1999.
- Janse, H., *Bouwers en bouwen in het verleden.* Zaltbommel 1964.

- Janse, H., 'Causes probables de la disparition des marques de tailleurs de pierre dans les Pays-Bas après la Réforme'. In: *Annales du cercle historique et folklorique de Braine-le-Château de Tubize et des régions voisines*. T. IV, 1980-1981, pp. 141-144.
- Janse, H., 'Hout onder golven: onderdelen van een kap met houten tongewelf op de bodem van de voormalige Zuiderzee'. In: *Bulletin KNOB* 85 (1986), pp. 87-89.
- Janse, H., 'Het bouwbedrijf en de steenhandel ten tijde van de Keldermans-familie'. In: Van Mosselveld 1987, pp. 173-182.
- Janse, H., *Houten kappen in Nederland 1000-1940*. Bouwtechniek in Nederland 2. Delft 1989.
- Janse, H., D.J. de Vries, *Werk en merk van de steenhouwer. Het steenhouwersambacht in de Nederlanden voor 1800*. Zwolle etc. 1991.
- Janse, H., 'Marques de tailleurs de pierre aux Pays-Bas et les communications entre les loges et ateliers'. In: *Actes du VIIIe Colloque International de Glyptographie d'Hoepertingen Euregio*. Braine-le-Chateau 1992, pp. 273-283.
- Janse, H., 'Steinzeichen und Steinmetzen'. In: Großmann 1994, pp. 89-99.
- Janse, H., *Van Aaks tot Zwei*. Den Haag 1998.
- Janse, H., *De Oude Kerk te Amsterdam. Bouwgeschiedenis en restauratie*. Cultuurhistorische Studies 7. Zwolle etc. 2004.
- Janssen, F., *De stadspoorten; historisch Nijmegen in pen en penseel*. Nijmegen 1966.
- Janssen, H.L., J.M.M. Kylstra-Wielinga, B. Olde Meierink (ed.), *1000 jaar kastelen in Nederland: functie en vorm door de eeuwen heen*. Utrecht 1996.
- Japikse, N., *Resolutiën der Staten-Generaal van 1576 tot 1609*. Part VII 1590-1592. 's-Gravenhage 1923.
- Japikse, N., *Resolutiën der Staten-Generaal van 1576 tot 1609*. Part VIII 1593-1595. 's-Gravenhage 1925.
- Japikse, N., *Resolutiën der Staten-Generaal van 1576 tot 1609*. Part IX 1596-1597. 's-Gravenhage 1926.
- Jappe Alberts, W., *Bronnen tot de bouwgeschiedenis van de Dom te Utrecht*. Part I en II. 's-Gravenhage 1976.
- Jappe Alberts, W., *Van heerlijkheid tot landsheerlijkheid*. Assen 1979.
- Jappe Alberts, W., *De Nederlandse Hanzesteden*. 2e dr. Haarlem 1980.
- Jong, J. de, 'Prosopografie, een mogelijkheid. Eliteonderzoek tussen politieke en sociaal-culturele geschiedenis'. In: *Bijdragen en mededelingen betreffende de geschiedenis der Nederlanden* 111 (1996), 1, pp. 201-216.
- Jong, J. de, 'Archiefsprokkels'. In: *Numaga* (1956), p. 94.
- Jong, J.A.B.M. de, *Het oud-archief van Nijmegen*. Nijmegen 1960.
- Jong, J. de, et al. (ed.), *Nederland-Italië: relaties in de beeldende kunst van de Nederlanden en Italië. Nederlands Kunsthistorisch Jaarboek 1993*. Zwolle 1993.
- Jonge, K. De, 'Architekturpraxis in den Niederlanden in der frühen Neuzeit; die Rolle des italienischen Militärarchitekten; der status questionis'. In: G. Bers 1994, pp. 363-383.
- Jonge, K. De, K.A. Ottenheym, *Eenheid en tweespalt; architectonische relaties tussen de Zuidelijke en de Noordelijke Nederlanden 1530-1700*. Project proposal, NWO 1996.
- Jonge, K. De, A. de Vos et al., 'Lucas Faydherbe als architect'. In: De Nijn 1997, pp. 70-122.
- Jonge, K. De et al., 'Building Policy and Urbanisation during the Reign of the Archdukes: the Court and its Architects'. In: Thomas, Duerloo 1998, pp. 191-219.
- Jonge, K. De (ed.), *Le Château de Boussu*. Etudes et Documents, série Monuments et sites. 8. Namur 1998.
- Jonghe, S. De, et al., *Pierres à bâtir traditionelles de la Wallonie: manuel de terrain*. Louvain-la-Neuve 1996.
- Jongste, P.F.B., *Het gebruik van marmer in de Romeinse samenleving*. Leiden 1995.
- Jurgens, N.H., 'De onderste molensteen. Molens in Rosmalen en 's-Hertogenbosch'. In: Willems et al. 2000, pp. 197-205.
- Juten, W.J.F., 'De koepelkerk in Willemstad'. In: *Taxandria* 29 (1922), pp. 11-25.

- Kalf, J., 'De kerk van Etten'. In: *Bulletin NOB* (1910), pp. 61-70, 210-223.
- Kannegieter, J.Z., 'Het St. Jansbeeld van het Bossche oxaal'. In: *Oud Holland*. LIX (1942), pp. 110-111.

- Kars, H., 'Early-Medieval Dorestad, Archeaeo-Petrological Study; part VIII: Summary of the Petro-graphical Results'. In: *Berichten van de Rijksdienst voor het Oudheidkundig Bodemonderzoek.* XXXIII (1983), pp. 83-94.
- Kasig, W., 'Die Nutzung der Gesteine des Aachener Unterkarbons durch den Menschen- ein Beitrag zur Anthropogeologie'. In: *Zeitschrift für deutsche geologische Geschichte.* 135 (1984), pp. 403-423.
- Kastler, J., V. Lüpkes (hrsg.), *Die Weser. Einfluß in Europa.* Band 2, Aufbruch in die Neuzeit. Holzmin-den 2000.
- Keblusek, M., J. Zijlmans (ed.), *Vorstelijk vertoon aan het hof van Frederik Hendrik en Amalia.* Zwolle etc. 1997.
- Kempen, P. van, *Tuf Stuf: de verspreiding van tufsteen in het Maas-Demer-Scheldegebied. Met het accent op de Middeleeuwen.* Doctoraalscriptie. Amsterdam 1997.
- Kennis, J.F.M., 'Meester Jan Darkennes (1485-1572); bouwmeester van de Sint-Janskathedraal'. In: *De Brabantse Leeuw* 46, nr. 3 (1997), pp. 138-148.
- Kerkmeyer, J., 'De waag in Hoorn'. In: *Het huis oud en nieuw* 9 (1911), pp. 235-246.
- Kesteloo, H.M., 'De stadsrekeningen van Middelburg van 1365-1810'. In: *Archief Zeeuws genootschap* 5 (1883) en 6 (1888).
- Kiem, K., *Die Waage als Bautyp.* Without place [1996].
- Kiem, K., 'Ideal und Wirklichkeit. Die Identifizierung des Entwurfs für die Waage von Haarlem: Lie-ven de Key, 1598'. In: *Architectura* (1996), pp. 24-32.
- Kiene, M., 'Zur Planungsgeschichte der kölner Rathausvorhalle'. In: *Wallraf-Richartz-Jahrbuch; west-deutsches Jahrbuch für Kunstgeschichte.* LII. (1991), pp. 127-156.
- Kinschot, G. van, 'Autobiografische stukken'. In: *Kronijk van het Hist. Genootschap te Utrecht* VI (1850), pp. 4-7.
- Klapheck, R., *Die Meister von Schloss Horst.* Berlijn 1915.
- Klaua, D., 'Petrographische Untersuchungen an den Bau- und Dekorationsgesteinen der Runnen-burg'. In: Meckseper 1998, pp. 207-228.
- Klein, P.W., *De Trippen in de zeventiende eeuw.* Assen 1965.
- Kleintjes, J., L. Sormani, *Rekeningen der stad Nijmegen.* Nijmegen 1910-1919.
- Kloes, J.A. van der, *Onze bouwmaterialen.* Maassluis 1893.
- Knoors, J.A., 'Maasvaart en Maashandel'. In: *Maaslandse sprokkelingen* 6 (1978), pp. 5-32.
- Knoors, J.A., 'De hertogelijke controle over de Maas bij Urmond'. 1993, pp. 271-292.
- Koldeweij, A.M. (ed.), *De bouwloods van de St.-Janskathedraal te 's-Hertogenbosch.* 's-Hertogenbosch 1989.
- Koldewey, A.M. (ed.), *In Buscoducis, bijdragen.* Maarssen etc. 1990.
- Kolman, Chr.J., *Naer de Eisch van 't Werck; de organisatie van het bouwen te Kampen 1450-1650.* Utrecht 1993.
- Kolman, Chr. en R. Stenvert, 'Nieuwe vormen en traditionele bouw: Het Vleeshuis te Kampen in het midden van de 16de eeuw'. In: *Bulletin KNOB* 93 (1994), pp. 81-99.
- Koning, J., 'Historisch bericht wegens Joost Jansz Beeltsnijder en de door hem vervaardigde stukken.' In: *Verhandelingen der Tweede Klasse van het Koninklijk Instituut etc.,* Part V (1831).
- Kooijmans, L., 'Risk and Reputation; On the Mentality of Merchants in the Early Modern Period'. In: Lesger 1995, pp. 25-35.
- Kooijmans, L., *Vriendschap en de kunst van het overleven in de zeventiende en achttiende eeuw.* Amsterdam 1997.
- Kossmann, E.F., 'Hendrick de Keyser als uitvinder'. In: *Oud Holland* 46 (1929), pp. 284-288.
- Kramer, A., *Schade aan natuursteen in Nederlandse monumenten.* Restauratievademecumbijdrage 08. Zeist etc. 1985.
- Krom, C.C.N., M.S. Pols, *Stadrechten van Nijmegen.* 's-Gravenhage 1894.
- Kuile, E.H. ter, 'Overheidsbouw in Leiden'. In: *Oudheidkundig Jaarboek* (1938), pp. 83-87.
- Kuile, E.H. ter, 'De werkzaamheid van Lieven de Key in Haarlem'. In: *Oud-Holland* 55 (1938), pp. 245-252.

- Kuile, E.H. ter, *De Nederlandse monumenten van geschiedenis en kunst. Deel IV, de provincie Gelderland. Tweede Stuk: het kwartier van Zutphen*. 's-Gravenhage 1958.
- Kuile, E.H. ter, 'Het ontwerp van de Leidse stadhuisgevel'. In: *Bulletin KNOB* (1964), pp. 89-106.
- Kuyper, W., *The Triumphant Entry of the Renaissance Architecture into the Netherlands*. Alphen a.d. Rijn 1994.

- L.L., 'Le métier des maçons et l'ermitage Saint-Fiacre'. In: *Annales de la Société archéologique de Namur* XXI (1895), pp. 377-392.
- Laleman, M.C., 'Steenhouwer Nicolaes Paternotte'. In: *Stadsarcheologie Gent* XIII (1989), pp. 37-53.
- Laleman, M.C., 'Bijzondere vorsten; hardstenen nokafdekking uit de 17e eeuw'. In: *Stadsarcheologie Gent* XIX (1995) nr. 3, pp. 21-33.
- Lambrechtsen - Van Essen, I.W., *De stadspoorten van Leiden en stadsbouwmeester Willem van der Helm*. Utrecht 1994.
- Langendonck, L. van, 'De Sint-Romboutstoren te Mechelen en zijn plaats in de laatgotische architectuur'. In: Van Mosselveld 1987, pp. 27-60.
- Leeuwen, A.J.C. van, *De maakbaarheid van het verleden; P.J.H. Cuypers als restauratie-architect*. Zwolle etc. 1995.
- Lefèvre, P., 'A propos de l'indification'. In: *Analecta Praemonstratensia* 3 (1927), pp. 427-429.
- Lefèvre, P., 'Textes concernant l'histoire artistique de l'abbaye d'Averbode'. In: *Revue Belge* 4 (1934), pp. 247-264, 335-348, and 5 (1935) pp. 45-58.
- Lemmens, G.Th.M., 'De oude inrichting van de Stevenskerk'. In: Diversen 1969, pp. 86-130.
- Lesger, C., L. Noordegraaf (ed.), *Entrepreneurs and Entrepreneurship in Early Modern Times: Merchants and Industrialists within the Orbit of the Dutch Staple Market*. Hollandse Historische Reeks XXIV. Den Haag 1995.
- Lindblad, J.Th., 'Louis de Geer (1587-1652). Dutch Entrepreneur and the Father of Swedish Industry'. In: Lesger, Noordegraaf 1995, pp. 77-84.
- Lips, C.J.P., *Wandelingen door Oud-Dordrecht*. Zaltbommel 1974.
- Lombaerde, P., 'Continuïteit, vernieuwingen en verschillen. Het concept van de stad in de Noordelijke en Zuidelijke Nederlanden rond 1600'. In: *Bulletin KNOB* 98 (1999), pp. 237-248.
- Lunsingh Scheurleer, Th. H., C. Willemijn Fock, A.J. van Dissel, *Het Rapenburg: geschiedenis van een Leidse gracht*. Leiden 1986-1992.

- Made, R. van der, *Contrats du XVIe siècle, annales cercle hutois*. 25 (1955-1957), 3.
- Mathias, P., 'Strategies for Reducing Risk by Entrepreneurs in the Early Modern Period'. In: Lesger, Noordegraaf 1995, pp. 5-24.
- Meckseper, C. (ed.), *Burg Weißensee "Runnenburg", Thüringen: Baugeschichte und Forschung*. Frankfurt Am Main 1998.
- Meinsma, K.O, 'De Sint-Walburgskerk te Zutphen'. In: *Oud-Holland* (1909), pp. 15-30.
- Meischke, R., et al. (ed.), *Delftse studiën. Een bundel historische opstellen over de stad Delft geschreven voor dr E.H. ter Kuile naar aanleiding van zijn afscheid als hoogleraar in de geschiedenis van de bouwkunst*. Assen 1967.
- Meischke, R., *Amsterdam Burgerweeshuis*. De Nederlandse monumenten van geschiedenis en kunst. 's-Gravenhage 1975.
- Meischke, R., 'De grote trap van het huis Honselaarsdijk, 1633-1638'. In: *Nederlands Kunsthistorisch Jaarboek* 31 (1980), pp. 86-103.
- Meischke, R., 'De modernisering van de twee grote zalen van het Huis Honselaarsdijk in 1637 door Jacob van Campen'. In: *Nederlands Kunsthistorisch Jaarboek* 33 (1983a), pp. 191-206.
- Meischke, R., 'Kasteel Honselaarsdijk te Naaldwijk'. In: *Het kleine bouwen. Vier eeuwen maquettes in Nederland*. Utrecht etc. 1983b, pp. 88-90.

- Meischke, R., H.E. Reeser, *Het Trippenhuis te Amsterdam*. Amsterdam etc. 1983c.
- Meischke, R., 'Het Mauritshuis te Willemstad'. In: De Heer 1984, pp. 265-294.
- Meischke, R., 'De stedelijke bouwopgaven tussen 1450 en 1530'. In: Van Mosselveld 1987, pp. 87-104.
- Meischke, R., *De gothische bouwtraditie*. Amersfoort 1988.
- Meischke, R., 'Een nieuwe gevel voor het Leidse stadhuis (1593-1598)'. In: *Jaarboekje voor geschiedenis en oudheidkunde van Leiden en omstreken* (1989), pp. 54-83.
- Meischke, R., K. Ottenheym, 'Honselaarsdijk: Tuin en park; speelhuis (1636) en Nederhof (1640-1646)'. In: *Jaarboek Monumentenzorg 1992*. Zwolle etc. 1992, pp. 118-141.
- Meischke, R., et al., *Huizen in Nederland; Friesland en Noord-Holland. Architectuurhistorische verkenningen aan de hand van het bezit van de Vereniging Hendrick de Keyser*. Zwolle 1993.
- Meischke, R., 'Het Amsterdamse fabrieksambt van 1595-1625'. In: *Bulletin KNOB* 93 (1994), pp. 100-122.
- Meischke, R., et al., *Huizen in Nederland; Amsterdam. Architectuurhistorische verkenningen aan de hand van het bezit van de Vereniging Hendrick de Keyser*. Zwolle 1995.
- Meischke, R., et al., *Huizen in Nederland; Zeeland en Zuid-Holland. Architectuurhistorische verkenningen aan de hand van het bezit van de Vereniging Hendrick de Keyser*. Zwolle 1997.
- Meischke, R., et al., *Huizen in Nederland; Utrecht, Noord-Brabant en de oostelijke provincies. Architectuurhistorische verkenningen aan de hand van het bezit van de Vereniging Hendrick de Keyser*. Zwolle 2000.
- Mekking, A.J.J., *De Sint-Servaaskerk te Maastricht*. Zutphen 1986.
- Merlos, J.J., *Kölnische Künstler in altere und neuere Zeit; Nachrichten von dem Leben und den Werken Kölnischer Künstler*. Düsseldorf 1895.
- Meulleners, J.L., 'De scheepvaart in het tegenwoordig hertogdom Limburg tijdens de beroerten in de XVIe en XVIIe eeuw, benevens bijzonderheden uit dat tijdvak over maasschippers, handel, zeden en rechtswezen in dit gebied'. In: *Publications de la soc.hist. et arch. dans le Limbourg*. XXIII (1886) pp. 89-160.
- Meyer, G.M. de, E.W.F. van den Elzen, *De verstening van Deventer: huizen en mensen in de 14de eeuw*. Groningen 1982.
- Miedema, H., *De archiefbescheiden van het St. Lucasgilde te Haarlem 1497-1798*. Alphen a.d. Rijn 1980.
- Miedema, H., 'Over de waardering van architekt en beeldende kunstenaar in de zestiende eeuw'. In: *Oud Holland* 94 (1980) pp. 71-85.
- Mierlo, Th. van, 'Alexander Pasqualini (1493-1559); architect en vestingbouwkundige'. In: *Bulletin KNOB* 90 (1991), pp. 157-175.
- Montias, J.M., 'A Business Partner and a Pupil: Two Conjectural Essays on Rembrandt's Entourage'. In: A. Chong, M. Zell, *Rethinking Rembrandt*. Zwolle 2002, pp. 129-158.
- Morreau, L.J., *Bolwerk der Nederlanden: de vestingwerken van Maastricht sedert het begin van de 13e eeuw*. Assen 1979.
- Morren, Th., *Het huis Honselaarsdijk*. Leiden 1909.
- Mosmans, J., *De Sint-Janskerk te 's-Hertogenbosch*. 's-Hertogenbosch 1931.
- Mosselveld, J.H. van, et al. (ed.), *Keldermans; een architectonisch netwerk in de Nederlanden*. 's-Gravenhage 1987.
- Muller Fzn., S., 'Getuigenverhoor te Antwerpen over het maken van ontwerpen van gebouwen in de 16e eeuw door schilders, goudsmeden, timmerlieden en metselaars'. In: *Archief voor Nederlandse Kunstgeschiedenis* 4, 1881-1882, pp. 227-245.
- Muller, S., *De middeleeuwsche rechtsbronnen der stad Utrecht*. 's-Gravenhage 1883-1885.

- Nagel, U., *Bauen ist eine Lust: Sprüche, Gedichte, Lieder und Bräuche vom Bauen*. Berlin 1996.
- Nanninga Uiterdijk, J., 'Nederlandsche bouwmeesters der 16e eeuw'. In: *Bijdragen tot de geschiedenis van Overijssel* 14 (1907), pp. 362-363.

- *Nieuw Nederlandsch Biografisch Woordenboek* 5. Leiden 1921.
- Neurdenburg, E., *Hendrick de Keyser beeldhouwer en bouwmeester van Amsterdam.* Amsterdam 1930.
- Neurdenburg, E., 'Het oxaal van de St. Janskerk te 's-Hertogenbosch en Nicholas Stone'. In: *Oudheidkundig Jaarboek* (1938) IV, 7, pp. 38-44.
- Neurdenburg, E., *Zeventiende-eeuwse beeldhouwkunst in Nederland.* Amsterdam 1948.
- Neurenbergh, J. à, *Disputatio juridica inauguralis ad Legem Rhodiam de Jactu.* Utrecht 1693.
- Nijn, H. de, et al. (ed.), *Lucas Faydherbe (1617-1697); Mechels beeldhouwer en architect.* Mechelen 1997.
- Nijs, R., G. de Geyter, *Geologie en petrografie van inheemse natuurlijke bouwstenen in onze historische monumenten.* Cursussyllabus. Gent 1985.
- Nispen, C.A.I.L. van, *De Vesting Willemstad.* Publicaties van het Archivariaat 'Nassau-Brabant' nr. 62. Willemstad 1983.
- Nispen tot Sevenaer, E.O.M. van, *De monumenten van geschiedenis en kunst in de provincie Limburg; geïllustreerde beschrijving.* De monumenten in de gemeente Maastricht. Eerste aflevering. 's-Gravenhage 1926.
- Noach, A., *De oude kerk te Amsterdam.* Amsterdam 1939.
- Noldus, B., 'De introductie van het Hollands classicisme in Zweden, aan de hand van twee woonhuizen van de familie De Geer'. In: *Bulletin KNOB* 98 (1999), pp. 141-151.
- Noldus, B., *Trade in Good Taste. Relations in Architecture and Culture between the Dutch Republic and the Baltic World in the Seventeenth Century.* Turnhout 2005.
- Nuyts, 'De voormalige schuttersgilden te Maastricht'. In: *Maasgouw* 1892, pp. 93-95.
- Nys, L., *La pierre de Tournai; son exploitation et son usage aux XIIIème, XIVème et XVème siècles.* Tournai etc. 1993.

- Oerle, H. van, *Leiden binnen en buiten de stadvesten: de geschiedenis van de stedebouwkundige ontwikkeling binnen het Leidse rechtsgebied tot aan het einde van de gouden eeuw.* Leiden 1975.
- Olde Meierink, B., 'De Gildehauser bouwmeestersfamilie Hagen'. In: *Jaarboek Monumentenzorg 1991.* Zwolle etc. 1991, pp. 139-158.
- Olde Meierink, B., 'Conflict tussen oud en nieuw; de zeventiende eeuw'. In: Janssen 1997, pp. 142-170.
- Oremus, J.M.S., *De bouw van het Sittardse stadhuis van Pasqualini (1560-1570) en magistratenfamilies in de 16e en 17e eeuw.* Monografieën uit het land van Sittard. Sittard 1993.
- Ottenheym, K.A., 'De bouwgeschiedenis van het stadhuis van Pieter Post te Maastricht'. In: *Bulletin KNOB* 85 (1986), pp. 145-160.
- Ottenheym, K.A., *Philips Vingboons (1607-1678) architect.* Zutphen 1989.
- Ottenheym, K.A., 'Architectuur'. In: Huisken 1995, pp. 155-200.
- Ottenheym, K.A., 'De correspondentie tussen Rubens en Huygens over architectuur (1635-1640)'. In: *Bulletin KNOB* 96 (1997a), pp. 1-12.
- Ottenheym, K.A., 'Bouwkunst op maet en regelen der Ouden'. In: Boonstra 1997b, pp. 18-39.
- Ottenheym, K.A., 'Van Bouw-lust soo beseten, Frederik Hendrik en de bouwkunst'. In: Keblusek, Zijlmans (ed.) 1997c, pp. 105-125.
- Ottenheym, K.A., 'Huygens en de klassicistische architectuurtheorie'. In: Blom et al. 1999a, pp. 87-111.
- Ottenheym, K.A., 'De Schilder-architecten van het Hollands Classicisme'. In: Brinkman 1999, pp. 34-53.
- Overeem, G.A., H.N. Karsemeijer, 'Steenhouwwerk'. In: *Restauratievademecum.* 1987/6 - 19.
- Ozinga, M.D., *Protestante kerken hier te lande gesticht.* Amsterdam 1929.
- Ozinga, M.D., 'Paulus Moreelse als architect'. In: *Oudheidkundig Jaarboek* (1931), pp. 18-25.

- Paczkowski, R., *Die Vorhalle von 1570 am Rathaus zu Lübeck; Überlegungen zu ihrer kunstgeschichtlichen Stellung und ihren typologischen Verbindungen.* Kiel 1975.

- Paczkowski, R., 'Funktionelle und politische Aspekte öffentlicher Architektur'. In: Bracker 1997, pp. 256-268.
- Paepe, P. de, M. Pieters, 'Petrology and Provenance of Unworked Stone from the Medieval Fishing-Village at Raversijde (mun. of Oostende, prov. of West Flanders)'. In: *Archeologie in Vlaanderen* IV (1994), pp. 237-251.
- Parmentier, R.A., *Documenten betreffende Brugsche steenhouwers*. Brugge 1948.
- Peeters, C.J.A.C., *De Sint-Janskathedraal te 's-Hertogenbosch*. De Nederlandse monumenten van geschiedenis en kunst. 's-Gravenhage 1985.
- Peeters, C.J.A.C., 'Het nieuwe werk als het bijna mogelijke'. In: *Bergen op Zoom, gebouwd en beschouwd*. Bergen op Zoom etc. 1987, pp. 157-169.
- Pelinck, E., 'Enige decoratieve reliëfs uit de Hollandse architectuur van omstreeks 1600'. In: *Bulletin KNOB* (1949), pp. 119-122.
- Philip, K.J., '"Eyn huys in manieren van eynre kirchen"; Werkmeister, Parliere, Steinlieferanten, Zimmermeister und die Bauorganisation in den Niederlanden vom 14. bis zum 16. Jahrhundert'. In: *Wallraf-Richartz-Jahrbuch* 50 (1989), pp. 69-114.
- Piot, Ch., 'Le jubé de la cathédrale de Bois-le-Duc'. In: *Bulletin des commissions royales d'Art et d'Archéologique* VI (1867), pp. 43-50.
- Plantenga, J.H., *L'Architecture religieuse dans l'ancien duché de Brabant depuis le règne des archiducs jusqu'au gouvernement Autrichien (1598-1713)*. Den Haag 1926.
- Pohle, F., 'Jülich und Batavia: ein Fallbeispiell für Theorieexporte im europäischen Kolonialismus'. In: Bers, Doose 1999, pp. 227-248.
- Pohle, F., 'Portal für die "Waterpoort" der Zitadelle von Batavia (Djakarta)'. In: Kastler, Lüpkes 2000, 51.
- Prak, M., *Gezeten burgers: de elite in een Hollandse stad. Leiden 1700-1780*. Hollandse Historische Reeks 6. 's-Gravenhage 1985.

- Riet, S. van, 'Lucas Faydherbe als beeldhouwer en altaarbouwer. Nieuwe gegevens en documenten'. In: *Jaarboek Koninklijk Museum voor schone kunsten Antwerpen*. (1996), pp. 141-225.
- Roding, J., *Christiaan IV van Denemarken (1588-1648): architectuur en stedebouw van een Luthers vorst*. Alkmaar 1991.
- Roding, J., 'De waag te Haarlem; een werck geduriger als ijser en stael'. In: Denslagen 1993, pp. 441-454.
- Roding, J. and L. Heerma van Voss (ed.), *The North Sea and Culture (1550-1800)*. Hilversum 1996.
- Roebroek, A.M.L., 'Oudheidkundig bodemonderzoek in de gemeente Sittard 2'. In: *Historisch Jaarboek voor het land van Zwentibold* II, (1981), pp. 136-148.
- Roorda, D.J., 'Prosopografie, een onmogelijke mogelijkheid'. In: *Bijdragen en mededelingen tot de geschiedenis* 94 (1979), pp. 282-296.
- Rousseau, F., *La Meuse et le Pays Mosan en Belgique: leur importance historique avant le XIIIe siècle*. Namur 1930. (Annales de la soc. arch. de Namur 39).
- Rousseau, F., 'Le Pays de Namur d'autrefois d'après les récits de voyageurs: V. Les impressions de Jean Sarrazin et de Jean Lhermite. 1582, 1587'. In: *Namurcum* XIV (1937) 3, pp. 17-27.
- Roy, A., *Theodoor van Tulden; een Zuidnederlandse barokschilder*. Zwolle etc. 1991.

- Sander-Berke, A., *Baustoffversorgung spätmittelalterlicher Städte Norddeutschlands*. Köln etc. 1995.
- Sarrazin, J. (ed.), *Spuren in Sandstein/Sporen in Zandsteen*. Coesfeld 1999.
- Sauer, H., 'Die Steinmetzzeichen des Aachener Domes'. In: *Zeitschrift des Aachener Geschichtvereins* 74/75 (1962-1963), pp. 467-476.
- Schepper, H. de, *'Belgium nostrum' 1500-1650. Over integratie en desintegratie van het Nederland*. Antwerpen 1987.

- Schevichaven, H.D.J. van, *Oud-Nijmegens, kerken, kloosters, gasthuizen, stichtingen en openbare gebouwen*. Nijmegen 1909.
- Scholten, F., 'De Nederlandse handel in Italiaans marmer in de 17e eeuw'. In: J. de Jong et al. 1993, pp. 197-214.
- Schroot, P.A., *Bouwkunde; de voornaamste Materialen der Bouwambachten: Steen*. D. de Vries' Handleiding voor Materialenkennis, eerste gedeelte. Groningen 1918.
- Schuttelaars, A., *Heren van de raad. Bestuurlijke elite van 's-Hertogenbosch in de stedelijke samenleving 1500-1580*. Nijmegen 1998.
- Schwarzwälder, H., 'Niederländer in Bremen im 16./17. Jahrhundert'. In: *Bremen und die Niederlande* 1995/1996. Bremen 1997, pp. 85-95.
- Simonis, A.H., et al., *Sittard, historie en gestalte*. Sittard 1971.
- Slinger, A., H. Janse, G. Berends, *Natuursteen in Monumenten* Zeist 1980.
- Slothouwer, D.F., *Bouwkunst der Nederlandsche renaissance in Denemarken*. Amsterdam 1924.
- Slothouwer, D.F., *De paleizen van Frederik Hendrik*. Leiden 1946.
- Snaet, J., 'De eerste protestantse tempels in de Nederlanden. Een onderzoek naar vorm en perceptie'. In: *Bulletin KNOB* 98 (1999), pp. 45-58.
- Staal, J.P., G. Berends, 'Het vroegere oxaal van de St.-Petruskerk te Boxtel'. In: *Bulletin KNOB* 75 (1976), pp. 1-18.
- Stenvert, R., 'Conveyed by Land, Returned by Ship; Mannerism and Sandstone'. In: Roding, Van Voss 1996, pp. 420-434.
- Stenvert, R., 'Von der Adelssprache zur Bürgerform: Aspekte der Renaissance in den neuen Habsburger Provinzen 1525-1575'. In: Bers 1999, pp. 449-470.
- Steppe, J., *Het koordoxaal in de Nederlanden*. Brussel 1952.
- Stevenhagen, E., 'De ondergrondse kalksteenwinning in Zuid-Limburg'. In: *Historisch-Geografisch Tijdschrift* 17, 2 (1999), pp. 37-48.
- Stone, L., 'Prosopography'. In: *Deadalus* 100 (1971), pp. 46-79.
- Stuers, V. de, 'Holland op zijn smalst'. In: *De Gids* 37, 3. Jrg. 11, 3 november 1873, pp. 320-403.

- Tacke, E., 'Die Hausdächer im braunschweigischen Weserberglande um 1760'. In: *Die Kunde* 7 (1939), pp. 195-210.
- Tacke, E., 'Zur Geschichte des Solling-Steingewerbes'. In: *Die Kunde* 9 (1941), pp. 139-152.
- Taverne, E., *In 't land van belofte: in de nieue stadt. Ideaal en werkelijkheid van de stadsuitleg in de Republiek 1580-1680*. Maarssen 1978.
- Taverne, E., I. Visser (ed.), *Stedebouw; de geschiedenis van de stad in de Nederlanden van 1500 tot heden*. Nijmegen 1993.
- Temminck Groll, C.L., 'De Cannenburch en de intree van de renaissance in Gelderland'. In: *Bulletin KNOB* 78 (1979), pp. 123-139.
- Terwen, J.J., 'Het stadhuis van Hendrick de Keyser'. In: Meischke et al. 1967, pp. 143-171.
- Terwen, J.J., K.A. Ottenheym, *Pieter Post (1608-1669) architect*. Zutphen 1993.
- Thurlings, Th.L.M., *De Maashandel van Venlo en Roermond in de 16e eeuw (1473-1572)*. Amsterdam 1945.
- Thomas, W., L. Duerloo (ed.), *Albert & Isabella (1598-1621)*. Brussel etc. 1998.
- Timmers, J.J.M., *Geschiedenis van het Spaans Gouvernement te Maastricht*. Maastricht, without year.
- Timmers, J.J.M., *De kunst van het Maasland: deel II, De Gotiek en de Renaissance*. Assen 1980.
- Tussenbroek, G. van, 'Een Italiaan in 's-Hertogenbosch; Alessandro Pasqualini en het bolwerk voor de Orthenpoort (1542)'. In: *Bossche Bladen* 1 (1999a) 3, pp. 83-88.
- Tussenbroek, G. van, 'Das Netzwerk der Steinmetzen als Bauinstrument; Pasqualini und die Steinmetzfamilie von Nürnberg bis 1570'. In: Bers 1999b, pp. 531-546.
- Tussenbroek, G. van, 'Bouwen in Bommel; een blik in de Zaltbommelse bouwwereld van de zestiende eeuw'. In: *Bijdragen en Mededelingen Gelre* XC (1999c), pp. 40-66.

- Tussenbroek, G. van, 'Over maatwerk en prefab. Het Bossche steenhouwersbedrijf in de zestiende eeuw'. In: Willems et al. 2000a, pp. 85-93.
- Tussenbroek, G. van, 'Geschiedenis van bouwhistorisch onderzoek. Een overzicht'. In: G. van Tussenbroek (ed.), *Bouwhistorie in Nederland: kennis en bescherming van gebouwen*. Utrecht 2000, pp. 28-49.
- Tussenbroek, G. van, 'Belgisch marmer in de Zuidelijke en Noordelijke Nederlanden (1500-1700)'. In: *Bulletin KNOB* 100 (2001) 2, pp. 49-71.
- Tussenbroek, G. van, 'Brood uit stenen. De veranderende sociaal-economische positie van steenhouwers in de vroegmoderne tijd: werken voor de kerk en werken voor de stad. Het voorbeeld van Jan Darkennes (1487-1572)'. In: *Bijdragen tot de geschiedenis*. De Brabantse stad. 84 (2001b) 4, pp. 467-496.
- Tussenbroek, G. van, *Onder de daken van Zaltbommel. Bouwen en wonen in de historische binnenstad (1350-1650)*. Utrecht 2003.
- Tyghem, F. van, *Op en om de middeleeuwse bouwwerf*. Verhandelingen van de Koninklijke Vlaamse Academie voor Wetenschappen, Letteren en schone Kunsten van België. Klasse der schone kunsten. 28, nr. 19. Brussel 1966.
- Tyghem, F. van, 'Het gebruik van mallen door middeleeuwse steenhouwers'. In: *Gentsche bijdragen tot de Kunstgeschiedenis en oudheidkunde* 19 (1961-1966), pp. 67-75.
- Tyghem, F. van, *Het stadhuis van Gent*. Verhandelingen van de Koninklijke Vlaamse Academie voor Wetenschappen, Letteren en schone Kunsten van België. Klasse der schone kunsten. 40, Brussel 1978.

- Unger, W.S., 'De bouwgeschiedenis van het Stadhuis van Middelburg'. In: *Oudheidkundig Jaarboek* 1932, pp. 1-41.

- Valvekens, E., 'Geeraard van der Schaeft (1501-1532)'. In: *Een praemonstratenzerabdij in het begin der zestiende eeuw*. Brussel etc. 1936, pp. 116-128.
- Vanaise, P., 'Note concernant le marbre de Dinant fourni par Jean Noël et Nicolas Duchesnoy aux sculpteurs parisiens Lheureux et Autrot à la fin du XVIe siècle'. In: *Namurcum* 41 (1966), pp. 8-16.
- Ven, G.P. van de (ed.), *Leefbaar Laagland. Geschiedenis van de waterbeheersing en landaanwinning in Nederland*. 4th ed. Utrecht 1996.
- Verburgt, J.W., 'Uit het particuliere leven van Daniël van der Meulen, Heer van Ranst'. In: *Jaarboekje voor geschiedenis en oudheidkunde van Leiden en Rijnland* 29 (1936-1937), pp. 73-88.
- Verhoeff, J.M., *De oude Nederlandse maten en gewichten*. Amsterdam 1983.
- Vermeulen, F.A.J., *De monumenten van geschiedenis en kunst. De Bommelerwaard*. 's-Gravenhage 1932.
- Vermeulen, F.A.J., *Handboek tot de geschiedenis der Nederlandsche bouwkunst*. 's-Gravenhage 1931-1941.
- Vermeulen, F.A.J., *Bouwmeesters der klassicistische barok in Nederland*. Den Haag 1938.
- Vierlingh, Andries, *Tractaet van Dyckagie*. Ed. by J. de Hullu and A.G. Verhoeven. 's-Gravenhage 1920.
- Vlaardingerbroek, P., *Het stadhuis van Amsterdam. De bouw van het stadhuis, de verbouwing tot koninklijk paleis en de restauratie*. Utrecht 2004.
- Vlieghe, H., *Flemish Art and Architecture 1585-1700*. Cambridge 1998.
- Vogts, H. (ed.), *Die Kunstdenkmäler der Stadt Köln*. Zweiter Band, IV. Abteilung: die profanen Denkmäler. Düsseldorf 1930.
- Voort, H., 'Die gräflich bentheimschen Bergmeister; ein Beitrag zur Geschichte des Sandsteinbruchs in der Grafschaft Bentheim'. In: *Jahrbuch des Heimatvereins der Grafschaft Bentheim* (1968), pp. 87-106.
- Voort, H., 'Die Holländischen Steinhandelsgesellschaften in der Grafschaft Bentheim'. In: *Overijsselsch Regt en Geschiedenis* 85 (1970), pp. 1-22.
- Voort, H., 'Abbau, Absatz und Verwendung von Bentheimer Sandstein in acht Jahrhunderten'. In: *Schriftenreihe des Sandsteinmuseums Bad Bentheim* 1, Bad Bentheim 2000, pp. 3-18.

- Vos, R. and F. Leeman, *Het nieuwe ornament; gids voor de renaissance-architectuur en -decoratie in Nederland in de 16e eeuw*. 's-Gravenhage 1986.
- Vos, A. de, 'Hof van Den Haag en hof van Brussel (1590-1630). Structurele organisatie van de bouwprojecten tijdens de regering van prins Maurits en van de aartshertogen Albrecht en Isabella'. In: *Bulletin KNOB* 98 (1999), pp. 198-213.
- Vrankrijker, A.C.J. de, *Geschiedenis van de belastingen*. Bussum 1969.
- Vries, D.J. de et al., 'Over pannen en daktegels: traditie en innovatie in de late middeleeuwen'. In: *Overijsselse Historische Bijdragen* 100 (1985), pp. 83-142.
- Vries, D.J. de, *Bouwen in de late middeleeuwen; stedelijke architectuur in het voormalige Over- en Nedersticht*. Utrecht 1994a.
- Vries, D.J. de, 'Naturstein im 15. und 16. Jahrhundert in den Niederlanden'. In: Großmann 1994b, pp. 113-126.
- Vries, D.J. de, 'Monumenten dendrochronologisch gedateerd (7). Huizen'. In: *Bulletin KNOB* 96 (1997), pp. 218-225.
- Vries, J. de, A. van der Woude, *Nederland 1500-1800: de eerste ronde van moderne economische groei*. Amsterdam 1995.

- Walle, A.J.L. van de, *Het bouwbedrijf in de Lage Landen tijdens de Middeleeuwen*. Antwerpen 1959.
- Wegener-Sleeswijk, C., *Vijftien jaar restauratie in de Oude kerk te Amsterdam*. Amsterdam 1970.
- Weilbach, Fr., *Frederiksborg Slot*. Kopenhagen 1923.
- Wendt, A., 'Das Schloß zu Reinbek, Untersuchungen zur Ausstattung, Anlage und Architektur eines landesherrlichen Schlosses, Kreis Stormarn und Stadt Reinbek. Ein Beispiel niederländischer Baukunst im Norden Deutschlands'. In: *Bulletin KNOB* 95 (1996) pp. 225-226.
- Westerman, J., 'Zwart marmer uit Doornik'. In: *Madoc; tijdschrift over de middeleeuwen*. 12 (1998) 1, pp. 33-42.
- Westermann, M., 'A Monument for Roma Belgica; Functions of the *Oxaal* at 's-Hertogenbosch'. In: *Nederlands Kunsthistorisch Jaarboek* 1994. Deel 45. Zwolle 1994, pp. 383-446.
- Weve, J.J., 'Nijmeegsche architectuur van voor het jaar 1600; hoofdzakelijk met het oog op de geschiedenis der vroegrenaissance'. In: *Bouwkundig Tijdschrift* (1889), pp. 1-16.
- Weve, J.J., 'Monumenten van Geschiedenis en Kunst in Nijmegen'. In: *Bulletin NOB* (1919), pp. 93-138.
- Weve, W., *Bouwhistorische documentatie en waardenbepaling Maarten van Rossumhuis Zaltbommel*. Rapport Rijksgebouwendienst 1986.
- Wezel, G.W.C. van, *Het paleis van Hendrik III graaf van Nassau te Breda*. De Nederlandse monumenten van geschiedenis en kunst. Zeist etc. 1999.
- Wijck, H.W.M. van der et al. (ed.), *Opus Musivum, een bundel studies aangeboden aan professor doctor M.D. Ozinga ter gelegenheid van zijn zestigste verjaardag op 10 november 1962*. Assen 1964.
- Wildeman, M.G., 'Guilloardius van Norembergen'. In: *Bulletin van de Nederlandsche Oudheidkundige Bond* (1901/1902), pp. 309-310.
- Willems, H. et al. (ed.), *De onderste steen boven: 25 jaar bouwhistorie in 's-Hertogenbosch*. Utrecht 2000.
- Wishaupt, M.C.M., *Inventaris van de archieven van de Maastrichter Ambachten en Ambachtsbeurzen*. Inventarissenreeks RAL 14. Maastricht 1976.
- Witteveen-Jansen, M., *Van het Kerkplein naar de Waterstraat; de restauratie van vroeg renaissance beeldhouwwerk in Zaltbommel*. Zaltbommel 1995.
- Worp, J.A. (ed.), *De gedichten van Constantijn Huygens*. Groningen 1892-1899.
- Woud, A. van der, *De Bataafse hut: denken over het oudste Nederland (1750-1850)*. 2nd. ed. Amsterdam etc. 1998.
- Wylick-Westermann, C.G.M. van, 'Het bouwmeestersgeslacht Keldermans'. In: Van Mosselveld 1987, pp. 9-27.

- Yernaux, J., *La Métallurgie Liégoise et son expansion au XVIIe siècle*. Liège 1939.
- Yernaux, J., 'Les de Hontoir, artistes namurois à Liège au XVIIe siècle'. In: *Études d'Histoire & d'Archéologie Namuroises, dédiées a Ferdinand Courtoy*. Namur 1952, pp. 723-733.

- Zuijlen, R.A. van, *Inventaris der archieven van de stad 's-Hertogenbosch, chronologisch opgemaakt en de voornaamste gebeurtenissen bevattende*. Part I, 's-Hertogenbosch 1863, part II, 's-Hertogenbosch 1866.

ABBREVIATIONS

AA: Archief van de abdij van Averbode
AS: Aachener Stadtarchiv
ARA: Algemeen Rijksarchief Den Haag
CBG: Centraal Bureau voor Genealogie
GAA: Gemeentearchief Amsterdam
GAD: Gemeentelijke Archiefdienst Dordrecht
GAM: Gemeentearchief Maastricht
GAN: Gemeentearchief Nijmegen
GAR: Gemeentearchief Roermond
GAS: Gemeentearchief Sittard
GAU: Gemeentearchief Utrecht
GAZ: Gemeentearchief Zutphen
KNOB: Koninklijke Nederlandse Oudheidkundige Bond
NA: Notarieel Archief
RAB: Rijksarchief Brabant, 's-Hertogenbosch
RAG: Rijksarchief Gelderland, Arnhem
RDMZ: Rijksdienst voor de Monumentenzorg, Zeist
RV: Restauratievademecum
SAA: Stadsarchief Antwerpen
SAH: Stadsarchief 's-Hertogenbosch
SAL: Stadsarchief Leiden

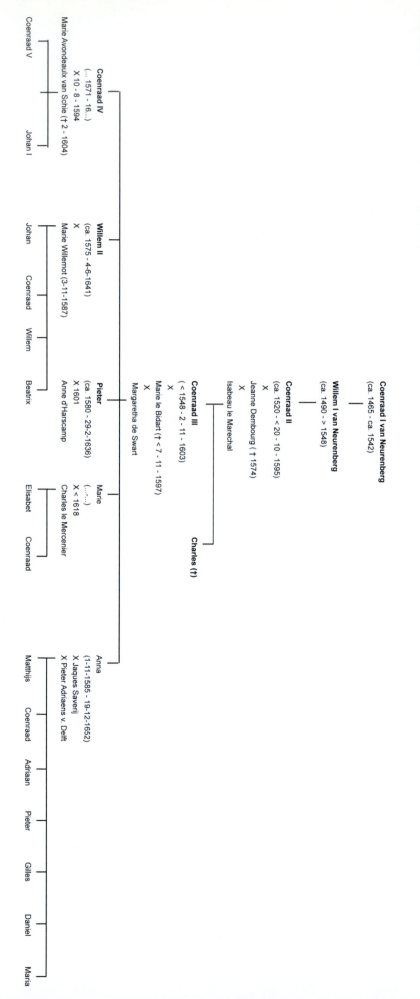

Coenraad I van Neurenberg
(ca. 1465 - ca. 1542)

Willem I van Neurenberg
(ca. 1490 - > 1548)

Coenraad II
(ca. 1520 - < 20 - 10 - 1595)
X
Jeanne Dembourg († 1574)
X
Isabeau le Marechal

Coenraad III
(< 1548 - 2 - 11 - 1603)
X
Marie le Bidart († < 7 - 11 - 1597)
X
Margaretha de Swart

Charles (†)

Coenraad IV
(... 1571 - 16...)
X 10 - 8 - 1594
Marie Avondeaulx van Schie († 2 - 1604)

Coenraad V   Johan I

Willem II
(ca. 1575 - 4-6-1641)
X
Marie Willemot (3-11-1587)

Johan   Coenraad   Willem   Beatrix

Pieter
(ca. 1580 - 29-2-1636)
X 1601
Anne d'Harscamp

Elisabet   Coenraad

Marie
(...-...)
X < 1618
Charles le Mercenier

Anna
(1-11-1585 - 19-12-1652)
X Jaques Saverij
X Pieter Adriaens v. Delft

Matthijs   Coenraad   Adriaan   Pieter   Gilles   Daniel   Maria

INDEX